Hope for the Oppressor

Hope for the Oppressor

Patrick Oden

LEXINGTON BOOKS/FORTRESS ACADEMIC
Lanham • Boulder • New York • London

Published by Lexington Books/Fortress Academic
Lexington Books is an imprint of The Rowman & Littlefield Publishing Group, Inc.
4501 Forbes Boulevard, Suite 200, Lanham, Maryland 20706
www.rowman.com

6 Tinworth Street, London SE11 5AL, United Kingdom

Copyright © 2019 The Rowman & Littlefield Publishing Group, Inc.

All rights reserved. No part of this book may be reproduced in any form or by any electronic or mechanical means, including information storage and retrieval systems, without written permission from the publisher, except by a reviewer who may quote passages in a review.

British Library Cataloguing in Publication Information Available

Library of Congress Cataloging-in-Publication Data Available

ISBN 978-1-9787-0915-7 (cloth : alk. paper)
ISBN 978-1-9787-0917-1 (pbk : alk. paper)
ISBN 978-1-9787-0916-4 (electronic)

∞™ The paper used in this publication meets the minimum requirements of American National Standard for Information Sciences—Permanence of Paper for Printed Library Materials, ANSI/NISO Z39.48-1992.

Contents

Foreword	vii
Acknowledgments	xi
Introduction	1
PART I: THE CONTEXT OF OPPRESSING	**21**
1 The Crisis of Social Identity	23
2 The Crisis of Self-Existence	45
3 The Crisis of Becoming	67
PART II: LIBERATING OPPRESSORS IN SCRIPTURE AND THE EARLY CHURCH	**85**
4 The Liberating Way of God	87
5 The Liberating Way of Christ	101
6 The Liberating Way of the Early Church	121
7 The Liberating Way of the Desert	139
PART III: CONSTRUCTING HOPE FOR THE OPPRESSORS	**157**
8 Hope from God	159
9 Hope with God	189
10 Hope for Transformation	209
11 Hope in the Kingdom	229

12	Hope among Community	255
13	Conclusion	275
Bibliography		291
Index		303
About the Author		327

Foreword

Let me begin with an event during a Mexico City conference in 1977, including Latin American liberation theologians and Hugo Assmann. I had criticized their academic Marxism, and they wanted to punish me. But then Jim Cone stood up and said, "As far as I know, more blacks live in Brazil than in the U.S. But no one among you is black." This embarrassed the Latin Americans, who were all white, and their Marxism did not help them at that point. Then Dora Arce Valentin from Cuba stood up and declared, "More than 50% of humanity are women, but I didn't see a single woman among you theologians." A long period of silence followed. We were beginning to see how much U.S. capitalism, white racism, and male sexism were allied with each other. Suddenly we could imagine what a liberation of the victims of these three powers, antagonistic to human dignity and human rights, could look like.

When I flew home to rich Germany and to my privileged position as a university professor, I wondered what a liberation of oppressors, racists, and sexists would look like. Oppression must be overcome on both sides, but the liberation of oppressed people is only the beginning. The end is the truly human community, or the "beloved community." In 1963, Martin Luther King Jr. had declared, in his famous speech, his dream "that one day, on the red hills of Georgia, the sons of former slaves and the sons of former slave-owners will be able to sit down together at the table of brotherhood."[1]

This happened almost sixty years ago. I am happy that Patrick Oden has taken up the idea of a "liberation of the oppressors" and applied it to our social situation. We are caught up in systems that regulate our minds and views. As long as we cannot break out of these systems, no liberation happens to us. Following this insight, Oden does not use Marxist analysis, but approaches liberation from the perspective of Niklas Luhmann's system-theory.[2] This theory is neutral to value judgments and also a-human. Luhmann was professor at an administration academy and views society as an administrative machinery. In this view, I am not a person, but a set of numbers, from my tax number to my passport. I am an "administered man," *ein "verwalteter Mensch."* I am a "controlled man," *ein "überwachter Mensch."* I function in the ways the systems in which I am embedded regulate me. The present digital revolution will foster the systems that dehumanize people and take their selves.

Thus, Charles Taylor has analyzed a "crisis of the self" in the West.[3] People don't know who they are. On this point, Patrick Oden finds the solution in Kierkegaard's existential theology of faith. Anyone who finds God finds also his or her true self. This theological personalism is in no way an individualism, as it constitutes a personal community where humans are free together. Faith in God liberates the oppressors and the captives from a-human systems. As an example and landmark, Oden takes Jean Vanier, who left his academic world in Canada to live together with handicapped people in France and founded *L'Arche*. Poor and rich is a central problem in the Old and the New Testament. Throughout church history, wealth and asceticism are theological topics. Liberation happened in a "patient manner" (Alan Kreider).[4] Oden examines Pannenberg and Moltmann, Sarah Coakley and Jean Vanier, under the leading idea of the holiness of God. This perspective is surprising and meaningful in allowing us to get a liberating distance over against systems of oppression.

This is a rich book, rich of thoughts and discoveries! Oden presents a "liberation theology" for our time, describing a liberation from our social and political systems. His voice is not "prophetic" as our voices were sixty years ago. He prefers the "patient manner." Perhaps his method is more effective than ours were at the beginning. The main thing is not to forget the oppressed and to overcome the oppression from both sides. Oppression of people and the earth is ending in catastrophes. The careful learn by faith and insight; others, by catastrophes. But humankind will ultimately learn humanity.

I am grateful to Patrick Oden: he picked up an idea of mine and carried it out in his own way, splendidly.

Jürgen Moltmann
Tübingen; January 15, 2019

NOTES

1. Martin Luther King, Jr., *I Have a Dream: Writings and Speeches That Changed the World,* ed. James M. Washington; foreword by Coretta Scott King (San Francisco: Harper San Francisco, 1992), 104.

2. Niklas Luhmann, *A Systems Theory of Religion* (Stanford: Stanford University Press, 2013).

3. Charles Taylor, *Sources of the Self: The Making of the Modern Identity* (Cambridge, UK: Cambridge University Press, 1992).

4. Alan Kreider, *The Patient Ferment of the Early Church: The Improbable Rise of Christianity in the Roman Empire* (Grand Rapids: Baker, 2016).

Acknowledgments

During a treasured week in 2011, Jürgen Moltmann graciously met with me in Tübingen, providing insight and inspiration as I was preparing an initial proposal for my PhD dissertation (which was published in 2015 by Fortress Press).[1] I am beyond grateful for his efforts in pursuit of liberation, as well as his counsel and his example to me over the years as he has responded thoughtfully through letters and offered tangible support through recommendations and connections.

As I entered into the process of writing, it became clear, first to my advisors and then to me, that I was really working on two books at once. The first was a discussion of Moltmann's ecclesiology; the second drew on this to explore Moltmann's understanding of liberation for both the oppressed and the oppressors. Veli-Matti Kärkkäinen and Bill Dyrness urged me to focus on the first goal for the dissertation, saving the topic of liberation of the oppressor for later. This was certainly good advice, as has been all the advice they have given me over the years. This book fulfills that goal, drawing on Moltmann's ecclesiology, as explored in *The Transformative Church*, and expanding the discussion of liberation well beyond the scope of that work.

The trek of writing this book has been accompanied by a heavy teaching load, without breaks, in three different homes and four different offices. While that may have prevented a smooth or efficient process, each setting offered its own insights. Frustrations can often be a way God teaches. That doesn't make them easier, but does redeem the experiences. In the midst of this, I have been thankful for the insights and direction those at Fortress Press provided along the way, as well as for their patience in waiting for a finished text.

This book is about liberation, but it is also an experience of liberation. As trials and frustrations arose, as chaos sought to discourage or co-opt me,

I realized I needed the lessons I was exploring in my own pursuit of God's wholeness in my life. Rather than getting caught up in the busyness, I have been again and again reminded of the need for *shalom*, a substantive peace that invites me to be attentive to the moment, to my setting, and especially my family. Amy, Vianne, and Oliver have been my co-travelers through the various settings and have inspired me to press on in every part of my life. They have provided balance and a tangible presence of hope. They are the music playing in the background of every chapter and every sentence of this book.

Without the support and investment of Fuller Theological Seminary, I could not have finished researching or writing. We are in a challenging era for Christian theology and evangelicalism in particular. There are a lot of forces trying to dilute the message of Christ and distort what it means to be a Christian in this world. We are seduced by power, politics, and culture wars, caught in dysfunctional histories, and contending with a dysfunctional present. Yet, those at Fuller exemplify what it means to pursue an evangelical faith, not giving into the distortions, not abandoning the possibility of thorough transformation. I am thankful for Fuller's example of persistent hope in pursuing often difficult conversations. With this, I am especially thankful for the women and men who have shared their journey with me as students in classes and other forums. I have learned from their insights, been inspired by their experiences and shaped by their questions. While there is much cause for discouragement in this world, my students have continually renewed my hope for liberation in every sense of the word.

I dedicate this book to my students and colleagues in Sacramento, where much of the book was written and where I experienced a renewed vision of hope, life, and community.

Yom Kippur, 2018

NOTE

1. Patrick Oden, *The Transformative Church: New Ecclesial Models and the Theology of Jürgen Moltmann*, Emerging Scholars (Minneapolis: Fortress Press, 2015).

Introduction

Hasten, O God, to save me;
 come quickly, LORD, to help me.

(Ps. 70:1 KJV)

In his tenth conference, John Cassian shares his continuing conversation on prayer with Abba Isaac.[1] Isaac notes that Ps. 70:1 is "the devotional formula . . . absolutely necessary for possessing the perpetual awareness of God."[2] "Not without reason," he adds, "has this verse been selected from out of the whole body of Scripture. For it takes up all the emotions that can be applied to human nature and with great correctness and accuracy it adjusts itself to every condition and every attack." In being suitable for "all conditions" this centering prayer becomes a tool for men and women experiencing a variety of circumstances, both of need and of success. "This verse," Isaac teaches, "should be poured out in unceasing prayer so that we may be delivered in adversity and preserved and not puffed up in prosperity."[3] Those who are in great need focus on hope in God, renewed by God's promise to work on behalf of his people. Those in prosperity remember they truly do need God, refocusing on the reality of God's presence, rather than the ephemeral state of their present successes.[4]

The centering prayer of Ps. 70:1 is an expression of hope to help each woman and man find their way back to God's perspective, a reality in which God seeks out all people and works to gather them together in unity.[5] Yet, people must learn to be open to the freedom and full identity that is only found in God. Without such a renewing vision, the oppressed fall into despair. The oppressors remain lulled by their apparent power. God seeks out people even still, working in Christ and through the Spirit in this world. This liberating work of God calls the oppressed out of their oppression and the liberating work of God calls the oppressor out of their oppressing. "Because oppression always has these two sides," Jürgen Moltmann writes, "the liberation process has to begin on both sides too."[6]

BUT WHAT IS LIBERATION?

The term is popularly applied to helping those who are poor experience less alienation in society. This is certainly an important goal and worthy of continued development in theology and practice. It is not, however, the whole of its meaning. There are ways of helping people that do not change their situation, such as charity, and there are ways of helping people that perpetuates their status, as happens with paternalism.[7] I suggest liberation is really about freedom. It involves freedom from that which constrains choice and limits expression. It involves freedom for a person or a group of people to determine how they will use their time and resources, giving them space to express their identity in full.

Liberation is thus different than charity or pursuits of justice which seek to address a particular need or to right a past wrong. These may be important elements along the way, indeed necessary, but are not themselves the fundamental expression of liberation. Those who are oppressed are often told what they must do to receive help, how they must do it; limited in their resources and constrained in their expression. They are helped but they are not liberated. Charity is offered but with certain expected behaviors or numbing bureaucracy or demanded political allegiance. A person's life becomes about receiving the charity, performing the expected obeisance to the duly appointed authorities.[8] Problems are addressed without an accompanying change in personal possibilities. Full liberation for the oppressed goes beyond helping immediate needs and involves changing patterns of society that allow for their free participation. Society is awakened first to the possibilities of change and then makes space in society for these changes to take shape. The oppressed become more than objects to be managed; they are recognized as persons with individual value.

I'm not saying anything new so far. Discussions about this kind of liberation are plentiful, defining a whole subset of theological discourse that illuminates how Christian theology, in particular, emphasizes freedom and participation by all.[9] The Salvadoran theologian Ignacio Ellacuría writes, "The goal of liberation is full freedom, in which full and right relationships are possible, among people and between them and God."[10] This emphasis on liberation as freedom was the core of Martin Luther King Jr.'s message, as expressed in his famous 1962 speech:

And when this happens, when we allow freedom to ring, when we let it ring from every village and hamlet, from every state and every city, we will be able to speed up that day when all of God's children, black men and white men, Jews and Gentiles, Protestants and Catholics, will be able to join hands and sing in the words of the old Negro spiritual, "Free at last! Free at last! Thank God almighty, we're free at last!"[11]

Freedom, of course, is likewise a tricky proposition and an imprecise term. King defined freedom as composed of three elements.[12] First, freedom is "the capacity to deliberate or weigh alternatives." Second, freedom "expresses itself in decision." A decision makes a choice, cutting off an alternative for the preference of the chosen path. Third, freedom involves responsibility, the ability to respond to why a choice was made, and the responsibility to respond as no one else can speak for that free person. These elements shape a wonderful ideal of freedom. We like the idea of it, the pursuit of it for others, and we definitely like our experience of it. Freedom as a lived reality is much more complicated. The trouble with freedom is how other people use *their* freedom, making choices we disagree with or making choices that actively undermine our choices or not taking responsibility for their choices.

For instance, I may choose to enjoy a quiet moment in my backyard, listening to the wind blowing through the trees. My neighbor may choose that same moment to mow his lawn or blow leaves from one side of his yard using very loud gas-powered tools. We both have freedom to choose, but the choice—the expression of freedom—is rarely expressed in isolation. My same neighbor may choose to put down his loud lawn equipment and enjoy a quieter moment of gardening, or reading, or smoking a fine cigar. Just at that moment, my kids decide to play in the backyard, yelling and screaming, exulting in the bounty of childhood. Expressions of freedom run head on into each other, in petty ways and in substantive ways. Herein lies the root of much division. On the surface, these are small matters indeed, but they easily fester.

Life with sharing backyards is one thing. The impact of multinational corporations controlling the natural resources of a nation and perpetuating cycles of abuse for many locals is taking it to another level.[13] The rise of mass-manufacturing led to unprecedented financial freedom for some in the modern era, thus expanding freedom beyond the upper classes, yet also led to human-caused social and environmental disasters. Those with power and freedom generally use their power and freedom for their own benefit, their competing claims for what is ultimately beneficial leading to intractable political debates. This is a human reality, existing across time and in very different political and social situations—though not always in the same ways. As Joe Kapolyo reminds us in speaking about the African challenges:

> Let us not forget that greed, exploitation, social and political elitism do not belong to any one social or political system. These evils are human characteristics that have the capacity to flourish under any guise. Unfortunately even the church is not immune: churches often shore up egotistical financial and political aspirations of leaders under some divine guise or other.[14]

Making it even more complicated, different kinds of oppression exist in the same context, and sometimes addressing one kind involves exacerbating others. The oppressed need to be liberated from oppression but doing this almost always entails a counter-oppression, a limitation of others or flipping the society so that the powerless gain power and the powerful lose it, switching parts in the same repeated drama. Oppression exists within categories as well. The oppressed oppress other oppressed; the oppressors are oppressed by other oppressors.[15] A limited freedom is thus often developed as a zero-sum game of competing interests, each trying to maximize their own experience of freedom in the context of others. We want freedom for all, on *our* terms. Liberation then becomes a pursuit of power.[16]

The unconstrained expression of freedom driven by the mantra, "*my* will be done" leads to rising tensions and maybe even conflict. Constraints are applied to mitigate these, and as such constraints limit freedom they become oppressive, at least in part, at least to some. Who controls the constraints? Who decides whose freedom has priority? What kind of freedom should liberation emphasize? Freedom that is unconstrained leads to choices that often oppress others. Yet the act of constraining freedom is itself an act of oppression, asserting choices by some over the choices of others. If we say that liberation is about freedom, and freedom involves the ability to make choices, then real and thorough liberation, as Martin Luther King Jr. expresses it, is an almost impossible prospect. Because those who have the ability to choose, will choose their own freedom over and against others. For these others to express their freedom, they will need to overcome the power and control of the establishment to become the new establishment.

This assertion of power may in fact result in liberation for some of the oppressed, but it is not actually liberation for the oppressors. Rather than being liberated from oppressing, the freedom of choice is removed, restricting them. This may rightfully stop oppression and is thus sometimes necessary. However, stopping oppression is different than liberating the oppressor. Just as charity is different than liberation, and paternalism is not the same as providing freedom. Slave owners, for instance, often argued the benefits of slavery for the enslaved, as they were given food, housing, and medical care.[17] Yet, that was not what the slaves themselves sought. They wanted freedom to buy their own food, live in their own houses, live life as they desired. True liberation for anyone is about their exercise of freedom, so if liberation is to happen from the side of the oppressor, it must be truly liberating as an expression of freedom.

That then is the challenge. If we define oppressing as the ability to make choices that oppress others, then the task of *liberating* oppressors is not to force them to stop oppressing. Rather, a liberated oppressor is one who retains freedom, yet makes different kinds of choices in how they respond to others. Oppressors must choose to not oppress, expressing their freedom in a new way of living. In being liberated from oppressing they choose to help others, to love their neighbor as themselves. Their liberation is expressed in the act of liberating rather than restricting, the making of space for others rather than the constraining of others. Liberation must begin in this side as well as from the side of the oppressed because only in this way can we keep oppression from perpetual cycles of application and inversion. "The goal," Moltmann emphasizes, "can be nothing other than the new and true communion of humankind, in which there are no longer oppressed or oppressors."[18]

How can such thorough liberation take place? In some sense, it is indeed an impossibility, as there is no reason an oppressor, someone with power, would voluntarily choose to let go their privilege and power.[19] It's not in human nature to do that. Yet, it happens. Men and women with power, with privilege, throughout history have chosen to let go that path and walk in other ways, often countercultural, finding a freedom of being that transcends those around them in the process. Do these unique specimens—prophets among us—live in ways that are impossible for the rest? Or have they awakened to a new way of life that points to possibilities for all of us? Is liberation a path all of us can walk, no matter our starting point? Must the rest of us linger in that liminality of guilt: leaning toward what is right but not able to ever achieve it?

WHO INDEED WILL SAVE US FROM THIS BODY OF DEATH?

This invites further discussion not only in determining whether liberation for the oppressor is possible but also how it may best take place. It is not enough to point to an ideal and say, "Do that." This is a good way to occasionally invoke guilt or shame, while also often being ignored. It becomes a religious transaction of sorts, just enough guilt to provoke response, just enough response to alleviate guilt. There are, after all, no end of calls for transformation in our era, highlighting injustices locally and globally, arguing for better use of resources and time. Awareness has been raised. We know what the problems are, but the difficulty is in leading people to change how they address them, to become aware of them in both thought and response. We have an orthodoxy, and we point toward an orthopraxy, but need an orthopathy—right passions and desires—in order to live out that which brings coherence to what we say we believe and know we should do.[20]

Liberation of the oppressor certainly needs a goal, an awareness of what it might look like in practice, but it also requires a renewed sense of method if it is to lead people to real transformation. For some, this discussion of method might seem like I am avoiding the driving issues that threaten our well-being. Yet, ignoring method and pronouncing judgments does not generally lead to change. It leads more often to division, frustration, alienation. The experience of the fundamentalists in railing against moral depravity did not, after all, lead to moral reformation. They could help enact prohibition but they could not end the attraction to alcohol or the social dysfunction it causes. They could point out what was wrong, why it was wrong, even as less and less people listened to them. Prohibition was overturned, but was widely ignored well before that; indeed, it engendered a new kind of organized crime. The fundamentalists lacked two key elements: they did not live up to their own standards so became known as hypocrites and they could not point toward a fuller life that made rigorous moral choices seem worth the cost. They expressed guilt and shame but did not offer experienced hope because far too often it lacked a Gospel that is actual good news. As Kierkegaard reminds us, "The good, of course, signifies the restoration of freedom, redemption, salvation, or whatever one would call it."[21] People heard their preaching and did not think it was good news in either rhetoric or practice.

Guilt and shame can highlight disorders for a time, and in a committed community these may even provoke a change of behavior.[22] But where trust is lacking and communities are fractured, simply highlighting how others should live their lives is more often seen as a grasp for power or empty scolding. That is our situation today. Competing factions asserting what is best for the other factions, fundamentalists with different priorities competing for power using the systems of this world. It is not enough because it simply does not work. Even if, and this is key, the statements themselves are right and should be said. The work of liberation has to be about more than scolding or invoking guilt and shame about *those* people who do *those* things and vote for *that* person. It must lead to a new way of living, choosing in freedom to live for others, choosing as a particular person to live in developing unity with others, accepting of their particularity. It must involve a path of love and reconciliation, so that foes become friends. Again, is this actually possible? My answer is yes. But it is not possible in our own power or as an expression of our moral will or rational discourse. It takes a broader perspective of freedom and an orientation in God's calling for this world.

Someone with infinite possibilities *can* voluntarily choose limitation for the sake of others, and Christ is the source for us of becoming this kind of person in our context. It's not a natural choice, to be sure. It's not a determinative result based on past experiences. Whether we are a titan of industry, in charge of multinational corporations, or a professor in a university competing for classes and recognition, we find it hard to relinquish our rights and power for the sake of broader thriving. Just as oppression became embedded in the work of the Church itself, so too does oppressing exist equally in nonprofits, and the academy, and other contexts that seek the good for others in rhetoric while oppressing them in method.[23] We need to find freedom from our desire to control, relinquishing demands to feed our egos and assert our wills over others. We thus all need, every one of us, liberation.

This book is an attempt to reboot the conversation, to enter into this long-standing discussion with a theme of hope, not only hope for changing contexts but hope for the oppressors themselves. It is a strange idea that the oppressors who already have privilege need hope, but that is exactly the problem we face. In his book on John Brown, W. E. B. Du Bois highlights the issue: "The price of repression is greater than the cost of liberty. The degradation of men costs something both to the degraded and those who degrade."[24] Repressing others may provide privilege in societal sense, but not necessarily real freedom, and in indulging oppression, they are cut off from the possibilities of fullness and life that is promised in Christ, both now and in eternity. The cost is hope, trust, and community, which are the cornerstones of life.

I propose a model that can more adequately define the context of oppressing, diagnose the underlying motivations and inclinations, and provide a theological analysis that gives both a Christian perspective and response. In doing this, I hope to offer a way of liberation that leads to a new pattern of life in our society, reflecting the values of the kingdom of God, one that is the task of individuals and churches to live out in their particular communities. In light of this latter goal, we discover themes that illuminate how liberation is, or should be, universal, diverse, and unifying. In expressing this more thorough understanding of liberation from both directions, the church can pursue its mission as a truly catholic church, working to actualize this liberation everywhere, in diverse situations and environments, pointing toward the Spirit of renewal that is infinitely complex and working in every setting and person, starting with each of us. As Oscar Romero reminded his listeners, "I also am a sinner and must take off my mask. I have offended God and society, and I must ask forgiveness of God. This is the call of Christ: the human person comes first."[25]

Indeed, it is the nature of personhood that is at the root of liberation. Liberation theology is concerned with the question of what it means to be human, and answers this in an expansive way. We are created in the image of God, each person is loved by the divine creator, and thus worthy of honor, respect, dignity, and equality.[26] Societal status does not affect this ontological value. Sin, however, does. In wrongly conceived patterns of meaning, we can pursue values and forms of identity that establish us in ultimately negating ways. That is, in fact, the original sin.

God continues to love us, but humanity seeks that which undermines our being. This sin is at the root of oppression and it is because of this we must talk about liberation for the oppressed and oppressors together. As Kierkegaard notes, "The bondage of sin is an unfree relation to the evil," so *both* the oppressed and the oppressors lack actual freedom.[27] The oppressed need to be liberated from oppression, and oppressors need to be liberated from oppressing, both being experiences of sin in need of salvation and renewal, a rebirth into a new way of life. Both experiences reflect the impact of structural and personal sin, so neither of these aspects can be ignored. Both experiences negate personhood, thus both require liberation into a new way of being, a renewed personhood. Borrowing Trinitarian terminology, such bi-directional liberation involves *perichoresis* for the oppressed, *kenosis* for the oppressor, each being reset into a more adequate expression of humanity in light of God's identity and mission in the world.[28] Each side needs freedom. The path to freedom is different for oppressed and oppressors, while the destination is the same: communion with God and each other.

In his text, *God for a Secular Society*, Moltmann has helpfully provided three "dimensions of human freedom," reflecting the tensions of our life in this world as well as the possibilities for a bigger vision of life together.[29] The first dimension is "freedom as domination," which approaches freedom in terms of power and control. This is a dysfunctional, zero-sum, approach to freedom, in which some are free while most are not. It is a very narrow understanding of freedom indeed, and not primarily interested in thorough liberation. The second dimension is "freedom as a free community." This dimension includes the values of friendliness and kindness rather than competition, exercising freedom as "neighborliness." There is a cooperative sharing, giving, and receiving; trust is maintained even as people may have very different roles. In this approach to freedom, solidarity is the core theme rather than domination, "where people intervene on one another's behalf, and especially for the weak, the sick, the young and the old."[30] This dimension begins the process toward liberation, though can become narrow in focus and limited in scope, even becoming defensive about changes.

The third dimension understands freedom as "the creative passion for the possible."[31] This is the dimension of transformation. Freedom is aligned toward the future, inviting movement that leads first toward reconciliation and then into new discoveries of human thriving. This dimension gathers the insecurities that may exist within an individual or community and rather than leading toward defensive postures or combative assertions, emphasizes the possibilities of individuals within communities. Freedom becomes defined by the acts of liberating and empowering, rather than restricting, the making of space for others rather than the constraining of others. Freedom becomes a way of hope for all, together—an expansive solidarity between formerly oppressing and no-longer oppressed.

How does this begin? First, by identifying who are oppressed and who are oppressors. The oppressed are readily identified. Identifying an oppressor is trickier, as they tend to resist the label, justifying their actions in some way that excuses any guilt. I take a broad approach in defining them. An oppressor is someone who is defined by a multitude of choices and options, compelled to engage life as a constant competition, and uses their choices to negate others.[32] These choices are not generally intended for the purpose of oppressing; more often, they are ways of seeking a kind of happiness. Even if not the intent, oppressing remains enacted, an effect of the kind of people we are in society. The context of choice and imposition of will remains constitutive of social identity. We expect something from others; we expect some influence over others. Ours is, after all, a society where we base someone's value on their ability to impose their will upon others. We are offended when we are imposed upon because that is a matter of another's will superseding our own.

Even in Christian circles, the "best" Christians are oftentimes the most influential leaders, the most charismatic speakers, the most rigorous academics.[33] We gauge the quality of their faith on the size of the building they preach in or the amount of books they have sold, pages they have written, how much sabbatical they are given, or any number of other societally validated metrics. The best leaders even compete about who is the best servant! They don't give up power, but frame it by how much they do for others. Of course, they set the parameters of what they do and how they do it as part of their leadership.

It is also true that oppressing happens across human society. Rather than limited to certain narrow spheres of definition, such as economics or race, it is increasingly clear that while liberation includes those categories—we can and should address issues of racism and economic oppression—it also transcends those categories.[34] Even those who may experience oppression within one or more categories may still be utterly in need of liberating from their own definitive context of oppressing. The rich young man of Matthew 19 was, after all, a Jewish subject of an occupying, pagan culture. He, like so many of us, was caught in traps of comfort and power. Even if we are not entirely successful at either comfort or power, we swim in the sea of these values, success at which makes us acceptable as people, failure of which makes us lesser beings, possibly not really considered a person at all by others or even, sadly, by our self. Comfort and power are lures that draw us to the hook. We are given a narrative of what it means to be human and live our lives so as to fulfill these in variously defined ways, even in Christian circles where the allure of consumerism is both preached against and indulged in, sometimes on the very same Sunday morning by the very same set of people.

Academia is certainly not immune. On the one hand, we can protest working conditions and abuse of workers in fields not our own. On the other, we overlook that a rising percentage of higher academia is being taught by adjuncts making less than a living wage. They are trapped because of their degree and the institutions that depend on such low-paid desperation to maintain a quality of life for full-time faculty and administrators. How can that change?[35] That is the problem. It seemingly can't. Academic institutions tend to be locked into a cycle of low-cost adjuncts teaching loan-crushed students in order to stay afloat in a system that resists easy transformation. It's the way things are and the way things have to be, lest the whole system collapse. Adjuncts and students become cogs in a system, not real people with status and commitment given to them for who they are.[36] Adjuncts do this, of course, with the hope of gaining a tenured position themselves, becoming a real person whose own freedom of scholarship is built on those who are being crushed.

Where is the way of life if we are all drowning in this status quo? What does it mean to be truly human in light of God's work rather than societal affirmation? Who are the truly human among us? The way Christ himself initiated gives a definitive answer to this. That is why simply restricting the oppressor is not enough. If the system of oppressing is itself kept in place, then once such restrictions are removed, the oppressing behavior returns as soon as the oppressor can restore their power. The oppressed may become new oppressors, justified based on past oppression.

Only true liberation, a transformation within the context of freedom, will result in a fundamentally different human experience for all. As Ellacuría writes, "It is not the freedom of base instincts, but a freedom of love that places the Christian at the service of others, because the entire will of God is fulfilled in the exact fulfillment of one commandment, to love your neighbors as you love yourself (Gal. 4:13–15)."[37] He goes on to note that it is the Spirit of Christ who accomplishes this work, particularizing each person, calling each person to a freedom that is a communal freedom where all are valued for their unique contributions.

How is it that the Spirit works? That leads the question from diagnosis to reflection. I like how Frederick Ware defines freedom as "a deep symbol of the fundamental reality of human existence" which makes the quest for freedom in sociopolitical terms "symbolic of a deeper quest for human fulfillment, as we consider our overall context of existence in the cosmos."[38] This reflection on the "deeper quest" reorients action, and the experience of the actions provides yet more resources for diagnosis and reflection.[39] If we stop short, we risk missing the mark altogether. Freedom for none. That is the destination of sin and death. The way of life is a way of freedom for all.

In what follows, I will develop the themes of oppressing and the pattern of liberation of the oppressor further. My goal is not to be comprehensive; that would be both too lengthy a task and indeed an impossible one since I am limited in my context and perspective. The current work is suggestive, encouraging different approaches that may move the conversations away from intractable political or religious stances. It is also an invitation, asking others in different traditions, with different expertise, in different contexts, to assess and contribute related insights. Thus, my goal is introductory rather than exhaustive, drawing from history, Scripture, and contemporary theology as a way of representing an alternative approach to this topic. The passages or figures I discuss are among the possible contributors. I actively invite an expanding conversation about how this may take fuller shape in our present world.

A second underlying goal involves arguing that oppressing is not limited to certain contexts or groups; rather, oppressing is part of human nature, and as such exists throughout society and throughout the world.[40] Rather than emphasizing someone else's sins, or the politics of *that* party, or the dysfunction of just the economically privileged, I echo Paul's statement in Romans 2:

> Therefore you have no excuse, whoever you are, when you judge others; for in passing judgment on another you condemn yourself, because you, the judge, are doing the very same things. You say, "We know that God's judgment on those who do such things is in accordance with truth." Do you imagine, whoever you are, that when you judge those who do such things and yet do them yourself, you will escape the judgment of God? Or do you despise the riches of his kindness and forbearance and patience? Do you not realize that God's kindness is meant to lead you to repentance?[41]

Liberation of the oppressor is something we all need, because we all engage in patterns of explicit or implicit oppression; some of us just rationalize it better or shield it with lofty rhetoric. Following the lead of Jesus, the challenge for us is to first look inward at our own selves and lives, seeing how each of us engages in patterns of oppressing, and in light of that, coming to terms with who we really are and who we need to be. If we cannot address this in ourselves and our specific context, we have little business suggesting change for others, and even less influence in getting anyone to listen.[42]

In part I, I lay the groundwork for my proposed approach, utilizing the work of Niklas Luhmann, Søren Kierkegaard, and James Loder to provide a picture of the social and psychological issues that underlie our societal tendencies. I propose their perspectives of sociology, philosophy, and psychology in theological perspective provide a fundamental answer to the present state of human society and personhood, developing models of the situation as it is and pointing to where we might find solutions. Why does a person oppress? Is it enough to tell them it is wrong? It doesn't seem so, given the direction of contemporary social life. What then are underlying problems that may require different kinds of solutions? "Every wound is not healed with the same treatment," wrote Ignatius of Antioch, so we must consider both the wounds as they are and the remedies in turn.[43]

In part II, I will engage in a retrieval of tradition. I begin with Scripture, focusing on how it addresses the liberation of oppressors within its overarching narrative. The experience of Moses, the messages of the Psalms, the event of the cross, the story of Ananias and Sapphira, Paul's journey from oppressor to martyr, and the hymn in Philippians 2 become helpful guides for our own journeys.[44] Following this, I will add insights from the early church, which saw the issues of wealth, power, and privilege as ever-present and crucially important to address in light of the radical call of Jesus and the Apostles. The work of Clement of Alexandria is especially instructive in addressing how we can understand the presence of wealth in our lives and society while continuing to participate within society. Anthony of Egypt provides concrete guidance from early monasticism, which, while oriented to those who have separated from society, still provides a road map of transformation for those of us with different callings.

Teachings on wealth and poverty are certainly substantial in early church writings and I am not attempting to be comprehensive in scope. My goal is to highlight a particular thread in early church writing that invites oppressors onto a new path, a thread that avoids condemning participation *in* society while also cautioning Christians about being co-opted *by* society. This approach encourages a fractal participation that emerges from below and expresses what Alan Kreider calls "the patient ferment of the early church."[45]

In part III, I make a constructive turn. Liberation for the oppressor involves highlighting the way of hope, what is gained in fullness of life and openness to community. Such a hope involves the deployment of a more adequately holistic theology, one that is simultaneously grounded in orthodoxy, orthopraxy, and orthopathy. Liberation involves a set of doctrines about God and the world; it also involves action, expressing what we know in our context by how we live our lives. What we know and what we do is intimately connected to our inner self—our emotions, our passions, our desires—and if we do not address this side of the human experience we become easily distracted or discouraged, co-opted back into patterns of oppressing. In light of this, the path to liberation involves more than an identification about current issues and actions we should take to solve them. Calling these out may seem prophetic in part, but it tends to be more preaching to a particular choir than enacting transformation in the streets.

Instead of jumping straight to the end—what must we do—we must first address issues of understanding about who God is and who we are in light of God's mission in this world. We must go back to the beginning of our assumptions about God and God's work in this world. Orthopraxy is important, but we should also involve orthodoxy and orthopathy in triangulating a better way of life. Ignoring these latter elements—or just one—results in being co-opted by other dogmas, and thus expressing that narrative rather than the narrative of Christ.

In chapters 8 and 9, I will focus on our concept of God. Our understanding of ultimate authority is mirrored in our conception of representative authority. How we understand God affects how we represent God to this world, and thus how we live in this world in light of God's identity and purposes. While oppression has many causes, oppression that arises in particularly Christian settings seems to reflect a prevailing understanding about God. If we conceive God in oppressive ways, we establish oppression in our contexts. If we conceive God in liberative ways, we establish liberation in our contexts. If God is defined by judgment, we emphasize judgment. If God is defined by hope and invitation, we express an inviting hope. I argue the way of God is a way of hope. Understanding this hope in our context involves a revision of our theology, before we can begin any other stage of liberation.[46]

In chapter 10, I build on this understanding and mission of God to point to the particular method of God illustrated in the work of Christ. This orients the discussion in terms of method, which cannot be separated from goals. Christianity, after all, is a way *in* this world, not simply a set of beliefs *about* it. The way of Christ for us involves living out a distinct story in the midst of the world, and this story depends on a particular view of reality. This way involves the cross and the resurrection together, a hope for renewal that begins in radical obedience played out in particular contexts. The resurrection teaches that transformation literally and metaphorically emerges from below, rising to encompass all that is.

In chapter 11, I expand on what this renewal means in light of God's plan in and for *this* world. The particular emphases of the Kingdom provide an orientation for liberated freedom. While this is a big picture perspective in part, it takes on more concrete expression in the experience of community, which I focus on in chapter 12. Liberation takes shape in our Christian communities so that we are not simply preaching about liberation to others, we are living within a field of liberation in our lives, a resonating transformation that displays what is possible through the work of the Spirit within this world. Such is not limited to isolated Christian communities but extends as transformed people live transformed lives within the contours of established society, living by a new set of rules in the midst of the established game.

In these constructive chapters, I draw from four theologians in particular. Each is a substantive contributor to theological discourse in our era and each points toward renewal in both theology and practice in productive ways. Wolfhart Pannenberg and Jürgen Moltmann provide a starting point in their theologies of hope that relates to a renewal of human identity. Pannenberg illuminates the goal, a transformative vision of holiness in renewed identity—exocentric in orientation and reflective of the triune being of God as the ground of being. Moltmann offers a more explicit consideration of contextual liberation: what does such a holiness mean for our assumptions and responses? With this, Sarah Coakley provides an example of a renewed approach to theology that in many ways expresses an embrace of diversity within its liberating emphasis on the work of the triune God through the holistic pattern of contemplative practice. Moltmann and Coakley serve especially as guides in orthopathy, orienting liberation in light of the fruit of the Spirit. They understand how the psychological and emotional experience of theology is as important for transformation as is reason and debate. Early monastic discussions emphasized this issue of "right passions" but it has been often left out of contemporary examinations.

Jean Vanier, founder of the L'Arche communities, offers a substantive example of liberation of the oppressor in his own life, showing theological reflection applied in practice that then provokes continued reflection and revision. For Vanier, orthopathy leads directly into orthopraxy. As he focuses on themes of becoming human, he prioritizes love and friendship in the context of a voluntary *kenosis*. Different passions *can* result in similar actions, but the particular passions shape how these actions are developed and the results that are pursued. In actions developed from love and peace, people let go oppressing because they discover something more profound in being open to the other, relating to the oppressed and shedding the cultural insistence on domination and control. This, I argue, needs to be taken up more thoroughly by the church in a variety of different ways and contexts, transforming it from a bastion of power to being a "community of becoming" for oppressed and oppressors together. Indeed, this is a theologically and scripturally substantive approach and so should be assessed in light of such.

In the concluding chapter, I draw together the various strands and point to a transformative move of hope and love that is initiated in a fully realized faith in the liberating God. We are liberated when we participate with each other in becoming fully who we are each made to be. We liberate when we help others become; we are liberated when we let others participate in our becoming. This is true freedom, a freedom that includes and invites, expanding the experience of humanity in particular contexts. Liberation into this kind of freedom happens for the oppressed and the oppressors together, the one taking up as the other lets go, each creating space for the other, resisting the depersonalizing tendencies of social systems as they engage in the truly personalizing movement of the Holy Spirit in their midst.

I begin this project with the contention that the systems in our society engender rather than mitigate oppressing. This involves the economic system but goes beyond that to involve the legal system, the political system, the education system, and the religious system. Even when our stated goals may seek something different, oppressing is incorporated and often even justified as being part of a perceived solution that never quite arrives. It sneaks its way back in, even in those places that purport to fight against it. Oppression is an insidious temptation, offering a fruit in exchange for wisdom about good and evil yet leading always to death. In a culture that has a long-standing Christian tradition, we cannot blame outside forces for our dysfunction. We cannot blame the snake.[47] It is our responsibility when we listen to bad counsel.

This is the continuing temptation we face. We are still, quite literally, creating habits of consumerism and competition that are modeled after dysfunctional ecclesial habits and teachings, though unintentionally. Having more "stuff" to show off to the surrounding world and attract more people is as much a church addiction as it is a personal one. As such, it is not enough to treat symptoms. The disease has infected our deepest parts. People who engage in oppression are reflecting the systems they are in, not generally making independent choices to oppress others. We must thus look at underlying dysfunction and treat the disease itself. My argument, which will take place in this text, is that theology (especially our doctrines of God, humanity, and the church) has oriented us into our current situation. We are living in one orientation but trying to convince ourselves to live out another. But it is impossible to go south and north at the same time. To be free, we must address these contradictory trajectories, and then and only then, can we shape people who live out their Christian life in transformative, liberating ways in which oppressors and oppressed find thorough and lasting community. That lasting community is the hope offered to all.

Especially relevant to this project, then, are the words of Henry David Thoreau:

> I do not mean to prescribe rules to strong and valiant natures, who will mind their own affairs whether in heaven or hell, and perchance build more magnificently and spend more lavishly than the richest, without ever impoverishing themselves, not knowing how they live if, indeed, there are any such, as has been dreamed; nor to those who find their encouragement and inspiration in precisely the present condition of things, and cherish it with the fondness and enthusiasm of lovers and, to some extent, I reckon myself in this number; I do

not speak to those who are well employed, in whatever circumstances, and they know whether they are well employed or not but mainly to the mass of men who are discontented, and idly complaining of the hardness of their lot or of the times, when they might improve them. There are some who complain most energetically and inconsolably of any, because they are, as they say, doing their duty. I also have in my mind that seemingly wealthy, but most terribly impoverished class of all, who have accumulated dross, but know not how to use it, or get rid of it, and thus have forged their own golden or silver fetters.[48]

NOTES

1. Or, at least, his stylized retelling of desert monastic theology in the form of personal conversations. John Cassian, *The Conferences*, trans. Boniface Ramsey (New York: Paulist Press, 1997).

2. Cassian, *Conference* 10:2.

3. Cassian, *Conference* 10:14.

4. Cf. Jas 4:1–5:12.

5. Though this is expressed in different ways. God's seeking after the poor, including them within his valued people, often involves God's calling the rich and powerful to let go their wealth and control. God's seeking after people, his option for all, calls some to rise up and some to let go. The trouble with much of Christian history is that the church often confused which method to apply to which group, calling the poor to let go and the rich to take up, securing the established power structures of the current political climate. This is why it is important to emphasize God's preferential option to the poor, because that is the message counter to much of the world's assumptions. However, this is not exclusive. Gustavo Gutiérrez writes: "The very word 'preference' denies all exclusiveness and seeks rather to call attention to those who are the first—though not the only ones—with whom we should be in solidarity. . . . I insisted that the great challenge was to maintain both the universality of God's love and God's predilection for those on the lowest rung of the ladder of history. To focus exclusively on the one or the other is to mutilate the Christian message. Therefore every attempt at such an exclusive emphasis must be rejected." In Gustavo Gutiérrez, *A Theology of Liberation*, 15th Anniversary edition (Maryknoll, NY: Orbis Books, 1988), xxv–xxvi.

6. Jürgen Moltmann, *Experiences in Theology*, trans. Margaret Kohl (Minneapolis: Fortress Press, 2000), 186.

7. On this, see Christopher Rowland and Mark Corner, *Liberating Exegesis: The Challenge of Liberation Theology to Biblical Studies* (Louisville: Westminster John Knox Press, 1989), chap. 5. See also W. E. B. Du Bois, "The Souls of Black Folk," 29 in *The Souls of Black Folk: With "The Talented Tenth" and "The Souls of White Folk,"* Reprint edition (New York: Penguin Classics, 1996).

8. See, for instance, Jack London, *The People of the Abyss* (New York: Macmillan, 1903), chap. 8.

9. For early accounts of Latin American liberation theology, see two key books by Bartolomé de las Casas, *Short Account of the Destruction of the Indies* (New

York: Penguin Classics, 2004), first published in 1552, and *In Defense of the Indians* (DeKalb: Northern Illinois University Press, 1974). In our era, Gustavo Gutiérrez, *A Theology of Liberation* is often considered the founding text, though he was certainly not alone in these discussions and there have been many written since. For the crucial conclusions of the gathering of Latin American bishops, see Louis M. Colonnese, ed., *The Church in the Present-Day Transformation of Latin America in the Light of the Council*, 2 vols. (Bogota: General Secretariat of CELAM, 1970). See also John Eagleson and Philip J. Scharper, eds., *Puebla and Beyond: Documentation and Commentary* (Maryknoll, NY: Orbis, 1979).

10. Ignacio Ellacuría, *Ignacio Ellacuría: Essays on History, Liberation, and Salvation*, ed. Michael E. Lee (Maryknoll, NY: Orbis Books, 2013), 244.

11. Martin Luther King, Jr., *A Testament of Hope: The Essential Writings and Speeches of Martin Luther King, Jr.*, ed. James M. Washington (New York: HarperCollins, 1991), 220.

12. See Martin Luther King, Jr. "The Ethical Demands for Integration," in *Testament of Hope*, 119–120.

13. One of the most heartbreaking pictures I've seen recently was a photo of a man staring at the severed foot and hand of his daughter, who was punished because he did not meet his quota at a rubber plantation owned by Leopold II. See "Father stares at the hand and foot of his five-year-old, severed as a punishment for failing to make the daily rubber quota, Belgian Congo, 1904," Rare Historical Photos, September 21, 2016, https://rarehistoricalphotos.com/father-hand-belgian-congo-1904/. The degree of one man's assertion of his power over the lives of others is overwhelming in its obscenity, and it is only one example among the myriad in history and the present.

14. Joe M. Kapolyo, *The Human Condition* (Carlisle: Langham Global Library, 2013), 18.

15. See, for instance, Cardinal Robert Sarah and Nicolas Diat, *God or Nothing: A Conversation on Faith* (San Francisco: Ignatius Press, 2015), 72–74.

16. Paulo Freire, *Pedagogy of the Oppressed*, 30th anniversary edition (New York: Continuum, 2000), 45–46.

17. See Peter Kolchin, *American Slavery: 1619–1877*, revised edition (New York: Hill and Wang, 2003), 111–118.

18. Jürgen Moltmann, "The Liberation of Oppressors," *The Journal of the Interdenominational Theological Center* 6, no. 2 (1979): 69.

19. For this reason, the dominant view among liberation theologians is that liberation of the oppressor can only happen by means of the oppressed. Virgilio Elizondo notes, "It is the Christian poor of today's world that will bring salvation to the Christians of the rich nations of the world, who because of the material wealth of their own nations are too blind to see the truth of the gospel." Virgilio P. Elizondo, foreword to *Mañana: Christian Theology from a Hispanic Perspective*, ed. Justo L. González (Nashville: Abingdon Press, 1990), 13–14.

20. On these categories, especially the less common one of orthopathy, see Theodore Runyon, *The New Creation: John Wesley's Theology Today* (Nashville: Abingdon Press, 1998), chap. 5. Clement of Alexandria writes, "The Instructor being practical, not theoretical, His aim is thus to improve the soul, not to teach, and to train

it up to a virtuous, not to an intellectual life. Although this same word is didactic, but not in the present instance. For the word which, in matters of doctrine, explains and reveals, is that whose province it is to teach. But our Educators being practical, first exhorts to the attainment of right dispositions and character, and then persuades us to the energetic practice of our duties, enjoining on us pure commandments, and exhibiting to such as come after representations of those who formerly wandered in error. Both are of the highest utility—that which assumes the form of counselling to obedience, and that which is presented in the form of example; which latter is of two kinds, corresponding to the former duality—the one having for its purpose that we should choose and imitate the good, and the other that we should reject and turn away from the opposite. Hence accordingly ensues the healing of our passions, in consequence of the assuagements of those examples; the Paedagogue strengthening our souls, and by His benign commands, as by gentle medicines, guiding the sick to the perfect knowledge of the truth." In Clement of Alexandria, *Pædagogus*, trans. William Wilson, ANF 2, reprint edition (Peabody, MA: Hendrickson), 1.1.209.

21. Søren Kierkegaard, *The Concept of Anxiety*, trans. Reidar Thomte (Princeton: Princeton University Press, 1980), 119.

22. See, for instance, Niels Henrik Gregersen, "Guilt, Shame, and Rehabilitation: The Pedagogy of Divine Judgment," *Dialog* 39, no. 2 (2000): 105–118.

23. This is not to say all churches, or all nonprofits, or the entire academy is oppressive. More that oppression exists, and may even predominate in some contexts. Such oppression stands out not because it is necessarily greater but because it exists where the rhetoric is about freedom from such oppression by others. On the debate about international aid efforts see, for instance, Dambisa Moyo, *Dead Aid: Why Aid Is Not Working and How There Is a Better Way for Africa* (New York: Farrar, Straus and Giroux, 2009); Gary A. Haugen and Victor Boutros, *The Locust Effect: Why the End of Poverty Requires the End of Violence* (New York: Oxford University Press, 2015); Jeffrey Sachs, *The End of Poverty: Economic Possibilities for Our Time* (New York: Penguin Press, 2005). For one of the more thorough discussions of the history of Christianity in Africa, see Ogbu U. Kalu, ed., *Africa Christianity: An African Story* (Trenton, NJ: Africa World Press, 2007). This is especially noteworthy as all the contributors are themselves African, thus it is truly an African expression of their own history and understanding. See also Kwame Bediako, *Theology and Identity: The Impact of Culture upon Christian Thought in the Second Century and in Modern Africa* (Oxford: Regnum, 1999). In regard to the academy, Richard Moser has recently written, "The increasing exploitation of contingent faculty members is one dimension of an employment strategy sometimes called the 'two-tiered' or 'multi-tiered' labor system. This new labor system is firmly established in higher education and constitutes a threat to the teaching profession. If left unchecked, it will undermine the university's status as an institution of higher learning because the overuse of adjuncts and their lowly status and compensation institutionalize disincentives to quality education, threaten academic freedom and shared governance, and disqualify the campus as an exemplar of democratic values. These developments in academic labor are the most troubling expressions of the so-called corporatization of higher education." See Richard Moser, "Overuse and Abuse of Adjunct Faculty Members

Threaten Core Academic Values," *Chronicle of Higher Education* 60, no. 18 (January 17, 2014): A19–A20.

24. W. E. B. Du Bois, *John Brown*, ed. David R. Roediger, new edition (New York: Modern Library, 2001), 4.

25. Oscar Romero, *The Scandal of Redemption* (Walden, NY: Plough Publishing House, 2018), 54.

26. The exact nature of the *imago dei* in humanity is a long-standing discussion. For a substantive overview and analysis of this concept in Christian theology, see, for instance, Stanley Grenz, *The Social God and the Relational Self: A Trinitarian Theology of the Imago Dei* (Louisville: Westminster John Knox, 2001).

27. Kierkegaard, *The Concept of Anxiety*, 119.

28. See Patrick Oden, "Liberating Holiness for the Oppressed and Oppressors," in *A Future for Holiness: Pentecostal Explorations*, ed. Lee Roy Martin (Cleveland, TN: CPT, 2013), 205–224.

29. Jürgen Moltmann, *God for a Secular Society: The Public Relevance of Theology* (Minneapolis: Fortress Press, 1999), 155–161.

30. Moltmann, *God for a Secular Society*, 158.

31. Ibid., 159.

32. Ellacuría, *Ignacio Ellacuría*, 29–30; 222–224.

33. Indeed, in a recent study, number eight on the list of careers with the most psychopaths was "clergy." See Kevin Dutton, *The Wisdom of Psychopaths* (New York: Scientific American, 2012), 162. Dutton, interestingly, does not see psychopathy as inherently a problem, indeed his text explores the idea of psychopathy as a potential "medicine for modern times" and taking it in moderation might be useful for success. The definition of success is, of course, a key element here. It certainly can lead to popularity, advancement, and recognition. One of the "leaders" of the recent Emergent church movement is a diagnosed narcissist, leading to a seeming divergent expression of life in public and private. This reality is, no doubt, also found in academia and theological studies. As Dutton, 163 asks could "twiddling those dials a little to the right on our respective psychopath mixing desks—at certain times, in certain specific context—actually be good for us?" The stories of how theologians, ministers, and other representatives of Christ have treated wives, other women, or many of those near them suggests that the answer, for reputation and profession, is yes. Indeed, it seems the case that oppressing is embedded in much Christian theology and so the challenge is to see how much Christian theology reflects the rationalizations of such psychopathic tendencies.

34. Ellacuría, *Ignacio Ellacuría*, 244 writes, "Certainly there are other forms of oppression besides the sociopolitical and economic, and not all forms of oppression derive exclusively and immediately from that one. Christians would be wrong, therefore, to seek only one type of social liberation. Liberation must extend to everyone who is oppressed by sin and by the roots of sin."

35. In seminary education, accreditation requires at least 30 percent of courses be taught by regular faculty. That means 70 percent of the courses offered may be taught by those who have no vote, little recognition. Many have to carry a heavy teaching load or a heavy alternative workload simply to survive so they do not have time to

keep up scholarship, thus falling further behind. A student could conceivable get an entire degree without taking one class from a tenured or tenure-track faculty at some institutions.

36. The term "community" is often utilized in higher education, but it is very much a pay-to-play system, where community is accessible as long as the payment is received.

37. Ellacuría, *Ignacio Ellacuría*, 50.

38. Frederick L. Ware, *African American Theology: An Introduction* (Louisville: Westminster John Knox Press, 2016), 16.

39. See Gutiérrez, *Theology of Liberation*, xxix.

40. John Wesley in his sermon "Original Sin" notes the increasing idealism about human nature among writers of his time, and how popular this line of thinking is for those in his time: "So that it is now quite unfashionable to talk another wise, to say anything to the disparagement of human nature; which is generally allowed, notwithstanding a few infirmities, to be very innocent and wise and virtuous. But in the meantime, what must we do with our Bibles? For they will never agree with this. These accounts, however pleasing to flesh and blood, are utterly irreconcilable with the scriptural." See John Wesley, Sermon 44, "Original Sin," in *The Sermons of John Wesley*, eds. Kenneth J. Collins and Jason E. Vickers (Nashville: Abingdon Press, 2013), 12.

41. See Romans 2:1–16.

42. See Kierkegaard, *Concept of Anxiety*, 138.

43. Ignatius of Antioch, *Letter to Polycarp*, trans. Michael W. Holmes, *The Apostolic Fathers,* 3rd edition (Grand Rapids: Baker Academic, 2006), 2.126.

44. Paul introduces the Philippians hymn with the words, "Let the same mind be in you that was in Christ Jesus," thus directly relating what follows to an admonition for our own behavior and identity.

45. Kreider, *The Patient Ferment of the Early Church*, 12. He writes that "God used not influential or powerful people but obscure fishers and hunters to achieve a huge end. . . . The churches grew in many places, taking varied forms. They proliferated because the faith that these fishers and hunters embodied was attractive to people who were dissatisfied with their old cultural and religious habits, who felt pushed to explore new possibilities, and who then encountered Christians who embodied a new manner of life that pulled them toward what the Christians called 'rebirth' into a new life. Surprisingly, this happened in a patient manner."

46. Indeed, I think it is a fair argument that the rise of atheism in our era comes more from the distorted expression of a dysfunctional theology than a direct rejection of a faithful presentation of God in the lives of those who claim to be in God's service.

47. See Harvey Cox, *On Not Leaving it to the Snake* (New York: Macmillan, 1969), xv–xvi. In writing about Adam and Eve he notes, "Their sin is our sin. It is not promethean. We do not defy the gods by courageously stealing the fire from the celestial hearth, thus bringing benefit to man. Nothing so heroic. We fritter away our destiny by letting some snake tell us what to do."

48. Henry D. Thoreau, *Walden or Life in the Woods* (Cambridge, MA: Houghton Mifflin, 1906), 17.

Part I

THE CONTEXT OF OPPRESSING

Chapter 1

The Crisis of Social Identity

INTRODUCTION

In this section, I look at the necessary starting point of liberation: the problem must be properly diagnosed in order to prescribe the most effective solution. What causes oppressing behavior? Answering this may seem an offensive task for many, as if to pursue understanding somehow coddles the seriousness of oppressing behavior and excuses the perpetrators. The goal is not to justify sinful behavior but is more like a physician who accurately diagnoses the problems in order to begin the process of addressing them.[1] If the problem is ongoing, treating only the symptoms allows the underlying problem to fester and even spread. To prevent oppression from continuing, or returning in another guise, it is important to develop a holistic perspective on human experience that recognizes why people who are not sociopaths oppress others as part of their social participation.

In this chapter, I examine the insights of sociologist Niklas Luhmann, as his model provides a useful description of how the world functions without imposing correlating judgments or supposed solutions that may conflict with thoroughly Christian proposals for response. Such conflicting models have the tendency to either negate or unduly syncretize with Christian ideals, leaving neither its form nor its power. So why include an outside model at all? Because while Christianity has an argument about who we are to be and what we are to seek, it does not necessarily provide insight into the particularities of modern society. In other words, it lacks a starting analysis that can enable contextual response. Luhmann provides that starting analysis without associating a prescribed solution. Even more, he actively resisted that task. Traugott Schöfthäler writes, "Luhmann seems to be motivated by his negation of blending sociological theory with ideals of human condition."[2] His non-prescriptive sociology provides a kind of cooperative analysis of society without being complementary, in a way analogous to the biblical distinction between the world and the kingdom.³ This approach helps explain even more clearly how oppressors are in fact oppressed by their oppressing, caught in expressions of life seemingly outside of their control and drawn into destructive social patterns.

Oppressors do not generally wake up each day with goals to oppress others. Yet, oppressing happens in the midst of daily life. It happens throughout our world and within our particular societies, in economics, health care, and the legal system. It also happens in academia, in politics, in social causes. The question at hand is not necessarily just why those *other* people—the people who voted for the wrong person—oppress, the question is why you oppress and why I oppress in the midst of trying to make our way in life.

Kierkegaard writes of a similar problem in his time:

> In Christendom, sermons, lectures, and speeches are heard often enough about what is required of an imitator of Christ, about the implications of being an imitator of Christ, what it means to follow Christ, etc. What is heard is generally very correct and true; only by listening more closely does one discover a deeply hidden, un-Christian, basic confusion and dubiousness. The Christian sermon today has become mainly "observations": Let us in this hour consider; I invite my listeners to observations on; the subject for our consideration is, etc. But "to observe" can mean in one sense to come very close to something, namely to what one wishes to observe; in another sense, it signifies keeping very distant, infinitely distant, that is, personally.⁴

In addressing how *others* oppress, it becomes easy to take the high road without acknowledging let alone transforming the conditions within our own environment. In "observing" the condition of others, we excuse ourselves and, as Kierkegaard highlights, leave ourselves. We decontextualize our actual self and incorporate a kind of gnostic disembodiment within our location. Our bodies continue to function, however, and our actions continue to resonate among others, just without a sense of moral responsibility about *our* environmental impact or the actions of the institutions we align with.

No matter where we turn, however, we are caught up in competition, in spheres of power, encouraged to assert our wills and minimize our inconveniences. We label this ambition, or as necessary elements of vocational advancement, or a privilege of our status. Yet, we are all caught up in the dysfunctional social and psychological realities of our society. Ignoring our context perpetuates the very problems we might think we're addressing in other contexts. By ignoring the problems that exist immediately before us and in us, we unwittingly perpetuate assumptions that drive oppressing within every person's particular "kingdom." As Dallas Willard defines it, "Our 'kingdom' is simply the range of our effective will. Whatever we genuinely have say over is in our kingdom."[5] But, of course, we have reasons why *our* oppressing is acceptable. Or do we? Is it just part of our role in the systems that have given us rationalization for our dysfunctions? This is what Luhmann helps us discover.

THE SYSTEMS IN THIS WORLD

As noted, Niklas Luhmann's systems theory describes how the world *is*, not how the world *should be*. Luhmann does not offer tools of response; indeed he does not offer a critique of the world as being either bad or good. It is what it is. While seemingly deficient if a person is looking for solutions to perceived problems, his theory has the benefit of flexibility in light of complexity. It does not have a correlative action that constrains the analysis. This lack of judgment and prescribed action allows space for a redemptive Christian response. By being descriptive rather than prescriptive, it provides a starting point for a new conception of holistic liberation that can then turn to a particularly Christian understanding of reality for a substantive response that reflects Christian priorities of goals *and* methods.[6] In beginning with a non-idealistic portrayal of the world before moving onto a theologically developed approach I am following what Moltmann writes, "Realism teaches us a sense for reality—for what is. Hope awakens our sense for potentiality—for what could be."[7] Luhmann provides realism. Christianity provides hope.

Utilizing Luhmann thus avoids the difficulty of syncretizing conflicting philosophies or sociological assumptions that assume society is fixable apart from the radical intervention of Christ.[8] Luhmann provides a picture of the state of society. Whether this is a problem to be solved, and how to respond if so, is a theological question as much as a sociological question. As Pannenberg has helpfully noted, the key question for many religious and sociological proposals is not necessarily about God but about the nature of personhood.[9] What does it mean to be a fulfilled person and what does it mean to be free as a person? Differing answers to this issue causes fundamental confrontation between different orienting philosophies.[10] Luhmann sidesteps this fray in how he conceives of the function of systems in society. Luhmann, after all, is not really concerned about people.[11] Which sounds rather harsh, except he argues he is reflecting what society itself constructs: society doesn't care about people either. And that creates a fundamental crisis between self and society.

A person is not the primary social element in Niklas Luhmann's systems theory. Society is not made up of individual human beings, each a rational player navigating life together with other rational players. Rather, society is made up of events, and these events involve communication. Particular people are participants in these expressions but do not construct or perpetuate them. People do not communicate to other persons, communication communicates. As Luhmann's interpreter Hans-Georg Moeller notes, "We can in communication only connect to the communication of others, but never to their minds or brains, much less to the 'human being' as such in any given case."[12] A relatively clear example of this takes place in the legal system. A lawsuit initiates over some issue. The lawsuit involves lawyers who file briefs and exchange arguments. The briefs respond to briefs, the lawyers are not concerned with the personal situation of each other or the litigants. Less clear, though no less present, is how communication like this happens in every system. A teacher communicates to the students, the students communicate back. The goal is not to build a community, but to transact knowledge. Freire's depiction of the "banking model" of pedagogy describes this well.[13] Freire emphasizes this as an oppressive oriented approach that encourages passivity and, while sometimes showing a paternalistic concern, maintains patterns of oppression.

In every sphere of life, we interact with the expressions of people, only very rarely with a person as their actual person. Interaction then involves participation in a *communication system*, which gives self-definition and guidance for behavior. The system shapes the people, rather than the people rationally choosing to shape a system. In effect, this cuts against a perception of personal agency, as participation in the system does not take note of a person's individuality. Participants are effectively anonymous. Moeller writes, "Systems theory recognizes that the world—or rather: *society*—can no longer be aptly understood as a human one."[14] People are expressions of the system's communication, a communication that is self-sustaining and self-creating.

Luhmann utilizes the term "autopoiesis" to describe this self-creating and self-sustaining nature of social systems, adopting it from the field of biology. Humberto Maturana and Francisco Varela first used it to describe how cells produce themselves, maintaining their own boundary within external conditions. An organism is operationally closed and thus organizes itself in an environment so as to perpetuate its own perpetuating. Or as Luhmann puts it, "Such operational closure is merely another way of formulating the statement that an autopoiesis system by means of the network of its own operations generates the operations that it needs in order to generate operations."[15] A cell creates in order to create, the functioning of itself the reasoning for the functioning. A cell makes a cell because that is what a cell does.

In biology, the term "poiesis" is used to describe a cell's actions rather than using the word "praxis."[16] Praxis involves reflective action: actions are pursued because such actions are meaningful, leading to virtue, or excellence, or other valued traits. The justification for these is built into their action: doing good because doing good is good. In much contemporary sociological discourse, it is assumed that people are rational participants involved in making distinct choices about their behavior. This is not necessarily the case, however. If people are more like cells in a system than wholly rational participants, then *praxis* is a goal oriented by intentional reflection while *poiesis* is the broader reality, the state of our social contexts as they are. It is the flow of the river, what we do when we live without intentional reflection on each action.

Poiesis does not have a moral or aesthetic goal; the purpose is making a product. In *autopoiesis*, then, the purpose is self-production. Luhmann argues that the various systems in society do not have an overarching goal. They exist in such a way that perpetuates their existence. He writes, "In the system, there is nothing but the system's own operations."[17] They simply operate as systems and work to continue such operation. "The operation is the condition for the production of operations," a producing of itself, thus involving a closed system of construction and maintenance.[18] The legal system creates and maintains the legal system, the economic system creates and maintains the economic system, the entertainment system, religion system, academic system substantiate and maintain themselves. This is their goal, each in their own separate sphere of values and meaning. These values and meaning are not the intent, but rather the elements that constitute the self-production.

Constituent parts contribute to the system for the sake of the system. This leads to a key problem: participants feel passive in a system that perpetuates without moral purpose even when there is significant critique or frustration with the system. The producing takes place in a context where the production is already presupposed, a factory of its own making, orienting every participant into the pattern of maximizing the production for its own sake. As Luhmann puts it, "At issue is the system that is its own work."[19] That is, systems organize themselves so as to perpetuate their own order, with different systems in society operating with distinct operational patterns. The phrase "this is how things are" is a way of saying much the same thing, revealing how easily moral intention can be subsumed in the process of participating. Everything, and everyone, is in service to these patterns and seemingly subservient to them.

The context of these systems is the environment, but the environment is not a preestablished reality, a supposed unity in which the systems fit like puzzle pieces.[20] The environment is more like a composite picture, where an image is made up of many individual images, themselves whole pictures. A system creates a distinction, maintaining this distinction even as it participates in the environment with other distinction-creating systems; it is a *difference* in an environment not a portion contributing to a unified whole.[21] Luhmann proposes three distinct spheres of systems, each a difference within an environment, contributing to sustaining the difference in their own manner: "systems of communication (social systems), systems of life (bodies, the brain, and so on), and systems of consciousness (minds)."[22] These exist in the environment of each other but maintain boundaries that keep each separately defined and ordered. They are linked by "non-reductive 'interpenetration.'"[23]

Our own participation in the environment is a useful analogy. An individual person is who they are in their body even as they may participate in communicative expressions and physical interactions. The body maintains the self as body without regard to these external elements, even as these external elements inform the body in contextual ways. We are a closed system that interacts with others and is affected by the environment without becoming integrated with the environment. In much the same way, the legal system shares an environment with the economic system, but operates within its own domain, always orienting itself in ways that self-produces itself. The economic system and religious system do the same, interacting in the environment but distinct from each other in operation and production. They are bodies, sharing the same space.

THE SYSTEMS AND OPPRESSING

As I participate in particular systems, I can attempt to maximize my experience in all these, but the more I do so, the less actually integrated I become, as each difference enables differentiation in my own expressed self. I can also choose, it seems, which systems bear the priority for my self-meaning but cannot fully disassociate from the systems themselves while still being part of a given society. Thus, there will always be a degree of dis-integration. In light of diverging self-meanings, I must thus rationalize how what one system requires does not bear on my attempt at self-understanding.[24] This is, of course, exactly what the brain is good at, providing us a sense of rational coherence when life is incoherent. For example, I can be a predatory corporate CEO, who pays an accountant a lot of money to reduce my tax burden to a bare minimum, while voting for progressive political policies and attending church every Sunday. This is not coherent, but it is often justified in social reality. The goal of the systems is perpetuation of each distinct system, not fulfillment of my selfhood, and part of that perpetuation involves providing a pseudo-sense of fulfillment and self, without actually providing actual fulfillment and coherent selfhood.

It is worth repeating: the self-perpetuating social systems are not *constructed of* people but, in effect, *use* people in society as the people are conformed within the autopoietic distinctions. The systems are constructed of communication and events. The systems assert identity priority in society, while a person is essentially anonymous in the system. For the purpose of the system, any person will do as long as they are fulfilling the system's goals. A person's social identity, then, is constructed in light of their participation in these distinct systems. There cannot be an individual in isolation nor an individual self-creating their being. Individualizing away from one system is more fully understood as prioritizing an identity in other systems while continuing to function in all the systems. Indeed, this even allows for very divergent identity expression.

The idea of operational closure reflects that the systems communicate within themselves, oriented toward their own self-production, rather than any cohesive expression of progress. Thus, the idealism that is present in Hegel and subsequent forms of social theory is not present in Luhmann's social systems theory, but neither is systems theory pessimistic.[25] As noted, social systems theory is descriptive, describing the mechanism of social systems as integrative within themselves and only determined by their own self-production or lack thereof.[26] For instance, we might say death is a judgment on a human body, which has ultimately failed in its self-production, but death is not necessarily a judgment in the political, legal, or economic systems as these can be maintained as communicating social systems without regard to particular bodies or people. Death may even be seen as a positive for the economic system as wills and trusts distribute funds, then energize economic activity by others. Such a death is, of course, also a boon to the legal system if the funds are disputed. The communication determines the communication and the communication takes place within each system. There is no universal valuation, only valuation determined within each system, and we are faced with the complications of integrating the difference within our own sense of self. It is both an impossible and necessary task if we are to be successful in this world.

This paradox of establishing self while anonymizing self is quite clear in the world of entertainment. If we see entertainment as its own system, then we can understand how fame can communicate without substantiating. Celebrity has the veneer of individuality but the reality of anonymous participation. People seek fame to gain a sense of self, but the fame is fleeting. The name or particularities of any individual singer or actor are negligible, as the system maintains itself with a bevy of replaceable participants, all who are conformed to the maintenance of entertainment as an entertainment system. Entertainment needs a "star" and every generation produces its own expressions, but the individual contributors themselves lose fame, while the entertainment system continues to self-perpetuate.

This is true for both the celebrity and the fans. What we find entertaining is, in effect, determined by the system of entertainment. Cultures become fans of that which perpetuates their roles as fans. We can describe a particular pop star and their devoted fans as being essentially the same as a small amount of red balls which gather and circulate a large amount of green balls. They are communicating within the system to each other's communication; they are not relating to each other as particular people. So too with the legal system and the religious system: participants are not extraneous but neither are they relevant as individuals. There is production and consumption, each with their own part, feeding into a continuing cycle, even after that cycle does not make contextual sense. They express the communication of the communication of the system and are conformed to the patterns the system maintains as itself, but the system does not confer or even encourage actual distinct personhood.[27]

A particular person is rarely integrated in their social context. Rather, they are expressing roles within distinct social systems. Thus, a person's expression as an individual is often effectively anonymous and incoherent. Someone can protest inequality in one system while dependent on the presence of inequality and even mandating it in other systems.[28] Each role has influence in the social environment and thus in the particular person. However, the systems themselves are not concerned with integration with each other, except as a matter of necessity in sharing an environment, and so are not concerned about a particular person's identity or integration as a whole person. This is worth repeating: systems are simply not concerned with people; they are an emergent social expression.

This is the problem when it comes to oppressing. An oppressor in society is culpable but not necessarily because of a choice they made. Participants in such societies are struggling for integrity in systems that shun such a possibility of reflective choice. A particular person can never be wholly integrated in society because society functions according to operationally closed systems, each with their own autopoietic patterns, concerned with their own self-creation not with any participants. Thus, a person in society is never a cohesive whole, but rather an amalgamation of anonymized participation, communicating the communication of the different systems. Each system seeks to perpetuate itself independently and is not oriented toward some moral, aesthetic, or social purpose. This has an oppressive element, but not necessarily a personalized one, in either source or reception. Appealing to guilt or volition increases the tension without providing effective salvation, functioning not unlike the law as Paul describes in Romans 7.

Inasmuch as some systems reflect social purposes, we can see the influence of the environment in creating a context that requires an apparent praxis, but this is not inherent to the system itself.[29] Praxis can be a posture of *poiesis* rather than genuine self-reflection. In which case, this pseudo-praxis is actually intended to avoid substantive change. It mimics praxis in order to mollify tension, like a politician promising help for the poor—thus gaining votes while maximizing their bank account. In Luhmann's framework, a sociology of morality should be able to deal with both "the obvious progress in formulating moral values like equality, fraternity, and freedom—and the obvious stagnation in their social implementation."[30] Morality exists as an aspect within a system but does not exist as a goal or as an end. Morality serves a function within the systems, but only so to perpetuate the systems, not oriented by some higher ideal.

Both the oppressor and the oppressed are then participating in this emergent social system in its own self-perpetuation. Their individual participation did not come through well-formed or malformed moral volition. They were born into this environment. Thus, the formation of amalgamated selves comes out of such operationally closed structures while dissipating personal responsibility in such systems. "It's just business," as is often heard, whether in business itself, or politics, or academics, or church politics, or social settings. Those who oppress are just as much "oppressed" by the system's patterns as are the oppressed, though admittedly often in a more environmentally congenial way. Given the high incidence of suicide or psychological dysfunction even in environmentally comfortable settings, it is clear that satiation of desires does not satisfy human longing or sense of personal cohesion. Likewise, focusing solely on one system in isolation can sustain patterns of oppression in other ways.[31]

Idealism, in this regard, is thus vulnerable to deception, as systems will adapt so as to appease while not in fact moving toward a more fully perfected humanity. Idealists can be deployed by the system to perpetuate the system rather than change the system, especially when addressing only one system in an environment or utilizing one system to change another. When threatened in other directions, systems will express different patterns, as Germany did in the early twentieth century, moving from a center of idealism to one of the starkest representations of human barbarity in recent history. Political systems are especially reactive in this regard, as participants will rarely emphasize that their goal is to further the system as system but will couch the operations in language that might appeal to voters, using the language of another system—such as economics or religion—while primarily perpetuating the political system. This is the communication of the system at work, a self-perpetuating operation of demand and appeasement. In systems, it is all *panem et circenses,* expressed in different contexts, appeasing different environmental stresses.[32]

This creates a curious situation: to argue within the system is to perpetuate the system, as systems are oriented toward their own self-production and thus have adapted to include dispute within their operations.[33] Politics and economics are established in light of internal conflicts and resolutions, such as political parties or supply and demand. To argue politics in light of the patterns of the political system perpetuates politics. There are, of course, occasional breakthroughs in which political action offers substantive answers, but this is historically rare and itself part of a self-perpetuating system. No one would play the lottery if there were never winners, but the appeal of winning is far too optimistic in light of actual chances. Just enough reward perpetuates a system by maintaining the illusion of benefit for those within the system.

SYSTEMS AND THE SELF

Systems are not separate from society, imposed structures from which one can easily find objective distance. They make up society as we experience it and how we assume it must be; the environment of the systems is the totality of our experience in life. Indeed, systems even welcome debate, within certain parameters. For instance, politics is debated through more politics, one side critiquing the others using established patterns of disruption. The disruption is part of the system. Political debate perpetuates politics. Critiques are built into the system *qua* system; the production of the system makes space for dissonance so as to produce itself further. This may result in reactionary models of government or heresy-incited orthodoxies or law-creating criminality.[34] It quite literally does not matter to a system as system. The systems absorb the critiques in defining and orienting the very definition of rationality and consensus. They constrain the discussion while maintaining the appearance of free engagement.

The rules are what they are, it is thought, and there is only the choosing of sides or navigating the established order in different ways. Rational consensus itself is always system specific and takes place with system operations. The rationality presumes a kind of constructive engagement and self-satisfying intent. Systems, after all, offer a kind of identity substantiation, not toward fully formed persons but as participants in a functioning society. Our societal value derives from our satisfactory acceptance in our system-specific roles. If the systems are all we know, then we assume that is how society must be. We then seek acceptance in these systems and compete over privilege or for power in these systems. In her recent book *Convenience Store Woman*, Sayaka Murata highlights this tendency through her character Keiko Furukura:

> If I went along with the manager when he was annoyed or joined in the general irritation at someone skiving off the night shift, there was a strange sense of solidarity as everyone seemed pleased that I was angry too. Now, too, I felt reassured by the expression on Mrs. Izumi and Sugawara's faces: Good, I pulled

off being a "person." I'd felt similarly reassured any number of times here in the convenience store.[35]

Legal, economic, religious systems tend to bear out the same underlying patterns and roles as life in retail sales, though in different enough ways as to disguise the consistency. This is true throughout history and across different contexts. Systems do adapt to changing environments, but changing these environments very rarely takes place through rational discourse arriving at a consensus for change. People's commitment to distinct operationally closed systems for identity substantiation precludes such idealism.[36] In other words, pure rationality is an illusion in light of autopoietic operations. We are not independent, functioning beings with fully formed identities able to consider and enter into a rationally considered pattern of behavior in society.[37] There are games to be played, credentials to be earned, resumes to build, hoops to jump through. We can be rational within systems but not across systems as different systems involve different rationalities.[38]

Within a given environment different people are prioritizing their roles in different systems, with each system providing its own autopoietic rationality, so consensus can never be fully achieved in an environment but only in a much more narrow sense. Within a single system, the rationality of a system is boundaried by operational closure.[39] Coherence is possible only within the bounds of a single system. As the definition of rational is distinct in each system, people prioritize their roles in the environment differently. This means the goal of any given system will reflect into the perceived identity of a given person but not necessarily to all people in a society in the same way, nor even into every part of a particular person. We can achieve great success in one system while being entirely dysfunctional or irrational in another. Likewise, different rationalities can experience similar success in a given system, even as debate over these rationalities radicalizes participants. Politics, for instance, does not thrive on consensus but on opposition, thus encourages heightened distinctions that, in order to keep the system moving, claim they are seeking consensus. It is a power that denies its goal in practice for the purpose of power. The quest for power perpetuates the system. The system does not care about the rationale as it commits to its own self-production. So different rationales can replace one another while the system itself endures without much change.

Adding to the complexity in an environment, a number of different rationalities can temporarily align with each other, with different rationalities in different systems promoting a shared general goal. For instance, consider a revolution against an oppressive government. Because particular revolutionaries are finding identity in different systems, they may in fact have very different outcomes in mind, not the same actual goal at all. Artists want freedom of expression, politicians want power and influence, the poor want food, lawyers want laws, police want order. A shared initial cause pointing toward a desired end—the overturning of a government—is only loosely cohesive and vaguely rational.

This is akin to what DeLanda calls an "assemblage" in which identity is structured around exteriority but does not actually reflect a substantive unity.[40] Those involved only rarely protest the systems as systems but more often protest their relative positions in the systems, leading to those sharing relatively lower position temporarily organizing together, assembling "as part of the antagonistic struggle of Us against Them, and antagonism is something that traverses each of these elements from within."[41] The goal of this assemblage is not toward wholeness or unity, however this does not diminish the continuing interest of each element to find meaning, and that embeds a tension within the assemblage. Slavoj Žižek writes:

> The desire-for-assemblage is thus proof that a dimension of universality is already at work in all the elements in the guise of a negativity, of an obstacle that thwarts their self-identity. In other words, elements don't strive for assemblage in order to become part of a larger Whole; they strive for assemblage in order to become themselves, to actualize their identity.[42]

This is why once a goal is accomplished there is rarely continued cohesion among the different players. A politician will use an artist as long as the goal is unmet, but an artist should not depend on the politician's continued advocacy once power is achieved. If the politician feels threatened by art, the system allegiance asserts itself. Thus, the revolution is distorted, abandoned, betrayed and a new revolution is called for. The systems endure even in a successful revolution, with different anonymized participants filling established roles.

To achieve societal validation in any given system a person participates in the system's communication. A person becomes effectively anonymous within the system but is not simply an automaton. Rationality is present, but it is only a small measure of our social functioning. Part of the systems functioning indeed involves a small measure of rational engagement so as to validate our sense of self in the system, even as the system anonymizes us as part of the system. We do not matter as our self, but we are convinced that our self is at stake in our relation to the system. We are concerned with our self as self, while the systems are concerned with their system as system.

In return for communicating within a given system, the system rewards us with a sense of self. We are never anonymous to our self, yet continually encounter the paradox of ultimate anonymity in the context of the systems, which we tend to both deny and obsess over. The fragile ego of a major movie star or recording artist is a clear example, both fully realized in the system and fully anonymous in the system (knowing their role as celebrity can and will be replaced by another at any given point in the system's functioning). The contribution of an adjunct professor in the education system is another, with little commitment or status in their place of employment. They are a role filling a role, not a person valued as a person.

Systems are ultimately anonymizing—autopoietic through the participation *of* people in the system but not *as* people in the system. This creates a tension if a person seeks real freedom and full identity as a coherent self. One solution is to leave society altogether. But that is not tenable for most of us nor is it a trend we see emphasized in Scripture. If that is the only hope for oppressors, then there is really no functional liberation of oppressors within society. Indeed, as history notes, when groups of people leave one society to live in another the same problems tend to arise. For those who seek to establish their particularity while remaining within their social contexts, people must engage in a transformative response: a meta-communication to the fragmented communication so as to integrate the systems toward a more holistic and emancipating praxis.[43] But the systems resist and restrict such an attempt, threatening the loss of what little integration there is, and that initiates a paradox: to become whole, a person must risk becoming nothing. To alleviate the tension of this paradox, yet another system steps in to bring order to the environment: the religious system.

SYSTEMS AND RELIGION

As a system, religion navigates the holy and profane (or secular), distinguishing between the transcendent and immanent, moral and immoral, or eternal and temporal.[44] It promises transformation or protection, while also organizing community in contrasting postures. Religion, Luhmann writes, "is the paradigmatic way to carry out paradoxization/de-paradoxization whenever such an occasion presents itself."[45] It provides meaning through contextual occasions, a medium of meaning that helps a person find substantiation in light of overwhelming questions that might otherwise lead to despair. Such substantiation is not, however, invoked in other systems but instead serves, in Western context at least, as a way for an individual to construct meaning alongside the otherwise anonymizing nature of every other system. However, as a system, religion likewise anonymizes its participants, something that is in fact embedded within many ecclesiologies. For instance, as noted in the church's response to the Donatists, it is not the presider who determines the validity of a baptism, but the event and communication. It is also not the confession of the person that validates the baptism but rather the act and the participation. Religion as a system thus emphasizes events rather than people, following Luhmann's definition of systems.[46]

Christianity is, not surprisingly, the primary example Luhmann uses in his discussion of religion as a system.[47] He notes that "in the Christian context, sin is the central notion of cosmology, referring to the first distinction of prohibition and transgression."[48] Questions, of course, remain about the nature of sin and whether Luhmann's conception of Christianity is an adequate expression of Christian theology.[49] That said, Christianity certainly has and does express itself in terms of a religious system, and in this way has situated itself in different environments among the different systems. Is this inherent to Christianity or, rather, an adaptation of Christianity as a religion replacing other religions within a given religious system of an environment? In other words, is it a distortion of Christianity to operate in terms of a religion system, and as such, perpetuating systems as systems rather than confronting society as a whole? This question addresses whether Christianity in its fullest sense is a net cause of oppression or if it can lead toward liberation.[50] A system cannot liberate out of itself nor liberate other systems. If Christianity is limited to the religious system, then it cannot offer fundamental hope to either oppressed or oppressors.

Is Christianity the problem to be overcome, as many have suggested over the decades? Inasmuch as Christianity is simply a filler for the religious system in some Western contexts, maybe so. When Christianity becomes subservient within a system, it becomes an anonymized religion. The system is lord, not Christ. Indeed, arguing that a system of Christianity is a problem is an argument made by both atheists and radical Christians. Roger William and George Fox, among so many others, certainly saw the dominating Christianity of their times as lacking spiritual authority and power.[51] Christianity that serves as a system helps maintain structures in an environment that are conducive to oppressing. Maybe religion itself is the problem. Of course, there's no simply getting rid of religion. The system endures, though maybe not with a deity or with a systematic liturgy, but as our postmodern world shows, people remain disoriented by the paradox of life, and the need to find integrative meaning in anonymizing systems. They turn to other orienting philosophies to give such purpose and meaning. The religious system endures, and maybe even more thoroughly once it has shed that anachronistic category of divinity.

If Christianity is not itself the problem, then why is it not a consistent solution? Maybe because it makes claims that it then does not follow through on. God loves everyone. Does Christianity reflect this? Does Christian history reflect the subsequent summary of the whole law: love God and love neighbor? What happened when Christianity has taken this seriously? For instance, the early church did seem to offer an integrative conception of the world. They did help the poor. They did take in the outcasts. They did live in a radically new way within this world. That suggests the issue isn't Christianity itself but more akin to Chesterton's famous comment that it has not been tried and found wanting, it has not been tried.[52] Christianity allowed itself to be co-opted, set into a box among the systems of this world, securing power for some, keeping the religious systems moving along. In this way it is, to adapt Wesley's terminology, an "Almost Christianity."[53] What went wrong? How can those of us who continue to assert fundamental Christian truths help steer it back on track?

How these important questions are answered radically affects the diagnosis of this world and the prescription for it. While there are other ways of assessing the world, and their accompanying philosophical proposals for fixing it, I find Luhmann's systems theory useful in how it highlights society in both a holistic and a particular way, showing how different systems express different aspects of our life, neither dismissing nor isolating one from the other. Whereas Luhmann's goal is to be descriptive, my goal is to better understand a starting point that led us into contexts of oppressing and find a way toward liberation. Luhmann highlights the fundamental problem is not about issues to be addressed between divergent parties. The very structure of society mitigates wholesale solutions or universal rational discourse. If Christianity itself is the problem, and ecclesiology inherently leads to oppression, then it is better to look elsewhere from the beginning. If, however, Christianity itself emphasizes freedom and liberation, whenever it has enabled oppression to take place, then that is a sign for when Christianity has become "anonymous" as part of a religious system.[54] If our ecclesiology has been co-opted by the systems, then we cannot find liberation by revision within the systems as they are currently expressed. That perpetuates the system. It is thus important to assess the theological issues that led to such a pattern and determine if these need revision or transformation.

CONCLUSION

Social theories that seek to resolve the crises within the systems are not adequate to the task of thorough liberation. Luhmann's systems theory is not up to the task of liberation either. Nor, of course, was it intended to be. This is where a more thoroughly Christian approach has a message of hope that goes beyond the way things are. Indeed, that's one key task for a liberation theology, to move from poiesis into *praxis*. As Ignacio Ellacuría writes, "Ideas alone do not change social structures; there have to be social forces that counteract in a process of liberation, the other social forces that established the process of oppression."[55] Other programs of social change—those that seek to transform from within the social structures—critique them in part but are also dependent on them. An "altogether" Christianity, however, proposes a transformation of "transcendent immanence" in which a new way of life is lived out in the midst of society.[56] Again, this insists on reassessing our definition of sin and the work of Christ in responding to it.

Christian theology is not limited to systems theory, the experiences of the past, or a presumed shared rationality. My argument, to be developed below, is that the kingdom of God is an integrative expression of being re-personalized in light of God's role of creator and savior.[57] It is thus not dependent on the social structures as they exist. In a thoroughly Christian vision for the world, we see a new perspective on the world and that which is beyond this experience of the world in the work of Christ. Theology becomes real engagement in this world as a transformative instigator. This work expresses a twofold response: confrontation of the systems as systems (the cross) and an invitation toward a new pattern of life in, with, and for this world (resurrection). This effort must understand both the context of how things are and the vision of how things should be. This vision is not a generalized ideal, it is inviting particular people into a complex interplay of many participants. After all, the experience of human life is not limited to broad social realities.

The participation of the individual in the social context adds significant complexity to any potential analysis, but without both the person and the context in mind there cannot be substantive liberation for either a person or society. Sin is structural and also personal, so a hope for the oppressor must address society and each participant. Christ is not someone to be admired, but rather imitated, and that is the substantive orientation of self that provides transcendent meaning in the midst of the world. In chapter 2, I will focus on the state of the individual person—the self—living in the context of society as it is. For guidance in this, I turn to Kierkegaard, who was particularly interested in a realized Christianity that took shape in an alienating world.

NOTES

1. In discussing the purpose of analyzing human vices, John Cassian writes, "Thus, penetrating the dark shadows of our vices with the most pure eyes of our soul, we shall be able to expose them and to bring them into the light, and we shall be in a position to disclose their causes and natures both to those who are free of them and to those who are still under their sway." In *The Institutes*, trans. Boniface Ramsey (New York: The Newman Press, 2000), V.II.3.

2. Traugott Schöfthäler, "Social Foundations of Morality: Durkheimian Problems and Niklas Luhmann's Systems Theories of Religion, Morality and Personality," *Social Compass* 31, nos. 2–3 (1984): 191.

3. See, for instance, Jn 15:19; Rom. 12:12; 1 Cor. 1:20–28; Jas 4:4. In using Luhmann, I am neither rejecting nor supporting Marxist approaches in liberation

theologies. Indeed, as there is an abundance of Marxist analysis, it seems especially worthwhile to propose alternative models as a constructive contribution.

4. Søren Kierkegaard, *Practice in Christianity*, eds. Howard V. Hong and Edna H. Hong (Princeton: Princeton University Press, 1991), 233–234.

5. Dallas Willard, *The Divine Conspiracy* (New York: HarperOne, 1997), 21–22. He continues on page 22 in regard to the depersonalizing realities of oppression: "Any being that has say over nothing at all is no person." This shows how oppressing really is depersonalizing, and how involuntary diminishment of our control feels like an attack on our personhood, which riles up defensive behavior: attempts at counter-oppression or resignation.

6. In a Christian sense, how the world should be must derive from biblical and theological resources rather than beginning with other models that perceive reality in a substantively different way and often do not include the revelation of God as the creator or re-creator of this reality.

7. Jürgen Moltmann, *Ethics of Hope* (Minneapolis: Fortress Press, 2013), 3.

8. Of course, it is certainly debatable whether such a radical intervention is indeed necessary, and that leaves open the possibility of other proposals and associated solutions as part of a broader analysis. However, it seems useful for a Christian theological response to contribute according to its particular Christian assumptions about reality, and not subvert Christian doctrine by emptying it of either its anthropology or soteriology. Doing such makes it "lukewarm" (Rev. 3:16). Cf. Søren Kierkegaard, *The Practice of Christianity*, 256. As Paul notes in 1 Corinthians 15, if the resurrection did not happen, then we're wasting our time talking about Christ at all. If it did happen, that changes everything and confirms what Christ taught. Cf. Wolfhart Pannenberg, *Jesus—God and Man* (London: SCM Press, 1968), 416–418. I venture forth in light of an affirmation of the resurrection and attempt to construct a theological response in light of it.

9. See, for instance, Wolfhart Pannenberg, "Christianity, Marxism, and Liberation Theology," *Christian Scholar's Review* 18, no. 3 (1989): 215–226. While a good argument can be made for utilizing elements of different philosophies, Pannenberg has argued that some philosophies have divergent enough conceptions of anthropology as to make the philosophies incompatible with Christian goals. Kierkegaard seems to agree with this in his response to Hegel, thus making it a coherent assumption for this current project. In his helpful response to Pannenberg, Stanley Grenz notes, "One dare not too quickly fault those Christians who, while ministering to the poor, are easily attracted to categories they find helpful in understanding their world context, regardless of those categories' sources." Stanley J. Grenz, "Pannenberg on Marxism : Insights and Generalizations," *Christian Century* 104, no. 27 (1987): 826.

10. I use the term "orienting philosophies" rather than "religion" because a lot of what in previous eras would have been considered religious is not categorized as such in our era. In avoiding that label, such proposals are given the veneer of objective secular analysis—allowed a voice where religions may be prevented—thus privileging their subjective perspective. To assume a religious perspective must involve a god or gods is a very narrow perspective indeed.

11. Indeed, very few philosophies are genuinely concerned about people, at least concerned about particular persons, though many show concerns for certain *populations*.

12. Hans-Georg Moeller, *Luhmann Explained: From Souls to Systems* (Chicago: Open Court, 2006), 9.

13. Freire, *Pedagogy of the Oppressed*, chap. 2.

14. Moeller, *Luhmann Explained*, 5. He continues, "The primary starting point of social systems theory—or its 'turning point' in comparison to its humanistic predecessors—is that it no longer holds that current society can be successfully analyzed on the basis that it is (or should be) fundamentally humane, and that it is, on principle an assembly of individual human beings."

15. Niklas Luhmann, *Introduction to Systems Theory*, trans. Peter Gilgen (Malden, MA: Polity, 2013), 77.

16. See Luhmann, *Introduction to Systems Theory*, 77–78.

17. Ibid., 70.

18. Ibid., 78.

19. Ibid., 78. Cf. Moeller, *Luhmann Explained*, 12–14.

20. "We live in a society which cannot represent its unity in itself, as this would contradict the logic of functional differentiation. We live in a society without a summit and without a center. The unity of society no longer comes out of this society. . . . Systems of functions can only legitimate themselves. This is, no system can legitimate each other." Niklas Luhmann, "The Representation of Society within Society," *Current Sociology* 2, no. 35 (1987): 105.

21. See Luhmann, *Introduction*, 63.

22. Moeller, *Luhmann Explained*, 9.

23. Peter Gilgen, "System—Autopoiesis—Form: An Introduction to Luhmann's Introduction to System's Theory," in Luhmann, *Introduction*, x. For this section as whole, I was greatly helped by Gilgen's concise explanations of Luhmann's often obtuse and sometimes intentionally dense terminology, prose, and main theses. Indeed, Hans-Georg Moeller, *The Radical Luhmann* (New York: Columbia University Press, 2012), chap. 2 highlights these latter elements by titling this chapter "Why He Wrote Such Bad Books." He notes that the style reflects the way Luhmann produced the texts, which was by a rigorous production of notes, stored in a cabinet, then assembled into bigger texts. His use of these notes, which involved key words and links, was a sort of mechanical "Internet." This pattern leads to a lack of linear development, being more of a collection of assembled musings. A second reason for his style comes from his attempt to develop a "supertheory" that addressed everything, which involved the use of a distinct vocabulary that reflects new terminology or old terminology used in new ways. With this is the fashion of some, especially European, academics to couch their concepts in intentionally esoteric expressions. Being inaccessible is then seen as a marker of academic superiority. Here Luhmann's approach is reminiscent of that of Radical Orthodoxy among other movements. Moeller, *Radical Luhmann*, 136 suggests that the style of writing is a major factor in Luhmann's lack of reception so far in North America.

24. The early church experienced this tension in an explicit way. The Roman Empire did not have a problem with early Christian devotion to Jesus as long as the early Christians also sacrificed to Caesar. That early Christians would not do so was a matter of confusion to Roman governors, who did not see any inherent conflict with what were clearly (to them) separate issues of concern.

25. On understanding Habermas as incorporating at least substantive aspects of idealism, see Maeve Cooke, "Realism and Idealism: Was Habermas's Communicative Turn a Move in the Wrong Direction?" *Political Theory* 40, no. 6 (2012): 811–821.

26. For a more detailed analysis of these elements, see Hans-Ulrich Dallmann, "Niklas Luhmann's Systems Theory as a Challenge for Ethics," *Ethical Theory and Moral Practice* 1, no. 1 (1998): 85–102.

27. Early Christianity was not uniform in embracing this expression of a religious system. Indeed, the Donatist controversy seems to especially reflect this. The debate was whether a particular person affected liturgical practices, and thus their behavior could impact the efficacy of such practices, or whether a particular person communicated the communication of the practices, but the practices were unaffected by the presider. As the latter approach was triumphant, the office rather than the person became the defining category. While this has theological justification, in part, it also strongly impacted the social influence of the church and, it seems, opened the door to overlooking injustices perpetuated by the church in later eras. See Zablon Nthamburi, "The Relevance of Donatism for the Church in Africa Today," *AFER* 23, no. 4 (August 1981): 215–220.

28. Again, I think here about the dependency on adjuncts in our higher education systems. This leads to the occasional incoherence of underpaid and overworked women and men, often in great debt and without other skills, utilized in unfair ways to help highly paid, highly privileged faculty take time off for writing about societal dysfunction. It takes a great amount of capital for students to pay for access to discussions about the evils of capitalism. This isn't an argument for or against such discussions, rather just highlighting the incoherence involved in our contemporary systems.

29. This might be most apparent in the economic system where corporations have recently expressed a strong interest in the environment, social causes, and so on. To see these as anything more than an expediency is to be naïve about the nature of such companies. Evidence of this can be found in how they act in contexts where such behavior is not socially or legally essential. Oil companies, for instance, that tout their environmental sensitivity in commercials in the United States perpetuate destructive environmental trauma in Africa and elsewhere.

30. Schöfthäler, "Social Foundations of Morality," 191.

31. See Moeller, *Luhmann Explained*, chap. 11 for study of Luhmann's response to Marx. Moeller, 178 writes, "According to Luhmann, Marx's understanding of the economy and its functioning as a social construct rather than a process based on some sort of natural law was groundbreaking." However, as he notes Marx "overestimates this social system in regard to its constituting power for all of society."

32. Niklas Luhmann, *A Systems Theory of Religion*, ed. André Kieserling (Palo Alto, CA: Stanford University Press, 2013), 101 writes that "one has to assume that the continuation of societal autopoiesis, the reproduction of communication by communication, brings up different problems depending on the level of historical evolution."

33. It is here we can see a logic to the response by Jesus in the trials leading to the crucifixion. The confrontation with the systems as systems did not come through his appeal to either Jewish or Roman law to acquit himself but by carrying through the

process according to the attempt by the systems to regulate their role as constitutive social powers. By dying on the cross, Jesus received the penalty of each system's judgment. The resurrection undermined their ultimate authority. They have no substantive power after all. By refusing to dispute with the system, Jesus left the door open to fundamental restructuring in light of the pattern of the kingdom of God.

34. On the role of heresy, see Hans Küng, *The Church* (New York: Sheed and Ward, 1967), 244–257.

35. Sayaka Murata, *Convenience Store Woman*, trans. Ginny Tapley Takemori, Kindle edition (New York: Grove Press, 2018), location 290.

36. Among the many other reasons history has shown us to distrust idealistic assumptions of human advancement.

37. See Nancey Murphy and Warren S. Brown, *Did My Neurons Make Me Do It?: Philosophical and Neurobiological Perspectives on Moral Responsibility and Free Will* (New York: Oxford University Press, 2009).

38. An academic may assume an education-system based rationality that assesses other systems, inviting other academics to discuss the assessments at conferences, writing articles and books that are read and critiqued by other academics. Success in academia leads to a protected position in a highly ranked institution, which in many cases was built and is sustained by the very systems the academic is critiquing. The academic assumes his identity from the academic system while participating in the economic (tuition, loans, endowments, donations), legal (contracts), political (government funding and education policy). Actions in these other systems are prioritized by the effect the academic receives in the academic systems, what will bring esteem or promotion or funding.

39. Following Luhmann in a slightly different way than he intended, we find potential validation still when he notes, "This might also explain why intellectuals talk mainly about other intellectuals, which is to say, why Habermas describes how Derrida describes Nietzsche or how Hegel describes Kant and why others, in turn, describe how Habermas and Parsons describe Weber, whereas Parson's critics describe how Parsons wrongly describes Weber. All of this takes place at the level of discourse as a description of descriptions, as an observation of observations. Realities enter into this autopoietic network of the intellectuals only as shocks. Thus the collapse of the socialist systems was a shock for the intellectuals, at least for many of them." Luhmann, *Introduction*, 117.

40. On this stimulating and creative approach to society, see Manuel DeLanda, *Assemblage Theory* (Edinburgh: Edinburgh University Press, 2016); Manuel DeLanda, *A New Philosophy of Society: Assemblage Theory and Social Complexity* (New York: Continuum, 2006). Although beyond the scope of this study, DeLanda's approach would likewise be a helpful interpretive partner for Christian theologians.

41. Slavoj Žižek, "Marx Reads Object-Oriented Ontology," in *Reading Marx* (Medford, MA: Polity, 2018), 22–23.

42. Žižek, "Marx Reads Object-Oriented Ontology," 23.

43. See Alan Kreider, *The Patient Ferment of the Early Church* (Grand Rapids: Baker Academic, 2016), 96–99 for the early Christian approach to this task.

44. See Luhmann, *A Systems Theory of Religion*, 89–91; cf. 95–99. See also Rudolf Otto, *The Idea of the Holy: An Enquiry into the Non-Rational Factor in the Idea of the Divine and Its Relation to the Rational* (New York: Oxford University Press, 1923).

45. Luhmann, *A Systems Theory of Religion*, 98.

46. Different ecclesial traditions emphasize different events, often though not always, characterizing these as sacraments. For the Catholic Church we can point to the Mass, for Protestants the event of preaching takes on a operational role. The person who preaches and the people who hear are effectively anonymous in light of the primary expression of the preached Word as Christ with us. Cf. Alasdair MacIntyre, *After Virtue: A Study in Moral Theory* (Notre Dame, IN: University of Notre Dame Press, 2007), 28–30.

47. There are certainly exceptions, throughout history, so this is not inherent to Christian theology nor a way of characterizing all ecclesiologies, or every aspect of any given ecclesiology.

48. Luhmann, *A Systems Theory of Religion*, 99.

49. This is not to dispute Luhmann's conception of Christianity as being an accurate portrayal in many cases but rather to say his goal is to describe it as within a system while there is more to it than this.

50. Cf. Kathryn Tanner, *The Politics of God* (Minneapolis: Fortress Press, 1992), 1–4.

51. "The essence of the Quaker message," Geoffrey Nuttall writes, "was that the Spirit of God was in everyman." In Geoffrey F. Nuttall, *The Holy Spirit in Puritan Faith and Experience* (Chicago: University of Chicago Press, 1992), 183. Claire Disbrey sums up Fox's "openings": "The four ideas that his early openings express were that Christians must have a personal experience of God, that Oxford-and-Cambridge-trained gentry should not have a monopoly of the priesthood, that the church does not consist of buildings but of people, and that God could speak directly to people's hearts." In Claire Disbrey, "George Fox and Some Theories of Innovation in Religion," *Religious Studies* 25, no. 1 (1989): 67. For excellent studies on Williams's contributions to the debate over the relationship between church and state, see Timothy Hall, *Separating Church and State: Roger Williams and Religious Liberty* (Urbana: University of Illinois Press, 1998) and Edmund S. Morgan, *Roger Williams: The Church and the State* (New York: Harcourt Brace & World, 1967). On George Fox, see George Fox, *The Journal of George Fox*, ed. Rufus Jones (Richmond, IN: Friends United Press, 1976).

52. In *What's Wrong with the World* (New York: Cassell and Company, 1910), 39, Chesterton wrote, "The Christian ideal has not been tried and found wanting. It has been found difficult; and left untried."

53. See John Wesley, Sermon 2, "The Almost Christian," §1 in *The Sermons of John Wesley*, eds. Kenneth J. Collins and Jason E. Vickers (Nashville: Abingdon Press, 2013), 96–99.

54. This enabling of oppression is a core critique of liberation theologies. In his introduction to the 15th anniversary edition of his groundbreaking book, Gustavo Gutiérrez writes, "The approaching five-hundredth anniversary of the evangelization

of Latin America should be the occasion for an examination of conscience regarding the immense human cost historically connected with that evangelization—I mean the destruction of individuals and cultures." Gutiérrez, *A Theology of Liberation*, xxii.

55. Ellacuría, *Ignacio Ellacuría*, 110. He continues, "If a real praxis of liberation is given, even if in an incipient manner, it is in relation to that praxis of liberation that philosophy can carry out its liberative function, first in respect to the liberative praxis as a whole, and later as an integral part of it, as much critically as positively, in favor of a liberative process and in search of a new social structure in which persons can reach the proper realization of freedom and communion."

56. See Oden, *The Transformative Church*, 235.

57. See Kierkegaard, *Practice in Christianity*, 238–239.

Chapter 2

The Crisis of Self-Existence

INTRODUCTION

What is the self? The answer seems obvious. The self is me. Or you, or any of the other innumerable accidents of human substance. The individual in contrast to the masses. Yet, the self in human reality is something more, both a perspective and an essence, our sense of being, meaning, and psychological coherence. Which is a curious reality to have, since we are also utterly social beings. We are self among other selves. We find our self enticed to *be* in a particular way. That was the promise in the Garden narrative, was it not? The serpent offered a way to *be*, without involving God in the process; to *know*, suggesting wisdom without sacrifice or relationship. Our environment does not have a tree of knowledge, but it does have a variety of systems, each of which holds out the promise of fulfillment—or at least satiation. The problem is that while we, as individuals, are concerned about our self, other selves are concerned about their selves. And the systems? They're not concerned about self at all. They don't care that I care, you care, or anyone cares. That is a big, multifaceted problem indeed.

Chapter 1 may be considered a sociological epidemiology, looking at the conditions that foster oppressing behaviors within a person's social environment. This chapter is about the crisis of being a self in a world that does not particularly care about our selfhood. It is thus much more particular in scope, resisting the urge to negate individuality in the quest for broad liberation. To accomplish this, I will examine the insights provided by Søren Kierkegaard, who saw the self and society in mutually determining ways and understood how the tension they bring to each other can engender a deep dysfunction in the self *and* in society. Kierkegaard offers helpful insights into the struggles of self and his writings point to the inner tensions and motives that often lead to outward oppression.

His piercing analysis engages the trajectory that began in the early part of the late modern era. The crises of self and society took on a new shape in his time and have since become entrenched throughout all of society in our era, making his insights still quite relevant. His analysis likewise involves a critique of the structural church, which is important in navigating our post-Christian response, as our context in the industrialized West has been shaped by ecclesial dysfunction resulting in ecclesial abandonment. Inasmuch as Christianity has functioned as a religious system, it has enabled oppression, serving the environment of systems to perpetuate anonymity. Because of a long history of such abandonment, people increasingly do not see the church as a solution, and that's a significant problem in constructing a Christian response.[1]

While it would be illuminating to study the whole of his writings, that is beyond the scope of the present work. I will thus examine *Sickness unto Death* in more detail, as this text was a mature attempt to clarify the conflict between self and society for what it is and thus what we must struggle against. Alongside this, I will first utilize introductory insights from his *Concept of Anxiety* and finally constructive responses from *The Practice of Christianity* as supporting material. In using these three texts together, I am following a particular thread of Kierkegaard's thought that seeks to analyze the human condition in light of God's calling.[2]

THE CONCEPT OF ANXIETY

While Kierkegaard has sometimes been labeled a strong individualist and existentialist, interpreters should consider his strong commitment to Christian doctrine and his strong opposition to Hegelian generalizations, both of which may better characterize him as emphasizing particularity rather than individualization.[3] He is not seeking to isolate individuals, but to identify them as particular subjects within a community that only has hope together with Christ. As such, he becomes a key contributor to understanding the problem a dissolved self in society and the problem of a dissolved society of isolated selves, both of which lead into oppressing behaviors.

"Dissolution" is an objective sounding word for a subjective experience. In Christian theology, "sin" is the term applied to such a state of things and indeed sin is the core concept in *The Concept of Anxiety*. Even though sin carries religious-system baggage, it is not limited to that system, even if the religious system often assumes such by narrowly limiting its definition and isolating it from other systems. In doing this, it hyper-individualizes the reality of sin as simply being a matter of wrong behavior or addressed merely by saying the right words in a stock prayer that leads to salvation. It can also become over-objectified, leading to disinterest about it or even knowing amusement about indulging in it. Sin is more complex and pervasive than this, however, individual while also social, involving what Alvin Plantinga calls the "culpable disturbance of shalom."[4] As the self is social, this disturbance has psychological realities that resonate into our contexts.[5] It is not a state, nor is it a disease.[6]

The study of sin does not, as Kierkegaard emphasizes, "belong to any science."[7] It belongs to sermons, he notes, but this does not imply it is only a religious category. Sin, using current analogies, is more like gravity; a kind of transcendent effect that is present without being wholly understood. In being transcendent, it is a resonating and shaping force that cannot be limited to mere behavior. There's something deeper about its presence with us that resists systematizing. This transcendent nature does not mean it exists on a plane of reality outside our experiences. "Now sin is precisely," Kierkegaard notes, "that transcendence that *discrimen rerum* [crisis] in which sin enters into the single individual as the single individual. Sin never enters into the world differently and has never entered into the world differently."[8] Just as gravity enters the world only through specific bodies, but resonates broadly out from the particular, sin disturbs our inner *shalom* as it disturbs our contextual *shalom*, disturbing the *shalom* of our entire social fabric as it resonates across time and geography.

The nature of sin is derived from the nature of freedom's possibilities. The encounter with possibility and the freedom to make choices engenders anxiety. In seeking to maximize our own self-being, we face a world that does not give a clear map to wholeness. It is uncertainty about who to be and what to do, what Kierkegaard calls "freedom's actuality as the possibility of possibility."[9] The anticipation is distorted by uncertainty, no longer ignorant about possibilities but overwhelmed by cognition of conditionality.[10] What if I did that? What if I went there? What if I pursued this? The apparent freedom is itself conditioned by prohibitions and limitations. This is not yet sin itself but creates the setting for sin in embracing the anxiety, succumbing to the prohibition or becoming stifled in indecision. Sin is pervasive not because it is a necessity but because freedom allows its possibility among our possibilities. When freedom becomes unmoored from its orienting reality, it drifts further into anxiety, getting freedom and prohibition and possibility tangled together, losing the ability to discern right from up, or left from down. Anxiety is an intermediate experience, a kind of ontological limbo, an "entangled freedom."[11]

This is where oppressing becomes identifiable as a category in need of liberation. When structural evils are enforcing oppression, those who are oppressed need freedom from those structures. But in the case of oppressors, the freedom of choice itself evokes an anxiety about being, and in this anxiety an oppressor becomes disoriented, expressing an inherited response to anxiety that restricts self and others. Cain kills Abel, not out of necessity but out of a choice due to anxiety. Outside the Garden, God's favor is in question. Innocence is lost. Why didn't God accept his sacrifice? The nature of this "inheritance" is beyond the scope of history, with its presence now so deeply embedded in our self and society that it seems part of what simply is. It reverberates from experience to act and back again, "hence anxiety is the dizziness of freedom," in which there is a loss of freedom rather than an embrace of it, succumbing in weakness to embrace the immediacy of prohibitions, or the distraction of desires.[12] Kierkegaard notes, "Sin entered in anxiety, but sin in turn brought anxiety along with it."[13] Anxiety is the background noise of the primordial sin. Sin is sustained, inherited even, through a feedback loop of anxiety produced by possibilities deepening our anxiety about our self. "As sin entered into the world, so it continues to enter into the world if it is not halted."[14] It does not even need an outside influence, as "anxiety about sin produces sin."[15] We worry about insecurities, insufficiencies, and worry about worrying itself.

In the unredeemed encounters with freedom, now these things remain: possibility, anxiety, and sin. Sin collapses the wave function of possibilities, restricting a sense of being into what must be because that is what we assume must be done. Such a collapse involves culpability but not necessarily volition, a consequence of choice that did not appear as choice because of the anxiety that clouded the scope of reality. Such anxiety resists repentance or reformation within the systems, because having despaired of hope, it can no longer acknowledge it as a possibility.

Of this status, Kierkegaard writes:

> The individual may repent of his wrath, and the more profound he is, the more profound is his repentance. But repentance cannot make him free; in that he is mistaken. The occasion comes: anxiety has already discovered it. Every thought trembles. Anxiety sucks out the strength of repentance and shakes its head. It is as though wrath had already conquered. Already he has a presentiment of the prostration of freedom that is reserved for the next moment. The moment comes; wrath conquers.[16]

Accusing an oppressor who is responding according to the system induces anxiety in them. Accusing an oppressor of inaction induces more anxiety. Orienting social salvation in light of new actions even contributes to anxiety. What if it is not enough? What if others attempt to prevent it? In all of this, guilt is invoked, and becomes a tool for partial reformation, but such an approach cannot provide actual liberation. Sin continues to remain, unhalted, creating division through variable expressions of attempts to tamp down the guilt, anxiety, insufficiency, all of which is experienced as wrath. Even attempts at good works falls short, as while they may have some positive effect, they continue in a dissolutive pattern. Kierkegaard notes, "The only thing that is truly able to disarm the sophistry of sin is faith."[17] But before getting to this solution, it is worthwhile to sit in wrath a while longer, for the state of wrath provokes oppressing, and the experience of wrath is that of despair. Only in understanding how anxiety and despair underlie persistent sin can there be a more adequate response to their cure and to liberation of those who are unfree in their experience of possibilities.

THE SICKNESS OF THE SELF

The systems coordinate a perception of self through nonrational operations in the systems to simulate rational participation: I want achievement because I have chosen this achievement to want, even as such achievement is socially determined and system maintaining. My rationality is conditioned by the systems. In this way, the human self is what Daphne Hampson calls "a derived, a constituted relation."[18] True objective awareness of such a state is certainly possible but by nature of such a paradox—authentic-identity fulfillment comes through derived-identity abandonment—it involves despair. Where is the true self to be found? The systems offer a paradox of being fully human while fully system. That is an impossibility. They cannot offer a cohesive identity because they lack any real cohesion between each other.

Modernity heightened the discord as progress advanced opportunities which did not fulfill the expected promise of wholeness. This was a driving issue for Kierkegaard, who sought to find coherence of self despite the competing claims and challenges. "Such a relation that relates to itself," Kierkegaard writes, "must either have established itself or have been established by another."[19] Self-establishment is impossible while subject to an identity establishing system. A system suggests there is no self outside the system, thus maintaining its authority over participants without inherent control. People do not have to participate but have been lulled into continued participation. Kierkegaard notes that "in relating itself to itself and in willing to be itself, the self rests transparently in the power that established it."[20] The self finds self in the system that does not care about self but only about the system. This encounter with impossible paradox eventually evokes despair.

Despair is "the misrelation in the relation of a synthesis that relates itself to itself."[21] Systems can promise systems but cannot promise either self or transcendence. Systems are always self-perpetuating, not creating something new. Confronted with a self that is not a self, it is all too common to embrace a pseudo-self which functions socially to provide meaning. "Meaning," Luhmann writes, "is a medium of autopoietic systems."[22] The systems offer a form of meaning, and we let the systems define who we are to be. To maintain our pseudo-self, we must produce within those systems. Better to be accepted as a pseudo-self than to be rejected as one's true self. To be anonymous is horrifying but to lack social meaning as defined by the systems leads to despair. These may be crumbs from society's table, but it is tempting for those who are starving. A person in this world "is ignorant of what is truly horrifying, yet is not thereby liberated from shuddering and shrinking—no, he shrinks from that which is not horrifying. It is similar to the pagan's relationship to God: he does not recognize the true God, but to make matters worse, he worships an idol as God."[23] Indeed, systems very often replace physical idols in the development of functions that orient the spheres of society, the service expressed through communication rather than supplication.[24]

The despair of self that Kierkegaard describes is not shallow or vague, it is a despair "over something." This something is a target, or goal, or achievement, or status but comes back to a despair within the self. "For example," Kierkegaard writes, "when the ambitious man whose slogan is 'Either Caesar or nothing' does not get to be Caesar, he despairs over it. But this also means something else: precisely because he did not get to be Caesar, he now cannot bear to be himself."[25] There is no going forward and there is also no going back. Where does one turn? The systems provide an allure but result in anonymity. Rejecting that path, without having a hope for something more, leads back to despair of self. The *something* that was going to give meaning is not achievable. These *somethings* need not be negative in and of themselves, rather they become dangerous inasmuch as they serve a system or as they provide a seeming path to achieve a sense of meaning. They divert from the pursuit of substantive meaning and in this they become death. Wesley highlights this distinction in his sermon "The Way of the Kingdom":

> Yea, two persons may do the same outward work—suppose, feeding the hungry, or clothing the naked—and in the meantime one of these may be truly religious and the other have no religion at all; for the one may act from the love of God, and the other from love of praise. So manifest it is that although true religion naturally leads to every good word and work, yet the real nature thereof lies deeper still, even in the "hidden man of the heart."[26]

This issue is certainly not limited to the religious system. One can sing because they love singing, that is a virtue; one can also sing because in singing a person gets the attention of others, finding fame or validation. Fame, however, is a fleeting target for those who can't find it and a dissipating target for those who do. One can love another as the other, for their own sake; one can also love another because of the status that person may bring. If a person loses status, it results in a loss of the love, and thus a loss of one's self-identity across different systems. Or the other may play the same game and seek a replacement in love that maximizes their own status, leaving one a winner and the other a loser. This leads to dissolution rather than trust. There are many marriages that involve love of the other and many marriages that involve love of the other for the sake of the self. Kierkegaard uses here the example of a young girl:

> A young girl despairs of love, that is, she despairs over the loss of her beloved, over his death or his unfaithfulness to her. This is not declared despair; no, she despairs over herself. This self of hers, which she would have been rid of or would have lost in the most blissful manner had it become "his" beloved, this self becomes a torment to her if it has to be a self without "him."[27]

People desire to be fulfilled most of all. In despair about fulfillment in their self, they seek satiation in the fulfillment of accomplishment, a semi-satisfaction that derives from validated participation in a complex of societal systems. They communicate the communications, congratulated in a suitable participation even as it conduces their anonymity, a dance of death. Such participation may involve a direct production in a given system or it may involve production in a producer, establishing identity in another person who has validation within a system. These two paths of sin are described as masculine and feminine tendencies: asserting oneself over another or losing oneself in another.[28] There are these two forms of sin that come out of false identity formation: hubris on the one side, apathy on the other side. Both of these have become models of virtue in our society, ways different people, usually defined in gender categories, are seen as acceptable to the rest of society. These, however, reflect underlying pathos of sin: to be desperate to oneself, or to be desperate of oneself.[29] "Thus" as Kierkegaard puts it, "sin is intensified weakness or intensified defiance: sin is the intensification of despair."[30] This is the sickness to death, an experience that underlies our various expressions in society, orienting us toward chaos.

Either way it is expressed, a person dismisses the despair by seeking an environmental fulfillment and, while it may not provide inherent value, it will provide a seemingly satisfying second best: a sense of fitting and purpose. People become servants to the systems, slaves unwilling to see any reason for freedom without being confronted with the dangers of a freed life.[31] Our self-awareness provokes a sense of value in us, we want life to be more than simply existing, yet it also exposes our anonymity. We must distract or satiate in order to mask its presence. No matter the path, despair never does leave. It is the wave crashing always behind us. As Kierkegaard writes:

> This is the state of despair. No matter how much the despairing person avoids it, no matter how successfully he has completely lost himself (especially the case in the form of despair that is ignorance of being in despair) and lost himself in such a manner that the loss is not at all detectable—eternity nevertheless will make it manifest that his condition was despair and will nail him to himself so that his torment will still be that he cannot rid himself of his self, and it will become obvious that he was just imagining that he had succeeded in doing so. Eternity is obliged to do this, because to have a self, to be a self, is the greatest concession, an infinite concession, given to man, but it is also eternity's claim upon him.[32]

Each path—intensified weakness or intensified defiance—offers the promise of a form of satisfaction, but, because both approaches are ultimately continuations of despair, they cannot orient a person as a person, but only as an object, class, or symbol. The person remains essentially anonymous—without a name—only serving to communicate the communication in the satiating system. A person's particular identity is not valued, only their service to the maintenance of the system as system. This can bring with it an appearance of success, of value, but it is only superficial as the value derives from the continued communication not the person as the person. As Kierkegaard puts it, "Themselves they are not; spiritually speaking, they have no self, no self for whose sake they could venture everything, no self before God—however self-seeking they are otherwise."[33] Nor is this masked only by apparent success in the system, but can also take place by what Kierkegaard calls the "philistine-bourgeois mentality," which is despair being masked through the trivial.[34] Lacking possibility, life instead is gauged through momentum, rejecting imagination in life while pursuing distraction. This is the comfortable life, the status quo life, which plays a steady role in all the systems without asking or taking too much.[35] Work hard, play hard.

Can this be categorized as an oppressing life as well? Inasmuch as the systems themselves orient toward oppressing and oppressed conditions this is likewise an expression of sin. One need not be culpable to contribute to a context where sin is perpetuated. Indeed, one may through this path find an even greater sense of winning in life: as a person seeks to avoid the highs and the lows of embracing tentative possibility, one is able to maintain a steady life. "The person who gets lost in possibility soars high with the boldness of despair; he for whom everything became necessity overstrains himself in life and is crushed in despair; but the philistine-bourgeois mentality spiritlessly triumphs."[36] Herein lies the challenge of someone caught in the trap of systems-oriented valuing. They may acknowledge the situation but cannot conceive of a resolution. If a resolution presents itself, it becomes an enemy to the apparent consolation of the system.[37] This is why using approaches like shame or guilt are rarely effective. They provoke feelings of insufficiency, entrenching the dysfunction or propelling into despair. Simply telling an oppressor to stop it, raising issues of moral virtue or Scriptural demands illuminates discrepancies without leading toward resolution. People may know what they are doing is wrong in and of itself, but rationalize it as being "how life is" and how it must be.[38]

At a certain point, attempts to induce guilt provoke a defensive response. Someone who communicates the communication of the system protects the system's communication, like ants or bees defending a hive. This reaction may very often be nonrational. About this, Kierkegaard comments, "to be in error is, quite un-Socratically, what men fear the least."[39] The person ignorant of their despair—or in light of systems, ignorant of their anonymity—secures themselves against awareness. They want nothing beyond the systems. Reminders that there is something else engages their operational defenses.[40] Kierkegaard sees this as the most common form of despair, an ignorance, whether it is a passive ignorance or an active ignorance that protects ignorance. Anxiety also lies underneath ignorance, both despair and anxiety appearing when ignorance is threatened. Rather than proceed through every negativity, thus confronting despair and discovering self as self, a person secures themselves in despair, embracing the ignorance of their anxiety, despair, and self. The system abides.

Who will save us from this body of death? Only the source of self as self, beyond the system, which cannot be resolved within the systems as the systems can only promise embracing weakness or pursuing defiance. This means that first one must become aware of the systems as systems, a cognizance of the environment, which might very well be included in the call for understanding the "signs of the times."[41] While a person can never observe the systems entirely from the outside of them, only a self-awareness derived from that which is outside the environment points to ways a critical engagement can begin to take place. In theological terms, this can be called an awareness of sin, sin being understood as those deficient ways of experiencing life as it is intended to be lived. Kierkegaard notes that "sin is despair; the intensification is the new sin of despairing over one's sins." For the oppressed, such awareness leads to greater perception of sins perpetrated against them. For the oppressor, this involves awareness of patterns where others are dismissed, alienated, overlooked, ways in which others are dehumanized, and how one participates in or expresses these in daily life.[42]

Sin, for both, also involves a despairing over sin, an intensification that leads to embracing the sin as sin or despairing over the forgiveness of sin. In the former, it is "an effort to survive by sinking even deeper."[43] This involves pursuing the sin for its own sake, a satiation, to embrace a coherence by giving oneself wholly over to sin, or submitting wholly to sinful structures, or in terms of the present discussion, submitting wholly and willingly to the system as system.[44] When the slave identifies as slave, insisting others do the same by resisting attempts at freedom, or when the tyrant embraces their tyranny, dismissing any critique, both are embracing the system as system, oppressed and oppressors working together in the production of the system.[45]

One might become aware of the despair and seek potential resolution, yet despair can counter even still with a protest against forgiveness, a rejection of the self as Christ-loved and a submission to the system as system. One might even protest within the system, embracing the system's own pattern of critique and resolution, not seeking real forgiveness or liberation, but rather seeking a new place in the system. We despair over our own sins being forgiven, so we flee from God. We reject the idea of an oppressor's sins being forgiven, so we flee from God.[46] Hope is turned toward embracing sin or seeking to become the oppressor. Either way, the invitation of the Cross is replaced by the despair of the system, that things are as they must be. There is no recreation, no rebirth from death into life. There is only submission or victory within the system itself.

This is why rational consensus is mostly impossible in practice across systems, as rationality can only take place within a particular system's communication, with closed boundaries preventing cross-consensus in an environment except as an adaptation of the system within its environment. Systems will adapt as a matter of *autopoiesis* but not for some greater cause or concern. Systems embed critique within their systems, so there can be an appearance of resolution, just as legalism can provide an appearance of holiness. However, because an individual is participating in separate systems they can produce within one system while really prioritizing another system for their sense of self. The resolution is not coherent. This is where corruption occurs; a system is manipulated by the values of another system. Politicians can seek their own economic benefit by emphasizing political rhetoric that brings wealth. Here, the economics system poses as politics, with those on the outside assuming the politician really is seeking political progress. Corruption, then, is akin to a disease, undermining, ultimately, the perpetuation of a system in preference of another. Or, maybe more apt, like parasitoid wasps which lay their eggs within a host.

Political or economic motives in the religious system undermine religious authority, leading to a breakdown of trust in the system, then less participation in the system. In light of that corrupted system, there seems to be a clear problem, even as there is not an effective correction for the person whose identity is in power or wealth. They are "right" in terms of their communication of the communication in the system they are prioritizing. They are not concerned about religion for its own sake: it is a tool to be utilized for different goals. They simply have a different "god" who belongs to a different system. If Christendom collapses, another kind of religion will take its place, and will continue to serve the goals of power or wealth.

Another dysfunctional though more mutually enforcing approach involves the judgments of one system used to judge another system, which results in substantiating the first system without actually provoking transformation in another system. Both systems effectively win, providing support within an environment for each other while continuing to communicate their own communications. Academics, for instance, communicate with other academics, forming councils and committees, writing serious texts, and attending conferences, sorting out the problems of the wider society through the education system's rationality.[47] When others do not adapt or respond, this then is a sign of the irrationality of those others, which is a cue for more conferences, publications, and committees.

There is little incentive to actually address breakdowns in other systems, as the existence of breakdowns in another system can perpetuate the communication in one's prioritized system. If society was doing everything correctly, there would be no need for analysis. Another system's dysfunction is a feature, not a bug; a boon, not a sin. It gives meaning to one's own sense of identity to critique others; remove the need to critique and one's identity as a critic is diminished. This is not just true for academia, of course; all systems have elements of this. The political system, for instance, is itself sustained by perpetuating critique about a context and proposing power as a solution. Poverty is not actually a sin to the political system, it is a driving theme that provokes further dependence on political production. This is why poverty is often discussed but rarely addressed through political action, or addressed in ways that alleviate just enough poverty to appear beneficial. This is offensive in light of other value systems, but each system contains its own driving values based on autopoietic impulse.[48]

Sin determined by a system is only truly understood as sin within the confines of that system's rationality. It is a sin to the system, not necessarily sin in a broader sense, just as a self is limited within the system. To be poor is a "sin" in the economic system, while it may be a mark of holiness in a religious system. The perspective determines self-assessment. "Qualitatively a self is what its criterion is."[49] A self can only be extended within the criterion of a system, and as systems are operationally closed, there is not a cumulative self that derives from the amalgamation of the different selves. They remain distinct, which is why a despair can be present even in light of other clear successes in other systems. One can only achieve what a system sets as a boundary, but this does not itself fulfill the self as a holistic self. The sin that is despair, a despair of self or rejection of self, is holistic but cannot be determined by a rationality that only reaches to the borders of a particular system. Thus, the despair itself resists being named for what it is, leaving it vague and seeking answers within established systems.

The systems cannot address this despair of an integrated self because they only produce within their operational boundaries. Their attempt at determining self is itself an expression of sin.[50] They are establishing themselves as lords, determining right and wrong, which is the province of God. Kierkegaard writes, in light of this, that "no human being can come further than that; no man of himself and by himself can declare what sin is, precisely because he is in sin; all his talk about sin is basically a glossing over of sin, an excuse, a sinful watering down."[51] Without an ability to declare what sin is, narrow approaches to liberation can only be partial goals in this life, an expression of contextual restriction that is identified within and resolved within a given system. This does not mean such partial goals should be dismissed or contextual restrictions ignored. By no means! We should indeed pursue such goals, albeit aware of the limitations for holistic renewal, lest we restrict human identity to a subset of the social environment.[52]

The goal of broader, holistic renewal must involve a perspective outside the systems in order to understand the self apart from the systems, thus leading to a renewal of self, and of broader liberation, that is not yet another production in a system's autopoiesis.[53] Transformation comes not by provoking despair without resolution but by initiating transformation. This follows, while expanding on, Kierkegaard in light of systems theory. He writes, "That is why Christianity begins in another way: man has to learn what sin is by a revelation from God; sin is not a matter of a person's not having understood what is right but of his being unwilling to understand it, or his not willing what is right."[54] Jesus was a true self, fully human, and as such he communicated himself to the systems as self, rather than communicating the communications of the systems in order to derive a self. We indeed can see his message as orienting within yet another system—this the kingdom of God, which as a system that perpetuates in eternity contains within it the only enduring source of identity for humanity.[55]

PURSUING PRACTICE IN CHRISTIANITY

Christianity is more than an orienting idea, a vision for how to think about the world and our lives within it. It is more than a topic for rigorous academic analysis or suitably raucous debate within classrooms or presentation rooms. It is an enacted expression of a holistic reality, a narrative that takes shape within the broader narrative of the cosmos. It is, thus, "a monstrous mistake to didacticize Christianity," to assume truth is limited to cognition, because "in original Christianity all the expressions were formed according to the view that truth is being."[56] It is, in its fullest expression, a way to think, live, and feel. This is a package deal. It is also an invitation, a way that has been prepared, a hope that has been initiated for those who are weary. Those who are burdened are not excused from every burden but are shown a way that is possible and freeing. "Come to me," Jesus invites, "all you that are weary and are carrying heavy burdens, and I will give you rest. Take my yoke upon you, and learn from me; for I am gentle and humble in heart, and you will find rest for your souls. For my yoke is easy, and my burden is light."[57] This is a way of liberation for both oppressed and oppressors. The invitation stands at the crossroads.[58]

To take up this way means to halt, to stop from going other ways. Which involves no longer trying to fit Christ within those other paths, using Christianity as a source of goals to be developed in systems-oriented patterns or to turn Christ into a religious figurehead, worthy of admiration but not emulation. That is the pattern of Christendom, the setting where Christianity is the majority faith in the religious system while maintaining the dis-integrity of the systems as they always have been. Of this state, Kierkegaard writes that "Christendom has abolished Christianity without really knowing it itself. As a result, if something must be done, one must attempt again to introduce Christianity into Christendom."[59]

Something must certainly be done. This involves understanding how we ourselves have been caught in the cycles of dissolution, continue to contribute to them, even as we excuse ourselves through highlighting the misdeeds of others, dismissing the radical calling of Christ in the process.[60] The invitation of Christ comes to each person, emphasizing that sin is a corruption of our being. That invitation creates a new space for a new absolute.[61] Kierkegaard insists on this point, preventing any coherent way of accepting his critique without the accompanying solution. "It is out of love that God so wills it, but it is also God who wills it, and he will as he wills. He wills not to be transformed by human beings into a cozy—a human god; he wills to transform human beings, and he wills it out of love."[62] The goal in this way is not comfort or immediate peace. As a confrontation with the systems, Christianity initiates a transformation, one that involves a breaking down and a breaking apart of a socialized identity within the environment.

This hearkens back to that prayer of Psalm 70, reminding each person of their fundamental status no matter their social experiences within a given system. A "consciousness of sin" is a wave that crashes over every person, dreadful and terrifying. This awakens possibilities but only in reference to the confrontational mission of Christ.[63] With Christ, one "bears their cross" and becomes, in effect, a contemporary with Christ. This is why honesty and understanding about our own self is so important, as it orients our present status within a zone of reference, "continually keeping the task in sight."[64] Kierkegaard thus vehemently rejects the idea of Christianity as a religion within a system—a comforting message about the sublime and the profound—calling this, effectively, blasphemy.[65]

The established order collides with the disrupting declarations of Christ. Society is not moving forward or upward or any positive direction in its own development—that deifies the establishment, and in doing so continues a revolt against God.[66] The only solution for ending oppressing is rejected even as oppression may continue to be frowned upon. Without God, a person wants to become that which they cannot become, to fulfill the hope of a coherent self without having a transcendent source of integration, leaving them with the transcendent dis-integration of sin. Rejecting cohesion in God, a person seeks an atheistic path of the systems. The systems prevent such cohesion but enable the illusion of its possibility, negating the personal in preference for the general.

The way of Christ offers the opposite tactic—God "uses the single individual to prod the established order out of self-complacency."[67] It is thus the particular that brings meaning to the whole, not the generalized pattern of a general theory of society. The established order seeks lordship, and Christ resists this. The systems do not seek to reject religion—or Christ—as much as relegate it to within their environmental patterns. The path of secularization is an enforced relativity that declares where Christianity can sit and where it can eat, as well as where it is not wanted or even allowed. It is a religious demarcation that itself is a religious assumption, framed in the guise of rational enlightenment. Yet, this attempt perpetuates the very patterns of oppressing, forming these patterns into states of society beyond the reach of judgment. And this approach is so convincing that even the religious—good, faithful men and women—assume the arguments as truth and perpetuate the patterns in noncoherent participation.

There is not, however, a middle way between Christ and the systems, as the "established order wants to be a totality that recognizes nothing above itself but has every individual under it and judges every individual who subordinates himself to the established order."[68] To argue against the established order—which I connect to the world systems—becomes, then, blasphemy to those systems. One must choose, then, which god to blaspheme: God or the world systems. As Kierkegaard asks in light of our response to Christ, "Now the issue is: will you be offended or will you believe?"[69] This is the choice given to each of us, in our particular place, not to be farmed out or dissembled.[70] Even though the help in Christianity looks initially like a torment, it is the way of liberation because it involves dismantling one's own systems-derived identity, and with it the kinds of oppressing behaviors these justify. Turning toward love enables integration, allowing a person a new way to encounter this world and their own being. "If there is to be any triumphant breakthrough, there must be faith, for faith is new life."[71] This is faith in the person of Christ, not the idea of Christ; faith in the power of the Holy Spirit, not the idea of the *Geist*.

In this faith is the hope of transformation, yet this faith confronts our very being because it argues for not being of this world. The hope is an invitation through a promise, the Spirit entering into the task of transformation "little by little."[72] The patient ferment of God's work is not instituted through the systems. This work resists the systems in a person's journey toward coherent integration of self and with God. The question for each person is whether they seek this path, whether they trust this hope, "whether one will in truth be a Christian or not."[73] Christ is truth, the only one who offers the possible paradox, a transcendent integration that allows for both divinity and humanity, and Christ seeks to draw all people to himself, not to oppress or to be oppressed, but to participate in a community as a self. Kierkegaard writes:

> Therefore Christ also first and foremost wants to help every human being to become a self, requires this of him first and foremost, requires that he, by repenting, become a self, in order then to draw him to himself. He wants to draw him the human being to himself, but in order truly to draw him to himself he wants to draw him only as a free being to himself, that is, through a choice.[74]

Such liberation happens through choice, expressed in freedom, so that a person is not oppressed or oppressor, but free in their participation and then freeing in their contributions. As Christopher Barnett notes, Kierkegaard "does not equate 'freedom' with the mere guarantee of autonomy; rather, it emerges when the self is in a proper relationship with others."[75] This journey is constantly tested, experiencing temptation and the attempts to co-opt. That is why it is beyond the power of human endurance. The hope of Christ's accompaniment is our hope, Christ's future our future, our end. Hope with Christ invites understanding how the Spirit works among us, enabling and encouraging and guiding this choice into experienced fulfillment.

This work insists on a participation, a joining in, becoming an imitator, not just an admirer, of Christ. "Salvation may be easy," Barnett writes, "since it is accomplished by God—but faith requires human cooperation and, with it, human struggle."[76] This means that to find the fullness of the hope, we have to participate in the methods. Christ does more than give a set of ideals that we should pursue. He is not to be admired, he is to be imitated.[77] In this imitation, there is a substantive confrontation with the world systems, but in this is also the hope of a genuine self, a genuine peace, a substantive community.

CONCLUSION

Kierkegaard's explication of the human condition has been highly influential over the last two centuries. Indeed, his influence has extended well beyond the boundaries of Christian theology, entering into wider philosophical and social influence. Nietzsche highly recommended his work, calling him, "one of the most profound psychologists who ever lived," and Heidegger noted that "S. Kierkegaard got furthest of all in the analysis of the phenomenon of anxiety."[78]

Yet, the idea that his proposals about the human condition could be separated from his solution would have shocked Kierkegaard. Sin as an assumption about the human condition was inherently accompanied by faith in Christ Jesus who provides a substantive salvation for human suffering *and* sinfulness.[79] This salvation requires faith, to act on that which we may not see for a goal that does not seem possible. But this goal is our hope, because it is the answer to our fundamental anxiety and an antidote for our despair. It is not a faith in a teaching or a concept. It certainly is not communicating the communication of a contextual religious system. As Kierkegaard writes:

> The God-man must require faith and in order to require faith must deny direct communication. In a certain sense he cannot do otherwise, and he does not want it otherwise. As the God-man he is qualitatively different from any man, and therefore he must deny direct communication; he must *require* faith and require that he become the *object of faith*.[80]

For individuals seeking selfhood in the contexts of anonymizing systems, the inability to recognize sin as sin, self as self, or others as other selves, perpetuates a depersonalizing reality that then embeds itself within the psyche as ego. We defend a false self for the sake of the systems that promise identity but only deliver anonymity. Trapped in the cycle of despair, caught in the middle of the impossible paradox of finding meaning in the self or in the systems, the only apparent way forward is deeper into the muck and mire. Christ who promises more of life shows the path of holistic liberation. This requires faith between two real persons, self to self, no longer anonymous in the systems. We call Jesus by name as a specific person and he recognizes us by name, providing a sense of self. Christ is the expression of the possible paradox, fully human and fully divine, a coherent self in unity with the divine reality. He can enter into the systems while not being defined by them, bringing an integrative hope that includes and transcends the environment. That reality, however, confronts the systems. The cross shows how the systems reject such confrontation. Christ shows how the cross leads to ultimate resolution. Our egos resist the path of the cross, leading to the call of dying to our impossible self. The interaction is not a transaction, but a relationship.

What is this self that has been constructed and orients its apparent self in light of ego? What is the nature of this defense that rejects a refutation of despair through substantive liberation? Resisting even if it knows the call is right and true. This psychological conflict expresses itself in social conflict, a developmental pattern of trying to exist in the midst of impossible paradox. If we can understand this, then we can more deeply understand the despair of the oppressor and thus point to where hope may lie and how they may be inspired to go in that direction. To help with this challenge, I now turn to James Loder, who wrestled with spiritual and psychological development together, finding resolution in the work of the Spirit, who makes the possible paradox of Christ our possibility as well.

NOTES

1. In saying the church is not seen as a solution, I am making a broad generalization, however one that addresses two different issues. One is the issue of waning participation in Christian organizations. The second, and maybe more invidious, is how a significant number of those who do participate in organized Christianity do not integrate their Sunday faith into the actions and decisions of the rest of their life. They see church as a spiritual response to an existential issue of private sin, not a wholesale solution to the broad scope of human longing, ambitions, and social conflicts. This raises resentment about the church as people identify as Christians then distort the image of Christ by acting in ways contrary to the integrated vision of the Kingdom. For instance, the popular media presence of televangelists is the most prevalent image of Christianity many people encounter. I wouldn't want to be a Christian either if that's all I knew about it!

2. Daphne Hampson, *Kierkegaard: Exposition and Critique* (New York: Oxford University Press, 2013), 129 writes that "*The Concept Angst* discusses a perceived need, angst, which it is suggested is overcome through the relation to God, a line of thinking that will be carried through in *The Sickness unto Death*." Meanwhile, Howard and Edna Hong call *Practice in Christianity* the "third part" of the two sequences begun in *The Sickness unto Death*, which addresses "the healing of the sin-conscious self and the indicative ethics gratefully expressive of the redemptive gift." In "Historical Introduction," in *Practice in Christianity* (Princeton: Princeton University Press, 1991), xiii.

3. There is significant debate about Kierkegaard's use of and response to Hegel. For a more complex summary, see Shannon Nason, "Opposites, Contradictories, and Mediation in Kierkegaard's Critique of Hegel," *Heythrop Journal* 53, no. 1 (January 2012): 24–36. Nason here argues that Kierkegaard rejects the idea that Christianity and speculative philosophy are relative opposites, that in fact Christianity resists mediation. For the conventional perspective which argues Kierkegaard's strong resistance to Hegelian thought, see Niels Thulstrup, *Kierkegaard's Relation to Hegel* (Princeton: Princeton University Press, 1980). Jon Stewart, *Kierkegaard's Relation to Hegel Reconsidered* (New York: Cambridge University Press, 2003), argues that

Kierkegaard was primarily responding to local Danish Hegelians, but on the whole was actually very influenced by Hegel himself. Stewart's view does not seem to have gained much support, for while most scholars acknowledge Hegel's influence on Kierkegaard (as if a scholar of his era could avoid Hegel's methodological influence) and some positive engagement, Kierkegaard ultimately takes a strong stand against Hegel based on both Christian theology and his perspective of the human individual in contrast to Hegel's world-historical approach.

4. Cornelius Plantinga, *Not the Way It's Supposed to Be: A Breviary of Sin* (Grand Rapids: Eerdmans, 1995), 16.

5. Theophan the Recluse writes, "Sin entangles a soul by its many nets, or hides itself from the soul by its many coverings; because sin is ugly in and of itself, and one glance finds it repulsive. The covering that is deepest and closest to the heart is comprised of self-deception, insensitivity and carelessness; over them and closer to the surface lie absent-mindedness and much-caring, the chief players, which hide sin and sinful habits and conditions. The upper-most covering is prevalence of the flesh, which is the most visible covering, no less strong and significant." In Theophan the Recluse, *The Path to Salvation: A Manual of Spiritual Transformation* (Forestville, CA: St. Herman of Alaska Brotherhood, 1996), 129.

6. See Kierkegaard, *The Concept of Anxiety*, 15.

7. Ibid., 16.

8. Ibid., 50.

9. Ibid., 44.

10. Such anticipation is neither a good nor a bad in itself, but only as it is directed, as while it can trap us in anxiety it also can awaken in us a sense of desire for God's fullness. Maximos the Confessor writes, "The intelligence recognizes two kinds of knowledge of divine realities. The first is relative, because it is confined to the intelligence and its intellections, and does not entail any real perception through actual experience, of what is known. . . . The relative knowledge that resides in the intelligence and its intellections is said to stimulate our longing for the real knowledge attained by participation." Maximos the Confessor, "Fourth Century of Various Texts," 29 in *The Philokalia: The Complete Text*, vol. 2, trans. G. E. H. Palmer, Philip Sherrard, and Kallistos Ware (London: Faber and Faber, 1981), 242.

11. Kierkegaard writes that "anxiety is neither a category of necessity nor a category of freedom; it is entangled freedom, where freedom is not free in itself but entangled, not by necessity but in itself." In Kierkegaard, *The Concept of Anxiety*, 49.

12. Kierkegaard, *The Concept of Anxiety*, 61.

13. Ibid., 53.

14. Ibid., 113.

15. Ibid., 73.

16. Ibid., 116.

17. Ibid., 117.

18. Hampson, *Kierkegaard,* 227.

19. Kierkegaard, *Sickness unto Death*, 13.

20. Ibid., 14.

21. Ibid., 15.

22. Luhmann, *A Systems Theory of Religion*, 34.

23. Søren Kierkegaard, *The Sickness unto Death: A Christian Psychological Exposition for Upbuilding and Awakening*, trans. Howard V. Hong and Edna H. Hong (Princeton: Princeton University Press, 1983), 8.

24. See Paul E. Capetz, "God and Religious Diversity: Toward a Theocentric Pluralism," in *Constructive Theology: A Contemporary Approach to Classical Themes*, 65–66. Cf. Luhmann, *A Systems Theory of Religion*, 88–91. He writes on page 90: "Religion guarantees the determinability of all meaning against the accompanying experience of constantly referring to the indeterminable." See also Jürgen Moltmann, *The Spirit of Life*, trans. Margaret Kohl (Minneapolis: Fortress Press, 1992), 206; Ignacio Ellacuría, *Ignacio Ellacuría: Essays on History, Liberation, and Salvation*, ed. Michael E. Lee (Maryknoll, NY: Orbis Books, 2013), 153.

25. Kierkegaard, *Sickness unto Death*, 19. I recently read a striking example of this. In 1995, *New York Times* reporter Lisa Belkin wrote of the suicide of Robert O'Donnell of Texas. He was the paramedic who rescued "Baby Jessica" from a well in 1987, an event that caught the attention of the nation. Belkin writes, "There was a parade, countless television appearances, a letter from the president, a handshake from the Vice President, a made-for-TV movie. But eventually, the cameras went away, the world's attention moved on and he was left alone—a man so changed by fame that he no longer belonged in his world, but not changed enough that he could leave that world behind." Lisa Belkin, "Death on the CNN Curve," *New York Times Magazine*, July 23, 1995, https://www.nytimes.com/1995/07/23/magazine/death-on-the-cnn-curve.html.

26. John Wesley, "The Way to the Kingdom," 5 in *The Sermons of John Wesley: A Collection for the Christian Journey*, eds. Kenneth J. Collins and Jason E. Vickers (Nashville: Abingdon Press, 2013), 56. Wesley is not talking here about the religious system, which he often protested as such, but religion as a wholesale encounter with God throughout life, transforming and expressive in love.

27. Kierkegaard, *Sickness unto Death*, 20.

28. While I am uncomfortable with such gender categorization, there is significant discussion using these distinctions. See Kierkegaard, *Sickness unto Death*, 49–74. See especially Valerie Saiving Goldstein, "The Human Situation: A Feminine View," *The Journal of Religion* 40, no. 2 (1960): 100–112. She notes that "masculinity is an endless process of becoming, while in femininity the emphasis is on being." The derives in part from the diverse experience in the sexual act and child raising. The *Journal of Feminist Studies* 28, no. 1 (2012): 75–133 consists of a roundtable discussion on Goldstein's work in light of more recent topics and approaches. In his theology, Wolfhart Pannenberg emphasizes the "masculine" element in his writings as I will discuss below. In an interview with the author, Moltmann states that he agrees with Pannenberg, but notes that Pannenberg's concept of egotism as the contrast of human identity in God is a "very male sort of sin." Pannenberg, he notes, developed his understanding in the 1960s, before a strong feminist perspective brought insight about broader issues of identity and sin in society. "To let go your identity," Moltmann notes, "is a very feminine sort of sin. Girls are educated to serve, to forget about themselves. But there is a healthy form to being yourself. So, there is egocentrism on the one side, apathy on the other side." In both of these, we discover the roots of more visible aspects of sin, as a person either wants to express themselves through

dominance or hide themselves in the dominance of another or other non-God reality. Cf. Sarah Coakley, *Powers and Submissions: Spirituality, Philosophy and Gender* (Malden, MA: Wiley-Blackwell, 2002), 66–68.

29. See Kierkegaard, *Sickness unto Death*, 77.

30. Ibid., 77.

31. This brings to mind a discussion I had with a friend who worked as a minister in Leipzig. She noted that while young people are embracing new patterns of life, those who are older, who grew up and lived in the formerly communist region of East Germany, had trouble with the transition and still have trouble coping with the results of reunification. There were, she added, a large number of suicides as people suddenly were confronted with an array of choices they never had before, while facing the loss of secure jobs which had been supported by the government. Cf. Num. 11:4–6.

32. Kierkegaard, *Sickness unto Death*, 21. Cf. Wolfhart Pannenberg, *Systematic Theology*, trans. Geoffrey W. Bromiley, 3 vols. (Grand Rapids: Eerdmans, 1991–1998), 3: 603–604. Hereafter referred to as *ST*.

33. Kierkegaard, *Sickness unto Death*, 35.

34. Related to this is what I call an "academic-bourgeois mentality" which likewise obsesses over minutiae in both subject and administration, ever-honing nitpicks of learning outcomes or methodology, caught in a trap of performance for the sake of approval and promotion within the system. Academic conferences abound in such a bourgeois attitude, hints of esteem in the midst of competition, invitation only hosted soirees, judged performances refereed by a panel of committee judges, saying who gets to speak, on what, making or breaking careers in the process, all in the guise of collegiality.

35. In a very interesting post, Venkatesh Rao has called this the "clueless" category of contribution in an organization. See Venkatesh Rao, "Ribbonfarm Experiments in Refactored Perception The Gervais Principle, Or The Office According to 'The Office,'" October 7, 2009, https://www.ribbonfarm.com/2009/10/07/the-gervais-principle-or-the-office-according-to-the-office/.

36. Kierkegaard, *Sickness unto Death*, 42.

37. See Ibid., 43.

38. For instance, the situation of dependence on part-time faculty for a substantive amount of higher education and the dependence on student loan debt to maximize student enrollment.

39. Kierkegaard, *Sickness unto Death*, 43. See also Kierkegaard, *Sickness unto Death*, 87–93.

40. Kierkegaard, *Sickness unto Death*, 44, notes here the connection of ignorance and despair is similar to the connection between ignorance and anxiety, both despair and anxiety lie underneath.

41. See Second Vatican Council, "Gaudium et Spes: Pastoral Constitution on the Church in the Modern World," 4–10 in *Vatican Council II: The Conciliar and Post Conciliar Documents*, ed. Austin Flannery (New York: Costello Publishing Company, 1975).

42. Jürgen Moltmann, *The Crucified God* (Minneapolis: Fortress Press, 1993), ix writes, "Wherever Christian hope makes people active and leads them into the

'creative discipleship' of Christ, the contradictions and confutations of the world are painfully experienced. 'When freedom is near the chains begin to chafe.' One begins to suffer with the victims of injustice and violence. One puts oneself on the side of the persecuted and becomes persecuted oneself."

43. Kierkegaard, *Sickness unto Death*, 110.

44. Cf. Rom. 1:18–32.

45. Other examples might include the strong class system in Victorian Britain, where no inherent laws but the laws of customs (and the use of wealth) helped maintain distinct divisions. Or, likewise, the caste system in India and elsewhere. The "lower" classes often enforce the distinction as much as the "higher" classes, each taking a pride in their "place."

46. See Kierkegaard, *Sickness unto Death*, 114. Cf. Rom. 7:7–23.

47. If we see the education system as an autopoietic system, then academics are in the business of producing the education system, rather than solving or addressing issues in other systems. That the topics may cover the ground of other systems is obvious, it is an environmental reality, but other systems are not the main concern of academia itself. This is where the "ivory tower" label is appropriate. The difficulty is that rationality for all is often gauged by academics in light of the academic system's own rationality. This then brings justification and meaning, authority of rationality, when other markers such as wealth or social power, may be lacking. I realize, of course, that this present text exemplifies the issue I'm highlighting. By writing on liberation, I hope to change the world but will settle for a permanent position and tenure that would allow me to write more "world changing" texts. My own writing confronts my motivations. This brings to mind a comment made by New Testament scholar Peter Stuhlmacher during a presentation at Fuller Seminary a number of years ago: "The renewal of the church will not come from academia." I was a M.Div. student at the time. This comment has served as an irritant in my vocational musings ever since.

48. This raises a question about whether poverty is functionally a "sin" in any system. The religious system has tended to substantiate poverty as a form of humility for the poor and the object of charity for the wealthy. The political systems, the religious systems, have a use for poverty continuing as well. It could be the entertainment systems is an exception, though the experience of poverty has been a significant driver in both creativity and ambition in developing entertainment.

49. Kierkegaard, *Sickness unto Death*, 114.

50. Of course as nonpersonal structural realities, this is not culpable sin. The sin becomes actualized as personal sin inasmuch as a person embraces the system's definition. In much the same way that a statue is not an expression of sin, but the worship of the statue is sin, as the statue represents a supposed divine reality in place of God.

51. Kierkegaard, *Sickness unto Death*, 95.

52. See, for instance, Pannenberg, "Christianity, Marxism, and Liberation Theology," 215–226. Cf. Ellacuría, *Ignacio Ellacuría*, chap. 6.

53. Cf. Janice McRandal, *Christian Doctrine and the Grammar of Difference: A Contribution to Feminist Systematic Theology* (Minneapolis: Fortress Press, 2015), chap. 2.

54. Kierkegaard, *Sickness unto Death*, 95.

55. See Wolfhart Pannenberg, *Systematic Theology*, trans. Geoffrey W. Bromiley, vol. 3 (Grand Rapids: Eerdmans, 1998), 580–586.
56. Kierkegaard, *Practice in Christianity*, 206.
57. Mt. 11:28–30.
58. See Kierkegaard, *Practice in Christianity*, 16–20.
59. Ibid., 36.
60. See Ibid., 38–53.
61. Ibid., 59–60.
62. Ibid., 62.
63. See Ibid., 195.
64. Ibid., 66.
65. Ibid., 68.
66. Ibid., 88.
67. Ibid., 90.
68. Ibid., 91.
69. Ibid., 115.
70. See Ibid., 140–143.
71. Ibid., 120.
72. Ibid., 186.
73. Ibid., 186.
74. Ibid., 160.
75. Christopher B. Barnett, *From Despair to Faith: The Spirituality of Søren Kierkegaard* (Minneapolis: Fortress Press, 2014), 32.
76. Barnett, *From Despair to Faith,* 56.
77. See Kierkegaard, *Practice in Christianity*, 256–257.
78. Quoted in Hampson, *Kierkegaard,* 136. Martin Heidegger, *Being and Time: A Revised Edition of the Stambaugh Translation* (New York: SUNY Press, 2010), 184 n.4.
79. Cf. Mt. 9:1–7.
80. Kierkegaard, *Practice in Christianity*, 143.

Chapter 3

The Crisis of Becoming

INTRODUCTION

As stated earlier, my goal throughout this text is to explore potential avenues of discussion rather than attempt a comprehensive analysis. In focusing on specific texts of certain authors, the present task is meant as a map, highlighting potential themes and contributors that may help develop a contributory stream. I am proposing a model of interpretation that invites further, and deeper, study in each specific direction. This is no more clear than in this chapter where, in focusing on the work of James Loder, I am also introducing the very broad field of human psychological development as an essential part of a potential liberation of the oppressor.[1]

Loder is especially useful in a couple regards. His main work on human development, *The Logic of the Spirit*, is greatly informed by his study of Kierkegaard and Pannenberg, two key interlocutors in this work.[2] Second, his intent is to begin with studies of human development in both faith and psychology as it takes place in most experiences. Along the way, he points to the transformative work of the Spirit in each stage. This constructive work addresses humanity as it is—formed by the conditions and systems in this world—and humanity as we are created to be—recreated in the power of the Spirit. For the purposes of this text, I will focus on two stages of human development, which are most directly related to the context of oppressing. This is not to say these are the only stages that relate, but rather the stages that establish and maintain the context of oppressing in people's lives and are the stages that may be most directly relevant in considering liberation from oppressing. Young adulthood is when we tend to lose a naïve idealism and fully jump into the systems of society for our own sense of self, while the middle years of life are when we become fully invested in these systems and are willing to defend these systems in protection of our amalgamated pseudo-self.

PSYCHOLOGICAL DEVELOPMENT IN YOUNG ADULTHOOD

Young adulthood spans the ages between approximately eighteen and thirty.[3] During this stage, a person begins to engage their vocation and their most serious relationships. The previous stages shape how this takes place. Ego-development establishes a defensive posture, protecting oneself against potential violation or dissolution. With the ego fully in place, well socialized for society as it is, we do not enter society uninfluenced or in an objective posture. As Volf writes, "The explicit will to be socialized already presupposes an initial, still rudimentary socialization."[4] Thus, we are not beginning afresh, able to create society anew. We enter into the systems ready-made to communicate their particular communications, segmenting and isolating our inner being so that by participating in each system our sense of self is secured in structures above and beyond ourselves. This sense of self is really an illusion, a societal form of smoke, mirrors, and misdirection.

Rather than oriented by love and openness to all—a non-naïve love that embraces the actuality of life with hope—we use love or other relational categories to more firmly establish a sense of ourselves. Other people become tools for our use rather than subjects with a distinct personhood. This is not how it should be, but it is all too often how it really is. Loder acknowledges such reality while pointing to the possibility of a different way, quoting Kierkegaard's *Works of Love*: "Love believes all things and is never deceived."[5] This quote is central to Loder's project, a hoped-for destination of fulfillment and participation. The love emphasized here is the love that derives from God, which reflects God's depth and relational embrace, a love that sent the Son into the world for the sake of the world. God is not deceived, that is certain. But what is it that God believes? God believes in life as it is meant to be lived, reflecting God's coherent order above the systems. This pattern of life becomes the new pattern of those who are redeemed by Christ, reoriented in their self through God's recreation—a rebirth that transforms the developmental patterns to reflect an eternal reality.[6]

Both Kierkegaard and Loder emphasize the vital importance of intimacy, a deep vulnerability that is affirmed in love itself, a proactive embrace of the other as other, and recognized as self by the other. For the conventionally socialized ego, the challenge of young adulthood is, from a Freudian perspective, *leiben und arbeiten*—love and work—or rather sexuality and productiveness.[7] Erik Erikson modifies this, arguing that the newly formed identity is challenged to risk fusion with the world around, with the option seemingly being to absorb or be absorbed.[8] This encounter threatens a loss of self but promises the potential of intimacy. We seek to be embraced as selves but are fearful of being co-opted, so may instead turn away into patterns of isolation. The yearning for intimacy is thus accompanied by the tendency for isolation. The ego attempts to navigate this paradox, attempting to provide a protective pattern of meaning, offering a form of intimacy without the vulnerability of potential dissolution.

For Erik Erikson, young adulthood is defined by this *intimacy versus isolation* construct.[9] A young adult's social encounters are accompanied by an increased cognitive awareness of self and indeed consideration of that which is beyond self. With this, there is a coordinating attempt to gain both meaning and guidance through an orienting philosophy. While systems are inherently distinct—interacting but nonoverlapping—a person tries to gain meaning through coordinating their participation in some kind of cohesive pattern. While this may not actually be integrative, it provides the cognitive perception of supposed integration; the pseudo-self only requires the veneer of cohesion after all, just enough to keep angst away from conscious awareness. This orienting philosophy is often religious in nature, but it is far too restrictive to say this is only found in nomenclated religion. People find orienting philosophies in different ways, and in an increasingly post-Christian society, these ways may not be conventionally religious in expression while serving the same basic function religion did in the past.

How we coordinate social encounters, then, is both expressive and formative, reinforcing our sense of self in the context of other selves. There are encounters that deepen intimacy and there are encounters that maintain a "role-structured distance or narcissistic self-sufficiency."[10] Oppressing comes out of these latter encounters, which are environmental reactions to internalized feelings of despair or self-danger. Again, liberation cannot come by simply presenting a person with alternative options, as if rational motivation were enough. The brain is quite literally structured to resist such alternatives.[11] Rather than being defined solely in economic terms, liberation must be seen as first providing hope that real intimacy is possible, then increasing the scope of a person's experience of intimacy and emphasizing encounters that deepen intimacy. Only this way can liberation be thorough and provide a sustaining integrity across systems.

Realizing the need for intimacy need not be, as indeed is often not, accompanied by coinherent action that brings such intimacy. We know we need it, but do not know how to find it or are unwilling to do that which it may take to get it. This quest for intimacy cannot resolve itself on its own. Intimacy requires others by definition. The conflict between a protecting ego and a desire for intimacy often results in dysfunctional expressions. We need closeness with others but want this on our terms. The ego cannot fix itself, the systems have no concern for such resolution, and other people are caught in their own cycle of conflict. The only way forward is to find perspective through an orienting philosophy or guiding concern.

SPIRITUAL DEVELOPMENT IN YOUNG ADULTHOOD

In light of this need for a transcendent orientation, faith development is concurrent with cognitive development, shaping a person beyond the immediate sensory data to compose a broader perception of reality. This is a fundamental nature of religion (however expressed) and a particular goal for Christianity. In light of the cognitive and social dissonance, Loder writes, "Thus, the stuff and substance of intimacy must be taken up and transformed by the Spirit of Christ so that the intimacy we most deeply long for may be found in our life in the Spirit of Christ with the people of Christ."[12] This leads Loder to look at the work of James Fowler, especially his *Stages of Faith*.[13]

Fowler argues that faith development is a universal trait to all humanity, defining it as "the person's or group's way of responding to transcendent value and power as perceived and grasped through the forms of the cumulative tradition. Faith and religion, in this view, are reciprocal."[14] Loder notes that these are less stages of faith in any meaningful biblical or theological way, but instead are "illuminating as stages of ego and the capacity of ego to construct meaning."[15] They are steps reflecting a more comprehensive perception of self as part of the wider world, integrating the self into this world rather than distancing the self from others. While "faith" is often understood as relating to a perspective or non-perspective on a divine being, the issue for Fowler goes well beyond that. Fowler writes that his task was to "clarify a developmental perspective on the human enterprise of committing trust and fidelity and of imaging and relating ourselves to others and to the universe."[16] Faith thus involves a comprehensive meaning for an understanding of self that is inclusive but not dependent on the systems in their autopoietic production.

The ego is reconstituted in each phase, constructing an ideological perspective that allows a person to make sense of themselves in their environment, often making choices of community and activity that are compatible with the coordinating beliefs and practices.[17] This person "is like those plants whose propagation is hidden—he breathes in God; he draws nourishment for his love from God, he is strengthened by God."[18] Thus, a person is both integrated and critical, finding peace with self and with this world, able to experience the world for what it is while perceiving inconsistencies and being willing to point these out. Such inner peace is certainly not passive.

The stages of faith involve a widening sense of the whole in a context of otherwise disparate goals. Peace and self-integration go hand in hand. Rather than dependent on a particular system, a person seeks to orient their self around a transcendent center. Patterns or assumptions of childhood are rejected or integrated into this developing pattern of meaning. This can be called "the dream."[19] Loder writes, "The understanding of dream here is like a vision of the future that gathers up deeply felt personal feelings and translates them into images of oneself in the adult world 'out there,' the world one is entering as a young adult."[20] This dream is transitional, orienting the past toward the future in the context of the present. It seeks resolution of internal conflicts through the pursuit of satisfaction of systems-derived meaning. By pursuing these assumed resolutions, a person finds meaning in this world and thus more secured as a self, preserved into the future and protected from dis-integration.

INTEGRATING SELF IN YOUNG ADULTHOOD

Underlying the particular orienting center is the dream of integration. A person seeks integration as self in the disparate systems, an integration that can be called wholeness. This quest is the driving hope, the developmental response to encroaching despair, a sense of meaning beyond the present that brings ultimate fulfillment. Momentary fulfillment is not ultimate.[21] The systems do not allow for actual integration as they have operational closure which prevents such overlap. The dream becomes an unrealizable possibility, a driving motive in a never-ending quest. The satisfied ego is the holy grail.[22] "Thus the primary authority in one's life as a young adult is the integrity of the dream, whether it is obeyed or not; to disobey is to pay a high price, as we will see."[23] Such a dream is often culturally conditioned, even as the underlying quest may remain the same. In a cultural sense, one thinks of the American Dream, for instance, the ability to establish one's own independence and creative engagement in this world without being obligated to the service of others.[24] In another setting, the dream is expressed in an opposite way, experiencing more thorough integration into society, becoming whole through absolute inclusion by a community. Such dreams may differ in expression while sharing the goal of experiencing something more than the mundane realities of present existence. It is, in a way, a form of anthropological eschatology, a desired future (the dream) interpreting the past so as to create a sense of self in the present that is not defined by the past but defined by the future.[25] Thus, rather than despair a person experiences hope.

Intimacy involves connecting this transcendent sense of self with another. A person attempts to integrate with others that share, or at least are agreeable to, a person's pursuit of coherence while within a multiplicity of societal meanings. In the journey toward transcendence, a person examines the suitability of their past in light of explorations of other options and interpretations. The tools of childhood and adolescence are included but also clarified. This involves coming to terms with truth as it has been mandated around them and truth as they perceive it, navigating between authority and relativism as one's own being comes into focus. A person learns to incorporate the past or the traditions of one's contexts as one's own, processed along a particular journey in space and time.

Of course, it may also mean rejection of such if the traditions do not endure the examination or negate preferred possibilities.[26] Thus, a self experiences vulnerability on the one hand and possibility on the other. One's sense of self is projected from the desired future but is not yet established fact, so there is a risk of dissolution at every point. Intimacy provides a place of trust and openness in sharing this vulnerability, both encouraging and securing risk. A lack of intimacy, however, can result in a closed off sense of exploration and possibilities, an experience of isolation, isolation from others and increasingly one's own self, resulting in forms of despair.

Such isolation may also derive from a dream that is not one's own, constructing a self that is integrated by another's "eschatology." This pursuit orients a person away from their own self, even as a person may not realize it at first. Or, it may be due to what Loder calls a "negative identity," a rejection of one life and investment into the supposed identity of another. Isolation may even be reactionary, defining the dream in terms of what one does not want to be rather than a positive embrace of a sense of true self.[27] Loder also notes that isolation may result from a dysfunctional model of parental patterns, not related to the issue of the dream as much as related to a lack of positive examples of true intimacy. The sins of our fathers (and mothers) in their relationships can be deeply embedded in our own attempts for relationships. Intimacy becomes thus disoriented in practice, even if one's sense of the dream is coherent.

Adding to Loder's list is another one that I think is key for those in more tentative financial situations. In contexts of stress, the dream can be deferred for the sake of immediacy. External factors can impede attempts to bring coherence simply because a person does not have the privilege of choices or exploration in young adulthood. This may create a functional intimacy without deep integration.[28] Should there be space to realize one's own self, one's dream, then the functional intimacy may be rejected in the newly opened vistas of potential meaning.[29]

Finally, in light of the previous discussions, it seems that the systems can serve as a parental proxy, imposing their perspective of a dream onto a person, which then engages the person's continued communication in the autopoietic productivity. The emergent nature of a system is not, of course, personal, but it does reflect a human vision of sorts, a collective emphasis on the present as somehow promising a fulfilled future. That the systems promise a form of advancement provides a nonintegrated sense of personal worth and progress. However, as nonintegrated and nonpersonal, such promises will not invite the kind of holistic intimacy that a more fully integrated dream can provide. The systems themselves not only guard against a deep intimacy, they at the same time hide or disguise the lack of such intimacy.

The *appearance* of community becomes the true opiate of the masses, which can take the form of any of the various systems. The experience of isolation in the context of assumed intimacy prevents a person from seeking true resolution or even realizing there is such a need for such resolution. As Loder writes, "In isolation the human spirit, so entangled in its constructions of defenses and its efforts to manipulate the environment, cannot create a world outside the egocentrism imposed by anxiety and flights into self-deception. The spirit has no choice but to move the person deeper and deeper into a well of well-defended isolation."[30] The response, "Am I my brother's keeper?" becomes the hallmark of human interactions.[31]

Contexts of oppressing develop from this pattern, reflecting what Erikson calls "distantiation," which is "the readiness to isolate and, if necessary, to destroy those forces and people whose essence seems dangerous to one's own, and whose 'territory' seems to encroach on the extent of one's intimate relations."[32] This can take the shape of prejudice, establishing a kind of intimacy through negating that which is experienced as foreign. The intimacy develops from a shared "enemy" rather than an authentic openness with each other. The prejudice then is not simply about a view of others, but carries a sense of placement within a community. Getting rid of the prejudice would likely involve the threat of social dissolution, as dysfunctional as such a kind may be. Thus, even where actual psychopathology is lacking, underlying psychosocial dysfunction may be present, and is likely much more common.

To simply say, "Stop it!" to an oppressor does not actually address the core issue, as it is not really an ethical decision at all, at least not at a conscious level. Oppressing is not often oriented toward the oppressed as targets; there is often an entire lack of animosity or even awareness of their personhood.[33] Loder rightly notes that "isolation is not from people or relationships; it is fundamentally the entrapment and isolation of the human spirit itself."[34] The attempt to secure one's own sense of self in the contexts of societal systems sets up a path of human interaction and response within those autopoietic models that causes oppression within those systems to endure. Those who reject such patterns reject, in essence, their whole sense of self and the dream that is built in the promises of such systems and thus the forms of intimacy that this pseudo-self developed.

This is a key issue in pursuing a holistic approach to liberation. Conventionally, only one element of liberation is addressed: the context. The liberation of the oppressed involves a transformation of the contexts. And that is often seen as enough.[35] Oppressors, however, require a transformation of the self, an impossibility that is deflected by the encounter with isolation and despair. They cannot or will not choose it in light of their standard trajectory, but they need it even still. Full liberation requires both liberation of self and liberation of context. Both aspects are important for each side, but the emphasis is different for each.

The oppressed need liberation from the context primarily, the self secondarily. The oppressors need liberation from the dysfunctional self primarily, the context secondarily. Without both elements, there is not actual liberation, just a change in situation that can easily revert to former patterns if given the chance. A wealthy person can lose all they have, but still fight and work in a way to rebuild their assertive power—learning nothing—if there is not an accompanying liberation of self. A poor person can find new freedom, and wealth, but be lost in the despair and negative identity imposed by former categories of oppression.

To argue the oppressed primarily need a change of self is to ignore the fundamental problem of wholeness. Our internal self is radically affected by our external circumstances. To argue for a liberation of the oppressor solely on the basis of changing the environmental context makes a similar mistake. Our outward actions reflect our inner self, and if we just change the environment we repress dysfunction rather than liberate being. Addressing the core issues in both directions can result in fundamentally different ways of living life, and this leads to a willingness to confront the systems rather than validate the forms of oppression they embed.[36]

Where is the way forward for the oppressor then if the self cannot fix the self, and the systems have no interest in the person as persons? The oppressed can find relief in a changed environment, but there seems to be no societal or internal recourse for the oppressor. Some assume the oppressors can only be liberated *by* the oppressed. For instance, Paulo Freire writes that "it is only the oppressed who, by freeing themselves, can free their oppressors. The latter, as an oppressive class, can free neither others nor themselves."[37] Yet, when the oppressed gain liberation, it often merely inverts the order of power and influence. The cycle perpetuates.

The alternative, the way of hope, is the promise of Christ, a path of deep intimacy that embraces a person as person, engaging their personhood in a community of other persons, a "true intimacy, Spirit-to-spirit."[38] The oppressor is liberated by this work of the Spirit, and then enters into a new pattern of life, the system of the kingdom, which personalizes and reconstructs the self in a pattern of eternal persistence. Fowler, writing from an a-Christian perspective notes that "the hallmark of the Kingdom of God is a quality of righteousness in which being is properly related to being, a righteousness in which each person or being is augmented by the realization of the futurity of all the others."[39] This is a mutuality of development, a community of those who seek the best for the others, without competition, with trust.

The pursuit of transformation for the oppressor highlights not what they give up, but what they gain if they enter into a new pattern. Emphasizing the new pattern before there is too much invested in the current systems is certainly ideal.[40] However, not everyone who participates in oppression or has investments in the systems as systems will be in this early stage. That is why it is also important to understand the developmental situation of the middle years. The continuing goal is to understand the problems of the self that resist liberation and perpetuate oppression, often even while rationally assenting to the need for change in both personal and societal patterns.

PSYCHOLOGICAL DEVELOPMENT IN THE MIDDLE YEARS

In discussing the developmental stage between roughly thirty to sixty, there are clear continuities with the earlier stages, especially the orientation set up in the young adult years. The ability to maintain a sense of self in increasing environmental complexity becomes a challenge, as does the realization that one's own self is not going to endure, a fact made clear by increasing health challenges and other physical issues—such as a slowing metabolism, menopause for women, loss of hair for men, graying hair for all, and other cues of advancing age. The rapid forward progress in life's stages slows down or even retreats. One is confronted by those who are more advanced in success as well as those who are younger and ambitious. The idealized future approaches ever closer without achieving longed for resolutions. This is the prime of life, but also the point at which responsibilities are their greatest. Responsibilities come from every direction, caught between the young of the next generation and the aging from the previous generation. Realism replaces idealism, but reality is hard to bear.

Erikson calls the development conflict "Generativity versus Stagnation." Those in this stage resist change even as the responsibilities of life increasingly sap spiritual strength. Such stagnation need not involve personal or professional rejection or stalling, with the overall stagnation related to a sense of self. "In essence," as Loder puts it, "over the years people build up unconscious drives that are working in one direction, an accumulation of unfinished business with any number of important people in their lives. But consciously at the ego level, they are working in an opposite direction."[41]

The momentum presses a person deeper into the places of prior investment even as, in many cases, it becomes clear these are not sufficient for identity and meaning. With this, resentments from the past may linger, perpetuating a sense of incompleteness that can no longer be resolved. These resentments can fester, or they can be sometimes addressed in attempts to regain the sense of loss: the prototypical midlife crisis.

The middle years often include the seeming paradox of experiencing both stagnation and the experience of engaged productivity. The ego responds with extra effort in motivating and propelling a person toward generativity. Stagnation can even involve a heightening of action and investment, deepening vocational pursuits so as to further the possibility of achievements in the chosen systems, doubling down in the course of previous investments, even as there's increasing awareness about the ultimate insufficiency about these investments. This is like revving the engine while keeping a foot on the brake.

More positively, the productivity also may emphasize others in light of responsibilities. Loder writes, "To be generative is a response to an instinctual power expressed in the ego through the virtue of caring."[42] The self orients its energy to assist future generations, going beyond the self in establishing security, resources, and meaning for others in one's line. A person is confronted with one's own mortality yet not necessarily in a despairing way. In a constructive encounter with mortality, a formerly self-focused individual often thus develops interest in the institutions of society.

This should not necessarily be seen as selfless exocentricity, rather the ego is itself involved in establishing one's own self through this outward investment, sustaining a legacy.[43] "Generativity," Loder continues, "represents a synthesis between personal and interpersonal insight and public responsibility, between the developing person and the social and cultural institutions that foster human development on its positive side."[44] For example, my interest in public elementary education was quite strong when I was young, then became mostly passive in my young adulthood, until my daughter started kindergarten. We can see this in church involvement as well, with church participation often dropping off in college only to rebound as parents want their children to attend church.[45]

SOCIAL RESPONSIBILITY IN THE MIDDLE YEARS

As a deep social investment is within the systems of an environment, then a call to transform or even dismantle such systems becomes much more than a call to individual sacrifice. Attempts to make changes confronts a person's defense of self by the ego, yes, but also a defense of others, a familial and tribal reaction to protect the persistence of the next generation within the communication of the systems, as it is the systems who promise identity, meaning, protection, and thriving. A pattern of reciprocal need is established, one that emphasizes individual development within the context of societal development and generational progress. In contexts of social fragmentation, there is a significant gap of trust between various groups. If a person does not trust those calling for change, they will not change, as they do not feel those calling for trust are concerned with their family or social welfare.[46] And often they are quite right!

Loder highlights here the work of Don Browning, who saw the generativity of the middle years as being "the ethical center of the descriptive system that has become normative for development."[47] In defining ourselves, we embrace others within a supporting context that bolsters this definition. The self becomes comfortable within a set environment, with various systems finding balance with each other and thus resistant to change. The contrast between individualism and community which is helpful in young adulthood to secure identity may, in the middle years, reinforce persisting dysfunctional patterns as community is embraced for the sake of a limited number—*pax Romana* writ local.[48]

These middle years tend to constrain a person within the narrative structure of an established environment rather than being open to others. Which may be a big reason why young and old have difficulty understanding each other's actions. What seems so clear to one stage is foreign to another; they are speaking a different ego-language. To see this purely in terms of purposeful oppressing is to misunderstand the psychological dynamics of most participants in these systems.[49] The young are willing to risk losing community to seek self-definition, thus breaking free of older patterns. Those who are older have gone through that stage and arrived at a self-definition established in a community of meaning, established trust in certain functioning.

To initiate risking self-definition for those who are older requires a promise of a more substantive reality. They have found a kind of coherence and purpose in their situation. Even more important, they have others they are responsible for. Jesus was unmarried and without children, and even he still found the path to the cross very difficult. This is why it is always much easier to be prophetic about changes other people should make, while rationalizing our own status and behaviors. It is far too easy to encourage others to sacrifice while maintaining our own trust-established functioning.[50] This is why the task of the liberation of the oppressor is not one for that *other* person, but for each of us in our particularity. As Jesus told his followers, "Whoever wants to be my disciple must deny themselves and take up their cross and follow me. For whoever wants to save their life will lose it, but whoever loses their life for me will find it."[51] Christianity is not in the business of sacrificing other people's lives to find our own peace. The core message of Jesus strikes home, and we resist it because *our* cross seems too difficult to bear, leading to sophisticated rationalization why those *other* people need to bear *their* cross while we remain supposedly righteous in systems-oriented peace.

CONCLUSION TO PART ONE

In choosing the particular voices in part I, I sought to provide representative social and psychological analyses that helps understand the context of oppressing as a way of reconsidering a response to oppressors that motivates their liberation. Each of these contributors serves as a layer of understanding; placed together they provide a holistic picture of the social and personal situation that fosters oppressive tendencies. Coming to terms with liberation involves more than addressing societal problems. Doing so is important—a hungry person needs food—but it is only a part. Liberation in a deeper sense addresses the underlying issues for what they are and offers a holistic alternative. While there are many worthwhile discussions on issues and crises of our era, the instinct has been more to attribute blame and tell people how they need to act better. This is only part of a prophetic call. Coming to terms with the root disease, the underlying issues that provoke people to respond to life in certain ways, is also an important issue. Oppressors, to be sure, generally do not lack material necessities or apparent freedoms. If we approach their status in a narrow perspective of liberation, it is easy to miss where they might need liberation at all. However, the material crisis is only one factor in life, alongside social, spiritual, and psychological factors. Dysfunctions in latter aspects may not only persist but even be encouraged, leaving a person dis-integrated while in a context of seeming privilege.

For oppressors, the problems are the self and the self in society, constructed in developmental paths and communicated to others in the process of productivity. These problems instantiate oppression and death in the day-to-day experience of social life. They also create a barrier to transformation, as a person perceives they are more rational and more integrated than they are because they are playing their part in the systems, and maybe even doing well within them. They also believe the promise of the systems to provide substantive resolution. These systems are not at all concerned with any given person, but instead include each person in anonymizing ways. They promise a self that is not wholly self, community that is restrictive within operationally closed boundaries: an amalgamated self and a tribal society that reproduces itself in adaptive ways across space and time.

A self constructed by the systems cannot be sustained through eternity and a person cannot live in a system-derived community without conformity. This amalgamated self reaches an impasse, and competing versions of identity then seek to dominate. Having lost confidence in dialog or reconciliation, a person can only perceive freedom as domination. Where else can such turn? Jesus offers a new way. The way forward, the way of hope, comes through a reconstituted unity of self in the context of diversity of other fully realized selves. In this way, liberation is salvation, salvation is liberation, for both the oppressed and oppressors. Salvation and liberation together orient a person with other persons into eternal communion with God, a communion that may begin at each moment.

To orient a trajectory in a path of liberation for the oppressed and the oppressor, offering a hope for both, and an invitation for both, we must first begin with our source and goal: God. Kierkegaard reminds us of this when he writes, "As soon as psychology has finished with anxiety, it is to be delivered to dogmatics."[52] How then, from within an environment of systems, do we understand God's perspective? This task will be the goal of part II. I will first draw insights from Scripture, a core source of God's revelation of self. Following this, I will seek guidance from key early Christian communities, who sought radical ways of disassociation from the systems of their day, in what they valued and how they lived.

NOTES

1. It is worth noting the potential weaknesses of these developmental theories in regard to their universal use. The major theories were primarily developed in Western contexts using almost exclusively those of European background. While this does not negate the potential of such studies for wider understanding, however, it is a caution worth noting. See Joel R. Sneed, Seth J. Schwartz, and Jr. Cross William E., "A Multicultural Critique of Identity Status Theory and Research: A Call for Integration," *Identity* 6, no. 1 (2006): 61–84. As this work is focusing my initial explorations on liberation of the oppressor in Western contexts, this is not a significant issue for the moment. Future studies examining a liberation of the oppressor in nonwhite or non-Western contexts should certainly keep these challenges in mind and address the problem of cross-cultural applicability. For helpful guidance in this task using Martin Luther King's emphases and sharing much in common with Loder's holistic approach, see Donald M. Chinula, *Building King's Beloved Community: Foundations for Pastoral Care and Counseling with the Oppressed* (Wipf & Stock, 2009). Chinula nicely emphasizes the vital nature of community in identity formation, while Western approaches tend to be highly individualistic. Chinula, 31 writes, "King views human identity as inextricably tied to human society; for him, this means human relationships and institutions. Further, it means global human and relationships and institutions. It is a central tenet of King's thought and belief system that human identity is inconceivable without this global human and relational web."

2. See James Loder, *The Logic of the Spirit: Human Development in Theological Perspective* (San Francisco: Jossey-Bass, 1998), 26–38.

3. There are different ideas about "young adulthood," what ages it spans and what issues it covers. I am here following Loder's range in this exploration.

4. Miroslav Volf, *After Our Likeness: The Church as the Image of the Trinity* (Grand Rapids: Eerdmans, 1998), 178.

5. Quoted in Loder, *Logic*, 251. See Søren Kierkegaard, *Works of Love*, trans. Howard V. Hong and Edna H. Hong (Princeton: Princeton University Press, 1998), 225–245.

6. See Kierkegaard, *Practice in Christianity*, 191. He writes, "In order to enter into the kingdom of heaven a person must become a child again, but in order that his life can express that he has entered into the kingdom of heaven he must become a youth a second time. To be a child and to be a youth when one is a child or a youth is easy enough, but a *second time*—the second time is what is decisive."

7. Loder, *Logic*, 252. See Erik H. Erikson, *Childhood and Society* (New York: W.W. Norton, 1993), 264–265.

8. Loder, *Logic*, 253.

9. See Erikson, *Childhood and Society*, 263–266.

10. Loder, *Logic*, 254.

11. See, for instance, Jonas T. Kaplan, Sarah I. Gimbel, and Sam Harris, "Neural Correlates of Maintaining One's Political Beliefs in the Face of Counterevidence," *Scientific Reports* 6 (December 23, 2016): 39589. For a broader perspective that includes neural and social issues, see Elliot T. Berkman, "The Neuroscience of Goals and Behavior Change," *Consulting Psychology Journal: Practice and Research* 70, no. 1 (March 2018): 28–44.

12. Loder, *Logic*, 255.

13. James Fowler, *Stages of Faith: The Psychology of Human Development and the Quest for Meaning* (New York: HarperCollins, 1995).

14. Fowler, *Stages of Faith*, 9.

15. Loder, *Logic*, 255.

16. Fowler, *Stages of Faith*, 292. Indeed, this highlights how a "religious perspective" does not need a referent to divinity at all to function as a religion. Any orienting philosophy that provides a sense of cohesive identity and understanding about the self and world can also be a religion, serving as the reciprocal ordering of life that reflects a person's particular "faith." Fowler, 31 writes, "The fact that one images the ultimate conditions of existence as impersonal, indifferent, hostile or randomly chaotic, rather than as coherent and structured, does not disqualify his or her image as an operative image of faith."

17. See Loder, *Logic*, 259.

18. Kierkegaard, *Works of Love*, 244.

19. Loder here is following the work of David Levinson, *Seasons of a Man's Life* (New York: Ballantine, 1978).

20. Loder, *Logic*, 259.

21. In this we see the pattern of immediacy substituting for ultimacy. The "next" thing becomes a sense of everything. If I don't get a job, I will be nothing. Then if I don't get married, then kids, then house, and so on. The leap of identifying the particular with the universal leads putting subsets of human behavior, such as sexuality, into the place of whole identity.

22. See Ellacuría, *Ignacio Ellacuría*, 153.
23. Loder, *Logic*, 260.
24. It is worth noting that even this dream can be contextually interpreted. The occasional academic disdain of such orienting goals in supposedly bourgeois American society is itself voiced from a context of the pursuit or experience of academic tenure—which offers the quite radical and rare experience of both security in a community and freedom from the censure of that community. This shows how people have a tendency to disdain how others are integrating their version of the dream, as it subverts our perception of our attempts as being truly universal.
25. This is precisely the rhetorical goal of Martin Luther King's famous speech, "I Have a Dream." He begins by noting the lack of freedom for so many even a hundred years after the Emancipation Proclamation, noting, "One hundred years later, the Negro is still languished in the corners of American Society and finds himself in exile in his own land. So we've come here today to dramatize a shameful condition. In a sense we've come to our nation's capital to cash a check." This "check" is the Constitution and the Declaration of Independence which promised real freedom. The promise had resulted in subjugation, not real freedom, and that can lead to despair by dwelling on the past as it has been experienced. Without negating these experiences, King calls his hearers to be defined by the dream of the promise, that what has been can change into a new pattern of life and living for and with all. This expression of a new pattern serves to instill a transformative hope in the frustrations and discouragements that were still experienced realities. The whole speech can be found in Luther King, Jr., *A Testament of Hope*, chap. 36.
26. This is a reason why there is a strong tendency to step away from the church in the young adult years, and a strong tendency to return when a person has children. One will risk one's own self in light of relativized tradition but the responsibility for another or others tethers a person back to more settled approaches to life. We feel a need to establish a strong foundation even if such a foundation was not fully sufficient for our own quest for self. It was sufficient enough to provide a starting place and we find that comforting in light of the dangers and mystery of leading another human through the stages of early development.
27. Loder, *Logic*, 262.
28. This may be a factor in the relationships between the World War II generation and their children, the baby-boomers. The dual crisis of the depression and World War II (whether active service or the stresses of life in the midst) led to a pursuit of a well-secured life and conformity to a societal standard without individualization, a "safe" life that often lacked emotional intimacy. Thus, many baby-boomers reacted against the perceived inadequacies of the "suburban" life and the associated conformity to the middle-class standards, which was seen then as the barrier between what they wanted and who they felt they were.
29. Erikson's theories are intended to illustrate a linear path along the lines of normal human development, however, one key critique of this is that such stages may not be in fact linear and often a person may revisit earlier stages that were not sufficiently engaged or for other reasons. This idea of revisiting earlier stages in light of later developments can be seen, however, even in Erikson, where he proposed an alternate path of adolescent development which he calls the *"homo religious."* Here,

a religiously defined adolescent moves into what is usually the final stage of development, integrity versus despair, rather than "ego identity versus role confusion." He used Martin Luther as an example of this, with Loder contributing Kierkegaard as another example. In an unpublished study, I argued John Wesley likewise can be best understood in this way. See also James W. Fowler, "John Wesley's Development in Faith," in *The Future of the Methodist Theological Traditions*, ed. M. Douglas Meeks (Nashville: Abingdon Press, 1985).

30. Loder, *Logic*, 263–264.

31. Most clearly expressed in contexts of individualism, as in the West, but may also be seen in more broadly construed examples that shelter community within a narrow boundary. This tribalism emphasizes a community identity but fiercely rejects those on the outside. A form of emergent human spirit that gathers a number of people within the same boundaries shares similar dysfunctions with individualism.

32. Erikson, *Childhood and Society*, 264.

33. That is a major part of the problem in both oppressing itself and in insufficient patterns of reconciliation that are more paternalistic and guilt-oriented. Which is why simply helping people become aware of others *as* people leads to much societal change and why a hallmark of oppression is rhetoric that intentionally lessens the personhood of the oppressed through religious or social categories.

34. Loder, *Logic*, 264.

35. Gutiérrez, among others, does indeed emphasize there is a holistic pattern of liberation, it is internal and external. The task of the Exodus narrative involved, it seems, both taking Israel out of Egypt and Egypt out of Israel. See, for instance, Gustavo Gutiérrez, *We Drink from Our Own Wells: The Spiritual Journey of a People*, trans. Matthew J. O'Connell, 20th anniversary edition (Maryknoll, NY: Orbis Books, 2006), chap. 5.

36. See below, chap. 9, for Sarah Coakley's understanding of reshaping our desires.

37. Freire, *Pedagogy of the Oppressed*, 56.

38. Loder, *Logic,* 264.

39. Fowler, *Stages*, 205.

40. Cf. Ibid., 181–182.

41. Loder, *Logic*, 287.

42. Ibid., 290.

43. Or, in a certain sense, an evolutionary instinct toward self-preservation past the age of productivity, when such institutions and descendants will provide care.

44. Loder, *Logic*, 290–291.

45. See Ross M. Stolzenberg, Mary Blair-Loy, and Linda J. Waite, "Religious Participation in Early Adulthood: Age and Family Life Cycle Effects on Church Membership," *American Sociological Review* 60, no. 1 (1995): 84–103. See also Richard J. Petts, "Trajectories of Religious Participation from Adolescence to Young Adulthood," *Journal for the Scientific Study of Religion* 48, no. 3 (2009): 552–571. Petts argues there is not a single trajectory, noting five different ones depending on the family and religious context.

46. This gives insights to the healing ministry of Jesus. In showing he genuinely sought their best, people trusted him with the more challenging messages. While this

may have a "show me" mentality on the surface rather than faith, there's an understandable element of trust development required in societies where different systems are certainly not concerned about a person's or family's particular welfare.

47. Loder, *Logic*, 289. It is here that Kierkegaard may arguably become less of a driving insight, as his own life neglected this developmental phase. He could speak in to the context of young adulthood that persisted into middle years, but was not in a situation where his self-considerations understood the issues of men and women who are invested in their setting for the sake of children and grandchildren.

48. As will be developed further below, I see *pax Romana* as a peace for some, built on the oppression of many, where one's own peace derives from the application of violence, oppression, or dismissal. In contrast, *pax Christi* is a peace that extends to all, with one taking on for oneself the burden of such peace. This is the fundamental confrontation of the cross itself.

49. While not the focus of this text, it is certainly true that much oppressing comes out of psychologically disordered individuals, such as those dealing with psychopathic or sociopathic issues. Response to those individuals must likewise be seen as involving very different strategies, potentially including force. Rationalizing psychopathy is an impossibility, which is at the root of a comment like Moltmann's that although he abhors violence in every way, if he had the opportunity to kill a tyrant, he would take it. Jürgen Moltmann, interview by author, Tübingen, Germany, May 18, 2011.

50. This is no better seen than in the wealth that many politicians, and even some pastors, pursue even as they may politically or spiritually encourage sacrifices and giving by others.

51. Mt. 16:24–25.

52. Kierkegaard, *The Concept of Anxiety*, 162.

Part II

LIBERATING OPPRESSORS IN SCRIPTURE AND THE EARLY CHURCH

Chapter 4

The Liberating Way of God

INTRODUCTION

"Now the works of the flesh are obvious," Paul writes in Galatians 5. While on the surface they seem to gratify life's cravings, they in fact lead to a narrowing experience of life. They lead to personal and social dissolution. The fruit of the Spirit is the contrast of these, orienting a new pattern of personal and social holiness in an expression of life in full. This new way resists primal gratification and pursues discipline, expanding fullness of being. The opposition to the flesh is not opposition to the physical, as Paul seeks to celebrate the possibilities of life lived in fullness of the Spirit. In a chapter on sanctification, Moltmann writes:

> Life comes from God and belongs to God, so it has to be sanctified through the people who believe God. The earth is not "unclaimed property" and nature is not "ownerless." It is God's beloved creation. So it must be encountered with reverence and drawn into the love for God. Today sanctification means integrating ourselves once more in to the web of life from which modern society has isolated men and women, and is separating them more and more.[1]

The work of the Spirit creates the personal within the communal and the communal out of the personal. It is, to use the language we have developed so far, an opposition to the anonymizing tendencies of systems with their overarching *autopoietic* momentum that treats physical people only as expressions of communicating. The claim in Galatians is that "the works of the flesh" actually dehumanize us, isolating us from community and our own self. In the work of the Spirit, we are re-personalized, becoming whole in who we are in the context of the wholeness of others in the overarching fullness of God's being. This is the biblical realization of liberation, a new beginning of real identity. We become persons in the freedom of Christ.

Abraham Heschel calls the Bible "a record of God's approach to his people."[2] As such, in what follows in the next two chapters, I will pursue a narrative understanding of the texts, with an emphasis on a unifying narrative arc. I will consider early Jewish narratives followed by later interpretations and applications by New Testament writers.[3] However modern scholarship has identified distinctions and even contradictions, it seems clear that the early church conceived itself in line with the history of God's work through Israel.[4] If we are to have a thoroughly Christian response to oppression, we must consider this record in a broad sense and how people navigated understanding this work.

In reading the Bible as a cohesive narrative, I return to earlier approaches of biblical interpretation.[5] While admittedly idiosyncratic especially as compared to the approaches in Biblical Studies departments, this is not absent either in their insights or in their methods.[6] Indeed, this approach is in keeping with some prevailing trends of hermeneutics.[7] With Galatians 5 as an interpretive key that draws the whole text together, we can see how God's pattern of liberation is inviting and inclusive, while well-exceeding the boundaries established for autonomous religious systems. Rather than being a restricting system, God's revelation is life-giving and life-affirming.[8] Indeed God's work does not have boundaries, providing a freedom in which only God is lord and a freedom in which God is wholly lord. God loves all that is within the *cosmos* and is willing to woo all that exists back into relationship.

The *pneumapoietic* activities bring freedom and promise renewal for life. This promise extends to all of creation, the *cosmos* which God so loved. Instead of promising autonomy it emphasizes community, the apparent freedom of the former falling away as the real freedom of the latter becomes increasingly—oft nonintuitively—realized. It is for freedom that Christ has set us free and this liberation reaches through all systems.[9] God is lord of all, integrative as well as enlivening, promising a liberation out of patterns of slavery and into a new pattern of holistic life. God's repeated self-definition in the Old Testament is "I brought you up out of Egypt and redeemed you from the land of slavery."[10] The revelation is tied to the goal of liberation— physical and social and moral and spiritual—a redemptive work that frees the oppressors from their oppressing and the oppressed from oppression. Examples of God's work in both these directions fill the pages of the biblical text. Throughout, we see God revealed in certain ways in how he acts. We learn that God frees because God loves, his promise is built on a commitment to reconciliation and lasting relationship. It is a love story.[11]

In this chapter, I begin with the initial narrative of the Fall, which introduces the contrasting effects of the way of life versus the way of death. I will follow this with a broad overview of the Exodus narrative and its contrast of the way of promise versus the way of despair. Finally, using Psalm 72, I will emphasize the way of compassion versus the way of domination as defining the covenant in terms of community.

FREEDOM AND THE FALL

While Genesis 1 emphasizes God's overarching lordship through the cosmic initiation, the narrative arc of the rest of Scripture really takes shape in Genesis 2–3. The creation of humanity is oriented within a particular structure of community and responsibility. Others are recognized as others through naming.[12] There is trust. There is no shame. Through God's intercession, community is created that invites unity with distinction yet without division. The human pair are exposed in full, being whole in their self in the company of another. This freedom resonates within the ecology of the whole created order. This freedom invites and includes, empowers rather than dominates. In the making of space, space is infinitely being made for and with others, a fractal freedom, world without end. This freedom extends throughout God's space, created within the context of what Gordon Fee calls, "God's empowering presence," extending deeply and broadly to resonate with all that has been made.[13] This is a vocational freedom, a relational freedom, a personalizing freedom.[14] Life is free and life is full. There is peace. Until temptation arises that speaks out of a different conception of human thriving.

In Genesis 3, the narrative moves into a confrontation between conceptions of freedom. Freedom within God's lordship is contrasted with an individualized freedom. Trust in God is replaced by suspicion. Participating together within God's space is replaced by seeking advantage, thus narrowing and isolating space. The appeal toward dissolution by the serpent involves two elements: a perception of God as a limited, insecure oppressor and an expansion of human potentiality as a self-secure identity. God is said to deceive because God is said to be afraid; the relational boundaries that establish a zone of trust (eat of everything, except this one thing) is framed as a limiting boundary impeding personal fulfillment.

The tree was good—the tree is good, within its boundaries of purpose. The suggestion by the serpent to take and eat of the only forbidden fruit invites the breaking of community for the sake of one's own non-mediated progress. Defensive ego resists perceived oppressive limitations. The pseudo-promise is to become like God in knowing good and evil, placing oneself as the arbiter of such in a self-centering perspective. Like God in *this knowledge*—but not like God in either wholeness, actual security of identity, or in love—the human fall is an egotistic embrace of a freedom limited to the self that orients apart and against other frames of reference. The person seeks wholeness absent the space of God's presence, absent the orientation within the community of others. Each frame of reference becomes a determining subject of the perceived cosmos. Everyone else is then perceived in terms of their orienting within or against one's own sense of self. The human pair ate. They saw their state. They saw each other, becoming aware of vulnerability and new needs prompted not by environment but by their now self-perceived inadequacies. The "desires of the flesh" are appealed to and self-indulgence ensues. Distrust and blame result, sin reaches into every part of the self and growing society. It continues its influence into history, death without end.

The dissolution of humanity, the old Adam, now determines the pattern of relational confusion that defines the rest of Scripture. Freedom is lost. Humanity is enslaved within a pattern of sin, seeking self-restoration in the pursuit of promised freedom that rather than fulfilling the hope, further traps and divides.[15] The freedom of the self-created self is a lie, begetting lies and initiating violence as a way of countering the attempt of other selves to dominate.[16] God does not abandon humanity, but history certainly becomes a lot more complicated. God then initiates a redemptive element within history, choosing a person—Abraham—and making a people—Israel—telling a liberating story within the world's story.

THE LIBERATING WILDERNESS

Genesis ends with triumph. Joseph the slave becomes Joseph in charge; Israel is saved and with Israel so is all of Egypt and the surrounding nations. The success provokes dismay. Exodus begins with frustrations, limitations, and negation. The people of Israel are now slaves. Indeed, Exodus begins in the style of the original sin in the Garden narrative. Pharaoh is said to be concerned about the people of Israel, jealous and nervous about how they will use their numbers in open freedom. He moves to restrict their personhood so as to protect his own. He cuts off their continuation as much as he can. Pharaoh is in fact what the serpent accused about God in the Garden: insecure and jealous about the potential of a foreign people. So, he enslaves. That is what systems do when their power is threatened.[17]

The people cry out. God, it seems, is silent. For a long time. Then he speaks. Not in the way hoped for or expected. Although the way of speaking is clearly stated as miraculous, it is also surprising in its lack of direct confrontation. It is a miraculous invitation to someone no longer in the midst of the conflict. Moses had killed. Moses was guilty and accused. Moses fled. He relinquished his place between Israel and Egypt and lost any previous sense of his own self. For those of us who know the later narrative, we can see this as a *kenotic* experience; involuntary *kenosis*, but still a "letting go" where brokenness replaces privilege. For Moses, the turn toward being a shepherd was simply his life. A way forged out of brokenness that led to a place of no longer waiting. Moses was not waiting for God to act and he was not waiting to go back into the game. He had lost any sense of that possibility, it seems.

God speaks to a man who has left behind his identity. Moses was not, after all, in a position of power or influence. He was broken, negated in his earlier attempts to address the injustice he saw around him. His violent response against the oppressing Egyptian overseer made sense according to his context. It was a response within the systems, but had no effect other than alienating him from both the oppressors and the oppressed.[18] He lost his voice to speak to either side. When God spoke, it was to a different Moses than the one who had struck the Egyptian. God spoke to a Moses who had lost his place in the system and so lost any confidence in the systems. Moses, in his brokenness, was free. In this freedom, he was able to begin to negate the negation, to communicate to the systems within his environment but not by means of the operations of those systems.

He certainly still had concerns and questions about God's choosing him. Moses was so far removed from being a social reformer that even when God called him out from a bush on fire, he resisted the calling.[19] God persisted. Why? We're not told, of course, but it is likely Moses was chosen because while a product of the systems, he was no longer caught in the ways of his former world. He could have a new hope because he had entirely let go of the hope of resolution from within the systems. He was not committed to those systems and they were not committed to him. His new path involved a cohesive communication in light of God's lordship over the systems, neither negating nor valorizing them. God was doing a new thing and this new thing involved undermining and confronting the systems themselves in the method of God's salvation. In this speaking, there was light and life. It involved a radical confrontation with the systems as they were.

Pharaoh is the systems personified as he represents both the personal and structural elements of oppression. The progression of challenges moves from pluralistic alternatives—one religion versus another—to inequality of possibility: God reveals himself to be much more powerful than the magicians and the other gods. The work of God emerges from below to overcome the assumptions of the dominant. Even still, the systems maintain their hold and assumption of power. Until the very persistence of the systems is at risk, then release is granted. The people of Israel depart, kept alive through the sign of the blood of the lamb, the Passover feast a commemoration of God's faithfulness and ultimate power in the context of a community.

While much of the Exodus narrative progresses as a liberation out of oppression, there is a continual subplot of liberation away from oppressing as well.[20] This again speaks to why liberation must happen from both directions. As Moltmann writes, "Because many persons are oppressed while at the same time they share in the oppression of others, and hence are 'oppressed oppressors,' it is important to recognize liberation on both sides of the oppression-situation."[21] The Exodus, then, is a new birth for the people of Israel, calling them into a new place and to be a different kind of people, neither oppressed nor oppressors, utilizing the terminology of blessing rather than winning. The law orients this new identity within a framework of social obligation and responsibility. The oft tediousness and specificity of much of the law suggests how deeply the new pattern of God's life was intended to reach into a person's experience.

Even the later narratives of conquest hold onto this. Jericho is overthrown, the narrative tells us, through a nonintuitive display of faithfulness in God—both by Rahab and Joshua in their respective ways—rather than a more rational pattern of conventional warfare.[22] In their victory, the people are reminded that the victory is God's and they should not assume a pattern of self-sufficient identity nor individualized consumption.[23] They are a people formed as a community in the conception of God's redemption. They are no longer the oppressed but they are not allowed to be the oppressor.[24] Good and evil is rigidly established in the holistic pattern of the law, patterns of obligation and confession provided so as to maintain an equilibrium. All are not equal in rights or privilege, but all are equal in terms of personhood, each person given meaning and worth despite their relative distinction in societal functions. The systems still exist but exist beneath the framework of God's overarching revelation of the people as God's people, and as God's people responsible to and with each other. The systems have coherence within the environment of God's rule.

This relegation of the systems beneath the overarching system of God is exemplified in the self-similar scaling of Sabbath rest. The seventh day enjoins all people to stop, to let go one day for the sake of rest, taking a risk by rest, trusting in faith of God's provision. This seventh day scales into a seventh year, letting the land itself rest, an ecological embrace that acknowledges the interconnectivity of humanity and environment.[25] People are not to oppress themselves, each other, or the land. This culminates in the Sabbath of Sabbaths, the year of Jubilee, where holistic freedom confronts the accumulation of pride, despair and objectification.[26] The people are freed, the land is freed, patterns are reset. Society is reborn.

From the ashes, a phoenix arises alive and fresh.[27] They are to rest, to let go, to be redeemed, to reset because humanity is not defined by politics, economics, or any other prevailing system.[28] As the end of Leviticus 25 declares: "For to me the people of Israel are servants; they are my servants whom I brought out from the land of Egypt: I am the LORD your God." They are servants of God, and this identity supersedes every other definition and obligation. The year of Jubilee is the year of liberation, the year in which identity as God's people relativizes every other kind of identity, liberating the oppressed from their oppression and the oppressors from their oppressing, reinvigorating the society by a lived declaration of God's lordship. In the acts of Jubilee, the people declare their trust in God's faithfulness rather than their dependence on the systems for meaning and security. Every system is relegated beneath the identity of God, the value of humanity, and goodness of the whole ecological context.

The liberated people of Israel were called into a new way of being, set free *by* God for freedom *with* God, a freedom that entailed responsibility, what Randy Maddox calls "responsible grace."[29] They were to be a people with a new narrative, a new meta-system that relegates the other systems of society beneath the overarching lordship of God. They were to be free, but not free to oppress. Free, but not free to depersonalize. They were to be free *with* the land, not free to do whatever they wanted *to* the land. If this sounds less like freedom, then it is because we have far too long equated freedom with doing whatever we want without regard to others around us, an individualized freedom.[30] A freedom within community has boundaries that maximize the freedom for all.[31] These boundaries need not be legal, and indeed the law itself can become yet another form of restrictive authoritarianism by those who interpret and arbitrate the law.

CONTINUAL LIBERATION

I opened the introduction of this text by quoting from Ps. 70:1, considered by early monastics one of the key verses in the whole Bible. It was considered especially useful because it could address various sides of oppression. Those who are struggling are reminded of God's goodness and grace. Those in power are reminded of their limits and how they need God's favor and grace. The same words provide a reorientation away from the assumptions of the present experiences in the systems and back into the narrative of God's promises.

The two psalms that follow address each side more specifically. Psalm 71 offers a perspective from the oppressed, written by one who is broken down and pursued. It is an expression of faith, seeking God's work in the midst of vulnerability. The writer has seen troubles and needs a restoration of life. God is a refuge, a protector, a liberator for the downcast.

Psalm 72 offers the counterimage. It is a royal psalm, attributed to Solomon, and consists of a prayer for blessing while in the position of responsibility, written from the perspective of the already powerful.[32] With this psalmic sequence, we see again the attentiveness of the Bible to orienting both the powerless and the powerful within God's redemptive patterns. Psalm 72 coordinates prosperity along with care for the afflicted, asking God to provide guidance and support in the tasks. God is asked to bring bounty from the land, a task beyond the king, and God is asked to defend those who are needy, a task given also to the king. This provides what N. T. Wright calls a "composite hope for Israel," in which there is hope for a new world, not just rescue, and this hope is placed in the rule of the righteous liberating king.[33] "May he crush the oppressor," the writer prays, a dangerous prayer for a potential despot.[34]

The Psalm orients the king within a form of success that is used to help those who are desperate for help. It does not dismiss the role of the king or call for a flattening of social classes. Instead, it places power within the scope of responsibility: the king as a caretaker. Verses eight through fourteen even have a covenant quality to them, asking for God's favor in politics and power, with this favor associated with the king's extension of the favor to those within the kingdom. The "may he" statements are followed by the "for he." Evoking the sentiment of the "golden rule," but orienting it in a divine way: may God help the King as the King helps the people. Or evoking a sentiment similar in the Lord's prayer: "forgive me as I forgive others" is expressed here as "bless me as I bless others." The one who could be the oppressor is continually reoriented with the scope of God's calling for him and God's love for all the people.

The powerful one is not framed as the oppressor but the guardian. The king will deliver, so he asks for God to deliver. The king will help, so he asks for God's help. The king will take pity on those who are needy and asks for a self-similar relationship from God. The oppressed are lifted up and protected. There is an expression of blessing that extends outward and inward, a blessing from God that blesses the king who blesses all the nations. This is a continual liberation, both for the king and for the people, a way of life that then expresses a new pattern of society, one that gives glory to God at each point.

We know this pattern did not persist. The ideal expressed in this psalm was swamped by other voices and other narratives. These two paths, the way of blessing or the way of oppressing, are presented starkly in 1 Kings 12, where Rehoboam, son of Solomon, is confronted by the people. Even Solomon, it seems, did not live up to his side of the agreement in the psalm, as the people come before Rehoboam, saying, "Your father made our yoke heavy. Now therefore lighten the hard service of your father and his heavy yoke that he placed on us, and we will serve you."[35] Rehoboam asks for advice, first from his older counselors, who encourage him to serve the people graciously. He then turns to his younger advisors, who counsel him toward more oppression. He listens to the latter. The stage is set for the dissolution of the united kingdom. "May he crush the oppressor," from Ps. 72:4 takes shape in the subsequent narrative. God moves to do so, a theme prevalent throughout the prophets.

CONCLUSION

In many ways the Old Testament narratives provide everything we need to know about God, God's work, humanity's response, and God's commitment. So much so it leads some like John Goldingay to ask whether we really need the New Testament.[36] We do—and Goldingay asserts this early in his book—but far too often we assume that what came later superseded what came before, as if there was a first attempt—an aborted attempt—and then a second try. This leads to a threefold use of the Old Testament in popular Christianity. First, to show how the Law didn't work—a reading suggested by Paul and made absolute by Luther. Second, to find isolated passages that highlight either God's promises that we can take as personal mottos (Jer. 29:11 for instance, or the now infamous prayer of Jabez in 1 Chron. 4:10)—which individualize our value and successes—or as proofs for New Testament revelation—proofs that tend to be circular in reasoning. Third, the stories are reduced to morality plays, flannel-board minimalism that suggests "we should be good people and here are some examples of good choices people with beards made in times long ago." These are not coherent approaches, as we are both warned against works and encouraged toward them. We are given stories of other cultures in other times, while co-opting these for our own supposed benefits, an egotistic move if there ever was one! In this way, in how the Old Testament is often taken in piecemeal or arbitrary ways, it is very easy to lose the central theme, one set up in the earliest chapters and continuing to the last: God opposes the arrogant ones, those who seek to establish themselves on the backs of others. God intervenes to set things right.

We need the New Testament because it takes this narrative—with its increasing tensions—and makes it personal. As Goldingay writes, "We need the New Testament because it tells us about Jesus."[37] But we can't understand Jesus without knowing what came before. All the New Testament writers assumed their readers knew these earlier teachings. The trouble is that the content becomes easily co-opted by the systems, and the reading of the narrative of God's work becomes another way to enforce, rather than dissipate, oppression. Which is why it is so important to continually return to the whole text, and to be especially committed to the pattern of Christ in interpretation and action. In this, in the revelation of Jesus and the engagement of society by the earliest Christians, we have hope in a new pattern of life in this world, teaching about how this can take shape, and a new freedom in the work of God to really live this out. If we are willing. If we are daring.

NOTES

1. Jürgen Moltmann, *Spirit of Life* (Minneapolis: Fortress Press, 2001), 171–172.
2. Abraham Joshua Heschel, *Moral Grandeur and Spiritual Audacity: Essays*, ed. Susannah Heschel (New York: Farrar, Straus and Giroux, 1997), 11.
3. See Lewis Ayres, *Nicaea and its Legacy* (New York: Oxford University, 2004), 38: "The narrative structure of faith shaped Christian discussions of human nature and transformation in teleological directions: discussions of human transformation came to be seen as appropriately focused on shaping progress toward the goals of life with God and the (increasingly eschatological) contemplation of the divine being. . . . At the same time those narratives also positions talk about God and the world by offering perspectives on human capacity and incapacity and the role of Scripture in aiding and shaping human reflection: Christian narratives thus also shapes epistemological concerns. Despite their constant debate about human capacity, Christians insisted that the text of Scripture is, as this stage in the drama of redemption, the fundamental resource for knowledge of God and a resource that shapes how we engage existing human perceptions of the world and all it contains." Cf. Ayres, 335–342; 416–420. On 335–336, he notes, "Like almost all early Christian writers, pro-Nicenes read Scripture as a providentially ordained resource for the Christian imagination. It is an intrinsic part of Scriptures' purpose to enable description of the God who acts *and* of the structure of the cosmos within which God acts: the reshaping of the cosmological imagination is a central aspect of the Incarnate Word's mission. Scripture shapes the description of the journey in the Church and in Christ toward full sight of the divine glory."
4. The book of Hebrews is the most explicit about this. Piotr Ashwin-Siejkowski highlights this approach in *Clement of Alexandria*, writing, "For instance, it is against Marcion's type of selective approach to the Scriptures that Clement strongly defends the coherence of God's revelation and asserts the continued relevance of the Old Testament and the law." Piotr Ashwin-Siejkowski, *Clement of Alexandria: A Project of Christian Perfection* (New York: T&T Clark, 2008), 9.
5. See Michael Graves, *The Inspiration and Interpretation of Scripture: What the Early Church Can Teach Us* (Grand Rapids: Eerdmans, 2014), 106–112. See also John Goldingay, "Biblical Narrative and Systematic Theology," 129 in *Between Two Horizons* (Grand Rapids: Eerdmans, 2000), 123–142.
6. For a more comprehensive study on wealth in the Bible which covers much more ground with closer attention to the exegetical questions and resources, see Craig Blomberg, *Neither Poverty nor Riches: A Biblical Theology of Possessions* (Downers Grove: IVP, 1999). Blomberg focuses very specifically on the issues of wealth and poverty in his wide-ranging survey of the biblical text. My goal is broader, including various issues of power and potential oppressing, and my discussion is thus less detailed.

7. See Robert Alter, *The Art of Biblical Narrative*, 2nd edition (New York: Basic Books, 2011). Alter, 11 notes that "in many cases a literary student of the Bible has as much to learn from the traditional commentaries as from modern scholarship. The difference between the two is ultimately the difference between assuming that the text is an intricately interconnected unity, as the midrashic exegetes did, and assuming it is a patchwork of frequently disparate documents, as most modern scholars have supposed." For Alter, of course, this interconnectedness does not necessarily mean a progressive unfolding of God's revelation, nor that this narrative should be taken literally, and his work is focused entirely on the Hebrew Bible. For help with an integrative interpretation approach for Hebrew and Christian Bible, see, for instance, Max Turner and Joel B. Green, "New Testament Commentary and Systematic Theology: Stranger or Friends?" in *Between Two Horizons* and Joel B. Green, "Scripture and Theology: Uniting the Two So Long Divided" in the same volume.

8. Moltmann, *Experiences in Theology*, 149.

9. Galatians 5:1.

10. See, for instance, Exod. 20:2; 29:46; Lev. 22:33; 25:38; 26:13; Num. 15:41; Deut. 4:37; 5:15: 8:14; Judg. 6:8; 1 Sam. 12:6; Ps. 80:8; 81:10; Jer. 34:13.

11. There is much to be said and has been said on this understanding. See, for instance, Isa. 5:1 and 55. Cf. Sarah Coakley, *The New Asceticism: Sexuality, Gender and the Quest for God* (New York: Bloomsbury, 2015), 96–97.

12. See Jürgen Moltmann, *Ethics of Hope* (Minneapolis: Fortress Press, 2012), 152–153.

13. Gordon D. Fee, *God's Empowering Presence: The Holy Spirit in the Letters of Paul* (Peabody, MA: Hendrickson, 1994), 5–9.

14. Moltmann, *Ethics of Hope*, 150–151.

15. Moltmann, *Ethics of Hope*, 160. In "Liberate Yourselves by Accepting One Another," in *Human Disability and the Service of God*, eds. Nancy L. Eiesland and Don E. Saliers (Nashville: Abingdon Press, 1998), 107, Jürgen Moltmann writes, "Egoism is born of the fear of falling short, and it is a battle a person has with herself and with others to make life hell and to destroy all the beauty of life. Egoism is not self-love at all, but rather a type of self-hate. Depression and aggression are closely related. And in the same way egoism and self-hate are merely two sides of the same coin: two aspects of a lost love of self."

16. Elisabeth Moltmann-Wendel and Jürgen Moltmann, *God—His & Hers* (New York: Crossroad, 1991), 8.

17. See J. Severino Croatto, *Exodus: A Hermeneutics of Freedom* (Maryknoll, NY: Orbis Books, 1981), 21–23.

18. See Exod. 2:11–15.

19. Exod. 4:1–17.

20. The Exodus narrative has a long tradition of uses by oppressed people in all kinds of settings. In its archetypical role in the biblical narrative, it points to how God truly does abhor oppression and seeks freedom for people, thus pushing back against the idea that the Bible supports slavery. Though, of course, the Bible recognizes slavery as a situation many may be in, and contains ethics about how to live in light of such a situation, it repeatedly emphasizes freedom as a good and slavery as an evil.

See Albert J. Raboteau, *Slave Religion: The "Invisible Institution" in the Antebellum South*, Updated edition (New York: Oxford University Press, 2004), 311–312. On the uses of Exodus in contemporary experiences of oppression, see R. S. Sugirtharajah, *Voices from the Margin: Interpreting the Bible in the Third World*, 25th Anniversary edition (Maryknoll, NY: Orbis Books, 2016), chaps. 17–22.

21. Moltmann, "The Liberation of Oppressors," 71.

22. See Joshua 2 and 6. While Joshua's role is more direct, Rahab's may be more profound. Both were examples of those saved by their expressions of faith in contrast to the majority of their peers who perished, either in the wilderness or in the city.

23. Earlier in their time at Shittim (Numbers 25), the Israelites prostituted themselves physically and spiritually, forsaking the covenant relationship to participate in unlawful activity. In Josh. 2:8–13, however, we find one who professionally is a prostitute, yet turns from her profession and loyalty to the Canaanite people and religions to claim the words of the covenant with YHWH. Thus, the story of Numbers 25 is reversed—the prostitute embraces the covenant—leading to the salvation and victory of Israel. In making this claim, Rahab was asserting in action and words that which the Israelite people were called to assert in actions and words. Their disobedience was highlighted by Rahab's obedience to a God that was not originally her own, but through this confession "grafted" her into the narrative (Mt. 1:5).

24. The tension in this statement, of course, lies in the acts of conquest performed by Israel. The indication is that such conquest is an act of judgment by God rather than oppression, though we are not privy to the narrative of God's work in these other nations. See Deut. 9:4–5. As Aslan told Aravis, "No one is told any story but their own." In C. S. Lewis, *The Horse and His Boy*, Reprint edition (New York: HarperCollins, 2002), 216.

25. See Lev. 25:1–7.

26. See Lev. 25:8–55.

27. Cf. 1 Clement 25–27.

28. See Adetoye Faniran, "Rest: The Biblical Model of Environmental Management and Its Implications for the Kingdom of God," *Ogbomoso Journal of Theology* 12 (2007): 43–58. Faniran, 49 writes, "The Sabbath Year and the (Golden) Jubilee extended the concept of rest to the entire creation, thus asking humans to recognize God's ownership, continued presence and abiding covenant. In other words, the period set apart for total rejuvenation, recovery, and sustained production/yield is meant to ensure the perpetual existence of God's creation as home of humans."

29. Randy L. Maddox, *Responsible Grace: John Wesley's Practical Theology* (Nashville: Kingswood Books, 1994), 19. He writes that this term "focuses Wesley's distinctive concern on the nature of God and God's actions, rather than on humanity. It makes clear that God's indispensable gift of gracious forgiveness and empowerment is fundamental, while capturing Wesley's characteristic qualification of such empowerment as enabling rather than overriding human responsibility."

30. So much so, that saying freedom is "doing whatever we want" seems obvious, and it would be almost Orwellian to say otherwise. However, freedom within community has always involved constraints, as the freedom of one person can easily overwhelm the freedom of others, leading to assorted forms of authoritarianism.

Boundless freedom of a religion becomes a theocracy, a boundless freedom of the extremely wealthy or corporations becomes an oligarchy, absolute freedom of a single ruler an autocracy, and so on. Thus patterns develop which blunt the absolute independence of rulers so as to maintain both their constructive role in the society and the actual freedom of those in the role. Kim Jong-un has absolute control, but few would argue he is more free than other leaders in Asia or Europe. Even the seeming boundless freedom of the people to choose their pattern of society in a democracy is itself constrained. The Constitution of the United States, for instance, is noteworthy in its attempt to navigate the various potential forms of authoritarianism, including that of the majority, by creating a model that involves popular and representational governance and a balance of government powers each with a distinct mode of responsibility. The freedom of the United States is a very carefully crafted and boundaried freedom, and even this, as history notes, is continually liable to distortion and abuse.

31. Cf. 1 Cor. 9–10. Jean Vanier, *Community and Growth* (New York: Paulist Press, 1989), 111 writes, "Many want community and a feeling of being together, but they refuse the demands of community life. They want both freedom and community; freedom to do just what they want when they want, *and* community, which implies certain structures and values. It's like wanting the cake and eating it too! People have to choose. But to be able to choose there has to be clarification."

32. This psalm may be more accurately described as Solomonic, rather than by Solomon. It may even be a prayer for Solomon by David, which is suggested by the last verse in the Psalm: "The prayers of David son of Jesse are ended." See Marvin E. Tate, *Psalm 51–100* (Dallas: Word Books, 1990), 222.

33. N. T. Wright, *Paul: A Biography* (San Francisco: HarperOne, 2018), 73.

34. Even more dangerous for Solomon's descendants, many of whom were despots.

35. 1 Kgs 12: 4.

36. See John Goldingay, *Do We Need the New Testament?: Letting the Old Testament Speak for Itself* (Downers Grove, IL: IVP Academic, 2015).

37. Goldingay, *Do We Need the New Testament*, 11.

Chapter 5

The Liberating Way of Christ

INTRODUCTION

Scripture tells us of God and tells us of humanity, how we are to live according to who God is, in our present contexts and beyond. This is not merely a set of ethical guidelines that show us how to be good people in a difficult world. It includes such at points, but the goal is much grander. The redemption of humanity is ontological as well as behavioral, psychological and spiritual, physicalized and intellectualized, a scope of holistic renewal that invites us to participate with God in every aspect of our life. Liberation is the fundamental effect of such communion as it transforms how such a people are comporting themselves in their contexts. This participation is the only path of resurrection, a new birth into a new life.

This new life is not, to be sure, immediately recognizable.[1] From the earliest narratives through the end of the Jewish Scriptures we find a tension between trusting God for identity and trusting more immediate narratives and examples. The giving of the law on Mt. Sinai was accompanied by the people abandoning God as they worshipped a golden calf. This now unoriginal sinfulness persists in every context, with the multiplicity of narratives providing a constant temptation for men and women, especially as God sometimes seems silent, distant, or seemingly insufficient. In many situations, it is not so much the abandonment of God as the relegation of God to being one among many: a god among pantheons or as the unifying object of a religious system in an environment of many operationally closed systems.

When these distinct systems are not clearly religious alternatives but their own pattern of apparent life and flourishing, seemingly positives even in biblical terms, it becomes difficult to see how the various narratives told by these systems are mutually conditioning each other toward oppression. It is truly a knotted thread. That is a key factor in this discussion, as many of those we might categorize as "oppressors" are really people who are trying to live their lives in the most fruitful way possible in their contexts. They are doing their duty—as they see it and as the world asks for it. While some may directly work toward the repression of others, a great many are simply people of relative privilege, who might even have a thriving, distinct, and influential religious element in their lives. They are not intentionally evil, though they are incoherent in their identity, thus enabling evil to persist. How to untie these tangled knots? That is the message of Christ to the disciples, and the disciples to the world.

In this chapter, I begin with the case of the rich young man of Matthew 19. Next, using John 3, I will point toward the liberative emphasis of new birth, a contrast way of experiencing life even in temporal terms. The new life is a putting aside of the old life, a new beginning in the midst of persistent living. Third, the narrative of the cross serves as the narrative of absolute confrontation between the way of the systems and the lordship of God. Christ stands between these two patterns in the ultimate example of kenotic liberation, one that resonates life out of death, freedom out of constraint, identity out of nonidentity.

Two examples from Acts will provide particularly religious expressions of oppressing behaviors, with two different results. Ananias shows the contrast of honest community versus performative pride, while the transformation of Paul reveals the contrast of legalistic zeal to humbled witness. With this latter narrative, the example of another Ananias exemplifies trust in God by extending peace to a former enemy. Finally, I will highlight Philippians 2 as an interpretive key for drawing the liberation narrative together. We who Christ calls into community are to follow the model of Christ that develops from *kenosis* into glory.[2] We are to let go of what we think we deserve so as to take up that which Christ offers in becoming a new people of God who celebrate the fullness of the work of God in, with, and for this world.

STEPS TO PERFECTION

The path of liberation always involves transformation. Our experiences of life need to change. For the oppressed, that means a transformation of the structures of society that enable oppression and a transformation of the psychological and social crises that oppression causes. What is the transformative call for those not in crisis, either moral or economic? The blind, after all, realize they need to see. How about those who do not realize what their issues are or where they may be off track? How does liberation come for those who do not realize their need for liberation? That seems to be the key issue in Matthew 19, where the rich young man is zealous according to his religious duties, seeking to do what is right in light of what has been revealed and ordained. Yet, there seems to be a lingering sense of incompleteness. For all his achievements and prosperity, he still encounters that ultimate crisis of mortality.

"Teacher," the man asks Jesus, "what good deed must I do to have eternal life?"

As he often does, Jesus subverts the question from the get go, noting that only God is good. This semi-aside is easily overlooked, but it points to a key approach of Jesus, and I would argue for Scripture as a whole. The question of the young man initiates in terms of tasks: What must be done? What steps are needed to accomplish the stated goal? This is an expression of privilege as it assumes anything can be accomplished if only one knows the right steps to take to do it.[3] The question "What must I do?" places the task within the abilities of the interrogator, once again that expression of the earliest sin.[4] Success is possible in any given system, one just has to know the rules. Jesus subtly pushes back against the question about "doing." God alone is good, there is no good isolated from the relational being of God. There is no good that bypasses God, despite human intent to discover the steps and strategies.

Jesus makes his point then proceeds to answer the question, not shifting his core orientation but rather approaching it in a different way. Jesus answers in the way the man seeks, a task-oriented ontology: keep the commandments.[5]

"I've done that," the young man says, likely honestly.

"If you want to be perfect," Jesus responds, "sell your possessions and give the money to the poor."

The man was likely expecting a confirmation of his goodness, a pat on the back of affirmation. Instead, the man who had seemingly done all the law required is given a task that strikes at who he was in society, "for he had many possessions." Did Jesus mean that possessions are themselves evil? Maybe, but I think he was emphasizing something else.

Matthew 19:13–15 is interpretatively important for the synoptic writers here.[6] In the passage that immediately precedes the conversation with the rich young man, Jesus discusses little children, offering a seemingly precious statement of their worth and value. The kingdom of heaven belongs to the little children, Jesus says. Yet, the young man had a much greater barrier to such acceptance. Children get in free, but the young man had to pay with everything he has. The distinction is not about ability, or about a supposed entry fee, but about identity, where meaning is found. As Emerito Nacpil notes, "The 'perfection' that is enjoined here is that of the Kingdom, not of the Law."[7] It seems the young man had to sell everything he owned so as to reset his self in, and only in, God.[8] He needed a Jubilee moment. Eternal life cannot be achieved by either actions or possessions. Only God is good, and the only way to fullness is in full openness to God. While there is much more to develop in the story of the rich young man, I will set it aside until the next chapter, where it becomes a key passage for how some in the early church understood the issue of wealth and identity.

STARTING ANEW

While certainly not linked in location or even contained within the synoptic tradition, Jn 3:1–21 is very apropos to the previous passage, especially if we see the statement about the children as an interpretive key for understanding the response to the young man. Near the very beginning of his ministry, as portrayed in John, Jesus has a secret conversation with a powerful man, an influential Pharisee named Nicodemus. While John places the conversation with Nicodemus near the beginning of Jesus's active earthly ministry, it anticipates what comes near the end, his death on the cross. The placement in the text is not as much about chronology as it is about theological interpretation: Jesus is pointing toward the exclusive nature of his ministry in light of the Exodus narrative. This exclusivity, however, is established in love and wisdom; there is no way to find life on one's own and so God offers a way of restarting one's identity. This is a way of cleansing and a way of pointing forward with a new hope.

Nicodemus acknowledges Jesus as being from God. With this confession in place, Jesus initiates the conversation about the kingdom. Participation in the kingdom requires being born again. In our era, this term has saturated Christian conversation to the point that it is almost without meaning, a tired euphemism for becoming a Christian. For Nicodemus, however, it is striking. How can a person be born a second time? This literal interpretation by an educated Pharisee is curious, with some suggesting more of a wistful than confused response: how can we put aside who we are and start over?

Leon Morris expands on this interpretation:

> A man, Nicodemus might have said, is the sum of all his yesterdays. He is the man he is today because of all the things that have happened to him through the years. He is a bundle of doubts, uncertainties, wishes, hopes, fears, and habits, good and bad, built up through the years. It would be wonderful to break the entail of the past and make a completely fresh beginning. But how can this possibly be done? Can physical birth be repeated? Since this lesser miracle is quite impossible, how can we envisage a much greater miracle, the remaking of a person's essential being? Regeneration is sheer impossibility![9]

We are who we are and this includes our context of both time and place. Our experiences shape us and this cannot simply be put aside. This is indeed the challenge of liberation, from either direction. There can be a change in situation but not necessarily a change in conception of one's own self, and whatever situation we are in, we carry this persistent sense of self.[10] The loss (or gain) of materials or power is not holistically transformative. A person can be freed from slavery but still have their sense of self defined by being a slave. A person can lose everything but still retain the sense of importance and priority due to their earlier state.

To find new freedom, a person needs a wholly new start in their sense of self. Rebirth is a restart, a letting go of those very "doubts, uncertainties, wishes, hopes, fears, and habits" which define the self in the environment of systems. The kingdom is not, then, yet another system among the systems but a wholesale reorientation of self. Life with Christ is not another chapter, but a whole new story. "In short," Jean-Marc Ela writes, "God carries human beings forward, toward a future characterized by a new reality."[11] Our past is not erased, of course, but the transformative work of God reshapes the narrative, the future giving new meaning to what has already happened so that everything that has happened becomes retold in the light of Christ's work in our lives. This, then, is not a choice within the system known as religion, but a renewal of our whole perceived environment. We see the world differently, our place, our past, our present, our whole self, our neighbor.

This is, ultimately, a reinitiation of trust, analogical to the trust the Israelites placed in the command to gaze at the bronze snake Moses held aloft. The object itself did not provide salvation, it was the obedience through trusting God for salvation.[12] Trust in Christ is placing trust within a new orientation.[13] This is not a choice to fit in with other perspectives alongside Christ. God is a jealous God. The narrative of Scripture pushes back against Christianity as another religion in the religious system as well as any idea that Christianity can be reduced to moral teachings, general pursuits of justice, genteel habits, or any other reduction that bypasses the cross. We cannot be, as Kierkegaard emphasized, mere admirers of Jesus. We are to be imitators.[14] The new birth initiates in the cross as the cross is the expression of *kenotic* obedience that strikes a mortal blow against any assumption of meaning through human systems.

God's love propels God's work, bringing the world back into relationship with God. But, one cannot live in God's narrative without a confrontation with the world's systems. God's salvation is a promise of renewed life, a liberated life, which by its very nature involves a new pattern and narrative of one's whole life and how it is lived in the context of community. This "abundant life," Marianne Meye Thompson writes, "looks back toward creation; it anticipates the blessings of the new life of the resurrection, especially the blessing of being in the divine presence; and it lies at the intersection of past and future, while in the present it offers communion with the living

God."[15] Providing this life is the mission of the Spirit, accomplished through a dynamic interplay within the contexts of this world. Like the wind blowing, going where it will, the Spirit leads according to God's rationality, not the world's. We are to interpret all that follows in the Gospel of John as a radical calling to participate with the Spirit. Indeed, wrestling with what this means in practice forms the rest of the New Testament.[16]

CONFRONTING THE SYSTEMS

While it would be instructive to walk through the whole of the life and teachings of Jesus to see this theme developed, such a task would overwhelm the goals of this book and indeed be more than any single volume could achieve.[17] So, as part of this task of providing narrative examples that represent the whole, I will jump to near the end of Luke.

In the narrative about the path to the crucifixion we find the starkest confrontation between the way of God and the ways of this world. The cross is an expression of obedience and trust, both of Jesus and then by those who trust in this obedience for their own salvation. It shows how whole trust in God resists being co-opted by the systems of this world despite their claims for absolute authority and meaning.[18] As this is a pattern established by both the writings and the prophets of the Jewish Scriptures as well as in the ministry and teachings of Jesus, the Gospels are not simply passion narratives with extended introductions.

The Gospels are a living example of what it means to live this out in real contexts among real stories. The narrative of the incarnation is the culmination of the whole narrative of Scripture thus far. The cross, then, is the end point, the fully exposed confrontation that exists throughout the ministry of Jesus, insisting on the ultimacy of God's lordship across personal, social, and societal systems.[19] This lordship is expressed in terms of love and commitment, but defining such in an absolute way that rejects syncretic attempts to see God as being another system among the systems, a god among the other gods.[20] God brings the people out of slavery, they are to have no other gods.[21] In contemporary terms, we are to have no other systems before him. God co-opts the systems, the systems respond, the result is the cross.

The confrontations of Jesus in the trials that lead to his seemingly untimely and certainly violent death are themselves imbued with theological and sociological meaning.[22] This is not a minor disagreement about political methodology or even a religious dispute. This is a wholesale cosmic confrontation. Judas is filled with Satan.[23] The priests are servants of evil.[24] The disciples are all at risk. Jesus thus asserts the priority of his narrative as the true expression of God's work. This narrative will be brutally assaulted, leading to the vulnerability of all those who align themselves with Jesus.[25] As the trial develops, there seems to be three distinct groups involved in the process, each of which represents an identity forming system that coexists with other systems in the same environment: the Jewish religious leaders, the Roman political rulers, and the zealots who are social reformers.

The first system initiates the process, as Jesus is arrested by the Temple guards under the orders of the chief priests. Jesus confronted the religious leaders and the religious system itself throughout his ministry, leading to their seemingly successful attempt to end his ministry. His call for a holistic pattern of expression across religious boundaries—which seemed to, but did not quite, circumvent the Jewish law—undermined their roles as judges and gatekeepers. Who speaks for God? Those with the scriptural mandate as priests or Jesus? Both assume they are the ones ordained to speak for God in and for the world. In this, Jesus was essentially confronting the religious system *qua* system. His message of the kingdom both confirmed and subverted the Judaism of his time, confirming the revelation while subverting how this revelation—the name of God—had been co-opted by those in power to establish a religious social strata. Thus, while he was accused of blasphemy in his trial he was effectively counter-charging his accusers with the same crime. They said they spoke for God through the system. Jesus rejected the system for the sake of God.

Jesus was not crucified by the Jewish religious leaders, however. He was crucified by Rome, the controlling legal authority of the time. Rome did not so much care about religious arguments—worship anything you want, just don't let it get in the way of the peace. Rome's concern was social order and they used violence—often extreme violence—to maintain this order. The *pax Romana* established peace for a great many people indeed, a peace that was established by expanding boundaries and brutal colonization. This was given a civilizing rationale, with those outside of Rome considered barbarians too ignorant to realize the benefit of Roman paternity. As the greatest power, Rome spoke for the world, the system of governance and social order. To cross Rome was to cross civilization itself, so the punishment was to be dehumanized, to suffer the cross.

Jesus was not himself a direct opponent of Rome, but his whole methodology and approach to this world was itself a confrontation of Rome. Most confrontations involved an argument about who was to be in power. The system itself stayed secure, people simply sought to change their situation in the system. That is how many liberation movements develop: people do not want to change the system of power, they want to be the power in the system. Jesus, in contrast, confronted the whole system which developed peace through violence and peace through obligating others to bear the burden. In this confrontation, the way of the world was at stake. Rome represented more than just itself, it represented a whole system and pattern of social order.

Jesus did not actively rebel against that particular expression and seek to be king of the system. The kingdom of God is more than a competing power to the system's status quo, it is an alternative to the system itself. Thus, we find Jesus not defending himself as he might have if he worked within the system. His silence was itself a confrontation against the ultimate power of the system. Indeed, his argument was not even against Rome (an important point to consider when Jesus is used in liberation discussions), but against the system of which Rome was yet another representative.

For Rome, Jesus was clearly not an immediate threat, certainly not like Simon bar Kokhba was a century later. Yet, he was still a secondary threat to social order, as he was a polarizing figure among the Jewish populace, some of whom threatened a disruption of the delicate peace (and Pilate's delicate situation). In good modern fashion, while predating it by over fifteen hundred years, the importance of a particular person was insignificant as long as Rome could maintain apparent "civilizing" progress. Jesus was one of Hegel's innocent flowers, crushed to pieces for the sake of supposed progress. To keep the peace, the Roman peace, which placed the burden of peace on others, Jesus had to die. That is how the system perpetuated. Jesus, in contrast, took the burden of his proclaimed peace upon himself, accepting violence against himself as a way of confronting the ultimate inadequacy of the rule of violence. Rome put people to death, the act of a worldly power. Jesus refused to stay dead, the ultimate rebellious act against the system that only had violence to commend it. The *pax Romana* was a peace for some, paid for by others. The *pax Christi* is peace offered to all, paid for by Christ only.

On the other side of Rome, within the same system, were the zealots, who did not so much protest the system *qua* system; they just wanted to be the ones who were the victors within the system. They saw violence as effective, the result of oppression that invites active and complete response—the justification for its perpetuation was the pursuit of justice. They intimated an end of oppression and coddled a never-reached anticipation that accomplishing the goal would bring an end to the violence. As Jesus seemed able to lead the people but did not raise a rebellion, it was clear that he was unwilling and thus irrelevant to the zealots' goals. Jesus spoke of a peace-making kingdom that brought peace through peace. That kind of thinking is clearly absurd, at least within the established systems.

Pilate realized, the narrative tells us, that Jesus himself was not a threat, but Pilate's main concern was social order. He needed a way to save both Jesus and his current peace. A custom presented itself that seemed just the thing. A prisoner was given a "get out of jail free" card, and the people could decide: Jesus the peaceful messiah or Barabbas, who was in prison for participating in an insurrection. Michael Wilkens characterizes him as a brigand, with brigands "popular with the common people because they preyed upon the wealthy establishment of Israel and created havoc for the Roman government."[26] When given an option to choose Barabbas or Jesus, the people chose Barabbas. He made more sense in light of the systems of their world and their environment. Jesus sought justice as well—and liberation—but by confronting the systems, not by participating in them to simply replace one power with another. Such confrontation meant, at its most basic level, not conceding the rules, definitions, or constructs of the systems. This kind of confrontation can look a lot like defeat. Which is what the cross seemed to be.

The cross is a definitive call to reject the patterns of identity formation offered by the various systems in an environment. This is a way of death: rejecting the systems entails a rejection by the systems who seek to preserve and replicate their fundamental place in a society. Death is the ultimate defeat. Jesus died, really and truly. In this death—a death encountered through obedience—death no longer has the final say. The one way through death has been initiated. The resurrection is the promise that rejecting patterns of this world will result in an even fuller life. Liberation of the oppressor, then, comes through a person's embrace of the cross but promises a new story. Which brings us back to Moltmann's admonition not to dwell on what people lose but what people gain. We let go of patterns and systems of death and dissolution because we do not need their promises of identity or security. We are freed from such anonymizing demands. Radical trust in God leads to radical realignment with the systems, embedded in them while oriented within the cohesive narrative of the Spirit's transformative power. That is the promise of the resurrection.

As a confrontation to the systems, the cross absolutizes the kingdom in contrast to the ways of society. These occupy the same environment—the world—but are expressing a substantively different narrative, a different way. It is absolute in that one cannot find a middle ground between the religious leaders and Jesus, the Romans and Jesus, the zealots and Jesus. Each side rejects such a synthesis. The systems want nothing to do with Jesus. Jesus rejects the systems. This does not, however, suggest that Jesus is a separatist, with the church called to isolation. Jesus does not abandon the world to itself; he enters the world in love. Separation may be a calling for a small number of Christians, but the church as a whole is embedded in the context no less than the systems are. They confront each other.

Because of the mutual exclusivity established by and through the cross, Christians could not be identified with both the systems and the kingdom of God. Either Jesus was right in saying he was speaking for God, or the Jewish leaders were right. Either Rome is the way of peace, or Jesus gives us a more expansive way. Either the methodology of the zealots is the way to social reform, or the way of Jesus. The curious nature of the cross, however, also mitigates putting these two patterns in direct conflict. The way of Rome, or any system, is self-protection and self-perpetuation, as is the goal of the human ego. The way of the Kingdom, however, is a fractal transformation. The story erupts from a manger and consumes the Empire from below.

FOLLOWING THE SPIRIT

By being defined according to a different narrative, a holistic and unifying, *pneumapoietic* narrative, the early Christians were committed to the world, in the world, through the Spirit of Christ. The experience of Pentecost took holiness into the streets, meeting each person in their own language, inviting them into this bigger story. This new life does not accept the world as it is, nor does it retreat from the world. Christians are involved *for* the world not defined *by* the world. It is a new way of being in the world, in which holiness is liberation. The power of the Holy Spirit inspires what Amos Yong calls "a vocational mandate directed for its redemption."[27]

As this is an issue of a new way and a new identity, a rebirth into a new story that transforms one's past, present, and future, it is not feasible to seek meaning in divided approaches. One is either with Jesus on the cross or with those who put Jesus on the cross. Those who sought to use Jesus for his teaching or his authority in pursuit of their own ends were always disappointed by him. Jesus refused to be co-opted. Likewise, we cannot co-opt Jesus for our goals, whether personal or social—even if these goals have elements of positive ambition. The way to hell is paved with good intentions, after all. While in our day, such an admonition seems either incredibly naïve or obtuse, this was not the case in the earliest communities. We see this distinction made, for instance, in the letter of Barnabas with the way of light and the way of darkness, in the letters of John and of Paul and of Peter, indeed in Revelation, where being lukewarm deserves being spit out.[28]

The call to be wholly with Jesus and the community of the Spirit may be most emphasized in the story of Ananias and Sapphira at the beginning of Acts 5. The end of Acts 2 notes with dramatic flair that those in the earliest church were radically generous, and this is emphasized again at the end of Acts 4. This generosity was not, it seems, a religious task intended to establish their position in a religious system; it was simply a new way of living life. As Everett Cattell has said, "I am impressed from study that life in the Spirit is hard to express, just because it is life."[29] They lived in a new way because this was the new way they were experiencing life. It was a generosity and openness derived from celebratory freedom. As is true in many cases, what is freeing and celebratory in such a context can easily become a marker of maturity or mandate of commitment for others. Some want to have the reputation of maturity without achieving such maturity through the Spirit, turning the free act into performance or obligation.

Luke does not tell us why Ananias, with his wife Sapphira, did not disclose the full selling price of the land they had. We only know they *said* they gave all the money from the proceeds, while *in fact* saving a little for themselves.[30] The trouble was they wanted to hold onto some of the money while receiving the acclaim for giving it all away. Peter would have been apparently fine with giving only a part of the proceeds; the key element here is the honesty rather than the financial decisions. In lying about it, they were lying about who they were within the community of the Holy Spirit. It was, effectively, a violation of holiness, an insertion of a false identity within the free and open body, a violation against the new kind of life.[31] Peter confronted Ananias. Ananias denied lying. A violation against the Spirit results in the reaction of the Spirit: life is removed.[32] The issue of community is more important than the issue of finances. Being authentic is part of the new narrative, as it is being open and honest with each other rather than posing for social advantage or other system-oriented gain.

Meanwhile in Damascus, there was another man named Ananias.[33] In contrast to the earlier Ananias, this Ananias was a trustworthy man, a disciple, spoken to at a very crucial moment in the narrative. Saul was on his way to Damascus. Saul had a very dangerous reputation, and Ananias knew this well. He was understandably dismayed. He even knew Saul's mission. God told Ananias to go and meet this Saul.[34] Ananias obeyed. This is risk. Risking life and likely his community in the trust that a vision was indeed from God. In contrast to performing for others and indulging dishonesty, Ananias risks his life for the sake of community with God and the community that God calls him into. This means community with even his enemy.[35] Ananias commits himself to the narrative of the kingdom of God, rather than the narrative style of Rome.

We see Peter in the next chapter likewise committing himself to the narrative of God's kingdom rather than the religious system.[36] This involves continued risk, putting trust in God's lordship over all rather than the identity promising systems, willing to face loss in the religious system for the sake of a greater gain, a gain of a broader and fuller community. Above all, this means committing to the work of the Spirit, not one's own goals or assumptions. "Careful study of the Acts of the Apostles," Jean-Marc Ela writes, "shows that there is *no* ministry except in the Spirit."[37] Indeed, without the Spirit there is no church. With the work of the Spirit comes a source of energy, empowering, for the creation process of the world.[38] The Spirit initiates among the particular, from below, and broadens outward, from within.[39] This new kind of community weaves its way through friends and former foes, drawing a diversity together into a cohesive complexity. Finite boundaries are replaced by infinite possibilities. The persecutor becomes the evangelist; a would-be target is the peace-bringing healer. Now *that* is liberation from both directions.

The Liberating Life

The story of Saul's transformation is itself worthy of much more consideration. Indeed, it may be the clearest example of the liberation of the oppressor in the New Testament. It clearly was important for the early church, as Luke repeats the story three times, the second two as testimonies of Paul in his trials later in his ministry.[40] Paul tells it himself in Galatians 1 and hints at it in other places. While a dramatic example, however, its striking nature makes it less useful for general application. Who would not have a reevaluation of their lives if confronted by the risen Jesus, knocked down, blinded, and admonished? This technique for liberation is both extremely rare and without need for further commentary. Those who experience something like this are immediately affected without need for convincing. If this was the only way such liberation could and should be realized, very few in positions of oppressing would be liberated until the return of Jesus in glory. This lends credence to the argument that, for most, the liberation of the oppressors can only come through liberation of the oppressed.[41] Without direct divine intervention, living life differently than the surrounding culture is viewed as irresponsible if not entirely impossible. It is assumed that some are called to radical contrasts, while most are to live in light of the various systems, with the religious system sharing an environment with the other systems so as to construct a socially rational life. Paul is fine, Jesus is great, I love the heroes of the faith, but I have a wife, kids, a mortgage, credit card debt, and social obligations.

In the letters of Paul, however, we do not see any expectation that liberation is only through direct divine intervention, nor that without it, Christians are absolved from living the narrative of Christ rather than the systems in the context of their environment. This was certainly not the case for Ananias or Sapphira. Again and again Paul admonishes his readers to live out their lives in a new way, the way of new birth, the way of Christ within the calling for which they have been called, whether or not there is a divine revelation. Paul saw his transformation as both entirely unique in its expression while broad in its calling. All those who were in Christ were called to live in a new way, no matter the path of their conversion.

To live is Christ, for Paul, and to die is gain, giving radical shape to both his mission and his hope, the life in the present fulfilling God's work in him, putting him in contexts of challenge and difficulty as well as success and advantage.[42] This defining passage rejects any relegation of Christ to a separate sphere of life, or internalizing salvation so as to refer only to a moment of resolved existential crisis. To live is Christ makes faith in Christ a new ontology, a new story that reframes every element of participation in this world.[43] It is a calling for all, that they live their life worthy of the calling of Christ in their contexts.[44] This calling involves challenge and suffering as well as progress and victory, the latter coinciding with the former as a new narrative takes shape from within the context of the resistant systems. Threatening the systems threatens the identity of those who find their identity and sustenance in the systems. Any who live according to the calling of Christ may experience the resistance shown Christ, something the early church knew all too well.

In contexts of Christian dominance, such experiences are either entirely unknown or reduced to simple annoyances or disagreements. It is, however, precisely in light of assumed privilege and power that the Christian message finds its most striking example. Paul presses this point in Philippians 2. Often referred to as the Philippians hymn, verses 5–11 mark some of the most profound Christology of the New Testament, a succinct statement of Christ's identity and mission. While the Christological questions are certainly worthwhile, they are beyond the focus of my present concerns.[45] What is important is the intent of Paul in writing these passages.[46] "Let the same mind be in you," he writes, then proceeds into the hymn. The pattern of Jesus, he emphasizes, is likewise a pattern for those who are in Jesus. This has personal and social implications, a pattern of engaging this world in contrast to the established powers or systems. He uses the theologically rich word *kenosis* alongside the pattern of Christ's victory. It was not through dominance or oppression that the mission of Christ took shape, even though Jesus was uniquely able to assert such privilege. By being obedient, God exalted him. We are not Jesus and his specific calling is different from ours; however, in having this mindset of obedience to God, we set aside any meaning or identity found elsewhere.[47] This is liberation from patterns of dominance, and into a place of serving from below and transformation within.[48]

We are to have the same love, finding unity with others rather than division. Instead of maximizing our ego and claiming the benefits of every last one of our supposed rights or potential exertions of power, those who have the mind of Christ are to voluntarily live in a pattern of openness and exocentricity.[49] The example of Christ is the transforming power of Christ that leads us from the way of the systems into the way of *letting go*.[50] The soteriological leads into the ethical: we are to be a new people because of the work of Christ in confronting the powers of the systems and orienting a new way that transforms the world from within.[51]

Like Christ, those who follow this way are not left lowly in a state of loss. *Kenosis* in God's work opens the door for a renewed victory. The validation of the resurrection is the power of new life within this life, the obedience of Christ transforming our very being in a salvation from death that initiates us into being able to truly live in a new way even now.[52] To live indeed *is* Christ. The systems promise more immediate gain but cannot sustain or perpetuate such promises. The apparent short-term loss found in a transformative pattern of living is counterintuitive but fulfills the promise of fuller life and community. We are to let go, because in letting go we gain everything, and find the many divergent pieces of our life becoming peace-filled and coherent. Stillness replaces frenzy, chaos is replaced by a new order. "For freedom Christ has set us free," Paul writes in Galatians 5. We should not succumb to a yoke of slavery anymore. We are called to stand firm within the power of the Spirit, in step with the Spirit, expressing the fruit of the Spirit in all of our lives. Such a way is indeed very good.

CONCLUSION

We read in Acts 2 that the believers "were together and had all things in common; they would sell their possessions and goods and distribute the proceeds to all, as any had need." They spent time together. They ate together. They were generous and they were glad, appreciated by their neighbors.[53] They worshipped God. The church grew. This summary repeats throughout Acts, a marker of the Spirit's movement in both depth and breadth.[54] Yet, as the story of Ananias and Sapphira shows, the early church was not perfect in its expression of this ideal. Neither was it *just* an ideal. It was an expressed reality at first and sporadically throughout history in narrow contexts. It is indeed a possibility, yet rarely realized as this reality involves the whole of a particular community living fully in light of the kingdom of God.

That is a difficult vision to sustain in this present experience of time and systems. The Way is not about the pursuit of the tasks and its lists of steps to take and rules to follow. Nor does the experience of previous saints somehow provide a shortcut for us now.[55] The Way is the living realization of a new narrative within this present life, where the new identity takes hold of a gathered community, weaving them together into a cohesive giving and receiving body.[56] It is not easily sustained. There are a multiplicity of narratives vying for attention and promising identity or simply pretty baubles. Just as the Israelites were caught in the tension between experiences and promise during the Exodus narrative—some holding onto the calling while others could not—so too those in the church are constantly pulled this way and that, sifted and challenged in their faith.

In order for a liberation of the oppressor to have integrity and coherence as a *Christian* theological response, it must be attuned to the whole testimony of

Scripture in describing both God's values and response, rather than wholesale adopting any pattern of sociological, philosophical, or psychological models.[57] Tertullian's question, "What does Athens have to do with Jerusalem?" is indeed apt for contemporary theologies of liberation.[58] In Christian conceptions, we should not separate the goal from the method, as they feed back into each other for a holistic vision of the future. The goal, in a Christian sense at least, is justice for the oppressed that leads to new patterns of living for all in a shared community. This is the ideal of *reconciliation*, a step that includes both justice and forgiveness.[59] Love must replace hate, hope must replace despair, joy for anger, life for death. The eschatological invitation of the kingdom is not derived from natural progression that derives from conventional responses, and that is why method is important as well. Precisely because it is not a natural progression is what makes it a particularly Christian proposal. It is an impossible proposal in much rational analysis. It does not only not make sense to the world, it may even seem entirely counterproductive.[60] That doesn't mean it's wrong. Such is the testimony of the Cross and the Resurrection.[61] Such is the testimony of the early church as well.

NOTES

1. See Kierkegaard, *Practice in Christianity*, 136–139.
2. See Ibid., 181–186.
3. The corollary, of course, is that those who are not successful in a given system have not, thus, performed the right steps. This then justifies, or at least excuses, patterns of oppression within a given system.
4. This is important because the oppressed are often judged according to what they could do but have not, or what they have done but should not. If accomplishment is purely based on chosen actions then there is resolution by performing those actions. Actions are important, as we see in Scripture, but are not absolute or determining in either success or failure.
5. While task oriented, these are also relational cues as expression of obedience. The Law serves as both a guide to human social behavior and as a way of showing intent to stay in relationship with God.
6. Important for interpretation because they are together in each of the synoptics. Matthew 19 and Mark 10 follow the same pattern throughout the chapter, while Luke leaves out the discussion about divorce.
7. Emerito Nacpil, *Jesus' Strategy for Social Transformation* (Nashville: Abingdon Press, 1999), 59.
8. Kierkegaard, *Practice in Christianity*, 190 writes, "In order to enter into the kingdom of heaven a person must become a child again, but in order that his life can express that he has entered into the kingdom of heaven he must become a youth a second time. To *be* a child and to *be* a youth when one is a child or a youth is easy enough, but a *second time*—the second time is what is decisive."

9. Leon Morris, *The Gospel According to John*, revised edition (Grand Rapids: Eerdmans, 1995), 190.

10. This may even extend prior to our own birth, as there seems to be a genetic component to memory. See, for instance, Brian G. Dias and Kerry J. Ressler, "Parental Olfactory Experience Influences Behavior and Neural Structure in Subsequent Generations," *Nature Neuroscience* 17, no. 1 (2014): 89–96.

11. Jean-Marc Ela, *My Faith as an African* (Eugene, OR: Wipf & Stock, 2009), 30.

12. For a fuller development of this theme in terms of atonement, see Patrick Oden, "'Obedience Is Better than Sacrifice': Atonement as the Re-Establishment of Trust," *Wesleyan Theological Journal* 50, no. 1 (2015): 100–115.

13. See Marianne Meye Thompson, *John: A Commentary* (Louisville: Westminster John Knox Press, 2015), 86.

14. Kierkegaard, *Practice in Christianity*, 254 writes, "Here again we see how Christianity has been abolished in Christendom. If there is to be truthful talk about Christianity, our sighting must be kept on the imitator; the imitator is the true Christian. But now the admirer become the true Christian, and the deniers of Christianity became Christians of sorts also, certainly not true Christians—the admirers, after all, became the true Christians—double confusion, infinite abyss of confusion. Only the imitator is the true Christian. The admirer really assumes a pagan relation to Christianity."

15. Thompson, *John*, 91.

16. This seems to be corroborated by Clement of Alexandria's highlighting a latter narrative *about* John in "Who Is the Rich Man That Shall Be Saved?" 42. John is said to risk everything in seeking out a young man who was lost in sin and to show him a way back to wholeness and community. The contrast with the local bishop is noteworthy, who abandoned the young man to his oppressing and corrupted lifestyle. John, though an old man, ran into the midst of a dangerous situation, to speak to the young man and invite him back into the community with Christ.

17. This acknowledgment is likewise Johannine, as Jn 21:25 notes: "But there are also many other things that Jesus did; if every one of them were written down, I suppose that the world itself could not contain the books that would be written."

18. This can be seen as a bookend to the temptation in the wilderness, where Jesus resisted the claimed benefits for the sake of sole allegiance to the Father. In the arrest and trial, he faces the counterpart to the ways sin and systems work: they first offer the promise of benefits and then, if resisted, turn to threats. If a person does not give into their apparent goodness, they will be cowed by their power.

19. Joel Green, *The Gospel of Luke* (Grand Rapids: Eerdmans, 1997), 744 notes, "Luke's narrative of Jesus' suffering and death is inexorably linked to the earlier chapters of the Third Gospel by the development of numerous motifs, the most pervasive and important of which is the motif of conflict. Conflict, too, has been a primary force driving the narrative plot forward to this point."

20. Reminiscent of multiple stories in the Old Testament, not least of which the narrative of Shadrach, Meshach, and Abednego in Daniel 3.

21. Exod. 20:1–3.

22. Or as Green, *The Gospel of Luke*, 745 puts it, "Luke has constructed a series of oppositions of pivotal importance."

23. Lk. 22:3. Cf. Lk. 22:31; Acts 5:3.
24. Lk. 22:53. Cf. Gen. 1:2–4; Jn 1:5 and 3:19.
25. Cf. Isaiah 7. I especially like v. 9: "If you do not stand firm in faith, you shall not stand at all."
26. Michael J. Wilkins, "Barabbas," in *The Anchor Bible Dictionary*, ed. David Noel Freedman, vol. 1, 6 vols. (New York: Doubleday, 1992), 607.
27. Amos Yong, *In the Days of Caesar: Pentecostalism and Political Theology* (Grand Rapids: Eerdmans, 2010), 201.
28. Rev. 3:16. See *Letter of Barnabas*, chaps. 19–20, which is very similar to *Didache*, 1–3; Deut. 30:11–20.
29. Everett Cattell, *The Spirit of Holiness*, revised edition (Newberg, OR: Barclay Press, 2015), v.
30. Cf. Josh. 7:1. Achan took from that which was to be entirely devoted to God. Ananias and Sapphira took from what they themselves had devoted to God. In saying they sold their land and gave all the proceeds, they were dedicating this money within the context of the whole community and thus they were not to privately benefit from it once so committed. This is the freedom of the Spirit rather than the compulsion of the law, but such freedom still entails responsibility. The new birth invites a pre-fall openness to each other while lying reinstitutes potential suspicion about motives and how we portray ourselves in public. It is likely a very good thing this lesson was not repeated as those of us on Facebook might likely be in a fair bit of danger. Of course, this story is passed down to us so we are still responsible for its lessons.
31. For more on holiness as a definitive category in liberation, see below, chapter 8.
32. Cf. Gen. 2:7.
33. See Acts 9:1–19.
34. Cf. Exod. 3:1–4:17. Saul's own call is more directly parallel to that of Moses and other Old Testament prophets. This seems to be Luke's intentional purpose. I greatly appreciate the insights of Lynn Losie for bringing this to my attention. This smaller narrative of Ananias, then, I see as a self-similar pattern contained within the scope of a larger scale validation of Paul as prophet. Cf. Gerhard Lohfink, *The Conversion of St. Paul: Narrative and History in Acts* (Chicago: Franciscan Herald Press, 1976), 61–69.
35. Cf. Jon. 1:1–3 and 3:1–3.
36. Acts 10. See also 1 Pet. 1–2.
37. Ela, *My Faith*, 55.
38. Jean-Marc Ela, *African Cry* (Eugene, OR: Wipf & Stock, 2005), 111.
39. See J. P. Heijke, "Thinking in the Scene of Disaster : Theology of Jean-Marc Ela from Cameroon," *Exchange* 29, no. 1 (2000): 79.
40. Acts 9:1–31; 22:1–21; 26:2–29.
41. Paulo Freire writes that "it is only the oppressed who, by freeing themselves, can free their oppressors. The latter, as an oppressive class, can free neither others nor themselves." In Freire, *Pedagogy of the Oppressed*, 56.
42. Phil. 1:21.
43. Cf. Col. 3:1–7.
44. See Phil. 1:27–29.

45. For a substantive, succinct discussion of this passage in terms of how the Christological issue of *kenosis* should be understood, see Sarah Coakley, "Kenosis and Subversion," in *Powers and Submission* (Malden, MA: Blackwell, 2002), 5–11. Coakley summarizes four contemporary approaches to this passage, adding a fifth one later, what she terms the "Alexandrian" interpretation, and then a sixth, which reflects the late-nineteenth-century approach by Gottfried Thomasius, which became a prevailing view that Jesus temporarily relinquished "certain characteristics of divinity." Coakley takes the position that *kenosis* here suggests Christ "choosing *never to have* certain (false and worldly) forms of power—forms sometimes wrongly construed as 'divine'" (emphasis in the original).

46. Coakley, "Kenosis and Subversion," 12 notes that however the passage was interpreted in the later patristic era onwards as critical to topics of preexistence or other Chalcedonian concerns, Paul's own purpose was "largely non-'speculative,' non-'dogmatic,' and arguably not even asserting substantial preexistence at all." She adds later that "if the majority of New Testament commentators are correct, then the 'hymn' of Philippians 2 was, from the start, an invitation to enter into Christ's extended life in the church, not just to speculate dispassionately on his nature." I suggest that Paul's contention was that those who entered into Christ's extended life in this way were those who made up the church, rather than a later assumption that Christ's life could only be found in an ecclesial structure *a la* Cyprian. The life of Christ in the believer is the location of the Spirit's primary work, which finds resonance among other believers who gather together in a Christo-formative community. This, however, is a debate for another time and place. See my *Transformative Church* for a more substantive development of this theme, although not one that touches on Pauline perspectives *per se*.

47. This is an important issue in terms of oppression as well. In taking on the mind of Christ, a person likewise should not see their identity lessened by societal categories. In this respect, this passage points toward a leveling of identity in the person of Christ, lifting up those who are broken and humbling those who might be societally powerful. There is a perichoretic inclusion as well as a kenotic calling. For more on this, see Oden, "Liberating Holiness for the Oppressed and the Oppressors," 205–224. Coakley, *Powers and Submissions*, 33 notes, however, the way in which such "letting go" can itself lead into proactive sense of self. See more discussion of this proposal of Coakley below in chapter 11.

48. See Coakley, "Kenosis and Subversion," 33–34.

49. See Craig S. Keener, *The Mind of the Spirit: Paul's Approach to Transformed Thinking* (Grand Rapids: Baker Academic, 2016), 199.

50. Ellacuría, *Ignacio Ellacuría*, 159.

51. Cf. 1 Thess. 5:1–11.

52. As part of his "Guidelines into Convictional Knowing," James Loder includes, "Transforming experiences initiated by Christ are characterized by a resulting sacrificial love in the one transformed." In James E. Loder, *The Transforming Moment*, 2nd edition (Colorado Springs: Helmers & Howard, 1989), 187–190. This sacrificial love is oriented toward reconciliation in previously broken relationships while contributing to meeting substantive relational needs. It is a sacrifice that is also filling, which

reflects how the Spirit works interpersonally, where there is both pouring out and restoring. Cf. Phil. 2:16–18.

53. These two elements together add a miraculous element.

54. Cf. Acts 4:32–35; 9:31; 12:24; 19:17–20.

55. Kierkegaard, *Practice in Christianity*, 207. writes that "what has completely confused Christianity and what has to a large extent occasioned the illusion of a Church triumphant is this, that Christianity has been regarded as truth in the sense of results instead of its being truth in the sense of *the way*." Kierkegaard emphasizes on 208–209 that this means there is no shortening of the way, like happens in the experience of an inventor and later user. The first person to turn on a TV took many years to develop it. Now I can turn it on with hardly any time or effort. Not so with Christianity. Simply because others have experienced results, does not then give later generations a short cut.

56. See Gerhard Lohfink, *Jesus and Community* (Philadelphia: Fortress Press, 1984), 99–106.

57. This is not to dismiss the worth of these but rather to orient the discussion within Christian tradition rather than adapting tradition to fit an alternative interpretation of reality.

58. See Tertullian, *Prescription Against Heretics*, trans. Dr. Holmes, ANF 3, reprint edition (Peabody, MA: Hendrickson), 7.246. This is itself an often misunderstood and wrongly critiqued quote. Tertullian, himself very educated, trained in rhetoric and law, was not being anti-intellectual, rather he was disputing the idea that interpretation of Christian principles can begin with an alternative system, in which Christianity is then situated. Christianity is more than a set of terminology and religious imagery, it is both content and method, describing a distinct picture of reality, the human condition, and a particular hope. It is, one might say, offering Christ as the constant in a construct of relativity.

59. Harvey Cox, *God's Revolution and Man's Responsibility* (Valley Forge: The Judson Press, 1965), 61 writes, "Jesus is the *shalom* bringer, and the church is a people that lives and demonstrates the *shalom* of God. But to understand what the church is for the world, we have to look at *shalom* and see what its component elements are. We will list three. 1. The first element of shalom is RECONCILIATION. Whatever else the church may be, it is a community which demonstrates and works for reconciliation." The second element of *shalom* that Cox notes is "freedom" and the third is "hope."

60. See Kierkegaard, *Practice in Christianity*, 170–178.

61. Desmond Tutu, *No Future without Forgiveness* (New York: Image Doubleday, 1999), 267 writes, "The death and resurrection of Jesus Christ puts the issue beyond doubt: ultimately goodness and laughter and peace and compassion and gentleness and forgiveness and reconciliation will have the last word and prevail over their ghastly counterparts."

Chapter 6

The Liberating Way of the Early Church

INTRODUCTION

It is easy to hedge one's bets, to ponder life informed by God's calling while also maintaining the security of a rational life in a given society. Sometimes the tension breaks and resolves one way or another: a Christian community seeks radical distinction from a culture, representing God's work in isolation as an outsider to the culture; or, on the other side, a Christian community all but abandons the transformative fundamental Christian narrative, utilizing only the rhetoric of the faith, not the reality. In both, Christ is framed in a different way than the man we read about in the Gospels. They present a different Jesus to the world. Pointing to a different Jesus will always devolve back into a systems-directed morass, as it is a very narrow road indeed that confronts all the systems without being co-opted by any one of them. In contrast to the systems of the world, the Jesus of the Gospels provided a holistic new way within this world, in confrontation with the systems of the world. As presumed disciples of Christ, Christians are called to convey in our community life this reality of God's work. They are to live in the tension of God's kingdom that is already among us. "It is right, therefore" Ignatius thus warns the Magnesians, "that we not just to be called Christians, but that we actually be Christians."[1]

What does it mean to actually be Christian? The early church certainly wrestled with this question, with varying success. Indeed, we have much of our New Testament precisely because the early church did not always live it out as intended yet sought constant reminders of its importance. The idealism and direct action of the early chapters of Acts very soon moved into reasoned exhortation or application of authority to bring outliers into line. The idealism in Acts itself was an intentional call to the early churches of their own earlier history. Whereas Paul writes direct admonishments that serve as corrections, Luke offers a vision of a cohesive community, albeit one that dealt with persecution, resistance, and incursions by world systems.

Even more complicated, it seems, are situations where there is no clear moral failing or conceptual misunderstanding, but instead the problem is one of not living fully into the calling to which Christians have been called.[2] Embracing what we *should do* in a complex situation, not just avoiding what we shouldn't do, moves a Christian life beyond legalism and into the realm of discernment. There often isn't a generalized answer to what we encounter, what should be done in light of a specific situation. Life involves more than red lights and green lights, there are also yield signs and cautions and even the occasional roundabout. Christians must be attentive to the particular signs of the times.[3]

The liberation of the oppressor involves correcting clear instances of oppression as well as commending a new way of life to those who are simply existing within the established narratives of the systems. We must clean house and also redecorate, to hearken back to the parable of Jesus.[4] It involves letting go of former patterns that are destructive to oneself and the community *while also* taking up patterns that are renewing for oneself and the community. To focus only on what a person should *not* do misses the fullness of the promise of God in rebirth. We live in a new way not because it is the obligation of a new set of rules, but because we are a new people for whom life is simply lived in a different way, the way of Jesus.

God seeks relationship with his people, and rebirth is only a start. Holiness is life as it is intended to be lived. This is a work of the Spirit to be sure; however, it is not, or at least it is only very rarely, an instantaneous process. Many of the early church writings, then, have this combined intent to both warn against wrong behaviors while pointing toward the patterns that reflect the new life in Christ. The latter is not a matter of putting more effort into specific tasks, but indeed becoming more open to the work of the Spirit in various ways so as to be more fully transformed. Those who are babies in the faith are called to be mature. This maturity expresses itself in thoughts, actions, and passions.[5]

In the next two chapters, I will point to a couple of key examples of early church teaching on liberation that leads to spiritual maturity. Led by the teachings of Scripture while attentive to developing concerns and established examples, those in the early church sought to exemplify the faith in what they said and how they lived.[6] As Tertullian notes in his Apology: "But it is mainly the deeds of a love so noble that lead many to put a brand upon us. See, they say, how they love one another, for themselves are animated by mutual hatred; how they are ready even to die for one another, for they themselves will sooner put to death."[7] The liberation of the early Christians was a liberation into a different narrative of the kingdom while living within the Roman Empire. This created the direction of much of the early Christian apologies, which sought to clarify and correct assumptions about Christians while commending actual Christian behavior as a being a boon to society. And while purportedly written for outsiders, such apologetics were mostly read by those already Christian, emphasizing the importance of a living witness by all in the Church. Of this, Alan Kreider writes,

> Indeed, the primary function of their apologetic writings was to contribute to the community's mission by building up the Christians and by strengthening their common life. Even if the outsiders didn't read the apologies, they would read the lives of the insiders! And they would read the Christians and their communities! As a result, when Christians lived a distinctive vision, they were challenging outsiders to investigate the Christian faith more deeply.[8]

Christians often sought to show how they were better citizens than others, commendable rather than blameworthy because of the quality of life they lived as individuals and together within society. They aimed to show that they exemplified that which Rome thought best about itself. Examples of various kinds abound because of these goals, to which can be added the goals of the significant writings intended to directly teach and correct those within the Christian community.

As with the previous chapters on Scripture, I will look at selected representatives rather than attempt anything near a comprehensive survey. The difference is that while Scripture tends to have a shared theme, the early church showed diversity of responses about what it means to be a Christian, and how to address wealth, power, and poverty.[9] As such, my choices are admittedly not representative of the whole teaching of the early church. Rather, my goal is to highlight a thread of teaching that emphasized transformation within a context for both oppressed and oppressors together. This is a prescriptive task more than it is a descriptive, albeit one that is informed by early teachers.

I argue that this thread of instruction offers a more liberative expression, even if it has less radical divisions between the world and those in the church. It is more liberative because it becomes within the range of expression of all, rather than focused on a limited number of "heroes" or reduced to securing salvation, both elements of which engage faith in more of a self-achieving way, rather than in a freeing expression of invited community. As Helen Rhee notes, "By virtue of the Christian love commandment, loving God through loving one's neighbor was not an option but an obligation; acts of mercy were acts of justice (and vice versa), which bound together the whole local community and different regional communities."[10] This means it is a community task of liberative freedom, an obligation that is also an invitation. And with this is the important goal of love as the foundation of giving, expressing how early Christians emphasized the genuine personhood of others.

This goal is seen throughout the works of Clement of Alexandria. He developed an approach to the pursuit of wisdom that was in reach of all people, and intended to be a priority for all people, calling them out as individuals within a true community in discovering the depths of Christ's calling.[11] He called this becoming a true "gnostic" in contrast to those who adopted that title without actually knowing God or reality. Those who "know" might better be called "saints," those who are made holy by the Spirit. However, when saints became a synonym for heroes of the faith rather than the people as a whole, the people as a whole increasingly left the heroics to others. Recovering the idea of the sainthood of all believers—those who are truly Christian—is a fundamental element of restorative liberation.

In this chapter, I will begin by looking at the role of Clement in his city of Alexandria, followed by a discussion of his work, "Who Is the Rich Man That Shall Be Saved?" which represents an early pre-Constantinian perspective. In chapter 7, I will look at the life and sayings of Anthony of Egypt, commonly called the Great and often credited with the establishment of Christian monasticism. In each chapter, I will offer a brief justification why I think these are particularly helpful places for understanding the theme of liberation of the oppressor for both their culture and ours.

CLEMENT THE CATECHIST

Clement is important for this present topic due to his influence in Christian theology as well as his key role in Alexandria. He was responsible for the teaching of Christians in this city, developing a pedagogy that pointed toward a progressive understanding and expression of the Christian life at various stages of instruction. Much later in history, his writings influenced John Wesley, whose project was in many ways itself a contextual expression of Clement's approach.[12] As Wesley's influence is profound for the shaping of much of the church in the Christian West over the last several hundred years, Clement has indirectly continued to teach us what it means to grow in Christian maturity. While his writings may often seem speculative and esoteric at times, he was foremost a teacher, with his audience divided between non-Christian Greeks, new Christians, and experienced Christians. Kwame Bediako writes that Clement's emphasis "consists in a continual effort to clarify and to elaborate a conception of the religious history of mankind that at once ensures the meaningfulness of all genuine quests for God and truth, and also secures the universal significance of the Christian revelation, particularly the centrality of the Incarnation of the Logos, Christ, the Saviour of all humanity."[13] This universal significance is revealed in the Jewish Scriptures, and also finds a place in the best of Hellenistic philosophy, which Clement sees as a preparation for the fullness of God's revelation in Christianity.

Clement emphasizes that Christianity no longer requires such philosophy but leads it to its sought-after destination in truth. Such a destination requires different maps, different patterns of explanation for those starting in different places. "Above all," Piotr Ashwin-Siejkowski writes, "Clement's project responded to the pedagogical need to educate his fellow Christian."[14] This goal of leading people to understanding is different than simply declaring a right way or a wrong way. Thus, Clement had to be attentive to not only speaking the truth but also how he was being heard. Each of his major three works seemingly target a different learner, and reflect a different style.[15] With each, however, there are unifying themes of commitment, persistence, and transformation. Osborn notes that Clement has three key relations in his writings: "the perfection of love between God and Christ, the total dependence of the complete Christian on God, and the relation of the believer to other humans in respect, concern, and love."[16]

CAN THE RICH BE SAVED?

In Clement's writing, "Who Is the Rich Man That Shall Be Saved?" he addresses to an important ethical question in light of the admonition of Jesus in Mt. 19:16–30: is there any place for wealthy Christians in the church of Jesus?[17] If salvation is impossible without first selling all of one's possessions, who indeed can be saved at all? This was the question the disciples asked Jesus right away. He responded with an emphasis on God's work, that God can do even the impossible. However, such an answer did not necessarily answer the question for those dealing with a similar situation as the rich young man. Were they also in fact *required* to sell all their possessions or be excluded from eternal salvation?

Peter's response to Ananias in Acts 5 suggests this isn't necessarily the case. He told Ananias that he was not required to sell his property and, with this, did not also need to donate the full selling price if he did sell it. As selling the property was a voluntary response, Ananias was guilty because he lied about what he did to bolster his own reputation. Nor do we see the example of selling everything being carried out by all the disciples or in every situation. Jesus, for instance, praised Zacchaeus and extended salvation to him, even though Zacchaeus stated he would give *only half* of his possessions to the poor, as well as pay restitution for fraud.[18] What is a rich person to think? Are they to sell all their possessions? Half of them? Is there another metric? Who is, we might ask, the oppressor who shall be saved? It is all too easy to revert to the idea that it is about what we are *to do*, which was the concern of the rich young man.

On the other hand, the early church was certainly not quick to dismiss the radical implications. Anthony of Egypt heard this passage preached and followed it literally. He transitioned from wealth to a radical expression of Christian devotion that was later praised by Athanasius as not only salutary for Anthony but also an example for all serious Christians. This later emphasis led to a seeming bifurcation of Christian response.[19] Some literally sold everything and became heroes of the faith. Others kept what they had and admired those who were more radical, arguing it was indeed salutary to sell everything, but not doing it themselves. Hagiographies became mythic tales of heroism rather than guidebooks for developing saints out of everyone.

In keeping with his priorities as a teacher for the Christians in Alexandria, Clement did not see this passage as limited to only a small number of heroes. He did not envision a bifurcated Christianity split between the so-called religious and casual devotees.[20] Nor does Clement dismiss the passage as a moral impossibility. Instead, Clement seeks the heart of the passage, the main thrust, arguing that Jesus is pushing toward a reorientation of life that includes a discussion about wealth and possessions, but is not limited to these. This reorientation applies to all those who follow him. It is not about what we should do or not do. It is not ultimately about wealth at all, but our disposition and focus.[21] Where, in other words, do we find our meaning and identity? If we find our meaning and identity in something other than God, *including but not limited* to *wealth*, we cannot see the kingdom of God. Where then is the kingdom?

Clement first establishes his approach to the narrative. He pronounces judgment on those who would praise the rich for their wealth. Those who do so are making it doubly hard for those with wealth. The wealthy must deal with the issues of wealth itself, which can corrupt in many ways. The wealthy must also deal with pride and false value, making them feel more secure in such an identity and less likely to find a more secure source of meaning in Christ. Wealth should not be a goal. Being fully in tune with Christ is the goal, thus Clement relativizes the discussion by prioritizing the perspective of God. Rather than praise people for their wealth, wealth should be seen as a potential distraction and trap. Those who truly love should express this love by seeing the rich as themselves in need of ministry. Christians from all backgrounds should lead each other toward prayer and a new disposition of soul.

As Clement moves to discuss the Matthew 19 passage, he points out that his goal is to teach those who genuinely seek Christ. He is not concerned with those outside the faith. "With those who are uninitiated in the truth I have little concern."[22] Not because they are without value but because those who are following a different story—caught in the world systems—will not care what Christ thinks. Teaching them involves a different approach. Those who claim life in Christ, however, are living in light of the hope that Christ will be all in all, and full freedom is found in the way of Christ. This is a teaching that can be assumed. They need to learn how to live this out as part of the consistent testimony of their whole lives. Be more than admirers of Jesus and become imitators.

Clement offers a rhetorical twist for those concerned with such hope, suggesting that wealth should not lead them into despair.[23] The Lord accepts anyone who seeks truth, but they must be willing to pursue it. There are many reasons why wealth interferes in more noble pursuits. These reasons insist on a disciplined response, akin to an athlete in pursuit of a prize, if a person is to follow Christ's calling in full.[24] Such a person must put themselves under the active lordship of Christ, using the message of Jesus as a diet, pursuing the fruit of the Spirit as exercises. Clement prays for help from Christ to offer helpful and renewing thoughts, "first with regard to the hope itself, and secondly with regard to the means of reaching it."[25] This approach highlights one of the reasons why I propose Clement is especially useful in our era.

As Moltmann has written, a liberation of the oppressor is better served by emphasizing what one must gain rather than what one must give up. While the idea that those with wealth and power above all need hope is counterintuitive, it is so precisely because of the defining narratives of the world systems that make wealth and power seem self-evidently good. In this perspective, then, the process of liberation both for the oppressors and the oppressed are defined by the inversion of wealth and power structures. The goal is still wealth and power. Christ is a means to this. The Gospel becomes a tool. However, Christ is not a tool; he is the source and the goal. By recognizing the need for hope as a path of transformation, there is a critique of the present systems and an emphasis on the alternative meta-system that redefines personhood in the conception of the Triune God, the very prayer of Psalm 71. The more conventional ways of responding to wealth and power by means of critical admonitions and guilt-emphasizing rhetoric have more immediate punch but are not necessarily as pedagogically useful for the whole gathered church and those who might be drawn into it.[26] Especially after Christendom, when perceptions of eternal value are increasingly dim, and the benefits of wealth are self-evident.

Because perfection is oriented relationally, there is not a task that must be done but *a disposition to pursue*. Only God is good, and only God can dispense eternal life. "We must therefore," Clement writes, "store up in the soul right from the beginning the greatest and chiefest of the doctrines that refer to life, namely, to know the eternal God as both giver of eternal gifts and first and supreme and one and a good God."[27] If performing an act was itself sufficient for a person then there would have been no need for the mission of Jesus, especially his suffering and death, except as a superfluous example. The very mission of Jesus pointed to the reality that there was a mission beyond the fulfillment of the law. Jesus highlights this in the way he continues the conversation with the young man. Only God is good, he tells him, but if a person wants to know what *to do* in order to come into the presence of this God, if one will be perfect, then they must abandon finding meaning in anything else. Clement notes this is where the young man showed his true self as not really wanting perfection but instead the appearance of it, busying himself with the apparent tasks but unwilling to pursue "the work of life."[28]

In making this passage about the *love of* money—the passion and concern it raises in us, rather than the wealth itself—some feel that Clement is undercutting the bold charge of Jesus. G. W. Butterworth writes:

> As a result of this exegesis, we are robbed of one of the most striking appeals to a man's heroism and contempt of consequences that even the Gospels contain. There can be no question that the Christian Church has suffered much, and is still suffering, from that avoidance of the plain meaning of historical records which is characteristic of the Alexandrine system of spiritual or allegorical interpretation.[29]

Though Butterworth ultimately judges Clement as mistaken, he commends his underlying goal to contextualize the Christian message: "The mission of Clement and the Alexandrine Church was to give Christianity a firm footing in the world, and to allow it to assimilate all that was good of human thought and culture."[30] While his critique is helpful in some respects, it misses the main vision of Clement throughout his works. As does Elizabeth Clark's trenchant comment that Clement "gladly widens the needle's eye to welcome the rich who generously give."[31] Clement is not seeking to justify the rich or to provide a social excuse for their ignoring biblical injunctions against wealth. In Clement's view, Christians are to live the narrative of Christ within their contexts, as a redeeming and enlightening presence, with this mission of God reaching into hearts and minds of those around them prior to their experiencing Christ, a *praeparatio evangelica*. This calling is indeed *more* radical not more accommodating, as it is a calling for every Christian.

Clement's goal is not to fit Christianity better into the world, but to emphasize throughout his works that Christianity is the fullest vision of the world, for this world, for everyone. This can be seen in his emphasis in recovering the term "gnostic" as one who truly knows truth in light of Christian teaching.[32] To know Christ is to know all of reality. To be perfect, a person must focus on God as the source of meaning and identity. Perfection is not defined in terms of activities but in terms of ontology. Christianity must, above all, be fully Christian. Those who are Christian must fully establish their being in

Christ. In doing this, the world changes. This certainly takes a very optimistic approach to God's work, but the key is that it is God's work. God is not a means to an end, but an end that awakens the means. Osborn notes, "Clement's optimism can be traced to his kerygma of the new creation, the ultimacy of divine love and the sovereignty of universal saving grace. He looks to the truly unique, one, almighty, good God who saves from age to age through the son and is in no way the cause of any evil."[33] Clement thus engages other philosophers in light of wholehearted belief in the universal lordship of God.

The goal of the Christian life is to be oriented in this radical vision of life itself. The goal of the Christian life certainly is not to be poor, as it is "no great or enviable thing to be simply without riches, apart from the purpose of obtaining life."[34] Being poor is not itself salvific, so there must be another quality that voluntary poverty fosters. Clement highlights other philosophies that prioritize poverty without pointing to the real fullness of life, "some to obtain leisure for letters and for dead wisdom, others for empty fame and vainglory."[35] Arguing that poverty is itself a good can easily instantiate poverty rather than transformation. For instance, the church in Latin America is criticized by liberation theologians for preaching that the poor were blessed within their poverty, while at the same time facilitating unjust structures and policies for the wealthy.[36] The wealthy, it seems, were more than willing to risk some eternal bounty for present power, while using Christian teaching to keep the poor mollified. A similar approach can be seen in how slave owners often emphasized how slaves should be content in their circumstances.

Clement's approach is certainly not validating wealth or the status quo nor dismissing the tenor of the passage. Rather, he seeks to understand why this narrative about the young man is contained in the Gospels. What makes it good news? Poverty is not a goal, and indeed the pursuit of poverty for its own sake can lead to the opposite direction of goodness. In thinking they are doing something of great moral worth, a person can increase the negative passions, becoming "supercilious, boastful, conceited and disdainful of the rest of mankind, as if they themselves had wrought something superhuman."[37] Poverty itself does not separate us from God, but neither does poverty in and of itself orient us in salvation. Or as Tevye memorably put it in Fiddler on the Roof, "*It's no great shame to be poor,* but it's no great honor either."[38]

Indeed, the presence of wealth, Clement argues, can be a good. "For what sharing would be left . . . if nobody had anything?"[39] While this may strike some as a rationalization for wealth, and similar arguments have been used as such, this is likewise not Clement's goal. He is arguing for the reality that those who are wealthy have the ability to share, to help, to contribute. Their wealth is not a sign of their importance but may be a blessing among other blessings a person may offer. This really is more of a common sense argument than a justification. Even in academic circles where it is common practice to protest the accumulation of wealth, such often coincides with the welcoming of grants, awards, sponsored lecture series, endowed chairs, tuition, and other expressions of income that allow for academic goals to continue.[40] If all were poor, who would pay our salaries or provide benefits or academic opportunities? We would be cast into the tasks of manual labor (which might indeed be a benefit for many academics!). The state of academic or church life, likewise, should not blunt all criticism of economic approaches or policies by academics. But it does relativize such critiques and point to how they can lack self-reflection when absolutized.

In support of his approach, Clement points to the examples of the tax collectors Zacchaeus and Matthew. Jesus did not command them to sell everything but rather to apply justice and rectify misdeeds. The message to the rich young man was not in fact the universal teaching of Jesus but indeed a contextual command for this particular person.[41] If selling everything was the rule, then we would expect at least *this* Gospel to be consistent in its application.

Clement offers a better test of righteousness. The true goal in the Christian life is to make wealth (indeed all elements of life) subservient to God's calling.[42] This includes whatever blessing we have been given, such as intelligence, good looks, opportunity, or any number of other benefits we possess that can be used poorly or properly. He writes:

> Are you able to make a right use of it? It is subservient to righteousness. Does one make a wrong use of it? It is, on the other hand, a minister of wrong. For its nature is to be subservient, not to rule. That then which of itself has neither good nor evil, being blameless, ought not to be blamed; but that which has the power of using it well and ill, by reason of its possessing voluntary choice.[43]

A person is assessed according to the pursuit of righteousness. Whatever leads to such righteousness should be pursued. Whatever undermines such righteousness should be abandoned. Such teaching undergirds Wesley's call to "earn all you can, save all you can, give all you can."[44] Wesley was certainly not one to excuse wealth for its own sake![45] And indeed, his approach to wealth throughout his life precisely illustrates Clement's teaching.[46]

Everyone, however, has a different hang-up, so for Clement and his Alexandrian approach, this leads the passage to say more than its "plain meaning." As it is included in the Gospels to speak to all its hearers, the message is likely broad indeed. He writes, "The renunciation, then, and selling of all possessions, is to be understood as spoken of the passions of the soul."[47] We all struggle with passions. For those who are caught up in the economic system, wealth itself is indeed a factor, but this does not limit the teaching only to economics. Any of the systems can be addressed here. If we are being consumed by politics, give up politics. If we are addicted to social media, give up all the social media. If we find our identity in what we eat, eat more simply. Again, the key issue is prioritizing the narrative of Christ in our lives above all. Whatever distracts or diminishes the defining narrative of Christ, even though it may seem good, is no longer good but a hindrance.[48] We can discern such priorities by being attentive to what holds onto our attention. "For where the mind of man is, there is also his treasure."[49]

This treasure is determined by our outward actions, following Mt. 12:33–37.[50] Like whether a tree is good or bad is determined by its fruit, so anything neutral can be expressed in either a righteous or unrighteous way. Clement again emphasizes that, at the core, salvation is not about works, it does not depend on external things "whether they are many or few, small or great, splendid or lowly, glorious or mean, but upon the soul's virtue, upon faith, hope, love, brotherliness, knowledge, gentleness, humility and truth, of which salvation is the prize."[51] It is this fruit of the Spirit that is the expression of righteousness and it is the pursuit of this Spirit that should animate our primary motivations.

God is not another system in the environment. God is the creator of the environment and the Lord of all the systems. To love God truly is to transcend the systems for their own sake and live in an integrated reality that takes shape according to God's lordship. We cohere in light of God's love and we are coherent in light of our love in return to God and to our neighbors.[52] This is neither passive nor a result of our actions. It is not something we can accomplish but it is something which we can pursue. In the transforming work of God's love, we are to pursue a life of love, expressing this with our whole being, and in this expression co-opting the way things are done in the systems of this world. This teaching very much echoes the Pauline admonition in 1 Tim. 6:17–19:

> As for those who in the present age are rich, command them not to be haughty, or to set their hopes on the uncertainty of riches, but rather on God who richly provides us with everything for our enjoyment. They are to do good, to be rich in good works, generous, and ready to share, thus storing up for themselves the treasure of a good foundation for the future, so that they may take hold of the life that really is life.

How do we do this? We are to be people who give, "not only to friends, but to the friends of friends."[53] When we see this in light of God's love, which Clement does, it reaches beyond our limited boundaries and opens our generosity to all. Our first generosity is friendship, which is community. "The Lord did not say, Give, or bring, or do good, or help, but make a friend. But a friend proves himself such not by one gift, but by long intimacy. For it is neither the faith, nor the love, nor the hope, nor the endurance of one day, but 'he that endures to the end shall be saved.'"[54] The persistence of a life of giving, of open generosity, characterizes the person of God because it first characterizes God. That which keeps us from such a model, then, is the barrier between life lived wholly in Christ and a life lived in the contradictions of the various systems.

We are to give to the friends of friends, and if we begin with the hope of being a friend of God, then we give to all those with whom God is friends. "And who is it that is the friend of God?" Clement goes on to ask.[55] This question is often determined by the valuation of other systems. I provide income to the worthy and truly desperate because I prioritize the economic system. I give education to paying students and learned colleagues because I prioritize the education system. I give friendship to those who will treat me well and offer reciprocity, like with like, because I prioritize a political system. Yet, in thinking in terms of the friendship of God, we are put outside the perspective of the systems. "Do not yourself decide who is worthy and who is unworthy," Clement writes, "for you may happen to be quite mistaken in your opinion; so that when in doubt through ignorance it is better to do good even to the unworthy for the sake of the worthy than by being on your guard against the less good not to light upon the virtuous at all."[56]

We are to be people who are generous in the pursuit of love, open to giving freely (even with potential loss or charges of gullibility), as our priority is the love of God with friends. The judgments or patterns of the systems are not determinative factors. If we are truly free in our identity with Christ, this is not a burden, as we give freely from what we have been given, which is all we have. The community of Christ is our new experience of living, our free space, expressed in a trustworthy reciprocity in the church. What we lack is offered to us, what others lack we give, each giving of what they have, in gifts and talents and skills, opening up the space of trust to an inviting expression of eternity itself.[57]

Other approaches to wealth tend toward placing the religious system in opposition to other systems. While seemingly a defense of Christian priorities, these tend to play into the very structures of the environment of systems. While resisting in some respects, the other systems do in fact operate relatively smoothly with a religious system as part of the environment. Those who might otherwise critique, restructure, or even dismantle such systems are shunted off into their own separate religious sphere, where such critiques are mollified by the religious system's own perpetuation, offering not so much as an alternative but a walled off citadel. Monasteries first served in this role and now, in theology and ethics at least, the academy offers a prophetic isolation. Even while the religious or education systems perpetually critiques other systems, the world system structure is still maintained. The systems use religion in effect as a "free speech zone," where a person can hand out flyers without disturbing the regular functioning of society. As long as academics are complaining about injustices to each other at conferences, they are not causing disruption in other systems, indeed maintaining forms of injustice within the education system that has a very unequal balance of privileges in who gets funding and invitations for conferences and promotion.

Clement, however, pursues a different goal than the systems. This is why his approach is more counterintuitive than a direct denunciation of power, wealth, and oppressing. He is not proposing contrasting systems, different tiers of commitment in Christianity, but instead seeks to instill in his listeners and later readers a new vision of a life under the lordship of Christ. Jesus is lord of all. Jesus not the head of one approach within yet another system, but the redeemer of all of creation. Jesus integrates the systems into a new way of experienced reality. There is still law, and politics, and economics, and even religion, but these are shaped by the cohesive Creator. Clement points Christians, all Christians, toward the new narrative of life in Christ. As it is only God who is good, there is no action itself which can lead to perfection, there is only the appropriation of the narrative of Christ in the whole of one's own life. Those who do this are the ones who experience the Kingdom, liberated and reborn, no longer operating in light of the world's values or patterns of identity. Whether rich or poor, male or female, Greek or Jew, they are part of a new humanity able to live in this new way in whatever context God has them in, able to bless and be blessed by God and others.

CONCLUSION

Dividing Christian service into the separate categories of the "religious" and the laity emphasized the idea that Christian perfection was a separate calling and could only be achieved in separation from this world. While this became a dominant view after Constantine, it was not this way for the early Christian communities. For Clement and others in the early church, the Christian life was animated by the context and offered distinct challenges, but these magnified the faithfulness of Christ as they continued to testify in their whole lives the truth of life in Christ sometimes even unto death.[58] With the dramatic shift of fortune after Constantine's rise to power, the opportunity for persecution fell by the wayside, and along with it rose the more pervasive mingling of earthly systems and Christian ideals.

Living a distinct Christian narrative in the context of the wider world had a radical emphasis when the rest of the world was so clearly pagan. When the same kinds of attitudes about the world persisted, but with ecclesial imprimatur, those who sought a more radical devotion could no longer find safe harbor in the established ecclesial structures, where persecution provided a kind of purification. They were drawn to the dramatic example of another Egyptian, Anthony, and sought the way of the desert for their spiritual perfection. While this separation likely helped them redeem their particular passions, it emptied society of its needed leaven, and drew Christianity back into the zone of a religious system rather than a transformative way. This was not Anthony's own goal, so it is important to now look at his vision of the radical Christian life and how it can inform our quest for liberation.

NOTES

1. Ignatius of Antioch, "Letter to the Magnesians," in *The Apostolic Fathers*, ed. and revised Michael W. Holmes (Grand Rapids: Baker, 1989), 4.94.

2. Wesley excluded such categories as ignorance, mistakes, infirmities, and temptations from his definition of perfection. See his sermon "Christian Perfection," in *The Sermons of John Wesley: A Collection for the Christian Journey*, eds. Kenneth J. Collins and Jason E. Vickers (Nashville: Abingdon Press, 2013), 611–614.

3. Second Vatican Council, "Gaudium et Spes," 4: "At all times the Church carries the responsibility of reading the signs of the time and of interpreting them in the light of the Gospel, if it is to carry out its task. In language intelligible to every generation, she should be able to answer the ever recurring questions which men ask about the meaning of this present life and of the life to come, and how one is related to the other. We must be aware of and understand the aspirations, the yearnings, and the often dramatic features of the world in which we live."

4. Lk. 11:24–26.

5. 1 Pet. 2:2. Cf. Coakley, *Powers and Submissions* (Malden, MA: Blackwell), 136–141. On the place of our affections, see Dale M. Coulter and Amos Yong, eds., *The Spirit, the Affections, and the Christian Tradition* (Notre Dame, IN: University of Notre Dame Press, 2016).

6. Alan Kreider writes this about the early Christian communities: "The churches grew because the faith that these fishers and hunters embodied was attractive to people who were dissatisfied with their old cultural and religious habits, who felt pushed to explore new possibilities, and who then encountered Christians who embodied a new manner of life that pulled them toward what the Christians called 'rebirth' into a new life. Surprisingly, this happened in a patient manner." In Kreider, *The Patient Ferment of the Early Church*, 12.

7. Tertullian, *Apology*, trans. S. Thelwall, ANF 3 (Peabody, MA: Hendrickson), 39.46.

8. Kreider, *The Patient Ferment of the Early Church*, 95.

9. For substantive analyses, see Helen Rhee, *Loving the Poor, Saving the Rich: Wealth, Poverty, and Early Christian Formation* (Grand Rapids: Baker Academic, 2012). David J. Downs, *Alms: Charity, Reward, and Atonement in Early Christianity*

(Waco: Baylor University Press, 2016). Susan R. Holman, ed., *Wealth and Poverty in Early Church and Society* (Grand Rapids: Baker Academic, 2008).

10. Rhee, *Loving the Poor, Saving the Rich*, 138.

11. See Ashwin-Siejkowski, *Clement of Alexandria*, 162. Ashwin-Siejkowski writes that Clement had a creative redefinition of the ideal, framed by Christian teaching of what is true about God and God's calling in this world. "Also," he writes, "according to Clement everyone may become a Gnostic, as the whole project is inclusive, never exclusive to a gender or ethnic group. This ideal is not an alternative option to the laity instead of clerical ministry. It does not depend on exterior conditions such as being celibate/married, young/old, wealthy/poor or ministering as a deacon, but is related to inner motivation (πίστις) and daily self-discipline."

12. David Bundy, "Christian Virtue: John Wesley and the Alexandrian Tradition," *Wesleyan Theological Journal* 26, no. 1 (1991): 139–140, writes, "The numerous citations in Wesley's works and the avowals of the importance of early Christian writers, especially the precise reference to Clement of Alexandria, have led Wesley scholars to affirm Alexandrian influence on Wesley. Harald Lindström observed, as early as 1946, that Clement's seventh Stromata 'On Perfection,' was important for understanding Wesley. Outler stated, in 1964: 'The "Christian Gnostic" of Clement of Alexandria became Wesley's model of the ideal Christian.' McIntosh argued that there are similarities between Wesley's and Clement's concept of 'perfect love.' Outler, discussing Wesley's interest in early Christian writers, affirmed, 'Clement of Alexandria was a favorite; Origen is cited seven times with sensitivity.'"

13. Kwame Bediako, *Theology & Identity* (Oxford: Regnum, 1992), 176.

14. Ashwin-Siejkowski, *Clement of Alexandria*, 228.

15. Eric Osborn, *Clement of Alexandria* (New York: Cambridge University Press, 2008), 14–15. Osborn writes, "Within his own writing the ideas of teacher and teaching recur. Clement gives a plan which is governed by stages of teaching. The *Protrepticus* precedes catechetical instruction. It is a handbook for Christians as missionaries, taking the gospel to those who do not believe. In the *Paedagogus*, Clement sets out a Christian *katêchêsis*. His programme is described in Stromateis 6.1.3. The work is clearly directed toward catechumens and presents a picture of the whole Christian life (*paed* 2.1.1). In this work Clement brings together the instruction which he has given to catechumens, pointing them on the Christian way and offering a handbook to guide them. The *Didascalus* was concerned to explain the propositions of faith and to interpret the words of scripture. The *Stromateis* fulfil this role by transmitting the teaching which Clement received, connecting oral and written teaching. The hidden element in them is a guard against their misuse by the mediocre or the bad. In his oral teaching, Clement imparted the seeds of truth and his writing recalls them. Non-Christians also can read because Clement edits his oral teaching to give it wider accessibility. However, the chief recipients of the *Stromateis* are those who are on the way to becoming Christian teachers themselves."

16. Osborn, *Clement of Alexandria*, 277.

17. In Greek, "Τις ο σωζόμενος πλούσιος" usually referred to by its Latin title "Quis dives salvetur?" hereafter abbreviated Quis div., in the notes.

18. Lk. 19:8.

19. See Kreider, *Patient Ferment*, 261–262.

20. See, for instance, Clement of Alexandria, *Pædagogus*, 209–296 and his letter *To the Newly Baptized* in *Clement of Alexandria*, Loeb Classical Library 92, trans. G. W. Butterworth (Cambridge, MA: Harvard University Press, 1919).

21. Downs, *Alms: Charity, Reward, and Atonement*, 188 writes that "*Quis dives salvetur* is addressed primarily to baptized Christians of some means who have not progressed very far along the path of perfection." While this may be the key audience in light of the title question, Clement has a bigger audience in mind: those who may idolize wealth or the wealthy; those who may have other seemingly desirable traits such as beauty or intelligence; those who may be mature in the faith but are challenged by the narratives of this world. On a personal note, this text immensely impacted me when I was a very poor sophomore taking a church history class in colleg. I had very little means and was not a beginner in the faith.

22. *Quis div.*, 2. All quotations will be from *Clement of Alexandria*, Loeb Classical Library 92, unless otherwise noted. Unfortunately, while there are newer translations of Clement's major works, this treatise has been rather neglected.

23. Thus establishing in his tone that the Christian message is a defining narrative. Of course, Christianity is not the only approach that is critical of wealth as undermining personal progress.

24. Cf. 1 Cor. 9:24–27; Ignatius, *Letter to Polycarp*, 2.

25. *Quis div.*, 4.

26. For early examples, see, for instance, Basil the Great, *On Social Justice: St. Basil the Great*, trans. C. Paul Schroeder (Crestwood, NY: St Vladimir's Seminary Press, 2009). Basil's sermon "On the Rich" contained in this volume is an especially worthwhile text both in its own right and as comparison with Clement's early treatment as they focus on the same passage. See also John Chrysostom, *On Wealth and Poverty*, trans. Catharine P. Roth (Crestwood, NY: St. Vladimir's Seminary Press, 1981). This latter volume collects sermons preached on the parable of Lazarus and the rich man as found in Luke 16.

27. *Quis div.*, 7.

28. Ibid., 10.

29. Butterworth, *Clement of Alexandria*, 267.

30. Ibid., 267.

31. Elizabeth A. Clark, *History, Theory, Text: Historians and the Linguistic Turn* (Cambridge: Harvard University Press, 2004), 173. Clark, 174 goes on to note that Clement's "social logic" in this text is to make sure the rich kept giving: "Despite the rigorous biblical injunctions to renounce wealth, the early Christian churches were dependent on the rich to support their extensive charity and other operations." The latter part may be true, but it's not clear at all the Bible encourages everyone to renounce wealth, let alone vigorously. It does strongly warn against misuse of wealth and assuming wealth is a sign of personal value. She rightly compares Clement with an anonymous, likely Pelagian, work that calls for more "rigorous renunciation." Such an absolute response essentially turns God's work into a legalism that then is relegated to a minority of elite Christians.

32. Ashwin-Siejkowski, *Clement of Alexandria*, 153 writes, "Clement's Gnostic, as a true Christian sage, is an individual who achieves not only freedom from

passions, but also lives by compassionate love for his or her fellow Christian. The Gnostic, though the recipient of spiritual gifts from the Holy Spirit as in Paul's ideal, also values rational investigation, philosophy and pursues advanced knowledge (γνῶσις)."

33. Osborn, *Clement of Alexandria*, 277.
34. *Quis div.*, 11.
35. Ibid., 11.
36. See Gutiérrez, *A Theology of Liberation*, 163–165.
37. *Quis div.*, 12. There is a useful analogy here with the topic of gluttony. Gluttony was seen to take two forms, either eating an inordinate amount or obsessing an inordinate amount about food. Both the person who ate too much and the person who ate only a little but was very fastidious or particular about it counted as glutton. Which, in our terms, means we can see gluttons as both the person who overeats at the buffet and the gourmand who is hyper-particular about ingredients and preparation. A person who is poor can be very obsessed by wealth or, likewise, obsessed by the wealth and status of others, signifying how they are not so much protesting the system as protesting their place or someone else's place in the system. The system itself still maintains its autopoietic functions in such protests. See John Cassian, "Conference 5.XI.1." in *The Conferences*, trans. Boniface Ramsey (New York: Paulist Press, 1997), 190–191.
38. "Ya ba dibba dibba dibba dibba dibba dibba dum." *Fiddler on the Roof*, directed by Norman Jewison (1971, MGM).
39. *Quis div.*, 13.
40. As well as increasingly relying on a class system for teaching where a small number of full-time professors carry the benefits while adjuncts (part-time, low pay, no benefits) carry the burden of much of the work.
41. In this way, we can see the teaching on wealth in the same way we see Paul's teaching on women in 1 Cor. 14:34. The tendency to universalize the teaching is undermined by the broader writings which show clear contextual distinction.
42. In this way he is following the text of the Proverb rather than the oft mistaken version, "Money is the root of all evil."
43. *Quis div.*, 14.
44. See John Wesley, Sermon 50, "The Use of Money," in Collins and Vickers, *The Sermons of John Wesley*, 304–411.
45. See John Galen McEllhenney, "Two Critiques of Wealth: John Wesley and Samuel Johnson Assess the Machinations of Mammon," *Methodist History* 32, no. 3 (April 1994): 147–159. Randy Maddox summarizes Wesley's economic ethics in four points: "(1) ultimately everything belongs to God; (2) resources are placed in our care to use as God sees fit; (3) God desires that we use these resources to meet our necessities (i.e., providing shelter and food for ourselves and dependents), and then help those in need; thus, (4) spending resources on luxuries for ourselves while others remain in need is robbing God!" In Maddox, *Responsible Grace*, 244.
46. For insight into Wesley's approach to wealth and poverty in his own life, as well as his emphases in his public ministry, see Henry D. Rack, *Reasonable Enthusiast: John Wesley and the Rise of Methodism*, 3rd edition (London: Epworth, 2002), 360–370.

47. *Quis div.*, 14.
48. Cf. Phil. 3:1–10.
49. *Quis div.*, 17.
50. See also Mt. 7:16–20.
51. *Quis div.*, 18.
52. See Ibid., 27–28. Cf. Jürgen Moltmann, *The Living God and the Fullness of Life* (Louisville: Westminster John Knox Press, 2015), 134: "Not every love is good. Love is always determined by what is loved."
53. *Quis div.*, 32. Though elsewhere, Clement seems to suggest that our "neighbor" is another disciple of the Lord (*Quis div.*, 30 and 31), here the conception seems broader (and more in line with the wider definition of Jesus). Giving also to a friend of a friend seems rhetorically analogical to the question in Mt. 18:21–22. When Jesus was asked how many times we should forgive, he answered, "Seventy times seven," which is not the numerical limit but rather expanding beyond limitation.
54. *Quis div.*, 32.
55. Ibid., 33.
56. Ibid., 33.
57. See Ibid., 35.
58. In his *Apology*, Tertullian highlights that Christians are part of society, and that their contributions provide a public benefit. "But we are called to account as harm-doers on another ground, and are accused of being useless in the affairs of life. How in all the world can that be the case with people who are living among you, eating the same food, wearing the same attire, having the same habits, under the same necessities of existence? We are not Indian Brahmins or Gymnosophists, who dwell in woods and exile themselves from ordinary human life. We do not forget the debt of gratitude we owe to God, our Lord and Creator; we reject no creature of His hands, though certainly we exercise restraint upon ourselves, lest of any gift of His we make an immoderate or sinful use. So we sojourn with you in the world, abjuring neither forum, nor shambles, nor bath, nor booth, nor workshop, nor inn, nor weekly market, nor any other places of commerce. We sail with you, and fight with you, and till the ground with you; and in like manner we unite with you in your traffickings—even in the various arts we make public property of our works for your benefit." In ANF 3, 42.49. He goes on in chapter 43 to note that "whatever loss your interests suffer from the religion we profess, the protection you have from us amply makes up for it." Tertullian here is emphasizing that Christians are already present throughout society and are committed to its thriving. This example is a testimony for why they should not be persecuted, but it is also an invitation to join a new lifestyle within society. As a text read by many Christian communities, this is also an exhortation to maintain a holy witness whatever a Christian may be doing.

Chapter 7

The Liberating Way of the Desert

INTRODUCTION

There are many different paths to power and fame. Some try for these directly for their own sake, while others garner them along the way in successful careers. It is the rare figure who finds power and fame after a life intentionally trying to avoid both. Such is the curious nature of Anthony of Egypt, sometimes called the father of Christian monasticism. He was not the first to go into the wilderness, nor the first to devote himself to isolated prayer and spiritual disciplines. His influence came through his rigor and, likely, his timing. After the rise of Constantine, there was a changing landscape for Christian devotion, with new needs for honing faith in the absence of persecution and new ways of spiritual rigor in an increasingly privileged church. The extent of Anthony's devotion, and his later calling to help guide others in their spiritual pursuits, initiated a groundswell of interest in monastic life. His efforts became an example for many who followed. That was not his goal. His goal was to find how to be who he knew Christ had called him to be.

After his parents died, and left him with significant resources, he heard the story of the rich young man as a call for his own life. He knew there was something more than the privilege and distractions of wealth. He sought perfection, a perfection in Christ, and to do this he left everything behind, all his wealth and privilege, all the world's stories. He sought a way of prayer and restoration within this present life. Discovering this way led him to a life of isolation in an abandoned fort in the middle of the Egyptian wilderness. He was reluctant about visitors because he was finding liberation, and it was because of this liberation that he was called back to be a teacher.[1] He didn't want to do this at first, but was convinced by God's continued calling in his life. This very reluctance likely helped him be the kind of transformative teacher so many were looking for. He did not seek honors but sought Christ and was willing to help others join in this same quest. In this chapter, I will explore his insights to learn what this instructor can teach our era regarding liberation. I will begin by looking at the famous biography written by Athanasius. Second, I will look at his sayings as they have been collected along with other early desert monastics. Finally, I will use his surviving letters to discover what he wanted to teach to those who sought to learn from him.

THE LIFE OF ANTHONY

Anthony became an important figure in Christian imagination in part due to his own reputation but mostly because of Athanasius, whose *Life of Anthony* became a very popular Christian work. Athanasius's goal is stated at the very end:

> Read this book very carefully to the brothers so that, when they learn about the faithful life of these outstanding monks, they may know that our Saviour Jesus Christ glorifies those who glorify Him and grants the nobility of fame to those who serve him and who long not only for the kingdom of heaven but also wish to lead a life of withdrawal in remote mountain places. They do this so that they themselves might win praise for their virtues and so that others may be spurred on by their examples.[2]

Winning praise for virtues and spurring others to similar achievements is an understandable ideal and, in light of a holistic liberation, a troubling one. It invokes vainglory as a motivation and embeds competition as a motivator.[3] Athanasius also notes another goal of the text is to emphasize Christ's lordship by providing examples of power encounters with spiritual forces. While there are mentions of Anthony's humility, the text is primarily framed as one of radical achievement in the pursuit of monastic ideals, one that represents more of Athanasius's views than is an accurate summary of Anthony's life.[4]

As with all hagiographies, the ideal model serves as an example for readers so they are convicted of their own weakness, spurred on to their own discipline, or encouraged to be followers of the topic's teaching.[5] There is very little relatable humanity. That was not the goal.[6] The occasional emphases on humility are more in line with passages like Num. 12:3, modeling a heroic godly virtue. With the list of ascetic heights, spiritual battles, intellectual triumphs over wayward philosophers, Anthony is portrayed as that ideal liberated man, consumed by a love for Christ, expressed in a life wholly dedicated to prayer and overcoming all temptations. While response to Athanasius's work has been mixed, especially relatively lately, there is no question it significantly shaped how many generations understood an ideal Christian life.[7] Indeed, this text likely set the stage for the explosion of monastic life for many centuries and gave a new model for Christian sainthood after the conversion of Constantine.[8]

Times have changed. In our contemporary Western context, monastic life is viewed as misguided if not outright rejected by many Protestants. For Catholics and Orthodox, it is popularly understood as a calling limited to a small number of specially called zealots. Overcoming sins is dismissed as impossible by a great many in both theory and practice, with that goal seen as reflecting a kind of Pelagianism.[9] Thus, nowadays as modeling an idealized Christian is no longer in favor, Anthony is little known and rarely studied in popular Christianity. Those who do know him rarely study him as a model for their own Christian devotion. This does not mean Anthony should be discarded as an influence for our time or relegated solely to discussions about church history or monastic life.[10] Rather, we should move beyond the *Life*, let him speak for himself, listening to what he taught and wrote his followers. There are two key sources for this task. The first is in the sayings of the desert fathers, a collection of short statements and stories from those who sought spiritual depth in the Egyptian wilds. The letters he wrote are the second and more substantive source, as they highlight his own priorities and patterns.

ANTHONY IN THE SAYINGS: WISDOM FOR THE LIBERATED LIFE

Like many of the desert fathers revealed in the sayings, Anthony comes across with a very curious combination of zealous spiritual maturity and a radical humility. Or maybe not so curious at all, given the nature of the target. By seeing God as the orienting reality, there is a constant awareness of imperfection and grace, a grace that extends to welcoming others. What must we do to please God? Anthony answers, "Pay attention to what I tell you: whoever you may be, always have God before your eyes; whatever you do, do it according to the testimony of the holy Scriptures; in whatever place you live, do not easily leave it. Keep these three precepts and you will be saved."[11] Useful advice to those pursuing silence in the desert or those of us raising a family in the suburbs! This is an example of how so many of the sayings provide a road map for spiritual progress no matter one's status or location.[12] In terms of a liberation of the oppressor, these sayings confront assumptions of grandeur or privilege by pointing a person back into an orientation of God's grace and calling. God is the goal *and* God is the lens by which we interact with our self and the rest of the world.

This orientation is not dependent on separation from the world (though Anthony sees benefit to such), rather it is about obedience.[13] The key task in obedience is discernment: "He also said, 'Some have afflicted their bodies by asceticism, but they lack discernment, and so they are far from God.'"[14] Indeed, even as Athanasius emphasizes Anthony's miracles, Anthony himself suggests a miracle is not in and of itself a sign of spiritual maturity or perseverance. Speaking of a young monk who had performed a miracle on a nearby road, Anthony tells those who reported it, "This monk seems to me to be a ship loaded with goods but I do not know if he will reach harbor."[15] Rather than signs, wonders, or ascetic triumph, Anthony points in a different direction. "He also said, 'Our life and our death is with our neighbor. If we gain our brother we have gained God, but if we scandalise our brother, we have sinned against Christ.'"[16] Spiritual maturity may involve leaving the world, but need not require it, and certainly cannot involve alienating or dismissing those around us. Quite the opposite. Spiritual maturity insists on having a right relationship with our neighbor oriented in light of God's love.

The Anthony of the sayings is thus much more human and approachable than the miracle worker of the *Vita*. The sayings invite people into a spectrum of response depending on their circumstances, while the rigorous all or nothing model we see in the hagiography leads some to emulation and others to resignation that their life can never follow such achievement. Thus, the *Vita* seeming to emphasize a radical liberation for some but not a call for all. Anthony's actual approach is more inviting than Athanasius indicates. In Saying 13, for instance, Anthony is critiqued by a nearby hunter for enjoying himself with the brethren. Anthony responds with an object lesson involving having the hunter repeatedly shoot arrows. After shooting for a while, the hunter who was initially bothered by Anthony exclaims, "If I bend my bow so much I will break it." Anthony then answers, "It is the same with the work of God. If we stretch the brethren beyond measure they will soon break. Sometimes it is necessary to come down to meet their needs." People who are caught in the systems may need time to develop paths to progress, and rather than being condemned (which tends only to leave guilt), there should be encouragement about a better way and about the progress that is made in an individual's life in that way.

We are to be oriented in God, which may involve a season (or longer) of asceticism. Anthony's path involved selling all of his possessions and giving the money away, the task Jesus gave to the rich young man. This is not the only path to such perfection. Indeed, an ascetic path easily becomes its own goal rather than leading toward the goal of Christ, thus losing its way while sounding very impressive. "He also said, 'Nine monks fell away after many labours and were obsessed with spiritual pride, for they put their trust in their own works and being deceived they did not give due heed to the commandment that says, 'Ask your father and he will tell you'" (Deut. 32.7).[17] Instead of emphasizing a specific gesture or task, the goal is obedience to God, for God's presence to be the defining reality, moving from fear into love.[18] In speaking of a man who was falsely accused of fornication, and hearing the monks were pressing his guilt, another Abba said to them, "I have seen a man on the bank of the river buried up to his knees in mud and some men came to give him a hand to help him out, but they pushed him further in up to his neck." Anthony commends this response, saying of this Abba, "Here is a real man, who can care for souls and save them."[19]

PROGRESSING TO PERFECTION

In turning to the letters of Anthony we continue to encounter a deep well of gracious wisdom that reflects the surprisingly balanced approach of the desert fathers.[20] Anthony reveals himself to be a thoughtful, and indeed likely educated, relatively independent teacher.[21] "Not, then," Tomas Hägg writes, "a loyal supporter of the Church and defender of orthodoxy, as in the Life, nor a saint, but a self-reliant master of spiritual teaching."[22] His words encourage his readers toward participation with God in a renewed, liberated, sanctified way of life.[23]

His first letter provides a set of frameworks for understanding the interactivity of our soul and bodies, and how we can progress toward perfection.[24] First, he talks about the three kinds of souls.[25] The first follows God readily, with Abraham as an example. The second follows out of fear, driven by themes of possible punishment. The third kind of soul is more stubborn, and the person persists in sin. So, God sends afflictions to break them down until they repent and seek God again. Anthony writes, "These are the three gates for the souls who come to repent until they obtain grace, and the calling of the Son of God."[26] However a person is initially called, it is the Holy Spirit who calls them and "who alleviates everything for them so that the work of repentance becomes sweet for them." The Spirit organizes their awareness and gives them control to do that which must be done.[27]

The path to perfection follows three steps. First there is the "cutting of all the fruits of the flesh" which involves disciplined fasting and vigils and other exercises meant to train the body into different habits. "Then," Anthony writes, "the guiding Spirit begins to open the eyes of the soul, to show it the way of repentance that it, too, may be purified."[28] The second step involves the mind discriminating righteousness, learning how to purify both the body and the soul, learning how to live in a natural way such as the body should "in its original condition." Third, the body is controlled by the mind, taught by the Spirit, becoming sanctified in every action, including food and sleep, indeed "in all its movements."[29] Anthony then goes on to specify what this might look like for each of the senses and bodily demands.[30] Everything becomes attuned to the movement of the Spirit, who reorients our whole being to become in tune with God's work. This path in progress is not easy but God provides grace along the way.

ENCOURAGEMENT AND EXHORTATION

In the second letter, Anthony seeks to encourage his readers. Since the creation of the world, he teaches, God has always embraced those who turn toward his promises. Those who seek other forms of identity have become irrational in their pursuits, but God continues to seek the eternal renewal of people "in his great benevolence."[31] In his love, God responds to our afflictions, giving us insight and wisdom and companionship with the Spirit. Anthony then in quick succession journeys from the prophets to Paul, quoting from Jer. 8:22 and 51:9, Ezek. 12:3, then Phil. 2:6–11, and Rom. 8:32 alongside Isa. 53:5. It is masterful summary of the story of God's work in responding to the needs of humanity throughout the whole of Scripture, tying it all into a focused theme. Such a mission of God leads us into response. Everyone "for whom the Saviour came" should examine their lives and see the good and evil in what they do, "so that he may be freed through his coming."[32] The goal is freedom, and this freedom is an expression of a new relationship with God. This Spirit of adoption leads out of fear toward love and wholeness. Those who resist or turn away from this progression will be judged. The encouragement of God's work, then, leads directly into an exhortation for our response. We are called to participate in the new work of the Spirit so that we reflect in our lives that which God has called us to be.

THE FREEING KNOWLEDGE OF SELF

The third letter develops the theme of freedom. Someone who is free in the Spirit, who has considered their self in light of the renewing life of Jesus "knows himself in his spiritual essence, for he who knows himself also knows the dispensations of his Creator, and what he does for his creatures."[33] The admonition to "know thyself" is not new to Anthony, of course, with the distinction being in how such knowledge is obtained and where it leads. This knowledge is given by the Spirit. As we participate with the Spirit, we are given discernment. The ways of the world being what they are, however, the "enemy of virtue always plots against truth."[34] Thus, God is persistent in reaching out to people, from the time of creation, meeting with those who "come to the Creator through the law of his Promise," and worshipping him accordingly.[35] But because of the difficulty, humanity was not able to persevere in such a task. God, then, responded with the Scriptures, giving the law so as to orient them in worshiping God as the one God, the Father whose oneness draws together all the world. Even with this, the deep wounds of humanity need yet more care.

Prophets were sent—including Moses—filled with the presence of the one Spirit. John the Baptist was the last of these and he pointed toward Jesus, the only one who could heal the great wound of humanity. In God's benevolence and for our salvation, Jesus died for our sins and thus brought healing. "Through the word of his power he gathered us from all lands, from one end of the earth to the other, resurrecting our hearts from the earth and teaching us that we are members of one another."[36] Anthony's feverish run through the Scriptural history of salvation establishes Anthony's exhortation: because of God's work in freeing us, we are free, and so we have to live this out "so that he can makes us wise through his ignorance, enrich us through his poverty, and strengthen us through his weakness, and resurrect us all when *he destroys him who has the power of death.*"[37] Because of this, we do not need to be caught up in the problems of the flesh, and essentially we are given power in the counter-narrative of the Creator so that we can live within this new way even in our present life.

For those who are thus preparing, this is a joy. For those who deny the power of Christ, the coming of Jesus is a judgment.[38] Anthony commends his readers as being better than the ignorant or dismissive. He encourages them to indeed know themselves, to know the time in a positive way rather than the negative way that comes through impatience or distraction.[39] Essentially, to think in terms of hope. He is writing to them "as to wise men, who are able to know themselves."[40] Again, repeating how he opened his letter, the person who knows their own self "knows God and his dispensations for his creatures."[41] This knowledge really is a liberation, a liberation of perceiving oneself entirely, seeing the self in the context of God's self. In doing this, a person understands one's place and role, being in this world as a reflection of God's creative actions. A person begins to own their own story and participate fully according to God's call for them in their particular time and place.

This knowledge calls each person to preparation, to be cautious and zealous. Each person must determine the right way in the midst of a dangerous world that offers either the power and life of God or the darkness and death of evil. Anthony thus ends by quoting the words of Jesus, "Lay not up for yourselves treasures on earth and take no thought for the morrow, for the morrow will take thought for the things of itself."[42] It is in the challenges we are tested, whether we are truly aligned with God, so we are to be vigilant and aware, and hold onto the freedom that we have been given. In other words, there are many ways to draw us out of God's promise, many kinds of identity that are offered, but in the liberation of Christ we find true freedom in our self and among others. We cannot couple a life that expresses freedom through Christ in one way while enslaved to the world systems in other ways. It is for freedom that Christ has set us free and this freedom must be expressed and exercised if it is to be an eternal reality.[43]

TO KNOW IS TO LIVE

Letters four and five continue these themes. We are to know ourselves as we truly are and live out this knowledge through God's work in our lives. God is angry with our evil deeds but loves us. We are not left to our own devices, the benevolence of God seeks us, then sends us the Holy Spirit to teach us about reality. To teach us about ourselves! Resisting liberation—moving away from the life-expressing freedom—is resistance to the Holy Spirit. The Spirit gives us identity so that we know our self. Not knowing our self is a sign of still being enslaved. In his one notable statement on a theological controversy, Anthony ends letter four with a condemnation of Arius, writing, "If he had known himself, his tongue would not have spoken about what he did not know. It is, however, manifest, that he did not know himself."[44] For Anthony, this is the ultimate wound.

CHALLENGES AND SETBACKS IN THE PURSUIT OF LIBERATION

In letter six, Anthony develops his theme of knowledge in a longer discussion, this time highlighting contrasting patterns of Christ and the devil. Those who participate with Christ must be zealous about their goals. He warns his readers about the "evil devices of the devils and their disciples" which they pursue because "they want us to be lost with them, so that we shall be with the multitude."[45] His readers, however, should know better, "as wise men," who recognize the Creator and the ways the Creator works in this world, the patterns that resonate life. We are, he writes, "called to be sensible, but have put on an irrational mind," so that we do not live as the world wants us to live, nor give attention to such ways. It is the counter-rational work of the Spirit that enables true understanding, living according to Christ, not in and for the systems. Anthony prays for his readers that they might have "a heart of knowledge and a spirit of discernment" able to rise toward the Father in all they do.

Anthony then goes on to talk about the ways such a task is resisted. The evil forces pull us down and distract us, orienting us away from our true self and against those around us, so that we are left alone and embittered. In an extended passage, Anthony writes:

> Truly, my children, they are jealous of us at all times with their evil counsel, their secret persecution, their subtle malice, their spirits of seduction, their fraudulent thoughts, their faithlessness which they sow in our hearts every day, their hardness of heart and their numbness, the many sufferings they bring upon us at every hour, the weariness which causes our hearts to be weary at all times, all their wrath, the mutual slander which they teach us, our self-justifications in our deeds, and the condemnations which they sow in our hearts, so that we, when we are alone, condemn our fellows, though they are not with us, the contempt they send into our hearts through pride so that we become hard-hearted and despise one another, becoming bitter against each other with hard words, and troubled every hour accusing each other and not ourselves, thinking that our struggle comes from our fellows, judging what is outside while the robbers are all inside our house, and [furthermore, with] the disputes and divisions we have with each other until we have established our own words so that they seem justified in the face of the other, and they incite us to do things which we are unable to do (and whose time it is not), and makes us weary of things we do and which are good for us.[46]

These forces lead us to wrong emotions and deceive us until we are enslaved to them, feeding on their lies as if they were nourishing food. Having done this, a person finds a false identity in these lies, a false expression of their self and the life they are to live. In living this way, a person arouses the anger of God. God calls the person back. But they have to listen, to return to the way of true knowledge and love. If a person is lost in their false self, delighting in self-delusion and a sense of self-grandeur, justifying themselves in the pursuit of such deception, then they are expressing evil itself, their mind, their soul, caught in a net.

Such a person is not free. Though they think they are free, their perception has been entirely undermined. Anthony writes that "over such a one the demons have great power, because he has not dishonored them before all men."[47] Such demons have many different strategies, so a person cannot just expect to know what they will do to undermine progress. This is why self-knowledge is so key: we are to discern God's work from demonic suggestions in the multiplicity of lived life, holding onto our identity in God and not being seduced toward the anonymizing patterns of death. We are to know who we are so we can constantly be in tune with God's calling in and for us. We have been given particularity by God. This gives us specific value and specific meaning, loved by God with specific names. God's work is an invitation to become such a person as we have been created to be. No longer enslaved, no longer anonymous.

This pursuit, according to Anthony, is inherently social. God is not vulnerable to our deceits or machinations or abuse, but other people are. God does not need our blessing or our encouragement or our help, but other people do. Thus, a person is to express their freedom in God by how they treat other people. He writes, "Whoever sins against his neighbor sins against himself, and whoever does evil to his neighbor does evil to himself."[48] We should "raise up God in ourselves by spurring one another," giving ourselves to one another, and living in a way that expresses the love and mercy of God to and with one another. This is not about loving self, but about becoming truly self, loving oneself in light of God's reality, oriented in this reality truly and wholly. In light of this reality, "he who is able to love himself, loves all."[49] This pursuit of self in love among others does not come about through our own work, but it is the work of God in us, supporting and raising us.

Essentially, we come to ourselves when we come to God. When we come to God we also go out from ourselves. If we retreat into ourselves, we become isolated from our true self and from God. We become isolated from the body, alienated from the head, experiencing an incurable wound. We who are saved are saved as a body, in a body, gathering us from all lands, and offering the salvation of the one whose wounds heal our incurable wounds. Christ has come to save and free us, so we should be aware of those ways we are enslaved and cry out to God for our freedom, living in this freedom as Christ calls us. As we are given freedom, we will be constantly sought after by demons who seek our downfall, to pull us back into places of darkness, even and especially those who are advanced. When a person is spiritually mature, then pride itself strikes, so a Christian must never lose sight of humility, our need for God, and constantly enact love and regard for others. Such is the way of wisdom, a life lived in the liberating freedom of Christ, constantly vigilant against that which will undermine our true self.

LIBERATION WITH CHRIST

In his final letter, Anthony opens with an emphasis on Christ, pointing toward how much he let go for our sakes, quoting 2 Cor. 8:9. Anthony emphasizes the kenotic mission of Christ, the counterintuitive activities that constituted confrontation with the world alongside renewal for those in Christ. We truly are made new in Christ and no longer subject to the rational assumptions of the world systems. In coming close to the Creator, we find salvation in the promise, but the ways of the world dimmed the light of the promise so people are unable to pursue it on their own. Christ is the life of every rational being, the true mind and immutable image of the Father—an image for us who have the mutable essence—a saving presence for us who no longer have any inherent virtues.

God saw our weakness and reaches out with his love, and in this benevolent expression invites us into the new pattern of life. Look at all that God has done for you, Anthony notes, all that he has given you. "Now, then, what shall we say to him on the day of judgement, or what good has he held back from us, that he has not done to us?"[50] We should live in light of God's goodness and grace. Again, Anthony walks through the history of salvation in Scripture, highlighting what God did, what humanity did and was not able to fix, and God's persistence, in doing that which was needed, working within the environment to give freedom to those in it.

In continuing this contrasting of wealth and poverty, strength and weakness, Anthony leads his readers more deeply into the counter-narrative, the true narrative of life with God that leads into a fullness of life. The weakness or poverty are not the goals, but in resisting the promises of this world that lead to death, we join in with the one who leads into fullness of life. "Therefore, Jesus divested himself of his glory and took upon him the form of a servant, that we might be freed through his servitude."[51] We become with Christ who we truly are, leaving behind that which constrains so as to join him in his way of life. Participation with God, then, is really an enlivening pursuit of our truest self. Sin makes us guilty, which is not so much a legal category as an ontological discrepancy. Sin is "alien to us and far from the nature of our essence."[52] As we set ourselves free in the life of Christ, we become disciples and receive the inheritance of God. Those who seek God will orient themselves according to God's patterns, seeking what befits us, "that which is after the nature of our own essence."[53]

The task is not easy and in this world there are constant temptations to pull us away from God and our true self, but God is with us and comes to our side to enlighten us and steer us into right awareness of our self and our contexts, not letting anything impede his mission. In light of all that God did and is doing, we must be prepared for his coming and offer all that we are for all that he is. This is a relationship of reciprocal freedom; God in his giving leads us in our giving. Anthony closes by urging his readers to prepare, to live in the holiness of Christ through the power of the Spirit, who "comforts us" and "will bring us back to our beginning." This Spirit of comfort teaches and renews us into a new expressed community, where we live as free among the free, men and women, master and slaves, brought into unity with and for each other. "Give occasion to a wise man," Anthony finishes, "and he will be yet wiser."[54] The Spirit is the Spirit of wisdom, and in this wisdom we too become wise, holy, and free.

CONCLUSION

I focused on the relatively brief works of Anthony because of the importance of his example and life to the history of Christianity. Throughout his teachings, his priorities focus on the work of the Spirit in transformation and encouraging us to live out the life of Christ in our lives, to be fully who we were made to be. What is striking is that while he was writing to those who lived in a monastery, there is nothing in his letters, and very little in his sayings, that emphasizes a purely monastic life. The council he gave is universal to all people, calling them to renew their minds by knowing their own true self. This is possible in the work and wisdom of the Spirit that frees each person from the bondage of the systems of the world. For monks, this becomes a single-minded devotion, though not without its own struggles and temptations. For those not in monasteries, this challenge is greater in some ways because of the more pervasive narratives and demands of this world, but such also offers more opportunities to come alongside others, to love God through loving those who are in need. All patterns can find community together.

In the sayings and the letters, we find three key elements of Anthony's teaching. First, he establishes the goal of perfection in the revelation of God. Second, he encourages and exhorts people to pursue this goal even in the face of discouraging setbacks. Third, he highlights the challenges that arise in this pursuit. This love of God leads us into a place of new identity, a defining reality that transcends the limited scope of world systems and seeks a holistic integration with God's mission in and for this world. As such, a liberated life may often lead to being embedded within the context of a city. Temptations from other identity-demanding systems are constant but opportunities to express love and community may likewise abound.[55] "It was revealed to Abba Anthony in his desert that there was one who was his equal in the city. He was a doctor by profession and whatever he had beyond his needs he gave to the poor, and every day he sang the Sanctus with the angels."[56] Such a person also seems to be exactly what Clement had in mind in his discussion about wealth, a true Christian gnostic.[57]

What Anthony writes is neither dismissive nor alienating, neither nagging nor lofty. Anthony is neither defeatist nor idealist. His hope is in the living God who seeks relationship with people in loving reciprocity. Anthony invites his readers to respond alongside God's overwhelming love for us, to be a new kind of person, the person we were always meant to be, living anew in the lives of others. We do not need to flee to the desert to find wholeness or holiness, though Anthony did. We do not need to be monks to pursue a sanctifying power of the Spirit, though Anthony did. What Anthony emphasizes is particular—know yourself—and universal—draw together in God's love.[58]

Clement and Anthony together represent major elements of the early church. The first was a great teacher of Christians in one of the more significant cities of the Roman Empire. The second is widely recognized as a great initiator and leader of early monasticism. How they understood the goal of the Christian life and the expectations of each Christian is entirely relevant for understanding what liberation of the oppressor might look like and how it might be achieved. They did not, after all, suggest there were some who were called to be specialists nor that such specialty should be manifested in a separated system outside of society. There were different callings and different locations, but a shared mission.

No Christian was given a pass to behave in any way they wanted. No Christian was given a pass to be an oppressor. To be an oppressor implies living according to passions and narratives foreign to Christ. True Christians—who are saved and living in the narrative of this salvation—find wholeness and coherence in Christ, who gathers together all of life in a new expression of living together. The calling to be "altogether" is predicated on the work of the Creator God in creating, the liberating Christ who frees all people to new life, and the empowering, comforting presence of the Spirit who gives gifts so they may be given to others in return.[59] The inviting and embracing pattern of God deprecates other attempts at meaning or power, orienting people to find themselves in the community of God's renewing narrative.

Both Clement and Anthony warn against the systems and the way they will seduce us, and if not seduce us, will mock us, and if the mockery does not work, may even persecute those who live according to their true identity. "Abba Anthony said, 'A time is coming when men will go mad, and when they see someone who is not mad, they will attack him, saying "You are mad, you are not like us."'"[60] It is not Christians who misunderstand reality, however, it is the world, lost in separation and isolation. But Christians have often been seduced by the world, indulging oppression in the name of Christ, and this draws Christianity back within the narrow bounds of a religious system. Both Clement and Anthony suggest that we are to stand firm in God's fullness even the while, holding onto our calling, empowered by the Spirit, the vision of the Holy God filling our vision.

The teaching of Clement and Anthony became an increasingly minor thread within a broader expression of ecclesial triumph in the West, which emphasized domination. This became the determination of "Christendom," lacking patience, dividing the Christian call into the religious and the laity, with both finding new patterns of justified corruption that asserted a righteousness under the ecclesial law. It was a kind of holiness that often lacked love, and thus lacked a coherent expression of who God is and how God wants us to live. This is the history we have inherited. The transformative task is to consider again the nature of God's holiness and the ways we can express liberation in a theologically rich and practically transformative way. As Elisabeth Moltmann-Wendel writes, "We must learn to love anew, with a love which helps others to come of age, does not oppress them and does not exalt them, a love which opens up a sphere that is free of domination."[61]

This means resisting the patterns of the world and especially the patterns of the world that have taken residency within our churches and within our very theology. That task takes us into a new section, in which contemporary discussions point to new ways of thinking *and* acting *and* feeling in light of God's method of liberation.

NOTES

1. "A hermit said, 'Anyone who wants to live in the desert ought to be a teacher and not a learner. If he still needs teaching, he will come to harm.'" In Benedicta Ward, trans., *The Desert Fathers: Sayings of the Early Christian Monks*, revised edition (New York: Penguin Classics, 2003), 111. See Ward, *The Desert Fathers*, xxix–xxxi, for a helpful discussion of the various collections of sayings.

2. Athanasius, *Life of Anthony*, 94. I am using the text from *Early Christian Lives*, trans. Carolinne White (New York: Penguin Books, 1998). Gregory of Nazianzus wrote that through this text Athanasius "composed a rule for the monastic life in the form of a narrative." Cited in David Brakke, *Athanasius and the Politics of Asceticism* (Oxford: Clarendon Press, 1995), 201.

3. Vainglory can be useful in spurring someone to purity but it is not a sufficient course, as it relates holiness to the ego rather than God. On this, John Cassian wrote, "Yet in one way vainglory is beneficial for beginners, for those who are still stirred up by carnal vices. . . . For it is better for a person to be troubled by the vice of vainglory than for him to fall into the fire of fornication, from which he could not or could barely be saved once he had been ruined. . . . As long as you are shackled by the praises of vainglory, you will never rush into the depths of hell and sink irretrievably by the commission of deadly sins." In "Fifth Conference: On the Eight Principle Vices," XII.1, in *John Cassian: The Conferences*, trans. Boniface Ramsey (Newman Press, 1997), 192.

4. It is likely Athanasius did not know Anthony very well. For more on this and the goals of the *Life of Anthony*, see Brakke, chap. 4.

5. See Tomas Hägg, "The Life of St Antony between Biography and Hagiography," in *The Ashgate Research Companion to Byzantine Hagiography: Volume I: Periods and Places*, ed. Stephanos Efthymiadis (Burlington, VT: Routledge, 2011), 27–28. In his introduction to a substantive study of hagiographic periods and places, Stephanos Efthymiadis notes that the origin of hagiography as a substantive genre can be traced to Athanasius's work, writing, "It was largely thanks to its message and original composition that this text generated a remarkable chain of imitators, successors and responses." In Efthymiadis, 9. For a very readable introduction to the use of hagiography, see Stephanos Efthymiadis, "Introduction," in *The Ashgate*

Research Companion to Byzantine Hagiography Volume II: Genres and Contexts, ed. Stephanos Efthymiadis (Burlington, VT: Routledge, 2014). For a broader perspective of hagiography as a genre, see Martin Hinterberger, "Byzantine Hagiogrpahy and its Literary Genres. Some Critical Observations," in the same volume.

6. Efthymiadis, *Byzantine Hagiography* v. 2, 3 writes, "The strong appeal to Christians of a literature inspired by the idea of renouncing the world in one way or the other should not come as a surprise. *Passions*, charged as they were with emotion and graphic intensity, and the monastic narratives, which explored the power of the extraordinary tale to the utmost and celebrated the feats of the mortified ascetic, broke with conventional descriptions of human experience and involved a close engagement with the emotions of their audiences."

7. Samuel Rubenson, *The Letters of St Anthony: Monasticism and the Making of a Saint* (Minneapolis: Fortress Press, 1995), 126 succinctly sums up more recent responses: "Although the verdict of scholars on the text has varied greatly, no one has ever denied the paramount important of the *Vita*. Scorned by Adolf von Harnack as the 'probably most disastrous book that has ever been written,' it is today hailed as 'next to the Gospel of St. Mark the most important biography of early Christianity' and as 'the most influential of Athanasius' writings."

8. This is not to suggest Athanasius saw Christian maturity as only possible through ascetic goals. There certainly were elements that all Christians could and should pursue which included temporary or limited forms of chastity and fasting as well as more consistent elements of giving to the poor and hospitality. Almsgiving, for Athanasius, was even at times equal to prayer and studying Scripture. See Bakke, *Athanasius*, 182–198.

9. The Wesleyan tradition, of course, is an exception to this trend.

10. Coakley, *The New Asceticism*, 124 argues for "deepening practices" for all Christians after all, and to better understand these practices we need those who explored their depths.

11. Anthony the Great, Saying 3. In Saying 7, he adds another key element of desert life: humility. It is humility that allows a person to escape the snares of temptation. Unless otherwise noted, quotations of the sayings will be from Benedicta Ward, trans., *The Sayings of the Desert Fathers: The Alphabetical Collection* (Kalamazoo, MI: Cistercian Publications, 1975), 1–9.

12. Indeed, this was repeatedly confirmed for me as I required my undergraduate general education students to read the desert fathers and write a weekly one-page reflection on a chosen saying from each chapter. I used the topical collection of the sayings: *The Desert Fathers*, trans. Benedicta Ward (New York: Penguin, 2003). The assignment had them discuss the passage in light of their own experiences with the topic, thus providing a kind of devotional exercise. While my mostly Evangelical students were initially resistant about using a text by monastics, they almost always found the assignment quite valuable within a few weeks. By the end of the semester, students regularly told me it was a favorite assignment.

13. See Saying 33 for an example of emphasizing the ascetic life.

14. Saying 8. For a more in depth discussion the importance of discernment, see John Cassian, "Second Conference: On Discretion," in Cassian, *The Conferences*, 83–104.

15. Saying 14.
16. Saying 9.
17. Saying 37.
18. See Saying 32.
19. Saying 29.
20. In the preface to *The Letters of Saint Anthony the Great*, trans. Derwas J. Chitty (Oxford: SLG Press, 1975), v, Metropolitan Kallistos of Diokleia writes, "We are listening here to the authentic voice of desert spirituality."
21. That Anthony was a teacher is without dispute, well attested in the *Vita*. Yet, the Vita tends to follow the tradition of de-emphasizing learning so as to emphasize a kind of instinctive sanctity. That this is more of a rhetorical goal than a historical fact is clear in the letters. Rubenson, *The Letters of St. Anthony*, 11, writes, "The content of the letter is . . . hard to reconcile with the traditional image of Anthony and the early monastic tradition gained from the *Vita*, the *Apophthegmata* and other sources. The obvious dependence on popular Platonic philosophy and Alexandrian theological tradition reveals that the author was no 'ignorant monk' who had simply exchanged the garb of the peasant for the monastic habit, but a teacher who wore a monk's garment as if it was the robe of a philosopher." As a child of wealthy parents, Anthony almost certainly had a good education. The suggestion by Athanasius that he refused to read and write like "the other little children" is almost certainly rhetorical. Athanasius sought to portray Anthony as wise in a different way than the typical educated man of his day, emphasizing that mere education is not sufficient for wisdom. As Rubenson, *The Letters of St Anthony*, 134, puts it, "When Anthony is repeatedly presented as an 'unlettered' man the alternative is not the man of gnosis, but the man of letters." See Rubenson, *The Letters of St Anthony*, 141–144 for further discussion. It has been a long-standing rhetorical move to de-emphasize one's own learning and rhetorical skills, a "simple-country lawyer" approach to argumentation. We can see something similar in Patrick's *Confessio*, where he bemoaned his lack of education and skill in writing, even as he was making a significant claim for spiritual authority from God in his ministry. To be sure, Anthony's letters indicate much more skill than Patrick, whose formal education was halted at age seventeen when he was abducted.
22. Hägg, "The Life of St Antony between Biography and Hagiography," 29.
23. Anthony is, in this way, likely aligned with Cassian's perspective on participation with God as discussed in his Conference 13. Grace is essential for salvation, but God invites participation as response. Cassian uses the analogy of a farmer planting a field. It takes much work to work the soil and plant the seeds, but without rain, nothing will grow. Rain is the required grace to help our contributions grow into spiritual fruit. In Saying 16 of Anthony we read, "A brother said to Abba Anthony, 'Pray for me.' The old man said to him, 'I will have no mercy upon you, nor will God have any, if you yourself do not make an effort and if you do not pray to God.'"
24. The letters are of questionable authorship, however there is a seeming consensus that Anthony is indeed the author. For a more detailed examination of the provenance of the letters, see Rubenson, *The Letters of St Anthony*, chaps. 1–2.
25. Rubenson, *The Letters of St Anthony*, 197–198. Cf. Cassian, *Conference* 11.VI.

26. Rubenson, *The Letters of St Anthony*, 198.

27. Anthony's pneumatology is striking throughout the letters. Here we see the work of the Spirit in a seamless expression of prevenient and sanctifying work in *and with* a person.

28. Rubenson, *The Letters of St Anthony*, 198.

29. Ibid., 199.

30. Cf. Moltmann, *The Living God and the Fullness of Life*, 161–171.

31. Anthony here seems to be providing a very succinct paraphrase of Romans 1–2.

32. Rubenson, *The Letters of St Anthony*, 204.

33. Ibid., 206. Cf. John Calvin, *Institutes*, I.1.i.

34. Rubenson, *The Letters of St Anthony*, 206.

35. Ibid.

36. Ibid., 207.

37. Ibid., 207–208. Emphasis in the original.

38. Cf. Pannenberg, *Systematic Theology*, 608–620.

39. Ignatius, "Letter to Polycarp," 3 writes, "Understand the times. Wait expectantly for him who is above time," in *The Apostolic Fathers*, ed. and revised Michael W. Holmes (Grand Rapids: Baker, 1989), 116.

40. Rubenson, *The Letters of St Anthony*, 208.

41. Ibid.

42. Anthony is quoting from Mat. 6:19 and 34. I am using the translation from Anthony's letter.

43. Gal. 5:1.

44. Rubenson, *The Letters of St Anthony*, 211.

45. Ibid., 217.

46. Ibid., 218.

47. Ibid., 219.

48. Ibid., 220.

49. Ibid., 221.

50. Ibid., 226.

51. Ibid., 227.

52. Ibid., 228.

53. Ibid., 221.

54. Ibid., 231. Quoting Prov. 9:9.

55. Indeed, the presence of such temptations may indeed be a boon. In Saying 5 we read, "He also said, 'Whoever has not experienced temptation cannot enter into the Kingdom of Heaven.' He even added, 'Without temptation no-one can be saved.'"

56. Saying 24. Cf. John V. Taylor, *The Go-Between God: The Holy Spirit and the Christian Mission* (Philadelphia: Fortress Press, 1973), 38–39.

57. On this in connection with Anthony, see Rubenson, *The Letters of St Anthony*, chap. 4.

58. This is not, of course, unique to Anthony. See Keener, *The Mind of the Spirit*, 46–49. What makes it unique is the source and orientation of this knowledge. In *Stromata, ANF 2*, 1.14.314, Clement writes, "The expression 'know yourself,' some

supposed to be Chilon's. But Chamælon, his book *About the Gods*, ascribes it to Thales; Aristotle to the Pythian. It may be an injunction to the pursuit of knowledge. For it is not possible to know the parts without the essence of the whole; and one must study the genesis of the universe, that thereby we may be able to learn the nature of man."

59. See John Wesley, Sermon 2, "The Almost Christian," §2, 99–101.
60. Anthony, Sayings 25.
61. Moltmann-Wendel and Moltmann, *God—His & Hers*, 11.

Part III

CONSTRUCTING HOPE FOR THE OPPRESSORS

Chapter 8

Hope from God

INTRODUCTION

Who God is shapes who we are. Our conception of divine life affects how we navigate our life. If the Christian God is indeed lord of all, then how this God chooses to work and how we communicate this work is more than a little matter. When our conception of God does not match God's nature, dissonance develops between how the world was created and how we are trying to create our world. A misconceived God leads to a misdirected life. Misdirected life runs into other misdirected lives, and conflict ensues as every side tries to gain the advantage. Misdirected lives pursue idols of our own making and lead to experiences of death. That is essentially the message throughout Scripture and Christian theology. Misdirected life is called sin, and sin requires God's intervention. This intervention is the hope for the world.

But can we trust that statement? Scripture tells us God is neither merely a clockmaker nor the object of our intellectual curiosity. We are told God is the living God who is engaged in this world and engages humanity with his works. This is all well and good in a vacuum—or in a theology seminar, which is often much the same thing. But it becomes more complex as we wrestle with the realities of this present world: pain, injustice, senseless violence, insatiable greed. The list can go on and on, each seeming to push back against the idea that there really is a god. Or, admitting this, it seems that God cannot be both all-powerful and all-loving. One of those must be abandoned in light of what we know about this world. God doesn't seem involved and maybe that means God wants people to accomplish the divine goals. The quest for domination then finds religious justification. The oppressors get away with oppressing, and so the only hope for the oppressed is to take power, to put things right. It is the *other* oppressors who need liberating, and the way to do that is to gain control. God is dismissed as powerless or becomes a figurehead to continuing cycles of revolution and revenge. Worse yet, God is framed as a tyrant who is on the side of the wealthy, while the poor are being judged for their supposed misdeeds.

Yet, the curious reality about Scripture is that it embraces the idea that there is a God who is almighty who is also a God who is love. Even more curious, in the midst of declaring this, Scripture also provides manifold examples of the messiness of humanity and this world. Neither Scripture nor Christian theology have run away from these seeming paradoxes. Yet, not surprisingly, wrestling with these issues practically and theologically has not solved all the problems.[1] While in the wilderness, there is always another problem offering new discouragement. Address one concern, and others arise. Later eras deal with different questions than were ever imagined before. Cultural assumptions change, shaping different expectations for life and adding new forms of syncretism. Old problems never do entirely die out.

That is why it is important to point toward transformative theology alongside arguing for changed behavior. If our orientation with God is misdirected, or if conclusions in one context are misinterpreted in another context, dysfunctional formation develops. We may have significant content, but lack discernment. We may have much knowledge, but lack love. Theology thus is always in flux. Elizabeth Johnson emphasizes this when she writes, "The profound incomprehensibility of God coupled with the hunger of the human heart in changing historical cultures actually requires that there be an ongoing history of the quest for the living God that can never be concluded."[2] This unending quest engages existential questions as well as dysfunctional expressions. If oppressing is indeed against God's call for humanity, and God reaches out to provide salvation through Christ, then why does oppressing still clearly exist in places with a Christian history? What has gone wrong? The message? The application? The appropriation? There's not a simple answer because there are a mix of answers given the situation. The context of oppressing in our era shares many elements with earlier eras, but there are enough differences that to simply assert blanket judgments results in either more dysfunctional application or ineffectual communication. Often both at the same time! This is, in many ways, the state of academic theology in the question for transformation.[3] The church, and those in it, does not so much disagree with academic theology as they pay it almost no attention. They pay it no attention because academic theology has not regularly sought integrity with lived experiences in living communication. As such, it may even be considered a separate system from the religious system.

In this section, I provide a small choir of theologians attempting to reorient theology in our era. Each is interested in how theology shapes the church, Christian practices, and societal transformation. In their theological and practical contributions, these contributors point to how theology can make a difference and why it is important to first reassess our religious assumptions and theological expressions so that we are no longer caught by a limiting religious or academic system. Likewise, while it is very useful to engage a much wider variety of thinkers, doing such does not highlight the internal coherence developed by a particular contributor. Thus, I take a risk in focusing more narrowly so as to emphasize a developed theological coherence that results in a liberative theology for oppressors as well as the oppressed. Such a narrowed emphasis is more programmatic in intent rather than comprehensive, with my goal showing there is a distinct thread which others certainly can contribute toward. It is also dialogical, attempting to learn from these contributors in their own work and as a shared chorus on the theme of liberation. While I am focused on their contributions, the implicit critique throughout is that they need each other to balance out their individual weaknesses.

In this chapter, I will focus on two theologians who encountered God in the midst of one the church's most challenging eras.[4] Theology certainly seemed to have met its match in World War II. Dazzling displays of rhetoric could explain most everything, but the Holocaust was a decisive expression of unjust oppression, perpetrated by a historically Christian nation, indeed a nation that was the center of academic theological thought. After the Holocaust and all the disasters of World War II, theology had to find a new way of talking about God, if it was able to talk about a God in Christian terms at all.[5] Pannenberg was among those who took up this rebuilding task. His peer and onetime colleague Jürgen Moltmann is another. Both were raised outside of the church, both found faith in Christ in young adulthood, both learned from the deep wells of German theological thought as it had continued after the war, both realized the lingering questions that were ignored by such thought.

Though they certainly differ in methodology, and often in their conclusions, they shared a common faith, a faith in a living God who could still be known, still be trusted. They found a way to talk about God after the Holocaust, in terms that anticipated postmodern developments. In these contributions, they emphasized a substantive hope that leads to present transformation.[6] They both argue that such transformation is not a natural step, as if we just have to convince people to take it; it is the embrace of a resurrection faith. Neither dismissed God, instead they found a resurging theology by digging deeply into Scripture, historical theology, philosophy, and other resources, all of which led them to a new way of speaking about God. While there have certainly been many helping to forge this trail, and many I could focus on fruitfully, the curious cooperation between Pannenberg and Moltmann provides a

GOD IS HOLY

Be holy, God says.[7] Okay, that is straightforward: don't drink, dance, smoke, tattoo, or go with those who do. That is how "be holy" has often been interpreted in popular church movements, dedicated to avoiding vices. Be holy because God is holy, the passage continues, which suggests something more interesting is at work. The people are representatives of the God they worship. How they represent God is shown by much more than what they *don't* do. It must also include how they live, all that they proactively do. God calls the people, effectively, to be his image to the rest of the world. Do this, because I do this. Be this, because I am this. It is important that we do not take this command in isolation from the rest of Scripture, separating ethics from theology, investing our own interests in the term and then making others live up to our interpretations. People should not be holy in the way they think they should be holy or holy in the way other people define holiness. This can lead to forms of oppression as holiness is applied in restricting or alienating ways. It can also embed divisions and justification for oppression against those who might be considered outside the fold. A more thorough understanding of God's holiness, however, leads in a different direction, one defined by love and engagement with others. The challenge to do this without being co-opted by the world's assumptions is perennial, however, and that is why it is important to begin not with what we should do—be holy—but begin with what it means to say God is holy.

The word "holy" is not included in Genesis. Rather, the root *qdš* makes its first appearance in Exodus 3. "Come no closer," God says to Moses. "Remove the sandals from your feet, for the place on which you are standing is holy ground."[8] The basic translation in the BDB is "apartness, sacredness." However, that is likely more of a derivation of the use of the word rather than its primary meaning.[9] This usage, no doubt, comes from passages like Exodus 3. Indeed, in the rest of the Pentateuch, there seems to be a clearly defined boundary between God and this world requiring specific steps to be taken in order to interact with the God who is. To be in the presence of God required a clear distinction between the common and the sacred. After all, the Law said, "You are to distinguish between the holy and the common, and between the unclean and the clean."[10]

To be in the presence of God—as Moses was before the burning bush and as the priests were in the Tabernacle—required a separation, one that made physical acts into an emotional and spiritual boundary. "This separation must be maintained," Robert Jenson writes. "Holiness is incompatible with impurity, and so walls and barriers protect the holy parts of the Tabernacle from encroachment upon it."[11] The law, as it is given, concerns itself very specifically with the separation between what is holy and what is unholy, so much so that the idea of separation itself becomes a derived meaning of the word. "God wishes to encounter Israel under certain circumstances" and so commands that they be placed "into a condition allowing them to approach God safely."[12]

But something changes in the New Testament. The Spirit comes, and we find the terminology particularly noteworthy. It is not the Loving Spirit, or the Merciful Spirit, or the Enlivening Spirit. It is the *Holy* Spirit. The definition as set apart, or separated, does not carry as much emphasis when we see the Spirit is the one who sends Christ into the world and sends the apostles into the streets.[13] Is this a transition of the word or does this entail a more exact understanding than "separated" or "morally upright" suggests? Procksch makes sure we do not assume a changing meaning of the term when he writes, "In the LXX, ἅγιος is used as the equivalent of the Hebrew in all applications of this Hebrew term, so that in the usage of the Bible we must everywhere recognize the Semitic background."[14] The word in the New Testament is not distinct from the Hebrew usage, and was used as a direct connection to the use in the Old Testament references. Which means, it seems, that as holiness never did primarily mean "set apart," it certainly does not have this primary meaning in the New Testament.[15] Holiness can thus never be used to justify division or oppression, imposing a kind of religiously justified self-protection.

Rather than being defined as "set apart," the definition of holy is better understood as applying to the nature of God himself, as his self. God is holy. God's holiness is a way of saying God's selfness. Hence, there is a strong need for separation within the Old Testament context. To be in the presence of the holy is to be in the presence of God, and to be in the presence of God, God demands certain safeguards so as not to expose his self to corruption. Or, maybe more importantly, not expose corruption to his self, as the corruption can't handle it. As Procksch notes, "His holiness denotes His innermost and secret essence."[16] God's holiness is his identity.[17]

GOD IS FULLNESS

The experience of God, the expression of the holy, is a "sense of the working and being of God in creation."[18] God reveals himself in history, Pannenberg argued, and it is his revelation in history that provides the foundations for our developed understanding of his self—his self as it truly is rather than how we might otherwise project our personalities upon him.[19] This is key in understanding how Pannenberg has reoriented discussions about God, incorporating history back into theological discussion. In the text that brought him theological fame, he writes:

> No one comes to the knowledge of God by his own reason or strength. This is not only true about the knowledge of God, but about other experiences we have. The divinely revealed events and the message that reports these events brings man to a knowledge he would not have by himself. And these events do have transforming power.[20]

The Holy is not something we perceive initially in our feelings or understand in our conflating human personality with God. Rather, the Holy, God's own self, reaches out to meet us, a thought in keeping with the biblical testimony, not least the first use of "holy" in Exodus 3.[21] This is a key distinction in holistic human formation. Rather than dividing the world into the holy, where God is present, and the secular, where God is not, understanding the being of God as holy itself is essential to understanding our encounter with the holy and our experiences in seeking God in this world.

Pannenberg contrasts the understanding of religious experiences in the proposals of Friedrich Schleiermacher and Rudolf Otto. Otto rejected Schleiermacher's existential understanding of piety as being "a mere self-feeling which is connected with the concept of God only indirectly by means of a conclusion from a cause."[22] Religious awareness is, instead, "oriented primarily and directly to an object outside myself."[23] Otto proposed the concept of the holy as a better way of understanding the common feature in religions. For Otto, however, the idea of holy as "set apart" or "separated" dominated his understanding of the religious perception, with the holy being defined as a contrast to the experience of the secular. Pannenberg notes, however, that "the concept of the holy shares with that of the *universum* the defect that it names not the concrete object of religious experience but the general sphere to which this is subordinated in reflection."[24] While emphasizing a seemingly less subjective understanding of religion, Otto relegates religious experience to its own sphere. This is now a decided trend within an understanding of religious experience, and a move Pannenberg is heartily against.[25]

If we insist on separating the holy from the secular parts of our experiences, our perceived distance from God is only overcome in the *cultus*.[26] Even though the distance is still dependent on God as the source of reconciliation, the *cultus* brings engagement with God into human control. "As we try to master the conditions of life in our dealings with the world," Pannenberg writes, "we do so also in our dealings with the power which meets us concretely in worldly forces."[27] In this way, by attempting to master physical and spiritual realities, religious people can actually be in opposition to the divine reality by engaging in the very definition of Pannenberg's understanding of sin.

Sin is the attempt to assert one's own ego upon another, or especially upon the Absolute.[28] The encounter with the holy in light of God's revelation is not limited to the *cultus*, as if God is dependent on our sometimes earnest, sometimes devious, attempts to encompass the all-encompassing reality.[29] Rather, "in our religious dealings with the Absolute, the true Infinite, the Infinite always meets us in the medium of worldly experience and its finite contents. It is important that Christian theology, too, should describe and discuss this fact."[30] The system of religion does not delimit the work of God. There may be overlaps of concern, but God's concern and his influence reaches far beyond the operational closure of a given system and even beyond the environment as a whole. Whereas systems, in effect, divvy up the effective sphere of control to different "gods," the creation narrative itself establishes the idea that God is the god of all systems, and limited by none of them.

God met Moses in the midst of the world, in the midst of Moses's vocation as a shepherd. God told Moses the steps to take in order to participate in a discussion with God, but these steps were part of God's reaching out, his embrace of Moses into his presence, a liberating embrace. This suggests a decided difference between "the biblical religion of revelation and all other religions."[31] This difference is emphasized in the first chapters of Romans, in which Paul seeks to take Jewish arguments against pagan religions and use them to judge Jewish aspects of religion. When the incorruptible Infinite is constructed or managed by corruptible things there is an attempt at human domination and control. God moves outside of this control, making himself known in history, in the reality of the finite world. God is likewise not limited by this revelation in the finite, or the objects he uses to represent his being. He undercuts attempts at control through the patterns he establishes. Yet, it is easy to fall back into a limited system of religion and take cues from this system.[32]

The religious tendency is to depict "the power of God according to the image of corruptible things and thus confuse God with his Creatures" (Rom. 1:25).[33] In separating so sharply the holy from the secular, the holy is reduced, made distinct only as it is defined by the overarching reach of the secular. "Identification of the divine power with one sphere of its manifestation always means restriction to one aspect of worldly experience," Pannenberg writes.[34] That is to say, seeing God as a religious topic embeds God in an environment of systems, where each preserves its own communication. God is separated out from the economic and political systems. In the revelation of God, however, the Holy opens itself up to participation in every sphere of life.

The continuing human tendency, beginning even in Exodus, is to take the name of God and form an understanding of his image in which devotion could be offered—but only, it seems, as a means of asserting a form of domination over the deity, seeking "magical control over the deity."[35] The systems seek to lord over the Lord, thus a tension develops within religion itself, as there is a push by the systems to restrict God and a push by God that denies the systems such control. Pannenberg writes that "this kind of attempt at control is not just a marginal phenomenon in religious life but so permeates religious practice in all its forms that polemically corruption of the relationship with God seems to characterize actual religious practice as a whole."[36] God will not be subsumed within the operational boundaries of a religious system that operates in a given environment. God makes claims for the whole of an environment. As Pannenberg emphasizes, "Misusing the relation to God so as to gain control over God with a view to self-security is always a perversion of faith."[37]

This misuse does not only pervert our faith, it perverts our relations with each other, with religious control and dominating religious hierarchy undermining open fellowship even as it promises holy pursuits. Rather than relationships built on trust—fellowship—people construct relationships built on control, thus embedding oppressing within categories that may otherwise speak of liberation (i.e., salvation). Pannenberg writes:

> A personal relationship can endure only as a relationship of trust, that is, only in respect before the uncomfortable personal character of one's fellowman. Yet, in striving to safeguard themselves, men repeatedly destroy the relationship with their closest companions. The same is true of man's relationship with God, with the counterpart toward which our question about the unity of reality and about the meaning of our existence is ultimately directed. This relationship is also destroyed when a person tries to replace trust with security. Yet men strive to extend the realm of their control even—indeed, exactly—to their ultimate concern. Man's religions are thoroughly characterized by the striving for security and by the effort to get hold of the deity and his saving power. This striving takes its point of departure in the religious man's grasping the infinite in something finite.[38]

This narrowed, system-limited version of holy has no bearing on the truly holy, which is God's self as his self, and thus demands our self in whole openness to God and to others, not our legalistic performance.[39] In Christian understanding, God is revealed to humanity—demonstrating power and perspective—in the process of salvation history.[40] Christianity, at its core, rejects the idea that God is one among the other gods, to be included in a diverse pantheon of varying responses to a shared pursuit of mythic wholeness. Humanity does not create God and define holiness. God reveals what holiness is for this world by revealing his self to others. God begins by revealing his self without beginning or end and as creator of this world

For Pannenberg, holiness is the key quality which characterizes the infinite as revealed by God. Holiness is who God is and is expressed as infinity.

Pannenberg places his main discussion of God's holiness within his section on God's infinity, seeming at first to prioritize the one under the other. Yet, this is more of a methodological issue rather than ontological, for as he writes, "Infinity is not a biblical term for God."[41] It is a convenient term to gather together the implied attributes of his eternity, omnipotence, and omnipresence.[42] "The confession of God's holiness," he writes, "is also closely related to the thought of his infinity, so closely, indeed, that the thought of infinity as God's infinity needs the statement of his holiness for its elucidation."[43] The extent of God is the extent of God's self as self, without limit or boundary or demarcated spheres of control. God is all in all. God is infinite in his being as God.

Thus, for humanity the holy is an issue of our being. The holy is threatening precisely because it is the power of God's identity who has chosen, in spite of the corruption, to reach out to this world, to transcend the supposed boundaries by entering into the environment. God is not otherworldly but continually manifested in the midst of what he created. The holy is God's being, as eternal self, which goes out into this world.[44] We are confronted by God, and in that encounter, we become fully aware of our finitude and the gap between our attempts to overcome our nonidentity. The finite is ontologically overwhelmed by the infinite. This can easily evoke despair or even dissolution. To approach humanity, then, God initiated patterns of relationship that were intended to orient people in ways they could encounter God. This initiation reached its culmination in the sending of the Son as a human, born in this world, showing the world what holiness truly is and how we can experience it.

Jesus is thus not the expression of God's love in contrast to the Father's holiness. This is a false division, asserting theological definitions as priorities over the divine essence. Jesus, as fully God, is the expression of God's love and God's holiness. To see Jesus is to see God's holiness, his identity, for what it is revealed to be. This was the continuing revelation of God's earlier revelation. Pannenberg writes, "The power of the holy, which is a threat to life in its destructive force, invades the human world in order to incorporate it into its own sphere. Thus Yahweh elects Israel to participation in his holiness: 'You shall be holy; for I the Lord your God am holy' (Lev. 19:2)."[45] This election is not about separating from God's creation, or to be removed from this world of profane physical corruption, a lifting out and away from what is common, and mean, and flesh. That was considered heresy by early Christians, not true knowledge of God at all. The election by God is an election *into* new life, an invitation of holy to the holy, to be with God as he is himself, in his future and in our present.[46] Our selves with God's self, in his eternity.

Pannenberg follows Plotinus in understanding eternity as an expression of "the presence of the totality of life."[47] Pannenberg describes it this way,

"Life for him was the enduring self which always has the whole present to it, not one thing at one time, another at another, but the whole simultaneously as undivided perfection."[48] Eternity is thus not about time at all, but rather is concerned with fullness of being, "the completed totality of life."[49] The eternity of God is the source of being, he is wholly himself in himself.[50] God's holiness is his self, his identity as a totality of fullness is both the hope and the terror of an incomplete human, who has no inherent identity but is continually confronted with the reality of incompleteness, something the human ego strives against in various forms.

In striving against this incompleteness, in experiencing such despair, people find meaning within the systems as systems, participating in the patterns of validation and oppression each system maintains for its own *autopoiesis*. The systems promise a sense of self, even as this selfhood is not substantive but serves only as yet another element of the system communicating itself. They give a *sense* of infinity as they promise a *scope* of reality within their operations. However, a system can only promise within its limited reach, all-encompassing a rather small pond indeed. This finite scope cannot extend across the whole of space or time. As the source of being, it is only God's self that provides a true self to each other in a wholly coherent way. Any attempt to derive selfhood from something or someone besides God results in judgment.

Judgment is a reality of human incompleteness that cannot exist apart from God's existence.[51] In this we continue to see the reality of God's holiness—his very identity as it is in himself—open up in love to his creation. Pannenberg writes:

> But beyond every threat of judgment the holiness of God also means hope of new and definitive salvation. In spite of human sin, God is faithful to his election. His holiness finds expression here, the difference between his attitude and ours: "For I am God and not man, the Holy One in your midst, and I will not come to destroy." (Hos. 11:9)[52]

Holiness is thus also the antithesis of judgment. It is inclusion into the life of Life itself that is God's self. Be holy, God commands, for our own sake. He reveals himself and invites others into that which transcends the systems and integrates people back together. The systems are not wrong in their existence but in their isolation and presumption of status and meaning. They are incoherent. God is not reactionary in response, even though humanity provokes self-destruction and social conflicts.[53] The human ego closes itself off or seeks domination over others in such experiences. Rather than closing himself off from an untrustworthy people as a person might, God's holiness acts in contrast to the human ego, choosing continued openness, continued exocentric fellowship, even as this, for the sake of the people, entailed certain initial rules for interaction. God, in his holiness, in his very self, continued to love, as an inherent reflection of his true holiness.

In God, holy and love are the same, not paradoxically interpenetrating, but unified in God's self.[54] God is love. God is holy. God is eternal. "Thus the holiness of God both opposes the profane world and embraces it, bringing it into fellowship with the holy God."[55] God's name is Holy, and it is this holiness that is also the quality of his kingdom that comes. "The holiness of God," Pannenberg writes, "which the high-priestly prayer of Jesus invokes (John 17:11), is the basis of the request that believers will be kept in fellowship with him."[56] God's love for the world is a complete reflection in unity with his holiness that reaches out, in exocentric fullness, to draw others from their incomplete state of isolation and into fellowship with God and with others. We are drawn by love into the holiness.[57] The holiness awakens our awareness of love and draws us to seek out infinity. Deep calls to deep.[58] God's love and God's holiness are inclusive, seeking fellowship, and his anger burns only when there are clear indications that this inclusion is being sidetracked by sin or by ego.[59]

God desires to be near, not distant. God continues to reach out in exocentric holiness through his love, to draw us back into the sphere of his being. This "reaching out" was first communicated in the covenant with Israel, the people of God who were to take hold of his promises, being formed as his people—whole and trustworthy. God's holiness was revealed in an indirect way, through the Law and the Prophets, expressing his values, his goals, his reality as giving life to all, and definition to the cosmos. This indirect revelation was likewise shown through his actions in history, revealing he is not as concerned with direct statements humans could misinterpret or abuse, but rather he proves himself in his actions that his holiness—his self—is of a certain sort.[60] God is indeed trustworthy, even when other people are not, and his revelation expresses this commitment to promise and commitment to people in holistic ways that provide a substantive hope for all.

GOD IS TRUSTWORTHY

Whereas Pannenberg was seemingly content to propose a methodology and construct a coherent theological system that reflects this method, Moltmann's emphasis has steered toward theological integrity. He does not have an interest in a comprehensive theology for its own sake, and thus his major works have approached theology from certain lenses, what he calls "contributions" to a particular systematic theme. While his overall contributions are well worth considering—indeed liberation is a significant theme throughout his writings—in this study I am going to take an unusual step of focusing on his more recent works, those published well after his last "contribution," *Experiences in Theology*. I am doing so for two reasons. First, because in my book *The Transformative Church* I reviewed his major works and highlighted his coherent, liberative ecclesiology. This text is a continuation and companion to that one. Second, Moltmann's more recent works are not necessarily breaking new ground in the ways his earlier ones were; rather he continues to hone his expressed theology and emphasize his developed priorities, often implicitly responding to criticism or explicitly connecting it to current events. That makes his recent works very important as self-summaries and indications of what he has sharpened over the decades.

Moltmann believes theology should have integrity with revelation. No less, it should also have integrity with our experiences in this world and our calling for this world. Thus, theology is also exhortation, a calling to the church that orients the church in transformative ways.[61] Good theology leads to rightly oriented participation. As Kathryn Tanner notes, "one's understanding of God and the world influences one's understanding of the rights and responsibilities one has toward others."[62] Wrong theology leads to disoriented expressions. Or, likewise, theological expressions that may once have been helpful for a given context may later undermine understanding what God is doing in other contexts. This becomes clear in church history where many abusive practices began with positive goals, then over time became disoriented. Debates about salvation later became divisions about God's favor, thus justifying uses of power to control the supposed outcasts. Debates about discipline later justified rigid divisions between laity and clergy, and sharply limited participation in ministry roles. Debates about the Eucharist turned love feasts into food fights.

In many ways, social oppression becomes embedded within ecclesial practices that deploy systems-oriented patterns.[63] The methods become theologized, speaking back into God, even as God has sought to confront such methods. The systems lend their support to this process, and like the serpent by the tree, speak smooth words of wise-sounding counsel. While seeming to offer advantage and fulfillment—the promise of the world systems—it really is anonymizing of our personhood. We are but cogs in the systems, even the religious system. The immanence of death always looms. Humanistic and materialistic approaches lead to what Moltmann calls "a diminished life."[64] No matter our importance in the systems of this world, we are in fact easily replaced. Moltmann continues, "A life that has forgotten God is a life without transcendence, a life without any light shed from above." The reality of Christian history shows how a person need not be ignorant of Jesus to have forgotten God.[65]

When we serve a God who is not the God as revealed in Scripture, we have forgotten the God who is, replacing God with idols. Such idols lead us into patterns of dysfunction even as we are convinced we are pursuing life.[66] Such a life is a mirage, a drinking of dust instead of water. Oppressors are dust drinkers. They are oppressed by their oppressing and need liberation. They need a life freed from isolated spheres of autopoietic activity, each with their own lords and their own conception of value. When everyone seeks to be lord, everyone competes for preeminence, while at the same time misunderstanding their actual role in and for this world. "There is so much unlived, unloved, even sick life that has failed and is lived without any point," Moltmann writes.[67]

The confession of YHWH as Lord is all-encompassing and defining for our sense of self and our interactions in this world. "Believers, lovers, and the hopeful take their bearings from the living God and, in their closeness to God, experience life in its fullness."[68] The comprehensive nature of the law given to Moses is only a beginning of such expressed understanding. Jesus includes this law within his own testimony, expanding it beyond the boundaries of containment with the overarching law of Love. This love is a love of life, with life, for life, the Spirit of Life drawing us into the life of God and the life of God pouring out in, with, and for us. "God," Moltmann writes, "draws to the divine self the people who are hungry for life."[69] So, Moltmann's theology is a theology of hope while also a theology of life, refusing to separate theology into a narrow pursuit of orthodoxy, incorporating themes of orthopathy and orthopraxy alongside. "What I wish to do," he explains, "is to present a transcendence that does not suppress and alienate our present life but that liberates and gives life a transcendence from which we do not need to turn away, but that fills us with the joy of life."[70]

The Christian experience of life is the Trinitarian experience of God. This begins with the experience of "undeserved and unexpected grace in the encounter with Christ and fellowship with him" and through "faith in Christ their life in the Trinity begins."[71] Such grace is a liberating grace, a way of being in this world that liberates the victims of sin and the perpetrators of sin, drawing them into the community of God, and by the very nature of this, into community with each other.[72] The theological awareness of God's work in Christ—"the brother in humiliation and suffering"—awakens us to a new pattern of living: our self is understood in light of God's Trinitarian self with expressive implications.[73] Awareness, then, must derive from the revelation of God by God, rather than starting with established definitions about what a god must be and seeing how the God of the Bible fits into these. Because the "immanence of the transcendent God brings all created things to their self-transcendence" the encounter with God involves a personal transformation if it is to be a truly Christian theology.[74] The triune God is the God of promise and empowerment; a participation with this God invokes the whole of self and the whole of one's life. We do not truly know God otherwise.

Who then is this biblical God? It is the God who "goes out of Godself and loves the beings God has created."[75] Rather than being the unmoved mover who attracts, God initiates movement in God's own self, the "self-moved Mover." With Pannenberg, Moltmann prefers Plotinus in regards to eternity, a fullness that separates from time while filling time, proceeding out of God and being into God, "like the water, which, in a Roman fountain, flows from basin to basin, from a single source."[76] There is no contrast between life and eternity, as if one demands the loss of the other, defining one through negating the other "by way of reciprocal exclusion."[77] The Spirit of God, the giver of Life, is continually outpouring into creation while never departing from the fullness of the presence of God, from being God in full. Eternity enters into time and time is drawn into eternity, deep calling to deep.

In all interactions the "Trinitarian persons offer one another reciprocally the inviting space for movement in which they can develop their own eternal livingness."[78] They relate to each other and are the living space for each other, neither closed off to each other nor even to the world. The Spirit works as the Spirit is. Which means that "the open Trinity is the inviting environment for the whole redeemed and renewed creation, which for its own part then becomes the environment for the divine indwelling."[79] This panentheistic emphasis is key for Moltmann's theological reciprocity between God and the world, God with us, and then us with each other. Such panentheism, however, must be considered within the scope of Moltmann's fully formed Trinitarian insights, especially his conception of the Holy Spirit. Moltmann's still-uniquely substantive discussions about the Spirit radically informs his theological project in a way that makes any discussion of his overall theology deficient without touching on his pneumatology. Indeed, he considers *The Living God and the Fullness of Life* as the continuation of *The Spirit of Life* and the *Source of Life*, taking up those ideas and bringing together themes from throughout his theological project as a way of offering his most mature expression of his conclusions.[80] Moltmann's theology is now thoroughly pneumatological and, as such, also more fully Trinitarian in developed scope than almost any other theological proposal arising from the Christian West.

GOD IS INVOLVED

The emphasis on beginning with the God of the Bible along with a developed pneumatology leads Moltmann to critique the classic attributes of God, offering an alternative to Greek metaphysical foundations.[81] He asks, "What has 'the Father of Jesus Christ' to do with Jupiter, the father of the Roman gods, in whose name Christ was crucified?"[82] In this question, Moltmann echoes the underlying declaration of Tertullian to resist beginning with Greek philosophy and try to fit Christian theology into its scope and terms.[83] This is not, again, anti-intellectualism, but a pursuit of coherence in light of the particularity of YHWH as the defining subject, not one god among a philosophical pantheon of potential claimants for the substance of divinity. God does not need to prove divinity to philosophy or philosophers, rather "I AM" defines both the divine self and divine actions in God's own terms. This is vital for the present consideration as how we live is shaped by who and what we define as characterizing the divine.

Moltmann begins a discussion on the characteristics of God with the topic of immutability. Immutability emphasizes God's consistency in contrast to changeableness, with change being classically understood in terms of potential deficiency. This trait came out of a desire to establish trust. We cannot trust that which is changeable. God is in fact trustworthy. But on what do we establish this trust? His nature or his identity? God as an object of divinity or God as the divine subject? These might, in classical understanding, be seen as synonymous. Yet, for Moltmann, the distinction is important because God as subject is truly free as God. "Immutability," he writes, "is an attribute of the *theion*, the divine substance. If we take it literally, there is no such thing as a *deus immutabilis*—an immutable God—but merely a *divinitas immutabilis*, an immutable divinity."[84]

Rather than immutability, which Moltmann calls a label of ancient physics, we should speak of God's faithfulness. Such faithfulness can incorporate and include those curious moments where God himself changes his intended course of action or even "repents" about an action.[85] God in his freedom can do what God wants to do, and it is not an anthropomorphism to highlight God's relational or volitional transitions. The nature of humanity as the image of God brings God's revelation within the scope of human understanding, while not suggesting God is changeable in the same ways that humanity is susceptible to change. The weakness or corruptibility of humans in changing—changefulness in light of the systems—is not God's changefulness. Rather, as Lord of creation, God is free in his faithfulness, a consistency in which God is free to be faithful in the midst of an active engagement with this world.

Second, Moltmann addresses the attribute of impassibility. In classical conception, the divine substance must be seen as incapable of suffering or it would not be divine.[86] This emphasis primarily reflects how human emotional responses are reactive to contexts and, because of this, reveal lack of control or inadequacy of self. To be without needs or passions is to always be in control. God is, by definition, always in control. Moltmann would not, it seems, dispute this statement in and of itself, but the statement is laden with assumptions about what constitutes control over the self and the environment. As discussed earlier in this chapter, God is not vulnerable to a loss of self.

God retains fullness of being as Being Godself. It is precisely because of this, then, that God can risk his self in ways that might make a human vulnerable to identity distortion or loss. Such loss reflects status within a given system, but God is not within the systems, so cannot be judged or measured by them. The fear of emotions should not then be a concern for theology nor are such emotions mere anthropomorphisms. They are part of the revelation of God who seeks intimacy, and intimacy always involves emotional interaction, even the experience of suffering.

The distortion of the passions should not assume that the passions themselves are outside of God's image. God is love. God thus loves. This is more easily accepted, as love is both positive and more easily intellectualized as a definition of God. Suffering, another experience of the world, is more difficult. Suffering is not itself an ontological category but an experience of a broken world. It is precisely for this reason theologians have been insistent about God's impassibility, as suffering suggests vulnerability to this world.[87] Such a suggestion is, of course, the very scandal of the passion. Christ suffers on the cross. Christ is God. God suffers both in and with Christ.[88] For Moltmann, then, this experience of suffering must be included in a doctrine of God; any attempt otherwise would "end up in a sum of contradictions."[89] Instead, "Christian theology must discover God in Christ's passion, and must think of Christ's passion in God."[90] How is this possible in light of preconceived assumptions about the divine nature? It is not possible. Moltmann thus suggests discarding the Aristotelian notion of divine impassibility and replacing it with Abraham Heschel's concept of *"God's pathos."*[91]

God's interaction with humanity precedes the mission of the incarnation through the presence of the Shekinah. God is a fellow traveler with Israel, participating in the victories and associating with the sufferings of the people. Whether or not the divine should be allowed to experience such interactions is not necessarily a concern for the God who is and does. This is a key issue as emphasizing a totality of *apatheia* in God conveys a certain pattern of what holiness is and should be for us.[92] Moltmann writes, "In the sphere of the divine *apatheia*, the wise human being will become an unshakeable and untouchable sovereign soul. In the sphere of God's pathos, the human being will become a *homo sympatheticus*, a loving person capable of suffering, a life-affirming person capable of participation."[93] The holiness of God that we are to model is a holiness of exocentric reciprocity, engaged and open to each other, in our joys and in our hurts, an exocentric sympathy that is modeled by the passion of Christ on the cross.

If we remove suffering from God, we deny the reality of Christ's experience on the cross. The early Christians knew this was a dangerous teaching, calling it scandalous. Yet, the scandal was tamed by theological massaging. Christian theology has been much more willing to dance with Docetism or

Arianism than acknowledge the experience of God's suffering in light of preconceived definitions about divine substance. Doing this, however, has led to an apathetic church and an apathetic people, for whom suffering is ignored or judged, presumed distance of affect incorporated even in supposedly good works.[94] Harvey Cox calls this apathy "the key form of sin in today's world."[95] He adds:

> For Adam and Eve, apathy meant letting a snake tell them what to do. It meant abdicating what theologians have called the *gubernatio mundi*, the exercise of dominion and control over the world. For us it means allowing others to dictate the identities with which we live out our lives.

The loving God loves and invites love. The loving God experiences suffering and promises hope. God is a relational God and real relationships involve actual engagement, real reciprocity of the whole self, real love. The experience of the Cross involved a wide experience of suffering, the Son on the cross, and the Father enduring the Son on the cross.[96] "People who are able to love are also prepared to suffer," Moltmann writes, "for they lay themselves open to the experience of others."[97] God in his freedom is, in fact, "a being rich in relationships," and engages men and women in the very depths of their lives, deeper than the systems and more thoroughly. Such a relationship is liberating precisely because of its openness and freedom. It is supremely personal—personalizing. The God who experiences suffering is the God of promise, the God who is not left in suffering nor leaves others in suffering, but opens people's lives up to the wideness of God's mercy and patience and compassion, a rediscovery of true life in its fullness.

In continuing his reevaluation of divine attributes, Moltmann considers omnipotence, asking "Is God Almighty?" Whereas "impassibility" is a questionable biblical concept, the Bible repeatedly utilizes the *idea* of "almighty" in describing God's ability to accomplish that which he wants to accomplish.[98] However, as Judith Krawelitzki reminds us, "There is no Hebrew equivalent for the word 'almighty.'"[99] The prevalence of this word in English translations provides a shorthand interpretation that then carries its own assumed meaning about God's power and our application of it, not unlike how the term "holy" is often misunderstood, then misapplied as a sort of religious control. The question with "almighty" is how the idea of God's *capability* is understood in coming to terms with God's method and application of power. Moltmann here makes use of Pannenberg's phrase "All-Determining Reality," as the essential definition of God's omnipotence, which is also God's rule.[100] This emphasis orients the possession and application of power in terms of God's mission rather than in terms of God's dominance.

As God is the one who rules, God is presumably free, but as kings, queens, and parents know, absolute rule is actually limiting. If God *must* rule, God is not free, and his lordship determines his identity. God is responsible for all, and the highest in the hierarchy of wielded power. The Lord then has a lord, and this lord is the definition of power. "Power is life," Moltmann writes, "weakness is death." So, the image of God as almighty brings his followers into representative rule. God rules; his people rule as representatives of his rule. This is the way of expressed and experienced reality, constraining even God. There are some who rule and some who are ruled. There's no use complaining about it.

Moltmann argues, however, that God is not determined but is determining, even over Godself. The theology that develops out of the category of "almighty" actually leads us away from God's ultimate freedom as God, and thus can be misleading and orient theology in a wrong direction. "The almighty God is not the living God," he writes about this problem, "for the living God has power over Godself first all."[101] The idea that God is not defined as almighty suggests a foray into Process Theology. Moltmann's purpose with his critique—which is key for the theme of liberation—does not lead in this direction. He affirms God's capability over all, but in a way that maintains real freedom.

God as "almighty" has often been understood as the ultimate oppressor.[102] Atheism is then pursued as a liberating move. People derive fundamental liberation as they perceive their subjugation to a religious system and seek to make space for themselves. God is not, however, revealed as oppressor in Scripture; he is revealed as liberator. God's determining, first of all, as Godself is the key element in the biblical understanding of God. It is, Moltmann writes, "decisive for the Israelite and Christian experience of God, for it is only in this way that the love of God can be understood."[103] God's primary mode of interaction is not power; it is relationship. Power defines two sides of experience: those with power over those without power. God as Most-Powerful-Power would, then, be the pinnacle of power always on the side of the experience of those with power. God is the victor in the ultimate bracket of reality. God always wins. God is on the side of those who win. Oppressors, then, are given implicit validation as gods within their own sphere of applied power. Humanity reigns over the earth, over creatures, and battles over who reigns humanity in manifold ways.

In the narrative of creation and in the mission of Christ, however, we find that this is fundamentally wrong. The creative act for God involves God's own initiative to create in a certain way, a way revealed as relational, full of patience, expressed in love, and enabling reciprocity. It is in this perceived weakness—what is often judged as weakness by the systems in this world—that God exhibits his enduring power. "God is not," Moltmann writes, "on the side of the mighty as 'the Almighty'—God is on the side of the weak, as the liberator who is in solidarity with them."[104] God's message to Job is to trust that God is capable and in control: an important message to those who are suffering. Jesus did not come as the conquering ruler but as the suffering servant. In entering into this world, God determines God's own actions and in revealing himself in the person and mission of Jesus, God determines his power as being on the side of the losers. The cross is loss. In the relationship of love, within loss, God creates space for others.[105] Such others do not have to pursue distance from God or community to find themselves in their own sphere of applied power. God is the safe place where trust can be restored.

God limits Godself in the expression of creation, respecting the other as other, working within the context of space, time, and autonomy of world systems. God is truly free, expressing this freedom in relationality rather than rule, inviting and making space for others to be free. God rejects the mighty in their attempts to assert their power or control. God's "weakness" is thus revolutionary in conceiving radical transformation and realignment within the sphere of God's relational invitation. God's power is asserted over the systems but negating their understanding of power. God does not negate; he invites those who seek the fullness of life itself in relationship with the truly living God. God's power is coordinated with his weakness as the cross moves into resurrection, and God's faithfulness is displayed in raising up those who have experienced defeat. This power is what Jose Bonino calls "his 'justice' in action" which is used "in defense of the weak, judgment of the unjust, protection of the powerless, and strengthening of those who he has given a mission."[106] Those who would truly be liberated align themselves with this God, thus with the God who worked through the cross, and only then in the kind of power displayed in new life.

The fourth category Moltmann addresses is that of omnipresence. Moltmann opens his discussion by quoting Psalm 139, offering it as a testimony to God's omnipresence. The idea that God is everywhere is commonly used to scare kids straight: "Jesus is always watching!" Indeed, I have a friend who talks about their well-meaning Sunday school teacher using imagery about final judgment in which we will all be given full replays of our lives as we stand in the crowd with others. All the happy and all the naughty scenes will be shown for all to see. Jesus forgives us but the cost is our future embarrassment. We are presumably to ask ourselves in a moment of temptation, "Do you want *that* on the jumbotron?" God becomes the ultimate surveillance state. He is the totalitarian ruler, a supreme potentate. This was an assumption of divinity, of a supreme god, which is precisely the image that Scripture disputes.

The image of Psalm 139 is not a police image or divine chaperone, rather it is an image of constancy and care. We are not crushed, we are sustained.

Attempts to negate or dismiss God certainly can turn God's presence into a perceived negative, but the reality of God's presence is one of being present *with* us. Presence is God's divine love language.[107] "Omnipresence . . . belongs to the divine subject, who desires to be present everywhere to all the beings God has created."[108] God is present even where God seemingly can't be present, those places of darkness, suffering, abandonment, even hell. "Because Christ has suffered the hell of separation from God, there is no longer any hell in which God is not present."[109] The only place, in fact, where God is not present is in the forces that orchestrated the suffering and death of Christ.[110] God is not present in the assertions of assumed power that seek to co-opt his intentions in being present with all people, valuing them, loving them, inviting them to fullness. This is why oppressors need liberation, why they need hope. Those who seek to be gods independent from God are the ones most distant from God. "Forgive them," Jesus still says, "for they know not what they do." The oppressors need forgiveness for they do not know what they are doing. God seeks their presence, but they are seeking somewhere other than God for meaning.

If God is present to everyone and everything, then it seems a natural correspondence that God is omniscient. God's pattern of relational presence, indeed, leads to a correspondence of knowledge, but not in the fashion of an eternal vault of security footage.[111] Moltmann thus embraces open theism more explicitly, arguing that "we now say that the living God does not know everything in advance, because God has no wish to do so."[112] God is not subject to a super-essential category of knowledge by which he must know everything in every moment to be divine. God is free, and this freedom involves the ability to not know as much as it does the ability to know. Here, the terminology becomes complicated by extracting our experience of knowledge into our understanding of God's reality. While this seems to be Moltmann's weakest argument in this section in relation to biblical testimony—which indicates God's divine knowledge in various universal ways—it continues his interest in reassessing how terms and ideas are used for the purpose of oppression.

Rather than seeing omniscience as a kind of *Encyclopedia Galactica*—or *Hitchhiker's Guide to the Galaxy* for the less sophisticated—which contains all the possible amount of facts available, it may be better to understand God's omniscience in terms of being a divine combination of all-wise and all-present.[113] Pannenberg notes, "When we speak of God's knowledge we mean that nothing in all his creation escapes him. All things are present to him and are kept by him in his presence."[114] God is not an absolute collector of facts who can dominate competition like a lawyer or scientist. The decisive trait of knowledge for God is that of promise. Like how Moltmann's pneumatology gives texture to his use of panentheism, so too does Moltmann's eschatology provide a substantive resource to how he understands God's omnipotence and omniscience.

Indeed, the idea of promise is central to his whole theological project.[115] God will fulfill his promise, and this is linked to providence rather than a passive awareness. God is not a Watcher, God is Father.[116] Promise "indicates God's intention, to which we can trust ourselves, as well as the trends in history, which we are supposed to realize."[117] This involves a participatory dialog, a conversation-act. The exocentric God invites exocentric reciprocity in return. "It is the advance knowledge of the living God intended for a cooperation with those God has created, especially with human beings, God's image, for a shared future."[118] This is the hope and this is the experience of liberation from both sides, drawing the oppressed and oppressors together in a healing community with the living triune God.[119] It is in this kind of liberation that real freedom is experienced.[120]

CONCLUSION

God is. God revealed himself to the world and reveals himself even still. We encounter this revelation in Scripture, where we learn of God's persistent interaction with humanity, despite the persistence of human ingenuity to try to avoid dealing with who God is and how God has made us to function in fullness. God is holy. This holiness defines God's nature as God, not a term that is first defined and then applied to God. What holiness is takes shape in the nature of God's being and expression. God created. He created all that is and is lord of all that is. God is outside of time but interacts within time, a history of interaction that comprises our past and present, orienting toward God's future. As such, our encounter with God is mediated by our context of time and space, not as a limitation of God but as a reality of our own limitations.

We do not exist as timeless, de-contextualized, neutral observers of God's being and God's work. The revelation of God is eminently translatable, but like with any work of translation, there is a tension between languages, experiences, and understanding. We can translate the Scripture into every human tongue, and each such translation brings out ever more nuance, while also being limited by interpretation. We are not limited to words on a page, fortunately, as the counselor that Jesus promised is not Scripture but the Spirit, who teaches us everything and reminds us of all that Jesus said. Scripture is an essential part of this teaching and reminding, but we also have the Spirit's work in tradition, in sanctified reasoning, in our experience with God's presence.

We also have our own narratives that intersect with God's grand narrative, and in this we come to Scripture and God's comprehensive revelation with different questions, different hang-ups, and different crises. That is why while the history of theology offers us wonderful tools for guidance and interpretation, we sometimes must confront how language about God has become unmoored from its original purposes and may have lost its instructive worth. In understanding how our conception of God shapes our conception of life, ourselves and others, it becomes clear that earlier goals to describe God in certain ways have led to problems in history, leading Christian leaders to incorporate patterns of hierarchy, authoritarianism, triumphalism, and, indeed, oppression within the Christian testimony. This is not the revelation of God, but the wayward way that language shows its insufficiency in light of God's eternal nature and our temporal experience.

We are thus ever drawn back to the testimony of Scripture and in prayerful reflection called to be faithful in presenting God's work and nature to our current contexts in ways that resonate with the Spirit's response to the signs of our times. In a context where Christian society has engendered systemic oppression, the task is not simply to address the symptoms, but to assess the situation at every level, being willing to go back to our core statements so as to remain faithful to God's eternal calling. As oppressing is often substantiated by misappropriated statements about God, it is important to recover language that better facilitates the kind of kingdom that God develops among us, a kingdom of love and a kingdom of life.

God does not wait for people to respond to the invitation of life, he seeks them out, drawing them toward the divine presence, and gathering them together in a community. This alluring and communal element of God's being is the topic of chapter 9, in which Sarah Coakley and Jean Vanier illuminate even more of God's liberating nature.

NOTES

1. God's response to Job beginning in Job 38 is decisive without being clarifying: "Did you make the earth?" God appreciates our asking but does not seem inclined to justify his work in this world.

2. Elizabeth A. Johnson, *Quest for the Living God: Mapping Frontiers in the Theology of God* (New York: Continuum, 2011), 13.

3. I am certainly not arguing against the place and importance of academic theology here. The tendency toward anti-intellectualism or reactionary pietism bring their own substantive forms of both dysfunction and ineffectiveness.

4. The word "challenging" can have many meanings, and World War II seems to package them together. It was a challenge for the church in its theology, in its history, in its mission, and certainly a physical challenge for all those who lived through it.

5. See M. Douglas Meeks, *Origins of the Theology of Hope* (Philadelphia: Fortress Press, 1974), 4–7.

6. See Jürgen Moltmann, *A Broad Place* (Minneapolis: Fortress Press, 2008), 105–107.

7. Lev. 11:44–45.

8. Exod. 3:5.

9. See W. Kornfeld, "קדוש‎," in *Theological Dictionary of the Old Testament*, vol. 12, ed. G. Johannes Botterweck (Grand Rapids: Eerdmans, 2003), 523.

10. Lev. 10:10.

11. Robert Jenson, "Holiness in the Priestly Writings," in *Holiness: Past and Present*, ed. Stephen C. Barton (New York: T&T Clark, 2003), 98.

12. Kornfeld, "קדוש‎," 544.

13. Mt. 1:18–21; Acts 2.

14. Otto Procksch, "ἅγιος," in *Theological Dictionary of the New Testament*, vol. 1, ed. Gerhard Kittel (Grand Rapids: Eerdmans, 1964), 89.

15. A difficulty with this phrase comes in how it is used. It may be better to understand "set apart" in terms of dedication to God's mission (i.e., Deut. 10:8), not "set apart" as separated from the world or put in contrast to it.

16. Procksch, "ἅγιος," 93.

17. *The God Who Is Triune* (Downers Grove, IL: IVP, 2007), 156, Allan Coppedge writes, "The extensiveness of the biblical data means that holiness is the first component of the essence, the *ousia*, of God's being."

18. Wolfhart Pannenberg, *Systematic Theology*, trans. Geoffrey W. Bromiley, vol. 1 (Grand Rapids: Eerdmans, 1991), 117.

19. This can be contrasted with the various pantheons of gods in Greek, Norse, or other cultures in which human strengths, foibles, desires were combined with a search for understanding both explanations of the finite and the infinite.

20. Wolfhart Pannenberg, "Dogmatic Theses on the Doctrine of Revelation," in *Revelation as History*, ed. Wolfhart Pannenberg and trans. David Granskou (New York: Macmillan, 1968), 137.

21. Which initiates a key moment in God's work of liberation, one that involves liberating the people from Egypt but with ultimately strict laws about the kind of people they were to become. It is a liberation that involves the oppressed to keep them from becoming new oppressors.

22. Pannenberg, *Systematic Theology*, 1:138. Otto, *The Idea of the Holy*.

23. Ibid., 1:138–139. Pannenberg notes that Schleiermacher's earlier understanding of religion in the *Speeches* is in contrast to the later form in *Christian Faith*, and that Otto has no issue with the earlier.

24. Pannenberg, *Systematic Theology*, 1:139.

25. See Collin Crowder, "Otto's The Idea of the Holy Revisited," in *Holiness: Past and Present*, 23–47 for a quite interesting discussion of Otto's project and the reception of him, and rejection of him, by twentieth-century theologians. While Pannenberg is not here noted, the article helps put Pannenberg's comments into a helpful historical perspective.

26. See Pannenberg, *Systematic Theology*, 1:173.

27. Ibid., 1:177.

28. "The image of the individual who takes himself or herself to be the center of his or her life aptly describes the structure of sin." Wolfhart Pannenberg, *Human Nature, Election, and History* (Philadelphia: Westminster, 1977), 26. Kam Ming Wong, *Wolfhart Pannenberg on Human Destiny* (Burlington, VT: Ashgate, 2008), 107: "Sin arises out of the tension in the interplay of two natural human drives, egocentricity and exocentricity, or, as discussed earlier, self-centeredness and openness to the world. Thus it is sin insofar as it falls into conflict with the infinite destiny of humanity, or as the ego adheres to itself rather than letting itself be inserted into a higher unity of life, beyond the individual and the community to the origin of the whole of reality. To the extent that this tension between egocentricity and exocentricity is seemingly unavoidable, sin is something that belongs to human givenness." See also Wolfhart Pannenberg, *Anthropology in Theological Perspective*, trans. Matthew J. O'Connell (Philadelphia: Westminster, 1985), 84–86. In this we can see how a religious "system" can work counter to the mission of God. This was a major element of the confrontation between Jesus and the religious leaders of the early first century. It likely still is.

29. On this tendency to demand God fit into our settings and schedules, see Chebon Kernnell, "Living Prayer, Living Worship," in *Coming Full Circle: Constructing Native Christian Theology*, eds. Steven Charleston and Elaine A. Robinson (Minneapolis: Fortress Press, 2015), 159–161.

30. Pannenberg, Systematic Theology, 1:179. Wolfhart Pannenberg, *Basic Questions in Theology: Collected Essays*, vol. 2 (Minneapolis: Fortress Press, 1971), 248: "Whoever has been gripped by God's future surely places himself, his trust, and his hope in it. But the ontological primacy of God's future over every presently existing form of human realization remains in force even here. For man will participate in the glory of God only in such a way that he will always have to leave behind again what he already is and what he finds as the given state of his world. Man participates with God not by flight from the world but by active transformation of the world which is the expression of the divine love, the power of its future over the present by which it is transformed in the direction of the glory of God." Cf. Wolfhart Pannenberg, *Faith & Reality* (Philadelphia: Westminster Press, 1977), 78–82.

31. Pannenberg, *Basic Questions in Theology v. 2*, 248.

32. Not unlike the Israelites of 1 Sam. 8:5, we want gods and kings like those other people!

33. Pannenberg, *Systematic Theology*, 1:179.

34. Ibid., 1:180; 184: "Sacred times and places restrict the deity and service of the deity to the spheres of life that are thus appointed."

35. Pannenberg, *Systematic Theology*, 1:180.

36. Ibid., 1:182.

37. Ibid.

38. Wolfhart Pannenberg, *What Is Man?* (Philadelphia: Fortress Press, 1970), 35.

39. Cf. Wolfhart Pannenberg, *The Apostle's Creed in the Light of Today's Questions* (Eugene, OR: Wipf and Stock, 2000), 24.

40. Pannenberg, *Systematic Theology*, 1:187. Pannenberg adds an important comment at the end of the chapter: "To the extent that this overcoming of the

perversion that takes place in the religious relation to God works itself out, through the consciousness of faith, in the life of Christians and the church, the human relation to God is set right by faith. But this does not protect the members of the church, as the experiences of history show, against the perversion of religion into magic." This sums up why it is so vital to come to a true understanding of the holy. There is nothing more destructive than a perverted understanding of holiness that offers only destruction and corruption in the name of service to God. And yet there is nothing more enlivening than a true encounter with the Holy, which is encounter with the very being, the very self of God himself.

41. Pannenberg, *Systematic Theology,* 1:397.

42. Cf. Dumitru Staniloae, *Orthodox Dogmatic Theology: The Experience of God* (Brookline, MA: Holy Cross Orthodox Press, 1998), chap. 8.

43. Pannenberg, *Systematic Theology,* 1:397. Stanley Grenz writes that Pannenberg "sees holiness as differing from the other three attributes, however, in that it renders the infinite a concept of the divine reality, whereas the others are concrete manifestations of God's infinity under the viewpoints of time, power, and space. In other words, the concept of infinity, which is not itself a conception of God, nevertheless becomes so in connection with the idea of holiness (or of the Holy One), which in turn implies infinity." In Stanley Grenz, *Reason for Hope: The Systematic Theology of Wolfhart Pannenberg*, 2nd edition (Grand Rapids: Eerdmans, 2005), 82.

44. Pannenberg, *Systematic Theology,* 1:398.

45. Ibid.

46. See Wolfhart Pannenberg, "The Working of the Spirit in the Creation and in the People of God," in *Spirit, Faith, and Church* (Philadelphia: Westminster John Knox Press, 1970), 24.

47. Pannenberg, *Systematic Theology,* 1:402. Moltmann, *The Living God and the Fullness of Life,* 29–30 points to Boethius in reaching a similar conclusion. On the similarity of Boethius and Plotinus on this issue, see Eleonore Stump, *Aquinas* (New York: Routledge, 2003), 500 n. 6.

48. Pannenberg, *Systematic Theology,* 1:402.

49. Ibid., 408.

50. Ibid., 410. Pannenberg writes, "God is eternal because he has no future outside himself. His future is that of himself and of all that is distinct from him."

51. Wolfhart Pannenberg, "Constructive and Critical Functions of Christian Eschatology," *Harvard Theological Review* 77, no. 2 (1984): 134: "On the one hand, the simultaneous presence of the whole content of one's life through participation in the eternal presence of God means judgment. This is because of the many self-contradictions within our lives that prevent its identity from becoming fully manifest. In the earthly history of our lives the awareness of what those self-contradictions are doing to our identity is mitigated by the temporal sequence of phases, so that we easily forget about what we promised yesterday or a year ago. In the eternal presence of our life as a whole all those contradictions will become fully evident. . . . Eternal judgment does not mean a violent reaction of a punishing God against his creatures. It rather means that the sinner is left to the consequences of his or her own behavior. In this way death is the consequence of sin, because already in

his or her separation from God the human person gets separated from the origin of life."

52. Pannenberg, *Systematic Theology,* 1:399.
53. Ibid.
54. See Ibid., 1:445–448.
55. See Ibid., 1:399.
56. Ibid., 1:399.
57. See Pannenberg, *The Apostle's Creed*, 17.
58. Psalm 42.
59. Cf. LeRon Shults, *Reforming Theological Anthropology* (Grand Rapids: Eerdmans, 2003), 74.
60. See Pannenberg, *Revelation as History*, 125–131. See also Kierkegaard, *Practice in Christianity*, 133–143.
61. I make this argument throughout my book, *The Transformative Church.*
62. Tanner, *The Politics of God*, ix.
63. This can be seen in manifold ways, from consumeristic instincts to competition between churches in a shared neighborhood.
64. Moltmann, *The Living God and the Fullness of Life*, ix.
65. While not phrased in the same way, this is the key element of John Wesley's sermon, "The Almost Christian."
66. Especially when these are idols sanctioned by theological construction, pouring the gold of philosophy or sociology or other academic disciplines into the fire and discovering the calf that comes out. To express it this way is not anti-intellectual, just as the rejection of the calf in the wilderness was not a rejection of the use of gold in decoration or worship. Cf., for example, Exod. 3:22; 20:23 and 25:11.
67. Moltmann, *The Living God*, ix.
68. Ibid.
69. Ibid., 24.
70. Ibid., x–xi.
71. Jürgen Moltmann, *Sun of Righteousness Arise!* (Minneapolis: Fortress Press, 2010), 158.
72. Moltmann, *Sun of Righteousness,* 158.
73. Cf. Timothy Ware, *The Orthodox Church*, new edition (New York: Penguin, 1991), 208. Ware writes, "Orthodoxy believes most passionately that the doctrine of the Holy Trinity is not a piece of 'high theology' reserved for the professional scholar, but something that has a living, practical importance for every Christian. The human person, so the Bible teaches, is made in the image of God, and to Christians God means the Trinity: thus it is only in the light of the dogma of the Trinity that we can understand who we are and what God intends us to be. Our private lives, our personal relations, and all our plans of forming a Christian society depend upon a right theology of the Trinity."
74. Moltmann, *Ethics of Hope*, 117.
75. Moltmann, *The Living God*, 26. It is worth noting that throughout this recent text, Moltmann seems to avoid the use of the masculine personal pronoun for God.

76. Moltmann, *The Living God*, 26–27.
77. Ibid., 27.
78. Moltmann, *Sun of Righteousness*, 154.
79. Ibid., 157.
80. Moltmann, *The Living God*, xi.
81. Cf. Staniloae, *Orthodox Dogmatic Theology*, chap. 9.
82. Moltmann, *The Living God*, 37.
83. Tertullian, *Prescription against Heretics*, 7.246.
84. Moltmann, *The Living God*, 36.
85. See, for example, Gen. 6:6; Exod. 32:12–14; 1 Sam. 15:11; 2 Sam. 24:16; 1 Chron. 21:15; Ps. 106:45; Jer. 18:8; 26:3, 13.
86. This is a very simplistic way of defining the classical usage. For a more complex analysis, see Richard E. Creel, *Divine Impassibility: An Essay in Philosophical Theology*, Reprint (Eugene, OR: Wipf & Stock, 2005), 9–12. In his analysis of multiple definitions, Creel follows Hartshorne in deciding the most adequate definition is that God "cannot be affected against his will by an outside force." This softens the meaning, making it more a matter of will than possibility. Cf. Richard Bauckham, "'Only the Suffering God Can Help': Divine Passibility in Modern Theology," *Themelios* 9, no. 3 (April 1984): 6–12. Cf. Daniel Castelo, *The Apathetic God: Exploring the Contemporary Relevance of Divine Impassibility* (Eugene, OR: Wipf & Stock, 2009). Castelo adopts Creel's definition and offers a rousing defense of *apatheia* and specifically addresses Moltmann's proposals in *The Crucified God* and *Trinity and the Kingdom* in developing his defense. While substantive, it too easily dismisses Moltmann's conceptual grounding and Scriptural influence, indeed the vast agreement given by biblical scholars, such as Richard Bauckham and John Goldingay. Castelo also ignores most of Moltmann's subsequent writings which address Castelo's concerns, especially those relate to issues of Trinitarian theology. This is again why I am utilizing Moltmann's later works, as his Christology and his pneumatology fills out his trinitarian perspective much more fully than his earlier works may have indicated. Moltmann understands the importance and meaning of *apatheia* for the early church, while seeking to find ways of speaking more adequately of God's being in our era, where we are not as concerned with passion driven whimsy as we are of rigidity and impersonal interaction. The worry in our era is not the fickleness of a ruler but the unbending rule-keeping of the bureaucracy, and that invites adaptation of our descriptions about God.
87. Moltmann, *The Living God*, 42 writes, "All that the apathy axiom says is that God is not passively delivered over to the finite worlds' fate of suffering and death."
88. Moltmann quotes John Paul II, "When sin brought forth suffering, Gods' pain found its full human expression through the Holy Spirit in the crucified Christ. Here we have a paradoxical mystery of love: in Christ God suffers." From *Dominum et vivificantem*, May 18, 1986, 41, http://w2.vatican.va/content/john-paul-ii/en/encyclicals/documents/hf_jp-ii_enc_18051986_dominum-et-vivificantem.html.
89. Moltmann, *The Living God*, 39.
90. Ibid., 40.

91. Ibid. He cites Abraham Heschel, *The Prophets*, 2 vols. (New York: Harper & Row, 1962).

92. Cf. Castelo, *The Apathetic God*, 32–38.

93. Moltmann, *The Living God*, 40.

94. One need only read the reports and testimonies about the poor houses in Victorian England. See, for instance, Jack London's first hand reports in *People of the Abyss* (London: MacMillan, 1904). Cf. Sofia Tolstoy, *The Diaries of Sofia Tolstoy*, trans. Cathy Porter (New York: Harper Perennial, 2010). I am intentionally using the contemporary understanding of apathetic here rather than classical meaning, so as to emphasize how language changes meaning and trying to assert an outdated emphasis is not helpful.

95. Cox, *God's Revolution and Man's Responsibility*, 48.

96. This thus avoids the issue of patripassianism, as it emphasizes the Father's suffering not in the pain of the cross but in the pain of watching a loved one experience suffering and death. The welcoming Father's joy upon the return of the prodigal son is a form of suffering that the elder brother lacked, who was only concerned about the justice of reward. This is a suffering of patience—a waiting for the other to find their way home—and a suffering of sadness on seeing a loved one enduring difficulties, even when the difficulties are brought on themselves. In this way, Moltmann sees the story of the prodigal as the story of the Father. He writes, "The Parable of the 'Prodigal Son' (Luke 15.11–37) is actually the Parable of the father, waiting in boundless patience. The son does everything to stop the connection to the father. He receives his inheritance as if the father were already dead. He gets the inheritance and ends up with the pigs. But the Father keeps his living space open in his house. When he sees the son from afar, he comes to him and picks him up with joy. . . . This is a parable for God's patience, His waiting and mercy and his joy in finding the lost man. But it is also a model story for parents whose children are 'lost.'" In Jürgen Moltmann, *Über Geduld, Barmherzigkeit und Solidarität* (Gütersloh: Gütersloher Verlagshaus, 2018), 14. My translation.

97. Moltmann, *The Living God*, 42.

98. Notably, this idea is prevalent in Genesis and Revelation, but especially in Job, where the NRSV utilizes the term "almighty" thirty-one times, more than uses found in the rest of the Bible combined.

99. Judith Krawelitzki, "God the Almighty?: Observations in the Psalms," *Vetus Testamentum* 64, no. 3 (2014): 434.

100. Moltmann, *The Living God*, 45. On Pannenberg's usage, see Wolfhart Pannenberg, *Theology and the Philosophy of Science*, trans. Francis McDonagh (Philadelphia: Westminster Press, 1976), 332–345. See also Pannenberg, ST 1:160–171.

101. Moltmann, *The Living God*, 44. Cf. Pannenberg, *Basic Questions in Theology*, vol. 1 (Minneapolis: Fortress Press, 2008), 156–157.

102. See Veli-Matti Kärkkäinen, *Trinity and Revelation* (Grand Rapids: Eerdmans, 2014), 301–302.

103. Moltmann, *The Living God*, 44.

104. Ibid., 47.

105. See Moltmann-Wendel and Moltmann, *God—His & Hers*, 9–10.

106. Jose Miguez Bonino, *Toward a Christian Political Ethics* (Philadelphia: Fortress Press, 1983), 96.

107. Not presents, despite what some "health and wealth" preaching may imply.

108. Moltmann, *The Living God*, 48.

109. Ibid., 49.

110. Moltmann does not refer to Mk 3:28–30, although it does seem apt here.

111. Moltmann, *The Living God*, 50: "But God's memory is not a heavenly video that mechanically records everything that happens. It is the remembering of the living God."

112. Moltmann, *The Living God*, 50. In this way, the discussion involves the now extensive debate over open theism. As this is primarily a North American argument, Moltmann should not be assessed in light of those debates, but rather his goal, again, is to reassess the terminology for the purposes of being more faithful to biblical revelation.

113. See Kärkkäinen, *Trinity and Revelation*, 300–302. Cf. Carl Sagan, *Cosmos* (New York: Ballantine Books, 2013), chap. 12.

114. Pannenberg, *Systematic Theology,* 1:379–380.

115. Moltmann's work on eschatology is, of course, extensive. In light of this discussion, see especially Jürgen Moltmann, *The Coming of God*, trans. Margaret Kohl (Minneapolis: Fortress Press, 1996), chap. 5; Jürgen Moltmann, *Theology of Hope*, trans. James W. Leitch (Minneapolis: Fortress Press, 1993), chap. 2.

116. In Marvel Comics, the Watchers are an ancient species of aliens who seek to observe civilizations throughout the universe. They have a policy of absolute noninterference.

117. Moltmann, *The Living God*, 51.

118. Ibid.

119. Pannenberg, *The Apostle's Creed,* 17 writes, "The love of one's neighbor which Jesus preached is nothing other than participation in God's own mind and activity, given beforehand to all human activity, and by which men ought to let themselves be possessed in their behavior."

120. See Moltmann, *The Living God*, 112–115.

Chapter 9

Hope with God

INTRODUCTION

Theology that purports to speak of God is very often developed within academic systems that promote frenzy, jealousies, competition, comparison, indulging of consumerism through library size, grant reception, or any other number of markers.[1] Tenure is based on such, but before tenure is even on the horizon, the very nature of procuring and sustaining a position involves a curious form of hypercompetitive collegiality. In my life, this tension between my seemingly natural (and at times indulged) bent toward contemplation has been variously challenged and subsumed by the requirements of doctoral studies and then professional tasks. I have sought to navigate my initial impulses and professional demands in pursuit of liberation as a topic and for myself while orienting with a priority of stillness, fed by contemplative retuning at every possible point.[2] Yet, oppressing is always calling to me: compete, control, demand, dismiss, dominate; curry favor for more power, influence, and attention. Indulge the frenzy of constant travel and perpetual self-publicity.

It is not enough to discipline my mind. That might offer resistance, but it results in being tossed to-and-fro, blown about as the demands of vocational advancement woo me back into the fray. My hope for stillness in the midst of it all is not through resistance or repression, depressing myself for some supposed noble goal. My hope is in a changing pattern of desire, realizing my calling in light of God's work in my life, shaping my whole being toward God, to live out the fullness of life in the midst of my various roles. In this, my hope is with a community of those gathered to pursue Christ in our contexts, not competition for the best way to talk about God *to* those who are likewise competing.

I note all of this as a way of introducing the next contributors in this constructive section, Sarah Coakley and Jean Vanier, who are theologians attentive to the passions and actions of life, calling those who walk with God into a more holistic perspective on what theology actually is in light of God's holistic revelation.[3] Sarah Coakley stands out in this book in two respects. First, she is a woman, while my other primary contributing voices are men. Second, while the other contributing voices have reached the end or are nearing the end of their life's work, she might be entering into her most influential stage, with three volumes of her planned four volume series still awaiting publication. At this point, any discussion about her overall theological contributions will be necessarily incomplete. Yet a key area of her trajectory seems well in place. This trajectory and developing methodology are key to conceiving a liberation of the oppressor. These have certainly resonated with my own quest for liberation as I have delved deeper into her works.

While Sarah Coakley is disturbing the theological production within academia, Jean Vanier was entirely outside of it and may not be readily identified as a theologian. Indeed, that was not his vocation or primary interest, and that is a big reason why he is important to include. Throughout this text, the approach has prioritized intellectual content and used this to suggest a Scriptural, historical, and theological understanding that can point toward a way of liberation for those of us caught in patterns of oppressing. Jean Vanier provides a different model of discussion. He developed liberation through reflection on life in this world and, even more important, through practice and example.

Together, Coakley and Vanier provide restorative insights to Christian theology. Coakley and Vanier remind theology it should not only be concerned with right thinking—orthodoxy. From the beginning, Christian transformation has wrestled also with right passions—orthopathy—and right actions—orthopraxy. These three elements reflect a holistic approach to human life. This holistic approach is essential if we are to provide a path toward thorough liberation for oppressors.

GOD IS ALLURING

In many respects, a theologian writing with feminist interests more conventionally writes from the perspective of the oppressed.[4] Coakley includes this interest among her perspectives; however, she is also plotting a different way to develop theological insight, critiquing theological conventions while in a position of great esteem and highly developed theological training. Coakley's experience as a scholar of early Christian and later mystical writings has led her to think about theology in the way that these early writers approached it, which, while often intellectually rigorous, was primarily established in the context of monastic life, persistent prayer, and pastoral intent. These were unified goals for these writers, and increasingly for Coakley's own approach. The pursuit of stillness and deepening understanding of God's revelation *can* go hand in hand, but only through devotional intent.

Taking up this mission in contemporary theology means pushing against the separated categories insisted on by scholars like Schleiermacher. It applies Christian theology to both content and method, arguing for an indivisible unity of expression. Coakley argues that our contemplative experiences of God reshape who we are, as well as how we encounter this world and others in it. This perspective leads to a reconception of the theological task and theological appropriation in the lives of those who pursue this task. As she puts it, "The central theme . . . is that the task of theology is always, if implicitly, a recommendation for life. The vision it sets before one invites ongoing—and sometimes disorienting—response and change, both personal and political, in relation to God."[5] It involves practice and transformation, internally and socially.

If theology is going to be something more than a contributing factor within a religious system, theology has to develop in light of its Christological impulses rather than limit itself to academic fashion or narrowed boundaries.[6] Theological studies, church practices, and lived expression of the Christian faith have increasingly diverged from each other in our contexts. In this divergence, these expressions increasingly reflect the operationally closed systems of contemporary life, the systems that instantiate patterns of oppression and resist integration or change. Theology, then, becomes a tool within these systems. This is most apparent in the academic system (departments of theology or religious studies) and the religious system (churches and the ecclesial industrial complex), while commenting on, but not transforming, the wide variety of other social systems that makes up the amalgamated self in our current societies. Theology has become specialized in its own narrow academic sphere and fragmented within the context of other systems, an anemic transversality.

Coakley offers a different way, which she calls "*théologie totale.*"[7] *Théologie totale* is itself a new approach to theology, informed by the earlier Christian writers and shaped in light of contemporary challenges and concerns.[8] Coakley's rediscovery of the holistic patterns of patristic writings, especially in Gregory of Nyssa, is the first key element of her proposed conception of the theological task, and leads her to a classic approach to theology that is not very common in our era where texts are either pastoral or academic, rarely both. Hers is not a version of radical orthodoxy that seeks a comprehensive Christian theology to dominate broader conversations, but rather is an inclusive conversation that resists being limited to separated systems or subjugated to the rules of those systems. Such a task is intellectual and ascetic, drawing in issues of orthodoxy and orthopraxy alongside an understanding that theology ultimately is reflected in and through our desires. Thus, there is an orthopathy developed along with orthodoxy and orthopraxy, offering a distinct third way between the entrenched perspectives of Left or Right, repression or libertinism. This is not a *via media*; it is rather a wholesale transformed perspective that reflects the reality of Christ's resurrection and the continuing work of the Spirit.

It suggests a theology *in via*, always in motion, including moments of transforming enlightenment and discouraging darkness, in which contemplative prayer is a formative experience of God's encounter with us.[9] Such prayer is itself a theological task, not relegated to the margins of spiritual disciplines but included within the development of a holistic theological discovery of life in all its facets. This contemplative experience derives from and feeds back into deepening practices, which reflect an ascetic encounter with the world, though certainly not in a separatist or isolating way. It is a theological version of eating healthy in a world filled with junk food. Such a task, to continue the analogy, can take the shape of dieting, which represses or rejects the appetites, or it can take the shape of a changed understanding of life and food's part in it. This loosely describes the difference between legalism—a resistance or repression—in contrast to holiness, where our minds are transformed into the pattern of Christ in our contexts.[10] The latter involves a change of desire, and it is this change that is at the core of Coakley's project, which highlights the element of sexuality (as this is a, if not *the*, featured debate in ethics these days) but does not see this as separated from any other element of life.

It is in our desires and expression of desires that we are at our most vulnerably theological. As the monastics realized, our desires express our true beliefs, those which actually drive our life course. It is not enough to have right thinking if our practices and behaviors speak out of a different narrative. To understand God we have to address the ways our passions, our desires, are misdirected and disoriented. This is not about repression for an authoritarian legalism; this is about transformation so that we participate in this world as a free people. Transformation of our desire involves deep liberation, a freedom to truly be who we are in tune with who God is and has made us to be. This latter element is a key point of why Coakley's contributions fit within a systematic theology framework. To develop all these themes in concert with each other and in light of Christian tradition she must walk us through such doctrines and traditions.[11] Christian mysticism is not a retreat into pietism but an embrace of the fullness of Christian teaching. The methodological developments took shape in her earlier works, with her new series showing how such contributes to a comprehensive systematic understanding.

GOD IS LORD OF ALL

Over the course of her career, Coakley has delved deeply in a wide variety of complex theological discussions, serving as an editor of many collections of essays and a contributor of essays to many collections. Her turn to a more contemplative and, indeed, ascetic goal is akin to Picasso's shift from portraiture to Modern art. It was in mastery of the field of his time that he was able to make a turn to what is often judged as more simplistic art "that my three year old could paint."[12] The seeming simplicity and less representational rigor masks an underlying complexity of intent and composition. Likewise, in her preface to *God, Sexuality, and the Self*, Coakley writes, "The method I here call *théologie totale* involves a complex range of interdisciplinary skills; and to link the theoretical to the pastoral in this way is a task of some considerable spiritual and intellectual delicacy, just as to write so as to be 'understood of the people' makes its own ascetical demands on the author."[13] Even the title of this volume suggests the overlapping, interdisciplinary intent as she enters into what she calls a systematic theology but would not likely appear to many as such in light of more commonly composed volumes of systematics.[14]

If we see theology as systematic when its goal is an "integrated presentation of Christian truth," then the goal for such a theology is to integrate as much, and as widely, as possible.[15] The critique against systematic theology for being narrowly intellectual suggests a problem with limitations of input rather than a limitation to the systematic task itself. Coakley sees the overall task thusly: "However briefly, or lengthily, it is explicated, . . . 'systematic theology' must attempt to provide a coherent, and alluring, vision of the Christian faith."[16] Coherence has long been the goal, while the task of being alluring is often seen as suspect or even resisted. To be alluring, theology should address broader topics of life and one's environment, discussing the issues raised by philosophy while expanding the discussion more broadly. Otherwise it is susceptible to being coherent only within a very narrow frame of reference and requires everyone to participate in, and only in, this narrow framework to find meaning and validation.

Theology is *totale* "not as a totalizing assault on worldly power, but as an attempt to do justice to every level, and type, of religious apprehension and its appropriate mode of expression."[17] This means to be truly systematic, theology should be inclusive in its range of influences, and transcend the limited boundaries of a single academic department or academia in general. In limiting theology to one kind of expression, conventional academic theology has limited the discussion about God to a narrow apprehension of God, constrained within the closed boundaries of a specific system. When theology is inclusive, it is also inviting, as Eugene Rogers emphasizes:

The phrase invites because it implies a theology that leaves nothing out, not Trinity, not sexuality, not science. *Théologie totale* invites scientists, too, to see their work as part of a larger whole. It implies openness to science, sacrifice, and feminist critiques of sacrifice, nothing relevant passed over, no artificial barriers, no self-insulation, but the Spirit-led confidence to encounter it all. It includes, as Coakley points out, the courage to push forward to meet the challenge and the refusal to withdraw into self-containment.[18]

Since a core statement of Christian theology is that God is the lord of all, then all that God is lord of speaks back into an understanding of who God is, how God works, and who God is calling us to be. It is this emphasis on life that leads theology to be a message of hope and liberation for the oppressors and the oppressed.

Coakley delineates nine elements of her *théologie totale* which form the methodological basis of her approach.[19] These also suggest a methodological path for a liberation of the oppressor, orienting a person through self-awareness and toward transformation. The first is *"Privileging contemplation."*[20] This involves submission and openness to the divine that is essential for developing awareness of the Real. Contemplation is open to all people, whatever their place in various systems, and as such retunes a person toward God's overarching narrative for their lives and their context. Second, Coakley emphasizes *"Theology in via."*[21] Such points to an openness to theological discovery rather than seeing theology as a way of establishing or limiting religious experience. Theology is thus always open to revision, not in a postmodern flight into absolute relativism, but as a way of taking the transforming and enlightening work of the Holy Spirit more seriously. Theology involves "an ongoing journey of purgative transformation and change" as well as reasoned exploration of new vistas of discovery.

Third, Coakley proposes a "counterpoint of philosophy, science, and *théologie totale.*"[22] Theology is not in pursuit of dominance of other fields of knowledge. That is not its task, and thus it is not queen. It is not theology that is outside the systems, that brings integration to them, but rather it is only God who integrates. "It is," as Coakley writes, "the Spirit's interruption that finally enables full human participation in God."[23] Theology is descriptive, searching out the integration as it can be understood, which is already taking place in the Spirit's work. How can this authentically occur if theology is developed solely in terms of established systems, whether in a position of power or not? It may not be impossible, but it certainly makes the task more difficult and less thorough. In seeking to speak of God as well as possible, theology must itself shift to toward contemplative purgation, put in "contrapuntal relation to revelation and grace" and "contrapuntal discussion" with secular philosophy and science.[24] Grace is constantly transforming the learner, and other patterns of knowledge offer contributory insight that may likewise lead to greater awareness and change. The Spirit can awaken insight in whatever way the Spirit desires and we must be open to that from any direction.

The fourth hallmark of Coakley's *théologie totale* is "Orthodoxy as goal."[25] This is the project of theology, project of truly *knowing* in full who God is and what God is doing. Coakley writes, "Orthodoxy is no mere creedal correctness, no imposed ecclesiastical regulation. At that horizon of true orthodoxy, theology, 'spirituality,' and ethics are fully united."[26] In developing more as intellectual elitism or for ecclesiastical control, the goal of orthodoxy has lost both its relevance as a living experience of our understanding of God and its integrity in engaging this world as God's world. In losing integrity, theology is significantly less likely to shape our lives, whether in our specifically spiritual formation or our engaged participation in this world in all its various systems.[27] At the same time, this emphasizes there is in fact a truth to be known, a right way of understanding God that reflects God's work and call for our lives and our contexts. Liberation thus does not find meaning through abandoning doctrine or minimizing specifically Christian testimony. Quite the opposite.

Fifth, *théologie totale* is "*socially located but not socially reduced.*"[28] Doctrines are not isolated statements from purely objective sources. We talk about Christianity in certain ways, with certain emphases, according to our contextual questions and concerns. All theology is contextual, something that has always been true, but we are only relatively recently expressing this in how the theological task develops. This does not, however, reduce theology merely to contextual expressions. We can talk about the universality of God's revelation and that implies a consistency across cultural boundaries. The goal, then, of theology is to bring in all the various tools of examination to sort through the theological and the social issues, discerning truth in the midst of social conflicts, biases, and contributions. As David Ngong puts it, "Theology that does not take the lives of people seriously is not worth having and mission that is not immersed in the lives of people is a waste of time."[29] This leads Coakley into historical, theological, and sociological resources to better discern the "'messy entanglements' of doctrinal truth and social reality."[30] Indeed, this approach to theology reflects the incarnation. Jesus was wholly a first-century Galilean Jewish man, but was not limited to this in reach and did not either wholly dismiss or wholly celebrate the understanding of God in that context.

Sixth, *théologie totale* includes the classical theological loci but not necessarily in the conventional order or limited to isolated theological concerns. For instance, in this first volume she is covering the doctrine of God with attention to the topics of gender and sexuality, highlighting theological perspectives through an analysis of iconography, and blending the discussions of the Trinity and Trinitarian persons.[31] This leads her text to be Trinitarian in theme and in methodology, with the persons always present in each other's discussions. Such an approach has led one commentator to describe the book as "theology in parts," reserving judgment of the whole project until the completion of all volumes.[32] Seventh, *théologie totale* is interested in broader human expression. That systematic theology has been located primarily in the halls of academia is neither endemic to the topic itself or Christian history. Theology has always been developed and expressed in a wide variety of mediums. While her text itself is, for the most part, reflecting her location as an academic, she is attentive to this broader issue by including "aesthetic attention" in each of her volumes, with art focused on in the first, followed by poetry, music, and liturgy in subsequent volumes.

The eighth hallmark of her theological approach is to overcome false divides. Modern approaches to theology, and almost any topic, tend to encourage binaries, *either* this *or* that.[33] Overcoming this involves proposing more options than two on a given theological question. It involves a diversity of content and method, themes and contributions. In some respects, this seems like a revisiting of Hegel's dialectic where thesis and antitheses lead us toward a synthesis. However, Coakley's approach is more complex, resisting the division from the beginning and, with this, resisting a supposed more adequate understanding based on the two poles. The contemplative task leads to a complexity of understanding of various perspectives rather than reduction of nuance into sides.[34] Again, the result is not some *via media*, but a reexamination of the whole issue informed by theological concerns, which in giving a more developed response likewise suggests the very questions may be in need of reexamination. When Jesus, for instance, was confronted with questions that were intended to have him choose a side, he often gave answers that placed him outside the assumed binary and changed the question into something new.

In this approach, Coakley thus looks to explore the core issues of any theological theme or relevant issue for the most pressing, yet often ignored, issue at hand, that of desire itself. Her last hallmark highlights this. Desire is "the constellating theological category of *théologie totale*."[35] In orienting her project in light of desire, Coakley leads theology back into the pressing experiences of contemporary life, experiences that are caught in a frenzy of desires and distortions. The definitions of self are driven by a need to determine one's self in the midst of a chaotic world, and if theology does not address these, it works to sustain their presence. Indeed, theology can often itself serve as a power play, enforcing a rigid and narrow kind of orthodoxy. The freeing experience of the church becomes instead a force for repression. These passions of the world disorient our communal participation and gut our proclamation of good news. This can be true even if theologians are addressing social problems in a society, seeming to have a prophetic voice, yet really communicating the communication of the system.[36]

This is why Coakley's new approach is important to consider in depth. Katherine Sonderegger calls it "altogether dazzling" in its aim "to cut across old distinctions, forge new alliances and refashion theological discourse in powerful and imaginative ways."[37] It is no longer enough to assume that theology will actually lead to transformation, let alone liberation, by means of the same sources and forms of discussion. To address a new kind of action for oppressors, a new way of expressing theology is essential, one that orients our desires and catalyzes knowledge for the purpose of continual transformation back into God's calling. "We are," as Sonderegger reminds us, "to begin and aim for wholeness, a totality, in which the full reality of creaturely life is held together with the mystery of God."[38] This begins in prayer, a way of orienting our life in tune with God's vision for this world. Of course, it does not stop in prayer, as the Spirit provokes transformation, orienting us in a new way with and for others, integrating our self and our environment in tune with God's community. Jean Vanier points to how such an integrating task can take shape in this world, as a counter-narrative for this world.

GOD IS COMMUNAL

In 1941, Jean Vanier approached his father, Georges Vanier—a decorated World War I soldier, diplomat, and continuing military leader in Canada—with a request. He wanted to join the Royal Navy.[39] Georges replied that he trusted his son and that he gave permission. Jean was 13 at the time. He left home and started at the Royal Navy Academy. He graduated with his commission and served in the Royal Navy and the Royal Canadian Navy.

In 1950, Jean Vanier resigned his commission as he sought deeper meaning for his life. He pursued graduate study in philosophy, eventually earning a PhD in philosophy from the *Institut Catholique* in Paris, with his dissertation on the topic of Aristotelian ethics.[40] He then began an academic career as a philosophy professor at the University of Toronto. Here he first came into greater contact with those who dealt with severe disability. Their struggles to find help and acknowledgment led to yet another change. In 1964, Vanier moved to Trosly-Breuil, France where he invited two developmentally disabled men to live with him. With this, he began the development of L'Arche, a growing network of homes where those with severe disabilities are joined by those willing to come alongside their difficulties, forming a community of care and mutuality that now reaches around the world.[41]

His biography suggests a driving momentum toward the kind of liberation I have discussed so far. His military career and academic posts offered significant boosts for his ego and meaning derived from application of societal success. He was born in a family of relative privilege, raised in a context where the application of power was part of the global struggle for justice and freedom. Yet in his journey into middle age, he did not see success as derived from such positions of power and intellectual achievement. He left these behind to pursue a less culturally powerful but more substantive path. He put aside his privilege to reach out to those whom society had often neglected, seen as a burden by their families, or even as a punishment for perceived sins. Such severely disabled men and women really have been treated as the "least" among us, historically ridiculed or left to die. More recently they have been institutionalized—not as much for their care as to absolve more active responsibility outside of the public and personal purview. Such asylums were often like prisons. Vanier sought something more alongside those who were treated in such deplorable ways. This was not a paternalistic goal to fix their problems, rather it was born out of a yearning for friendship and meaning, one with another, the to-and-fro of love expressed in the struggles of real community.

The difficulty with discussing Jean Vanier is similar to the problem of Anthony of Egypt: it is such a striking example that it becomes very easy to dismiss as a practical impossibility for the rest of us. We can easily affirm, indeed, celebrate Vanier's life and contributions while staying within the systems and identity that mark our lives thus far. Yet, Vanier teaches that it is not such an extraordinary expression at all, almost the contrary. He spoke of his own journey as being very regular indeed, as he sought to live in the way that reflected his calling. "It's not so much a question about courage, it's about knowing *this* is right," he said in a recent interview, "something you feel is right, and things fall into place . . . and then the realization that this is God's work, not my work."[42] As such, the expression of liberation can take shape in many ways, most of which are not as dramatic as Vanier's experience, but all of which may reflect the exact kind of life we are to live in light of God's calling for us in the community of which we are a part. It begins by having a renewed understanding of who God is and what God values. Vanier emphasizes that we reflect this understanding to those around us by how we encounter them.

GOD IS COMPASSIONATE

In his study of John 14, Vanier focuses on the title of paraclete. The paraclete is the counselor, the "Spirit caring for the weak." This is like a mother with a child, or any experience of real relationship where cares are addressed in the context of commitment with each other. God responds this way with those who are poor, pointing toward their importance and meaning to him through compassionate love.[43] It is an expression of the value of the person and God's presence with that person enabling healing, growth, and participation in meaningful ways. "This is also the reality of L'Arche," Vanier writes. "At L'Arche, we are not there just to take care of people with disabilities, or do things for them; we are there to live with them, so that each may discover this truth: 'You are loved as you are. You have the right to be yourself. Our desire is to help you rise up so that you may develop your gifts and become fully yourself.'"[44] From this, one may easily assume that the caretakers are there to love the handicapped residents and to help them in their needs. This is only partially true.

Those who are disabled are helped by the assistants, but this is not a one-way help. In living together, they all help each other discover the truth about love, living together in a holistic experience of reciprocity. "We eat together, we work together, we have fun together, we pray together, and sometimes we fight together," Vanier notes, emphasizing that those with disabilities are called "core members" because their service to L'Arche and the assistants involves mutuality.[45] The L'Arche community in Orange, California describes their existence this way: "The structure of the community is unique because there are no roles of patient or client; the core members and assistants live in the household as a family and share all aspects of daily life."[46] Vanier emphasizes mutuality through recognition of the other as a real person, beloved by God and so a person is both a giver and receiver of love.[47] It is this expression of recognizing love that transforms subjects into being an expression of the Spirit's work, a work that liberates by giving freedom and life to each other.

Liberation, then, is about relationship above all: we become the kind of people who are open to relationship and enter into relationship with both like and unlike. For the oppressor, those with power and identity in the world systems, this requires a *kenosis*, which includes a revised understanding of self and others as defined by the love of Christ rather than by the value in any given system. Because of their handicaps, the core members have often experienced radical exclusion and isolation, leading to profound experiences of despair that they often cannot adequately convey. "If someone," Vanier writes, "cannot live according to the values of knowledge and power, the values of the greater society, we ask ourselves, can that person be fully human."[48] The systems, of course, don't care. Nobody is important as a person as long as they are communicating the communication of a system. Lacking that communicative participation, there is no value at all according to the systems and those who find meaning in the systems cannot conceive of meaning for any who do not fit.[49]

When we are in full communion with Christ, we are in communion with the Father, and that "communion changes my heart, so that I will open my heart to the friends of Jesus: the poor and the weak."[50] Communion is not simply an intellectual or ecclesial act; it is a reflection of God's love to us outwards to those around us. For those in L'Arche, the transformative love of Christ reflects one to another, the assistants and the core members learning from and coming alongside each other in the process of recovery from past hurts and becoming a new person animated by compassionate love.[51]

The source of our identity is revealed in how we treat people. If we can enter into a compassionate mutuality with those with severe disabilities, who have no system identity, this is an indication that our love reflects the love of Christ, who loves each person because they are a beloved person, worthy of love.[52] It is easy to love or honor someone who can help advance in social and professional goals, after all. To love for love's own sake, for the sake of the other, is a liberative love. "First and foremost, L'Arche members understand themselves as the beloved of God," and it is this understanding that leads to transformative meaning for all involved.[53] God enters into community with each person, and thus shows that God is not represented by the powerful to the lowly, or that only certain people have special access. God shares his self with all and gathers all together into a community that is formed in light of his love.

Those who seek to enter into this process encounter what Kevin Reimer calls "downward mobility," which is "the idea that our deepest human potential lives in simple relationships."[54] This pursuit resists the invitations of the systems, describing the process of stepping away from system-derived rationality and their sense of importance. It is a new way that only makes sense in light of the divine narrative. Contrasted with the more well-known "upwardly mobile," which emphasizes competition and vocational achievement above all, being downwardly mobile emphasizes descending in sense of self, giving up or not living up to one's potential as defined by the values of the broader social environment. More deeply, the downward mobility of someone caught in oppressing patterns involves redefinition, letting go of the identity forming systems while still a participant in the environment. It is, basically, a form of asceticism without separation, thus not taking on the commonly understood models of monastic or eremitical life.[55]

The transition evokes communally oriented passions. "The downwardly mobile," Reimer writes, "manifest everyday compassion in a manner that is surprising, at times groundbreaking, and occasionally profound."[56] Downward mobility is not about resignation but about a quest for deeper meaning and way of life, fundamentally about hope and expressed in community. "L'Arche redeems difficult hope" as the communities include and celebrate people, honoring their uniqueness as people and highlighting their contributions and preferences.[57] Such hope is learned and such learned hope is infectious, a way of life that transmits value and renewal of life to all involved.

Those with disabilities find value in these communities and in the expression of hope and love that comes with such valuation become essential teachers to the assistants. "Hope is the gift of disability to moral maturity."[58]

The process toward such hope is different for the assistants in comparison to the core members, even as the journey and destination are shared. For the assistants this journey involves different goals depending on which stage of participation they are in. For newer members, the goal of a more cohesive identity involves self-consistency, openness, adventure, empathy, and a transformed lifestyle.[59] For long-term assistants, the cluster of transformative goals include balance, groundedness, self-care, interpersonal responsibility, and "awe and ethics."[60] These are not learned as a systematic set of steps, as if there was an organized ladder of advancement; rather these are part of what Reimer calls a "narrative identity." At L'Arche, and other transformative settings, "Humans create narrative identities of enduring coherence where hope and awe are present reminders that moral commitments to real people (such as core members) celebrate compassionate possibilities that make the problems of our world bearable."[61] These narrative identities are formed in the experience of living, involving both manifold lessons of practical and spiritual engagement with others and with God. Daily actions lead toward deeper self-reflection, a mutuality of maturation of inner and outer life.[62] Simply getting along with others is itself a significant trick, especially when people are dealing with significant personal issues—which includes both core members and other assistants.

The continuing process of contemplative engagement—realistic and often discouraging encounters—reveal the limitations of self and others. Active, committed engagement built on priorities of trust and vulnerability lead to a transformative experience of life that recasts a person increasingly out of system-defined identity and into the widening, empowering, and freeing waters of the Holy Spirit. This is not a quick process, and it is easy to become discouraged. While the core members can never leave their disabilities, the assistants can move on and away, sometimes carrying their lessons onwards into new phases of life, and sometimes leaving those lessons behind. Such transformation is a lot to ask of a person, even if the ultimate hope in a coherent, integrated personality is a substantive promise. The challenge of liberation of the oppressor thus involves persistence and patience.[63]

Reimer notes three features of compassionate love that mark the challenges those at L'Arche must journey through.[64] First, "Core members and assistants must realign expectations of community life based on immediate realities." Community is messy and will involve both joy and hurt in engaging others and in the realities of life's struggles. Expectations tend to exist in a binary, either idealism or despair, with neither reflecting the process of real transformative interactions. Second, "compassionate L'Arche members at times resign themselves to the physical and emotional limitations of their love." We all are but human, and in this humanity can do and be only so much. The constancy of engaged community in service with those who are significantly disabled and other assistants can be immensely draining.[65]

This draws discouragement and exhaustion into the realities of liberation. Indeed, disappointment and exhaustion should be expected rather than be an indicator of wrong or deficient progress. We simply do not have the resources to carry on in a new pattern of life without honesty about our own need for rest, renewal, and encouragement. As Jean Vanier says, "L'Arche is impossible," it is an "ever-widening paradox" that requires transcendent awareness in the midst of oft messy and challenging immanence. This leads into the third feature, in which "durable compassionate love requires practitioners to find *meaning* in action."[66] Such meaning is the reflective task, going beyond just inspiration into discovering the bigger meaning and purposes of seemingly unending trauma. "Without meaning," Reimer writes, "the fragile ark is easily pushed sideways in the deepening trough."[67] The waves crash over, the vessel is overturned.[68] Such meaning must itself bear a coherent and integrating insight in order to sustain fragile transformation, bringing to mind Paul's admonition to the Ephesians: "We must no longer be children, tossed to and fro and blown about by every wind of doctrine, by people's trickery, by their craftiness in deceitful scheming."[69] Discernment is necessary, along with continued engagement, with the to-and-fro of praxis and reflection providing a holistic, supportive expression of love that can endure.[70] This is not our task to initiate or to design, as it is the work of Christ that we participate in through the power of the Holy Spirit. Life emerges from darkness.

CONCLUSION

Who God is shapes who we are, and our conception of God shapes how we engage with the world. Roberto Goizueta writes, "An authentically human praxis is, by definition, a participation in a *theo*praxis, God's own praxis on history." God isn't just involved in this world, God is committed to it, drawing people closer—with God and with others—empowering them to live in a new way together. Goizueta continues, "Our ability to act as historical agents, our freedom, our very identity are themselves given us by the God who loved us first, the God who is fully revealed in the wounded body of the crucified and risen Christ."[71] God gives us freedom. This isn't about our own whims nor limited to concepts in a narrowed religious system. All our responses within this life show what God we believe in, and inasmuch we have developed patterns of division, abuse, or negation, we have lost a vision of the

God who invites people into a new kind of reconciliation and liberation. Life is given so that life can be lived in full, and this fullness of life reaches into every area of human understanding and calls us to live in a new way. Our desires are reformed so that our practices can be transforming. This leads toward an ever-increasing depth and breadth of liberating life.

The work of God reaches into us, shaping us, revitalizing us, creating openings for participation in God's presence through prayer and contemplation. But God does not seek our settled communing, as if we have been given a pass for an existential spa and resort. God works so that others can work, initiating a moment of radical intervention that overcomes barriers and calls those who seek fullness to live in new ways, ways that benefit the lives of others, ways that invite others into this new kind of life. The cross that is the stopping point—the radical confrontation between systems and death—is not the end of the great story. Nor is our understanding of God, our participation with him, the end. Even more, our doing of good works is not the end, if we try to do these out of feelings of guilt or assumptions of deficiency. The work on the cross offers a radical forgiveness *and* a radical reordering of society. The promise of resurrection invites people into a new life, awakened to who God is. In this new vision of possibilities, there is a freedom of being in this world that resonates deeply and broadly. The radical intervention of God in the mission of Christ is truly an enacted *théologie totale,* giving us guidance and orientation for taking the steps to realize liberation in our contexts.

NOTES

1. This is not to say *all* theologians reflect this, nor that there is a binary of enlightened and debased academics. It is a spectrum on which our ideals weigh against our perceived vocational demands, with each person landing at a different place in between these seemingly divergent goals.

2. I note this not as a matter of pride but as an expression of my desired discipline. There are many points at which such retuning was not possible and other points at which it was possible (if not always easy) but I neglected the goal and the practice, leading to deflation and discouragement within my calling.

3. It was after writing the first part of this chapter that I encountered Coakley's description of her own formative years in relationship with God and in the academy. Her description, while quite different in many respects from my own, reflects the same tension of being drawn by God in a certain way and feeling discouragement in the seeming need to conform to established approaches. For her brief autobiography see Sarah Coakley, "Prayer as Crucible: How My Mind Has Changed," *Christian Century* 128, no. 6 (March 22, 2011): 32–36.

4. See, for instance, Sarah Coakley, *God, Sexuality, and the Self: An Essay "On the Trinity"* (New York: Cambridge University Press, 2013), 47. Hereafter "GSS."

5. Coakley, *GSS*, 18.

6. See Ibid., 52–55.

7. She gives a helpful introduction to this theme in St Johns Timeline, "Sarah Coakley, God Sexuality and The Self," *YouTube Video*, December 18, 2014, https://www.youtube.com/watch?v=Y0gxtpmlgBg.

8. Coakley, *GSS*, 62 acknowledges her terminology is derived from the well-known Annales School of history pioneered by French historians in the mid-twentieth century. She goes beyond this movement, however, in including an even broader range of fields. In this, she is more akin to Pannenberg's understanding of public theology. On his approach, see Pannenberg, *Anthropology in Theological Perspective*, 13–23.

9. See Coakley, *GSS*, 15–20.

10. Legalism and holiness are often considered only in light of practices, but also are quite present in each of the categories I listed above. We can see a contrast between legalism and holiness in orthodoxy and orthopathy as well as orthopraxy. Christians who insist on projecting a happy demeanor to the world no matter their inner status are legalists in terms of orthopathy, an artificial assumption of the fruit of the Spirit rather than actual transformation that leads to inner joy and peace. Christians who argue over doctrine but do not act in a way that shows they *know* it, are legalists in terms of orthodoxy, an assumed intellectual stance that is generally deployed to browbeat others for their ignorance or faulty positions.

11. See Coakley, *GSS*, 12–13.

12. Indeed, not too long ago my three-year old did draw a picture of our family that is reminiscent of Picasso's works. It recently sold at auction for $23 million dollars (just kidding, though I am open to such offers). As an example of Picasso's early, representational works, see, for instance, *First Communion* (1896) and *Science and Charity* (1896).

13. Coakley, *GSS*, xvii.

14. Coakley may be better understood as being distinctly non-Thomist in her organization and development rather than non-systematic. Coakley, *GSS*, 47 notes that "systematic" often is interpreted as a strategy of power, where the system reflects embedded patterns of oppression or hegemony. Recently I had an online conversation with a Master's level theology student who argued that "constructive theology is where it is at" because systematic theology is only concerned with the perspective of white, European males. Coakley, *GSS*, 51 notes that the objections to systematic theology presume that "the systematician idolatrously desires mastery." This leads into her discussion of the need to transform desire, something theologians are often in need of as well as the broader world.

15. Coakley, *GSS*, 41.

16. Ibid., 41.

17. Ibid., 48.

18. Eugene F. Rogers, Jr., "Sacrifice Regained in the Light of God, Sexuality, and the Self and 'Flesh and Blood': Objections and Replies, or How I Changed My Mind," in *Sarah Coakley and the Future of Systematic Theology*, ed. Janice McRandal (Minneapolis: Fortress Press, 2016), 51–52.

19. This list overlaps with the elements I noted earlier. This is not a repetitive list, however, as here she is specifically noting elements of her systematic approach in her new series while my list contained the traits I noted in reading her works more broadly. The overlap suggests how her method has been developing and forming throughout her contributions over the last decades.

20. Coakley, *GSS*, 88. Emphases for these nine elements are in the original.

21. Ibid., 88.

22. Ibid.

23. Ibid., 89.

24. Ibid. She adds, "There is a paradoxical double counterpoint here between secular reason, theology's reason, and that reason still *in via* to God."

25. Ibid., 89.

26. Ibid., 89–90.

27. Cf. Oden, *The Transformative Church*, 33–38. Moltmann exhibits this interest in the integrity of theology as well, though not without attention to the question of coherence. The core question and the root of *The Crucified G*od, "Where was God during the holocaust," is a key expression of this goal, and each of his various "Contributions to Systematic Theology," likewise suggest a core concern in their prefaces that initiates the exploration.

28. Coakley, *GSS*, 90.

29. David Tonghou Ngong, "The Theologian as Missionary: The Legacy of Jean-Marc Éla," *Journal of Theology for Southern Africa* no. 136 (2010): 16.

30. Coakley, *GSS*, 90. She makes a fuller claim for the use of social sciences in chap. 2 of this text. While Coakley discusses the contributions of feminism in that chapter, this raises the issue of global theology as well. While not absolutely the rule, the tendency is for theology in former Christendom to rely primarily on philosophical foundations while global theologies tend to reflect sociological guidance.

31. While stimulating it also has made it difficult to assign readings for a theology course, as she does not fit within the boundaries of topics. It also has made her text difficult for seminary students who are generally used to more conventional patterns. They have trouble understanding where she is going or even why.

32. This was stated in a faculty meeting when the professor was asked to describe this book for other colleagues upon it being proposed for use in theology course by an adjunct professor. That the professor who said this also uses the text in his course suggests critical intrigue with her ultimate aims. See also Stephen Burns, "From Evelyn Underhill to Sarah Coakley: Women Teaching Theology and the English Context," in *Sarah Coakley and the Future of Systematic Theology*, ed. McRandal, 215–217.

33. See Coakley, *GSS*, 91.

34. Such modernistic reductionism always does violence to both history and thought, ultimately oppressing in how it constrains and generalizes.

35. Coakley, *GSS*, 92.

36. Primarily in the education system, promulgating the furtherance of academic conferences and organized discussions.

37. Katherine Sonderegger, "A Review of God, Sexuality and the Self," *International Journal of Systematic Theology* 18, no. 1 (January, 2016): 35.

38. Sonderegger, "A Review of God, Sexuality and the Self," 36.

39. The details from this brief biography were culled from a variety of interviews and sources. The official biography on the L'Arche website serves as the primary resource: https://larchelondon.ca/story-jean-vanier/.

40. Published as Jean Vanier, *La bonheur; principe et fin de la morale aristotélicienne* (Paris: Desclée de Brouwer, 1965). His later book *Made for Happiness: Discovering the Meaning of Life with Aristotle* (Toronto: Anansi, 2001) is based on this earlier research and writing, adapted for a broader audience and given insights by his subsequent work with L'Arche.

41. See Zoe Orsazoxia, "Love and Belonging (50 years at L'arche with Jean Vanier)," *YouTube Video*, 45:18, February 4, 2015, https://www.youtube.com/watch?v=vDnfdHQu-rg. This is a documentary on the founding and goals of L'Arche.

42. TempletonPrize, "Templeton Prize Student Roundtable (Compilation)," *YouTube Video*, 32:40, June 15, 2015, https://www.youtube.com/watch?v=dz31RUnjCRs.

43. See, for instance, Exodus 22:7; Psalm 78:38; Matthew 9:36; Philippians 2:1; James 5:11.

44. Jean Vanier, *The Gospel of John, the Gospel of Relationship* (Cincinnati: Franciscan Media, 2015), 103.

45. Jean Vanier, "Foreword," in *Living L'Arche: Stories of Compassion, Love, and Disability*, ed. Kevin Scott Reimer (Collegeville, MN: Liturgical Press, 2009), vii. Vanier, *Community and Growth*, 18, writes, "Communities are truly communities when they are open to others, when they remain vulnerable and humble; when tee members are growing in love, in compassion and in humility. Communities cease to be such when members close in upon themselves with the certitude that they alone have wisdom and truth and expect everyone to be like them and learn from them."

46. "Who We Are: Orange, California," L'Arche USA, http://www.larcheusa.org/who-we-are/communities/orange-california/.

47. See Vanier, *John*, 86. Reimer, *Living L'Arche,* 105, writes, "Dozens of caregiver assistants insist that disabled core members are the prophets and teachers of L'Arche. Core members provide instruction on living well with disability. This unexpected characterization anticipates movement from shame to moral maturity."

48. Jean Vanier, *Becoming Human* (Mahwah, NJ: Paulist Press, 2008), 77.

49. This does not include just the severely handicapped. As every system gives value in light of its own autopoietic motivation, a person can have widely varied valuation in different contexts. An assistant professor of theology may have a grand sense of value in an ecclesial setting but not in the economic system. We tend to depersonalize and devalue those who do not rank high in our own sense of identity substantiation. The severely mentally handicapped tend to not fit well within any system so have historically been devalued in every system.

50. Vanier, *Becoming Human,* 29.

51. Reimer, *Living L'Arche,* 55, states that his initial impression of compassionate love was as a "tit-for-tat altruism, sprinkled with a desire to achieve inspired notions of care described in poetry and spiritual writings. To put it baldly, we care for others because we expect good things in return and feel better aspiring to our highest goals and ideals." In contrast to his "educated prejudice," Reimer notes being enlightened by the insights of an assistant named Katherine. He writes, "Her love required little

reasoning or planning to enact, seemed unconcerned with consequences, and was shockingly vulnerable. Far from the jungle or the theologian's desk, compassionate love involved relationships characterized by raw and elemental honesty. Compassionate love was about the other person who makes relationship possible, about security and trust liberating each individual to learn about the other more completely."

52. This is, of course, not just limited to how we respond to the severely disabled. A person's character and value system is indicated by how they treat other people in any setting. If a person only treats the wealthy, educated, powerful with value, they reflect the values of a particular world system. The ways Jesus responded to the wealthy and the poor, the included and the outcast, is a major element of his ministry.

53. Reimer, *Living L'Arche,* 48.

54. This definition is from Marilyn, an assistant with L'Arche, quoted in Reimer, *Living L'Arche,* 4.

55. Reimer, *Living L'Arche,* 10 notes that it is not ascetic, though his meaning here suggests more of a separatist understanding than that suggested by Coakley which can be expressed in the context of "regular" life.

56. Reimer, *Living L'Arche,* 10.

57. Ibid., 126.

58. Ibid. Reimer goes on to add, "L'Arche is an incubator for loving character, celebrating life in the midst of disability. Caregiver assistants come to understand their own disabilities even as these are hidden from external view. With this wisdom comes hope of reconciliation and healing which pushes individuals more deeply into the practice of compassionate love." Cf. Irenaeus, *Adversus haereses,* V.3.1.

59. Reimer, *Living L'Arche,* 147.

60. Reimer gives examples of all of these in his text. Most are generally self-explanatory so I will not repeat those examples here, except the last one which is not quite as evident in meaning. In describing "awe and ethics" Reimer points to examples like looking at stars, living in gratitude, and being a godly disciple, expressions that might fit into a description of contemplation as well as including any helpful practice that is not neatly contained within the other goals. The idea that formation includes both practical steps and a revised awareness and excitement about God's work in this world is important to highlight.

61. Reimer, *Living L'Arche,* 146.

62. See Ibid., 147–148.

63. Which are elements of the fruit of the Spirit in Galatians 5.

64. These are listed on Reimer, *Living L'Arche,* 166.

65. Again, the experience of having significant disabilities is also immensely draining, but the core members do not have the option of leaving their disabilities behind, so are not confronted as readily with the choices of continued engagement, instead having to deal with the realities of living with persistent oppression brought on by their own bodies.

66. Reimer, *Living L'Arche,* 166.

67. Ibid., 167.

68. Vanier, *Community and Growth,* 136 highlights four great crises of community life: "The first—which is certainly the least hard—comes when we arrive. There are always parts of us which cling to the values we have left behind. The second is the

discovery that the community is not as perfect as we had thought, that it has its weaknesses and flaws. The ideal and our illusions crumble; we are faced with reality. The third is when we feel misunderstood and even rejected by the community, when, for example, we are not elected to a position of responsibility, or do not get a job we had hoped for. And the fourth is the hardest: our disappointment with ourselves because of all the anger, jealousies, and frustrations that boil up in us. If we are to become totally integrated into a community we must know how to pass through these crises."

69. Ephesians 4:14.

70. Vanier, *Becoming Human*, 16 notes the worth of the academic studies with this reflection, while also warning against their potential misuse. He writes, "Philosophy, anthropology, theology and those sciences that tell us what it means to be human can be dangerous if they become ideologies that dictate reality; instead the need to be understood as the means by which we humbly listen to and marvel at reality."

71. Roberto S. Goizueta, "Knowing the God of the Poor," in *Opting for the Margins: Postmodernity and Liberation in Christian Theology*, ed. Joerg Rieger (New York: Oxford University Press, 2003), 147.

Chapter 10

Hope for Transformation

INTRODUCTION

Thorough liberation is a seemingly impossible task. Things are the way they are, and the way they are is the way they will stay in the natural course of events. The oppressors will never give up power and the oppressed will never be given power. That is the way of history, the way things have been and the way things are now. Change thus seems to require overthrowing the establishment in a revolutionary fervor, with this the only way to properly acknowledge injustice and pursue transformation. Yet Christianity is a religion of history and a religion of eschatology, teaching that one is within the other, pointing to the possibility of change that is radically unexpected. Slaves are given freedom. The blind see, the deaf hear. What "must be" can change in a blink of an eye. The crucified one is risen from the dead. This resurrection impulse is central to Christian teaching, orienting the whole methodology of liberation in Christian teaching. We can commit to the method of Jesus in the hope that the past and the powers do not have the ultimate say. This way is more than a set of tasks to accomplish; it involves a whole pattern of being that hopes in a transforming work of the Spirit.

In this chapter, I will highlight the transformative way of Jesus Christ that is shown through his mission into death and into life. This expands the confrontation beyond the powers of this world and addresses the fundamental problem we all face—that we will die. The work of Christ also addresses the despair that develops within a negated life. I begin by discussing how Jesus confronts the powers, which builds on the definition of holiness as being more than existential. It is engaged and it is empowering. Next, I will argue how this reality shapes our perspective on the past and the future, providing a hope that radically changes our perspective of self and others, invigorating us for this life, not just giving us something to wait for in some supposed next stage of reality. Third, this hope reaches deeply into our being, reshaping our desires and passions. No longer constrained by the definitions of the systems, we *want* in new ways. No longer striving after self-definition, we share with each other in new ways. Is this just an idealistic vision? Not in the experience of those who have pursued this in their own lives. Thus, fourth, I will show how this can take place in the midst of our life, giving an example that also is a motivation. Substantive peace and solidarity are possible, and this communal peace is a hope for oppressors that can defy historical trends, leading them to use their freedom for the sake of others.

CONFRONTING THE POWERS

The coming of Jesus into this world is an act of God's love expressing his holiness to the world, his exocentric holiness. God's love draws people into his holiness, even as they are lost in the systems. God does not wait for a person to awaken on their own and become sanctified in order to participate in God's community. Jesus is not the "good cop" to the Father's "bad cop," appeasing the anger and fury of a separated judge.[1] Jesus is the expression of the love of God, and indeed the very revelation of God's exocentric identity, which is holiness. Indeed, he is the true human and the true God, fully formed in identity.[2] Jesus is the fulfillment of the law, which communicated God's holiness and the ways in which humanity could be formed in this holiness, and so be trusted to interact with him.[3]

This enacted holiness is evident throughout the life of Jesus. A key illustration of this is in passages such as Mt. 8:1–4:

> When Jesus had come down from the mountain, great crowds followed him; and there was a leper who came to him and knelt before him, saying, "Lord, if you choose, you can make me clean." He stretched out his hand and touched him, saying, "I do choose. Be made clean!" Immediately his leprosy was cleansed. Then Jesus said to him, "See that you say nothing to anyone; but go, show yourself to the priest, and offer the gift that Moses commanded, as a testimony to them."

The law was very clear about leprosy and its absolute uncleanness.[4] Following the understanding of holy as "set apart" and the reality of God's holiness as abhorrence of corruption, it would seem that Jesus, as God among us, would have made sure not to soil his identity with the uncleanness that was prohibited from Temple interaction. Lepers could not participate with God, with others, in the fullness of their calling, even as they were often part of the called people of God. Those who knew holiness only from the law were called to reject such people, lest the uncleanness of the corruption spread. Yet, Jesus was a man in the street, walking about, touching, talking, teaching those who came near him, without regard to their own inherent status of identity.

His love is his holiness, an inviting holiness that does not demand people make themselves whole, which is impossible, but instead reaches out, as holiness, to deliver restoration.[5] His holiness was not corrupted by the disease or uncleanness. Rather, his holiness made clean that which was unclean. Healing is, in essence, exocentric holiness, making whole and restoring to fullness. Jesus did not reject the leper, as the law did, but as God present, he restored the identity of the leper. The leper was no longer defined by his disease, but by Jesus who could and did make him clean. As Pannenberg notes, "The sending of the Son to save the world (Jn 3:16) aims at the bringing of the world into the sphere of the divine holiness."[6] This is a healing of the world, not a separating from it.

This overcoming of impurity works in every aspect of human identity and relationship. Jesus is the expression of God's love and God's holiness among us, living a life expressed in exocentric fellowship, which overcomes the sin induced by contradictory egos colliding.[7] "The victory over sin," Pannenberg writes, "had not been attained before Jesus' birth, but only in the entire accomplishment of the course of his existence."[8] When we see the Son, we see the Father. This revelation—this direct revelation of God's work in the work of Jesus—has to transform our perception of God's holiness and embrace this identity as the fount of our own.[9] This is true about how Jesus lived, what he valued, and certainly true in the work of the cross. In the cross, Jesus shows that he is not, in fact, reacting to the world as other people might react, in defensive support of their unformed ego. He does not need validation by the priests or the rulers, does not need to defend himself even from the injustice. This injustice of his crucifixion is itself a reflection of sinful humanity, a clash of egos that collide against each other in exocentric deformation.

Jesus takes on these sins of the world.[10] He does what only a fully formed identity can do. He stops the cycle. He shows his holiness in his acceptance of the injustice, not demanding separation or satisfaction but instead revealing his nature as the true human, in trusting fellowship with God the Father.[11] He trusts the Father, and the Father trusts the Son. This trust extends to people through the work of Christ. Pannenberg writes:

> In "ecstatic" being with Christ, believers are not in bondage to another, for Jesus as the Son of the Father is for his part fully God and therefore the man who gives himself up for others. . . . Those who believe in Jesus are thus not estranged from themselves, for with Jesus they are with God, who is the origin of the finite existence of all creatures and their specific destiny.[12]

Humanity in Christ is reconciled to the Father. Identification with Christ allows for participation in the trust that God shows his son. This work of God in the person of Jesus is not fully realized in the cross, but is only expressed as God's holiness in the resurrection.[13] Death is not holy, so God does not stop at death. God, as his self, takes on the sin that is thrust against him by human egos, and does not succumb to this attempt to identify and control him. The ultimate attempt to define Jesus by others does not work. Instead, he is who he is. He is not subject to their verdict of death, even after dying. In himself, he is made manifest in the life that is not overcome by that apparent path of human corruption. God is so clean, so whole, so himself that even death itself has no sting. He overcomes death, a hope fully realized so as to express the holiness of his full identity. In identifying with Christ in his death, those who follow Jesus let go attempts to form ego-driven identification, trusting God in this life for the fullness of life which is the only true life. Pannenberg writes, "According to the New Testament message the holiness that invades the world is mediated by Jesus Christ."[14] In joining with Christ we show trust.[15] We die to our self. We are reborn, with Christ, to participate with God and in doing that freeing us to more fully participate with others, as we continue to abandon our egos' attempts at redefinition.

This continued reformation of our inner self, this rebirth into a new stage in which we learn basic trust without the interference of a defensive ego "is also the work of the Holy Spirit, who is called the Holy Spirit because he is the Spirit of the holy God."[16] The Spirit brings holiness to us in this present life and leads us into God's identity, which is his future, our future, and all future. "As the Spirit who is identical with the divine essence (John 4:24) he is opposed to the world (Isa. 31:3), but he is also at work in creation as the origin of all life, and he sanctifies creatures by giving them a fellowship with the eternal God that transcends their transitory life."[17] This is not to say that the Son hands off the work to the Spirit. "The Logos and the Spirit work together in creation in such a way that the Word of creation is the fashioning principle, while the Spirit is the source of the movement and life of creatures."[18]

We are reconciled to God through Jesus, whose life expresses the fullness of God's identity and allows participation with God and also clarifies God's attributes, pointing us toward his work, teaching, and sacrifice to what it means to be fully realized as participants in God's openness.[19] God's own Spirit enlightens us to the reality of God, "deep calling to deep," rebuilding our identity into truly free beings, participants with the source of life. Those who trust God, in Christ, live out this trust in the power of the Holy Spirit, not to become automatons, mindless drones of some impersonal power, but rather to become whole, particular beings. The Spirit invites and empowers in light of God's continued exocentricity. The people of the Spirit take on the attributes of Jesus as noted in Philippians 2, no longer defined by independently construed identity and ego-driven attempts at domination.

The law, as noted in Romans 7, was not sufficient for identity formation. It gave a ground of understanding of God's nature and being, that he was a holy God and this was to be respected by our actions and interactions with him. But our passions blocked real participation with him. We want to be that which we cannot be. As Keener notes, "Paul depicts here a divided person."[20] The law caused us to realize our incompleteness—the chasm between possibility and actuality—and this provokes our ego even more. The gift of the Spirit is freely given, though working with synergistic expectations. "The form of the gift," Pannenberg writes, "does not mean that the Spirit comes under the control of creatures but that he comes into them and thus makes possible our independent and spontaneous entry into God's action of reconciling the world and our participation in the movement of his reconciling love toward the world."[21] This is essentially what Paul wrote in Romans 8.

The Spirit brings real freedom, not freedom to sin, nor a narrowed freedom constrained by operations of the various systems. This freedom is to truly live as exocentric beings within true reality, becoming free from our ego's distortion, and becoming free to live for God, with others, in openness to this world.[22] We live free with God and we bring this true freedom to others in our participation with God in this world.[23] Pannenberg writes that the "content, however, by which such freedom lives, is love. Only the person who loves is free."[24] Our living in freedom is our holiness that is expressed in love.[25]

Here we see the role of the Spirit in judgment. The Spirit is God's being with us, freeing us, revealing to us the identity of God as shown in Christ's life and work. God's being is eternity.[26] "Eternity," Pannenberg writes, "is judgment."[27] But this judgment is not, as noted earlier, a judicial decree based on impartial evidence considered by a neutral magistrate. The Spirit is the Spirit of life. God is the creator God and so for "creatures, then, confrontation with eternity means judgment only insofar as they have made themselves autonomous in relation to God, separated themselves from him, and thus become involved also in conflict with fellow creatures."[28] Sinners are left to the consequences they have chosen, left to the ego which they have embraced, and left to the identity which they have sought as their own.

In the moment of eternity our life comes together as a whole, one moment with all the other moments. The inner contradictions that our flow in time could ignore become present all in that moment.[29] These contradictions expose a "shrill dissonance."[30] The systems integrate in tune with God's rule. If we are not already integrated in the Spirit, we experience fundamental dis-integration along with the elements of the systems that are counter to God's rule and prevent operational openness. Our participation with the Spirit in the present and in eternity offers harmony for our existence rather than dissonance, as our rebirth in Christ reconfigures our contradictions into a new, free identity that finds its ground of being in God.[31] Our life with God is based on our trustworthiness, which is our holiness, conformed to the likeness of Christ by the Spirit. We become holy, just as God is holy, by letting go our attempts at domination and identity. God is God; we are God's people. Instead of embracing our self in contrast to others—the nature of the oppressor—we let go our ego, embrace the work of the Spirit, and show trust in acceptance of Christ's life and work as real, transformative realities in our life. We walk according to the reality of God, by the Spirit, and so our holiness is an eschatological identity which celebrates in hope and faith the love of God even in this not-fully revealed portion of history.[32] In this way, in participating with the Spirit, we experience true freedom.[33]

RESURRECTION HOPE

This experience of freedom in God leads to an embodied expression of renewed life. The hope is not for a vague, ethereal, and essentially gnostic desire for redemption that leads us, as individuals, away from the world. In the Old Testament, the Exodus narrative is the archetype, and God defines himself by this liberating act throughout the text. In the Gospels, the archetype expands to emphasize the resurrection.[34] The experience of resurrection transforms our expectations that derive from the past. It provides hope that expresses itself in a transformed way of life, in the present, oriented by the defining future of God's eternal life.

As such, the resurrection is an eschatological event that happens within even our experience of time. It fills history with divine meaning, even as it was not a result of historical events: one thing leading to another. It is a work of God in which the one who was dead—a state of determining reality—is now alive, a reflection of God's promise. Moltmann writes, "Raising is a historical event that has taken place in Jesus of Nazareth, but it is at the same time an eschatological happening, anticipating the raising of the dead in this one Person, and the new creation through that one Person."[35] If the cross is a prism in which we see the trinitarian persons in distinct activity, the resurrection brings these persons into shared focus once again, drawing all people into the new way of being. This new way of being leads to a rebirth to the fullness of life. Moltmann continues, "Through the transforming power of divine love mortal life will come alive from within. The experience of God will become the experience of being loved and affirmed from all eternity. That is the fullness of life."[36] Such an experience "is the greatest experience of God's love." The bodily resurrection is an expression of divine love and divine promise.

People can experience this before they can even begin to comprehend it, and so theology is a second order task reflecting on the experienced love of God among us, transforming us. What does such transformation entail for us? In his book on whether there is indeed a gospel for the rich, Richard Harries emphasizes that it is not enough to confine faith to an internal piety or isolated morality, or even to our interpersonal relationships, all of which turns the Gospel more into a self-help approach, one among many others. The gospel for the rich involves substantive transformation, which has three elements according to Harries:

> The way to transformation is: first, a willingness to come before God with our own personal needs; secondly, a willingness to subject our understanding of faith to a critique about its context and effects; thirdly, the development of a sense of spiritual solidarity with all those in need of different kinds.[37]

Without this concomitant transformation, we cannot comprehend God's being or work. If we think we can comprehend God without such transformation, our sights are not on the living God. If our sights are on the living God, then the promise of the resurrection inaugurates a new sense of identity that lives out the new narrative of Christ's fullness in the context of life and its various struggles and temptations. The threat of death or identity dissolution is no longer compelling. This has social, political, and vocational implications that resist the boundaries of the systems and the values they establish in order to perpetuate their functioning in the world-environment. Such a perspective "indicates the beginning of a fundamental change in the conditions of possible experience."[38] This, again, is precisely why Paul is adamant about the resurrection in 1 Corinthians 15. Either it is true or it is not true, and if it is not true, then Christianity does not offer a new narrative for the world. If it is true, then everything, literally everything, changes.

In the presence of the coming One, we experience reality differently from the way we experienced it in the conditions of death and transience. "We see mortal life in the light of the life that is eternal; we experience history in the light of God's kingdom, and nature in the perspective of its future perfecting in the eternal creation."[39] This experience is the foundation of hope and the orienting factor of Moltmann's ethics of hope. In light of the transforming reality of the resurrection, change becomes possible for any situation, and where change is possible, then transforming action in the pursuit of change becomes a mode of anticipatory faith, practicing our trust in God in manifold ways within our contexts.[40] More than the possibility of change, the resurrection orients such responses in a way that affirms life in this world.[41] The active work of God begins in the isolation of death turning forsakenness into a new invitation of inclusion, a way of life that participates in this world neither conformist nor separatist. "It is," Moltmann writes, "guidance for changing the world."[42]

Such guidance is oriented by an orthopathic transformation: we become filled with joy at the new possibilities God has initiated. Our actions derive from this hope we have in God for this world and the joy we have in participating with God in this new reality. This is why resurrection is a central concept for those who are oppressors as well as those who are oppressed. In this new experience of life, people are no longer stimulated by that which offers temporary distraction or unfulfilling accumulation. That life simply holds no appeal.[43] The fullness of life replaces anemic satiation, and community with the living replaces the isolating constructs of consumption. We become alive in a new way even in the midst of this present experience, lovers of life because the promise of life is a promise that we can trust wholeheartedly. "All the senses become awake, the understanding and the heart become open for the beauty of this life."[44] Such a renewal certainly involves delight and joy, but in becoming awakened to this life, we also become aware of the patterns of death in this world. Our rightly ordered passions experience the fullness of emotions, the positive and the negative, open to hurt from others in a new way, and only in the light of the resurrection can we maintain hope and a sense of identity without dissolution ourselves.

Even if there is the hope of resurrection, death is indeed still tragic. After all, Jesus wept just before raising Lazarus. Experiences of death include physical death and all the various forms of emotional and social death. Persistent experiences of death often lead to apathy, which is then expressed in various ways. The fullness of resurrected life pushes against the tendency for either idealism or apathy, not ignoring the tragedy while refusing to be defined by it. This leads into lament but not despair, that sickness unto death. Lament spurs a person to prayer, to continued struggle, to perseverance in hope, enduring an actuality that is not yet God's fulfilled promise. We do not see that which we need, but we do not lash out at others or ourselves because of it. Despair evokes panic. Lament sustains patience. The fulfilled promise awaits. Death is seen for what it is; life itself is justified. Resurrection affirms the human will to survive without the accompanying demand that it survive at the cost of others.

Resurrection gives the possibility for victory in any moment, a daily affirmation to always pursue life and not succumb to death-orienting patterns in order to maintain a semblance of self. "Christ's resurrection," Moltmann writes, "comprehends God's 'yes' to life and God's 'no' to death, and awakens our vital energies. 'Jesus is the defiance against poverty, against sin and misery,' wrote Christoph Blumhardt. And for that reason Christians are 'protest people against death.'"[45] Resurrection protests the world as it is and the way it says it must be, but does not lead us away from this world and its experiences. Resurrection embeds us even further into this world in light of God's overarching mission. "The hope of resurrection is part of the seeking for the kingdom of God, since the abolition of death is an irrelinquishable component of that kingdom."[46] This hope is a confrontation with what the systems say life must be like. The mission is the kingdom of God among us, the will of God being done on earth as well as in heaven.

THE PASSIONS OF NEW LIFE

The Christian message always contains the promise, a hope for redemption that emphasizes the value and personhood of everyone. It can speak out of contexts of privilege—who is more privileged than God, after all—but it can never justify oppressing based on its declarations of God's truth and power. It can speak out of contexts of alienation—the light of the world was born in a colonized stable, and not long after was a refugee from political persecution. These shared truths invert and blend the power structure toward a new realization of human identity that cannot find substantiation in itself while finding absolute validity through the love of God. Communicating a seeming paradox of meaning is a theme throughout Scripture: "Blessed are the poor for theirs is the kingdom."[47] The hope of God is a hope of transformation without repression or oppression, and theology must express this in both content and methodology, reflecting the kind of lordship that God reveals in this world.

For some, the task of theology is inherently oppressive: a patriarchal God that demands worship and subjugation to the bounds of an approved contingent of chosen religious representatives (generally men and of a single culture). The question is whether this is inherent to Christian theology itself or if Christian theology has often been co-opted by the religious system, utilizing orthodoxic themes in the service of that system's autopoietic perpetuation. In contrast, a liberation which emphasizes libertinism is likewise not sufficient. The Bible is filled with warnings about behavior and limits for what it means to be in relationship with God. That this is a relational rather than legal approach does not necessarily make things easier. After all, as Sarah Coakley argues, the ideal is a proper understanding of submission, itself a delicate and even dangerous topic in contemporary discussion. It is in submission, obedience to the cross, that the resurrection becomes a possibility, but such a path strikes against our sensibilities.

Coakley has noted that her emphases on contemplation and submission have received strong resistance.[48] A feminist emphasizing submission is no true feminist at all according to some. Yet rather than submitting to the critique, Coakley presses her point. The challenge is, ultimately, connected with our theology of the Trinity, which historically has seemed to reflect, adequately or inadequately, the economy of God within the social structures of the church. When the Father is understood as the source of the other two persons, there is an assumption of hierarchical ordering, which has varying scales of expression but tends to emphasize subordinating women.[49] "This hierarchical Godhead is . . . symbolically charged with social implications for women: for how is the ceding to the Spirit in the contemplative quest not also implicitly, for a woman, the ceding to potentially repressive and patriarchal structures in church and society."[50] In the Christian West, the tradition of the *filioque* exacerbates this issue, subordinating the Spirit beneath both Father and Son in linear procession, with the representatives of the Son, in the church and clergy, essentially arbiters of what the Spirit can do and in whom the Spirit can work and in what ways.[51] Trinitarian theology has thus provided a theological instantiation of oppression at the very core of Christian thought. Yet, how can we understand theology as particularly Christian except through a posture of submission and obedience to God?

For oppressors to be liberated, they must abandon their oppressing, but because such a status offers perceived meaning and worth, they are not likely to do so. They must be shown a better way, given hope to more substantive meaning and experience of life. This is not a small task, especially when the theological audience includes both those with power who do not want to give it up and those without power who want it. Neither wants to hear messages of submission or dependence. This is why explaining *how* Christian theology develops these themes in an empowering way is a key part of Sarah Coakley's theological contributions. In her prologue to her collection of essays titled "Powers and Submission," she writes, "At the heart of this book is an insistence that the apparently forced choice between dependent 'vulnerability' and liberative 'power' is a false one."[52]

The challenge is that the meanings of both power and submission are not truly established and that these must be understood in light of divine revelation and human calling if we are to utilize these for a truly liberative expression of Christian freedom. What is power and where does it reside? Is submission possible without suppression or repression? These have widely varying responses, and history mostly provides examples of oppressive answers. In our experience of God, however, we are provided a new way of life and understanding of ourselves that radically shapes our perceptions of others, and it is only in this experience of God that we can be free to perceive others in an open and non-oppressive way. The world—or rather the world systems—invites us to experience power through the binary of subjugation or domination. We, however, are not to submit to the world. This is exemplified in the third temptation of Jesus in Mt. 4:8–9: "Again, the devil took him to a very high mountain and showed him all the kingdoms of the world and their splendor; and he said to him, 'All these I will give you, if you will fall down and worship me.'" That is the false promise: worship another for ultimately limited gain. The way of holiness involves neither libertinism nor repression. Each expresses a misunderstanding of how we are to live in community, and in this misunderstanding insist they are the only alternatives to which all people must submit.[53]

Our posture before God does not negate our personhood in the context of other people, precisely because the persons in the Trinity do not negate or subjugate each other. Here, Coakley offers a modified perspective on social trinitarianism: the structure of the Trinity is not a model *for us*; rather, she argues that by participating with the Trinity we become shaped as a new kind of people, a transfigured community, opening us up in freedom with and for other people.[54] A right encounter with God empowers and enlivens and unites. The Son is "sourced" in the Spirit, as the Spirit is "sourced" in the Son, as the Father is Father from the other two "persons," "precisely via the Spirit's reflexive propulsion and the Son's creative effulgence."[55] Our participation with the Spirit is the empowering and transforming Trinitarian life with us. Thus, our experiences of the Spirit form us to be a self-similar expression of community. As Dumitru Staniloae writes, "The Spirit creates communion among us because in him there is the unconfused communion of the entire Trinity."[56] We live through the Spirit as the Spirit experiences and expresses life.

Again, this is not social Trinity as a model *for us* but sociality as the experience of the Trinity in participation *with God*. Only God offers such a result from otherwise oppressive behaviors of submission. The Trinity can never be understood as patriarchal and thus lead to patriarchal (or other oppressive) models if it is to be a truly Christian understanding of God.[57] The nature of God involves a "perfect mutual ontological desire that only the Godhead instantiates—without either loss or excess. Here is a desire not of need or imposition but of active plenitude and longing love."[58] This transformation of our sense of place and participation is, to use Pannenberg's terminology, exocentric relationality that frees us from oppressing and oppression, as oppressing can never be joined with a submission to God. If we submit to the God who loves humanity, there can be no justification for depersonalizing or subjecting others without essentially trying to replace God with our own self. Oppressing is heresy. It seeks to represent God to the world in a way that God does not express God's own self.

The passion of life is to be encouraged, not repressed or rejected, as it is the Spirit of life who leads us into being and in being leads us into God. This is the resurrection of whole self including our physical self, intellectual self, and emotional self. We become more alive. "The central theme is that the task of theology is always, if implicitly, a recommendation for life."[59] In life there are desires, and in new life the intensification of desire orients toward the source of life and eternal substantiation. This new life can still be co-opted however. For liberation to avoid either oppression or repression is the "paradox of power and vulnerability" of waiting on God. Just as the *kenosis* of the Son in the incarnation does not result in the Son's repression or subjugation, indeed results in his glorification, so too the model of kenosis as a posture before God in this world involves an opened vulnerability. Just as fasting is different than starving, so too does this waiting and patience reflect a proactive freedom, not an oppressive limitation.

In a life oriented by God's promise, a person does not need to dominate in order to avoid despair and secure a sublimated self that rejects forms of "weakness" as defined by the systems. In a life dominated by systems, vulnerability opens us up to abuse and subjugation, a reality in which might makes right—the law of club and fang as Jack London famously called it—inviting unjust suffering as our honesty of self before others becomes a way for their domination and control of us.[60] So, we repress our self, fight for domination, or descend into despair. This is not, however, the experience of the cross that contains the promise of resurrection. Just as the cross does not end with self-abnegation of Christ, but rather leads into the fully expressed identity and obedience of the Son in the redemption of the world, so too our "self-emptying" in the pursuit of liberation "is not a negation of the self, but the place of the self's transformation and expansion into God."[61] Such expansion is an invitation for our self fully realized, realized only in and through God, always in concert with others who are likewise being so recognized and realized.

Is this even possible?

Jean Vanier suggests that it's not only possible, it is radically inviting.

NEW LIFE AMONG OTHERS

After more than fifty years of developing, leading, and living in L'Arche, Jean Vanier expressed a very learned humility about the challenges and possibilities of what it means to be a liberated person in our society. This new narrative is the process of becoming human, no longer anonymous or a cog in the systems, but empersoned by the Holy Spirit to be who we truly are. For Vanier, this involves two realities: "It means to be someone, to have cultivated our gifts, and also to be open to others, to look at them not with a feeling of superiority but with eyes of respect. It means to become men and women with the wisdom of life."[62] In entering into these realities, we become aware of our common humanity, an awareness that transitions us from egocentricity to exocentricity while maintaining a coherent sense of self as self. We respect others in light of their value, able to come alongside without demanding reciprocity, no longer driven by our hurts or insecurities that require constant self-regard and consolation from others. We are fulfilled in our self and in this fulfillment engage others in an open and free way, forgiving our enemies, loving all without a sense of superiority and contributing without competition. This is what it means to become truly human.[63] It is the journey of a lifetime.

Vanier begins with an honest and direct assessment. As people, we need others. We are social creatures, yet the nature of our society often leads us to significant experiences of loneliness. Such loneliness is more than a mere unfortunate situation, it is a fundamental experience of life that drives our psychosocial development from the earliest stages. It is the experience of death in the midst of life, because life is intended to be a social experience. It "can appear as a faint dis-ease, an inner dissatisfaction, a restlessness in the heart," sometimes almost imperceptible, yet like flowing water, causing great fissures in our being.[64] Vanier suggests that even though loneliness can seem absent when life is going really well, it can never really go away because it is essential to human nature.[65] This does not make it an inherent evil, however, as like with any fundamental need, it drives us to the kind of nourishment we need. Vanier highlights how loneliness often drives the arts and revolts against injustice, as the fire activates a willingness to disrupt the status quo. Such loneliness is a common human experience that exists across cultural and physical distinctions, with each particular context and experience pushing toward patterns of resolution. In order to avoid insufficient patterns of development that lead to expressions of oppressing, Vanier notes five principles from his own journey that help him navigate the challenges of loneliness while retaining an exocentric, fulfilled identity.[66]

First, we must understand that "all humans are sacred" no matter their abilities or contributions, and this is not a passive valuing but an active importance. We need each other and everyone has something to contribute to our becoming. Second, we and the world are in the process of evolving, learning from and incorporating the past in new ways that help us encounter our present and future. This highlights the interpretive importance of eschatology, as Moltmann and Pannenberg have long argued. The future we anticipate affects what we see as important for continued coherence. In light of Christ's future, and the work of the Spirit, our evolution is oriented by values of "openness, love, wholeness, unity, peace, the human potential for healing and redemption, and, most important, the necessity of forgiveness, so everything that permits and encourages the flow of life and growth is necessary."[67] Third, the progress to maturity always involves others, as we become whole in our sociality when in dialog with others on the same journey, secure in a sense of belonging and exploration. Fourth, the ability to choose is vital. We can coerce a social regimen, but results in repression rather than transformation. In making space for options and choices, becoming responsible for one's self and others, a person realizes the importance of others, losing the self-centeredness and defense strategies of the ego. "In other words," Vanier writes, "we humans need to be rooted in good earth in order to produce good fruit. But for this we need to freely risk life in order to give of ourselves."[68]

Finally, this process of development is oriented in truth, the right perception of reality. The goal involves coherence with our created self and the created world, accepting our context while working toward a more developed experience of fullness, neither idealistic nor fatalistic. We abandon being closed up in the systems, "of being closed up in illusions, dreams, and ideologies, frightened of reality" instead choosing to "move toward connectedness."[69] Reality in and of itself is neither crushing nor something to be forced into the shape we think it should take. Reality is both a context and an opportunity for the promise to take shape within our experiences, something we can commit to in finding its fulfillment. "Time," as Reimer notes, "is transformed from a commodity to an expression of love."[70] These principles, again, are part of a continuing journey, an orienting set of patterns that help us navigate the challenges and opportunities more fully. They are not themselves the hope, but they express the signifiers of the hope. The hope itself is more fully in the experience of belonging. The experience is that of the kingdom of God among us.

CONCLUSION

A life that is caught in the struggles of definition and determination, trying to find some way of contesting the inevitable reality of looming death, is a life defined by protest. It is not yet a life defined by hope. It is easy to say what is wrong—wrong in the world if not always easy to say what is wrong in our own self. It is easy to highlight the evils of others, creating categories of unclean behavior or unclean being. Even as trust is at the root of human longing, our ability to perceive injustice is part of our core as well. Injustice certainly abounds, and we are bombarded with its presence in ways large and ways miniscule, though sometimes the latter loom largest for us when they are closest to our experiences. Caught in the valley of the shadow of death, we fear every evil, turning to strike against it or turning away in despair. Either way, this reality of shadow life causes us separation and isolation, if not as sole individuals, then in groups, or tribes, or departments.

God does not need the world to provide definition of who he is or what he can do. God does not rely on the world to define others or their value. As such, the holiness of God is an interactive one, giving meaning, value, and hope. Jesus entered this world as the revelation of holiness. This holiness healed. This holiness invited. This holiness participated in even the most unclean of contexts. Rome was powerful, but it was not holy. The Law was influential, but it was not God. In Christ, we see what holiness does and what holiness calls others to do. This is the messianic mission, a mission that did not end with the death of Jesus. He is risen. This mission certainly did not end with the ascension either. The mission is spread through the Holy Spirit, who invites and empowers people to new life, a life of hope and a life of real freedom. This is a resurrection life, transforming our way in this world and transforming our experience of it. Those who participate in this way are transformed, their desires reshaped not repressed. Those in the Spirit are not doped; they are awakened. Everything is new. Life is thoroughly possible. Once we are aware of its possibility, it actually can take shape in the nitty-gritty realities of our particular context, among our families, friends, neighborhoods, and so on.

While transforming our particular experience of life, resurrection goes beyond our individual experience of it. It is God's work and, as God's work, resurrection encompasses the whole of history and the whole of the cosmos. Space and time are themselves subject to the will of God. What can the systems do in light of that lordship? They can distract humanity, seeking to limit the scope of possibility through narrowed visions of immediacy or claims of human inadequacy. They ask, "What is the point of change?" They tell a story in which the world is how it must be. There is a different story, however, for those who seek life in full. God's work is a divine meta-narrative, an integrated understanding of coherence and integrity in this world and under God's lordship. This is the nature of the kingdom of God.

NOTES

1. See Iain Taylor, *Pannenberg on the Triune God* (New York: T&T Clark, 2007), 127.
2. Kam Ming Wong, *Wolfhart Pannenberg on Human Destiny* (Burlington, VT: Ashgate, 2008), 46.
3. Mt. 5:17.
4. See Lev. 13.
5. Dunn writes, "What Jesus did seem to object to was the application of purity rules simply to exclude from community, without anything more being done for the person(s) thus reckoned unclean. And what made him even more angry was the factional use of purity rules to dispute right of access to the holy to others who did not share the factions' interpretation of the purity laws. In such circumstances, purity of heart rendered such factional disputes irrelevant; the humble confession f sin to God by the sinner was what assured the sinner's acceptance by God, not the Pharisee's testimony of halakhoth observed (Luke 18.10–14). Holiness was more important for Jesus as a power which cleanses uncleanness and dissolves impurity than as a status (of a person or place) constantly threatened by the 'common' and profane." James D. G. Dunn, "Jesus and Holiness: The Challenge of Purity," in *Holiness: Past and Present*, ed. Stephen C. Barton (New York: T&T Clark, 2003), 192.

6. Wolfhart Pannenberg, *Systematic Theology*, trans. Geoffrey W. Bromiley, vol. 1 (Grand Rapids: Eerdmans, 1991), 399.

7. Wong writes, "According to Pannenberg, in the second century the Old Testament view that God created human beings in his image and likeness was interpreted in the sense that God bestowed his *logos* on humans, the same *logos* which was to appear fully and completely in Jesus. This means that only by Jesus is the human destiny, the true humanity, fully realized. This is compatible with the New Testament teaching that only Jesus Christ is the perfect image of God." Wong, *Wolfhart Pannenberg on Human Destiny*, 40. This suggests an element of recapitulation in life and mission of Jesus as understood by Pannenberg.

8. Wolfhart Pannenberg, *Jesus—God and Man* (London: SCM Press, 1968), 416.

9. Wolfhart Pannenberg, *Faith and Reality* (Philadelphia: Westminster Press, 1977), 48–49: "In this way the Christian finds in Jesus the image of the God revealed by him, the God of fatherly love. As God's image, Jesus is the prototype of true human perfection, and every individual human being approaches his human destiny to the extent that his life is transformed into the likeness of the love of God revealed in Jesus' deeds, in order in that way to become truly human and truly free."

10. Pannenberg, *Jesus—God and Man*, 298: "God has made Christ to be sin for us, that we might become in him the righteousness of God. That Christ has been made to be sin means that the misfortune following from our sin has fallen upon him." Stephen Barton, "Dislocating and Relocating Holiness," in *Holiness: Past and Present*, 206 writes, "Holiness as separation—of life and death, male and female, priest and lay, Jew and Gentile, purity and impurity—is displaced by holiness as solidarity: the solidarity of Jesus the great high priest in sharing human nature as flesh and blood and, above all, in accepting the defilement of death (cf. Heb. 2.14–15, 17)."

11. See Wong, *Wolfhart Pannenberg on Human Destiny*, 43.

12. Wolfhart Pannenberg, *Systematic Theology*, trans. Geoffrey W. Bromiley, vol. 2 (Grand Rapids: Eerdmans, 1994), 452.

13. See Wong, *Wolfhart Pannenberg on Human Destiny*, 55.

14. Wolfhart Pannenberg, *Systematic Theology*, trans. Geoffrey W. Bromiley, vol. 3 (Grand Rapids: Eerdmans, 1998), 200.

15. In Oden, "Obedience is Better than Sacrifice," 100–115. I argue this is the central element of the atonement. The obedience of Christ expresses a relationship of trust between Father and Son. We do not trust the Father and the Father does not trust us, but we can trust each other through the trust in the work of Christ.

16. Pannenberg, *Systematic Theology*, 1:400.

17. Pannenberg, *Systematic Theology*, 1:400. Cf. Ibid., 3:197.

18. Pannenberg, *Systematic Theology*, 3:4. Christiaan Mostert writes, "Only through the Son and the Spirit can human beings attain the perfection of human existence. Only in fellowship with God, in the relationship of sonship to God mediated by the Spirit, can the perfection of this relatively independent existence be achieved." Christiaan Mostert, *God and the Future: Wolfhart Pannenberg's Eschatological Doctrine of God* (New York: T&T Clark, 2002), 199.

19. "The Spirit glorifies Jesus as the Father's Son by teaching us to recognize the revelation of the Father in Jesus' words and work." Pannenberg, *Systematic Theology*, 3:5.

20. Keener, *The Mind of the Spirit*, 97.
21. Pannenberg, *Systematic Theology*, 3:12.
22. See Ibid., 3:583.
23. "The Spirit is not only the source of the new; it is also the Spirit of unity, who integrates, reconciles, and unites, and who brings the cosmos to its consummation in the eternity of God." Mostert, *God and the Future*, 172. Cf. Pannenberg, *Systematic Theology*, 2:102.
24. Pannenberg, *Faith & Reality*, 47.
25. "In relation to the God of the power of the future, man is free: free for a truly personal life, free to accept the provisionality of everything, free with regard to nature and society, free for that creative love that changes the world without destroying it. This creative love proceeds from freedom and is directed toward affirming and creating freedom in the world." Wolfhart Pannenberg, *Theology and the Kingdom of God* (Philadelphia: Westminster, 1969), 69.
26. See Pannenberg, *Systematic Theology*, 1:401–410.
27. Ibid., 3:610.
28. Ibid.
29. Pannenberg writes that "the simultaneous presence of the whole content of one's life through participation in the eternal presence of God means judgment. This is because of the many self-contradictions within our lives that prevent its identity from becoming fully manifest. In the earthly history of our lives the awareness of what those self-contradictions are doing to our identity is mitigated by the temporal sequence of phases, so that we easily forget about what we promised yesterday or a year ago. In the eternal presence of our life as a whole, the destructive impact of all those contradictions will become fully evident. . . . Eternal judgment does not mean a violent reaction of a punishing God against his creatures. It rather means that the sinner is left to the consequences of his or her own behavior. In this way death is the consequence of sin, because already in his or her separation from God the human person gets separated from the origin of life." In Pannenberg, "Constructive and Critical Functions of Christian Eschatology," 134. Cf. Wolfhart Pannenberg, *What Is Man? Contemporary Anthropology in Theological Perspective*, trans. Duane A. Priebe (Philadelphia: Fortress Press, 1970), 78–79.
30. Pannenberg, *Systematic Theology*, 3:611.
31. Pannenberg, "Constructive and Critical Functions of Christian Eschatology," 135: "The Presence of God means glorification as well as judgment, and whether it will be on or the other depends on the relation of the creature to God and to his kingdom. Therefore the beatitudes are addressed to those who are not satisfied in their situation so that they would not cease being concerned about God, but who because of the frustration inherent in their condition have no other hope but God. The message is not different when, in line with the early Christian Gospel, it is said that those who have communion with Jesus will be saved from the eternal wrath, to the effect that the discord of contradictions destroying the unity of our life will be overcome and transformed into the harmony of that whole that God intended us to be."
32. See Pannenberg, *Systematic Theology*, 3:193.
33. See Taylor, *The Go-Between God*, 159–163.

34. It is noteworthy that Paul, in 1 Corinthians 15, makes the truth of the physical resurrection of Jesus as the make-or-break issue in Christian faith. If it happened, everything is possible. If it didn't, Paul and his readers are to be greatly pitied as there is nothing of worth in Christian faith.

35. Moltmann, *The Living God*, 146.

36. Ibid.

37. Richard Harries, *Is There a Gospel for the Rich?* (New York: Andrew Mowbray, 1992), 166.

38. Jürgen Moltmann, *Sun of Righteousness, Arise!: God's Future for Humanity and the Earth*, trans. Margaret Kohl (Minneapolis: Fortress Press, 2010), 48.

39. Moltmann, *Sun of Righteousness*, 48.

40. Moltmann, *Ethics of Hope*, 40–41.

41. Moltmann, *Sun of Righteousness*, 55.

42. Moltmann, *Ethics of Hope*, 50.

43. In talking about his weight loss, the magician Penn Jillette has said that after following a very dramatic shift in his eating habits, losing about 100 pounds, "I now eat whatever I want, but what I want has changed profoundly." See "How Penn Jillette Lost over 100 Lbs and Still Eats Whatever He wants," https://www.youtube.com/watch?v=NelIXCuuSZ0.

44. Moltmann, *Sun of Righteousness*, 54.

45. Ibid., 76–77.

46. Ibid., 81.

47. Mt. 5:3.

48. See, for instance, Coakley, *Powers and Submissions*, xii–xv.

49. See, for instance, the recent debate among Evangelical theologians: Caleb Lindgren, "Gender and the Trinity: From Proxy War to Civil War," June 16, 2016, https://www.christianitytoday.com/ct/2016/june-web-only/gender-trinity-proxy-war-civil-war-eternal-subordination.html.

50. Coakley, *Powers and Submissions*, 57.

51. See Coakley, *GSS*, 330. Such subordination is often coupled with adulation: women are given a supposed honor while not being allowed equal participation or allowed to be their whole self. Such honor is given to Mary—an idealized mother who is essentially de-sexed. It is noteworthy that Moltmann (e.g., *The Spirit of Life*, 306–309) and Pannenberg (e.g., ST 1:317–319) likewise each vehemently rejected the *filioque* clause.

52. Coakley, *Powers and Submissions*, xv.

53. For a fuller discussion of this, see Sarah Coakley, *The New Asceticism* (New York: Bloomsbury, 2015), chap. 5.

54. Coakley, *GSS*, 321–322. On the correspondence and limitations of using the Trinity as an analogy for human community, especially that of the church, see Veli-Matti Kärkkäinen, *Hope and Community*, vol. 5, *A Constructive Christian Theology for the Pluralistic World* (Grand Rapids: Eerdmans, 2017), 284–291.

55. Coakley, *GSS*, 333.

56. Staniloae, *Orthodox Dogmatic Theology*, 77.

57. See J. Scott Horrell, "The Eternal Son of God in the Social Trinity," 77 in Fred Sanders and Klaus Issler, eds., *Jesus in Trinitarian Perspective: An Intermediate Christology* (Nashville: B&H Academic, 2007). Horrell writes that "those who on the basis of a hierarchical model of the Trinity justify political oppression or autonomous masculine rulership in familial and ecclesial settings do not grasp the self-sacrificing nature of the Father as well as the of the Son and the Spirit." Horrell also argues that those who project Western definitions about equality and freedom into the Trinity are likewise missing the mark.

58. Coakley, *GSS*, 333.

59. Ibid., 18.

60. See Jack London, *The Call of the Wild* (Mineola, NY: Dover Books, 1990), chap. 2.

61. Coakley, *Powers and Submissions*, 36.

62. Vanier, *Becoming Human*, 3.

63. See Ibid., 5.

64. Ibid., 7.

65. Ibid.

66. These are found in Vanier, *Becoming Human*, 14–15.

67. Vanier, *Becoming Human*, Cf. Moltmann, *Experiences in Theology*, 149–150.

68. Vanier, *Becoming Human*, 15.

69. Ibid.

70. Reimer, *Living L'Arche*, 24.

Chapter 11

Hope in the Kingdom

INTRODUCTION

The experience of God's will on earth as it is in heaven is the transforming presence of the Kingdom already among us. God's will for us is to love truly and deeply—the fundamental experience of the kingdom—in keeping with God's own purposes and shape of created reality. Because God is holy, he is love. God's being is God's love. The kingdom is liberating because it is established in God's identity, thus overriding the patterns of colliding egos and disintegrating systems. Our being with God, our holiness, is the fount of our love. Love is more than an intellectual theme for theological pondering. Love is inherently relational. Love is inherently communal. Our holiness is not about conforming to a certain morality or legalistic code. Our holiness that is from the Spirit of life is about becoming who we truly are, finding our real identity within the scope of God's being, identifying with Christ, becoming trustworthy in his work, and so finding our own exocentric identity in fullness with God and with others. Love God. Love neighbor: in the fullest sense of the term, because God is fullness.

Our holiness is our love. Our love is our holiness. Love, after all, covers a multitude of sins. Holiness is not contrasted with love; a severe rule countered by a grace-filled gesture. Holiness is the state which allows a person to love. When a person is freed from the bondage of the ego, no longer seeking after self-assured identity but instead is free to be who they truly are in their participation with the God who truly is, they can express their talents, gifts, blessings, and all their being in positive support of all others. As this holy love begins to define every part of life, being reaches from the particular into the universal, from an atom of time into eternity. In this holiness that is love, we grow into ourselves, and in this participation, we begin to participate in the kingdom of God, God's will being done on earth as it is in heaven. In this chapter, I will explore the shape this kingdom takes and how this kingdom is expressed in our lives. Once again, I gather insights from Pannenberg, Moltmann, Coakley, and Vanier to create a dialogical chorus. I begin by examining characteristics of the kingdom and how this shapes our participation with God, with this world, and with our own self. The kingdom orients a new way of being and offers a substantive experience of belonging for those who are gathered within it.

THE NATURE OF THE KINGDOM

Our participation with God's being in holiness is our identification with his rule—with his eschatological presence in this present and future world. Our participation in holiness is only possible through the work of the Holy Spirit, who is God's being in exocentric expression, reaching out and drawing in, transforming us to conform to God's being, and thus God's rule.[1] As Pannenberg writes, "God's being and existence cannot be conceived apart from his rule."[2] God's being is his rule.[3] With this perspective, God's Spirit is likewise God's kingdom.[4] We experience his kingdom in the acting out of our holiness, which is our fellowship with God and our identity that is not dependent on ego, but on God's identity.[5] This holiness transforms us and transforms the world as we move toward the world in holistic love. "The key to understanding the inextricable connection between love for God and love for fellowmen is the identity of God's being with the coming of his Kingdom."[6] This rule is not entirely manifested in our contexts. Pannenberg would even say God's being is not fully realized.[7] As God's reality as God entails his full rule over this world, the proleptic kingdom manifested by the Spirit awaits full revelation of both ourselves and God together in open, *perichoretic* fellowship.[8] This kingdom is our hope because God's full expression of his identity is an absolute. Because this kingdom is the experience of love, it not only insists on community, it consists of community as its fundamental and proleptic expression.

PARTICIPATING IN THE KINGDOM

The hope for the kingdom among us can easily drift into a form of idealism, and indeed historically has drifted this way. Impatience can provoke shortcuts toward transformation, "having a form of godliness but denying its power."[9] Likewise, ignoring such a goal can lead people into a gnostic form of individualized redemption out of the physical world. Moltmann navigates these two dangers in following the lead of Christoph Blumhardt and Dietrich Bonhoeffer. Both offer a renewed Yes to the earth in light of God's kingdom that engages—indeed loves—the *cosmos*. The kingdom does not involve a wait and see approach for an otherworldly and disembodied expression. In a world filled with much that speaks of negation and loss, God's kingdom is a Yes by God to the world as it *should* be. "At the centre of Blumhardt's hope for the kingdom of God on earth is not the Kantian idealism of nineteenth-century liberal German Protestantism, but the overcoming of death in the resurrection of Christ from the dead."[10] Bonhoeffer has the same center.[11] Both are seeking a new world that is "already beginning in the midst of the old one" in the work of God through Christ.[12] In being faithful to Christ, Christians are to be faithful to that which God is faithful toward, participating with God who is faithful to his promise to creation. The resurrection sends a person more fully back into this world to live out the narrative of the kingdom at work. We become people of the Promise. The Promise is more real than the supposed reality expressed by the systems.

Participating in this kingdom involves three initial aspects for Moltmann, each helping the people of the Promise to avoid deficient responses.[13] First, they "must free themselves from the world around them and resist its pressures." Second, they "must find a new identity and fellowship." Third, they can then enter into an alternative way of living that links the ethos of change with "solemnity of the new era." Such an alternative life is an intervening alternative that is defined by the new narrative of the kingdom of God and is shaped in its activities by constant referral to its empowering modes of transformation. The key element in this kingdom involves "resistance against the forces of death and unconditional love for life," characteristics of a resurrection ethos. Such an ethos can only maintain its trajectory in light of faith in God, which is the "trusting self-surrender to the coming Kingdom and an experience of freedom in its proximity." It is only when we are truly free in our new identity in Christ and becoming established in the patterns of meaning derived by such a holistic encounter that we can avoid the controlling and dehumanizing tendencies of other models of social change. In *The Spirit of Life*, Moltmann address this latter tendency:

> But the people who throw themselves into practical life because they cannot come to terms with themselves simply become a burden for other people. Social praxis and political involvement are not a remedy for the weakness of our own personalities.
>
> Men and women who want to act on behalf of other people without having deepened their own understanding of themselves, without having built up their own capacity for sensitive loving, and without having found freedom towards themselves, will find nothing in themselves that they can give to anyone else.

Even presupposing good will and the lack of evil intentions, all they will be able to pass on is the infection of their own egoism, the aggression generated by their own anxieties, and the prejudices of their own ideology.[14]

Without an orienting internal transformation, a person may seek to fix themselves through fixing the world. This may sound worthwhile at first, but the problem is that because it draws from dysfunction it will express either an anemic or destructive solution. Moltmann writes, "Anyone who wants to fill up his own hollowness by helping other people will simply spread the same hollowness."[15] The work of transformation is more than simply getting things done, and indeed those who may seem like they are the most engaged in social action may in fact be motivated by significant dysfunction, which undermines the possibility of lasting liberation. This more often creates added tensions, as impatience, anger, frustration are fueled by both the need for change and inner dissatisfaction. Resistance in either goal or method bumps up against the person's ego, that very element of oppressing defense. And then transformation becomes a battle of egos, raising tensions, heightening divisions. The response is to then reject the possibility of patient change, because others do not seem to be listening. "Why?" Moltmann asks. "Because people are far less influenced by what another person says and does than the activist would like to believe. They are much more influenced by what the other *is*, and his *way* of speaking and behaving."[16]

Engaging in oppressing tactics—even for good reason—continues the cycles of social and psychological defenses. Egos bump into each other. The systems press forward, utilizing this competition for power and control. This is the substantive expression of an earthly kingdom, battles of wills by people who are following the leading of anonymizing systems. The way of the kingdom, however, is a way of peace, in which transformation is possible precisely because it is no longer an attempt to address inner anxiety or despair through outward action. When a person is full of peace—not just talkers about peace—people begin to trust them. When a person speaks of hope and freedom for all—people find themselves awakening to the possibilities.

This new way of encountering the world isn't without its challenges, making it all the more important for those who share this mission to support each other. Evagrius writes that there are three groups of demons who offer opposition to those who pursue this kind of life: "those entrusted with the appetites of gluttony, those who suggest avaricious thoughts, and those who incite us to seek the esteem of men."[17] Moltmann does not use the subject of demons in his approach but he does emphasize these same elements throughout his ethics as fundamental barriers of a truly free life, implicitly taking hold of Kierkegaard's understanding of the demonic as an "anxiety about the good" and that it "is unfreedom that wants to close itself off."[18] The kingdom of God is a contrast to these patterns. It involves a way of living in freedom alongside others, making space for others rather than hoarding or competing for limited goods.[19] We live in freedom because we are open to others through our trust of God. If we fear starvation or lack, we pursue gluttony. If we fear loss of security or the greed of others, we are avaricious. If we fear our own lack of identity or meaning or purpose, we seek the esteem of others to provide us value and meaning.[20] On this role of fear in sin, Gyula Simonyi writes:

> Fear is like rocks in the soil: power that hides headstrongly in the depth of our personality. It is not sin, for we do not want it; in fact, we would rather like to be free from its rule, but its consequences are often sins. . . . Fear can chase love out of our heart; in fact, it can cause great wickedness and hatred within us.[21]

The contrast of fear is trust. If we trust others in light of God's promise, we become free to be ourselves. The kingdom is characterized by this trust, a trust that is exemplified in the obedience of Jesus on the cross, fulfilled in the resurrection, and pressed forward in the work of the Spirit. "Trust is freedom's essential living space."[22] We are fully ourselves when we are free to trust. As Moltmann puts it, "Fish need water to swim in, birds need air in which to fly, and we human beings need trust if we are to develop our humanity and our powers."[23] In this trust, Jesus really is truly human. Jesus is the new Adam, his trust begets our trust, and the Spirit engages our trust in the life of this world.[24]

The context of trust is initiated in the trust in God, God's will being done in full among us, and only in this trust can we be people who live out a different narrative in a coherent world system, one that is oriented by the *pneumapoietic* transformation in us and around us.[25] God initiates this trust in the development of the Promise, "we trust God because God trusts us."[26] The tension, of course, is stepping out into this faith before we see and experience the validation and security of an assured future. The kingdom of God that is trust is also, thus, faith. We have faith in the hope of the Promise and in this faith of hope we live out lives of love that radiate in every direction and enter into every sphere of our experienced reality.[27] Such orientation can never be artificial or coerced. Coercion is the tendency of theocracies or fundamentalisms, in which freedom is lost, trust is nonexistent, and all that survives is an increasingly tenuous connection with perceived religious values which must then be rigidly enforced by asserting power over others.[28] Coercion is the indication of impatience and faithlessness. These have little or nothing to do with the kingdom of God as they have rejected the faith, hope, trust, and love that resonates in the lives of those who participate with the Spirit.

As these religious patterns seek control not trust, instead of drawing together the various systems into a coherent expression of God's lordship, they seek the dominance of the religious system over the other systems, taking control of separate functions and elements of life, but not integrating them together. The other systems become restrained and restrain those within them. "To replace trust by control," Moltmann writes, "means destroying creative life."[29] It is easier to control, and it is often very validating to control. Moltmann highlights the element of trust versus control in the issue of academic freedom: where there is control there is not progress but continued commodification. Free expression is diminished in the pursuit of producing the production of the academic system. Everyone does what is expected and what is expected is enforced by powers who control grants, employment, promotion. Oppression and commodification turn everyone and everything within a system into an object for control and use.[30] Trust involves risk, and we prefer not to risk when we think there is much at stake. That is why breakthroughs are often developed by those who have been cut out of the system.[31]

God trusts rather than controls.[32] A shocking development, but one that is displayed throughout the Bible. God, in trust, continues to place the mission of renewal in the hands of broken and insufficient people. God's trust in us is certainly a risk.[33] God bears this risk in the pursuit of the promise of the kingdom that is truly one of freedom, a freedom expressed in the context of others, a hope in God who hopes for us. In hope we are open to God's freeing work. In hope we participate in freeing of others. In God's hope, we are open in trust and thus initiate societies that are participatory and anticipatory, living out the promised kingdom in the fullness of the present, a prevenient love that invites others to love in response, expressing what Veli-Matti Kärkkäinen has recently described as "salutary communion."[34] Humanity is never considered a commodity by God and so humans can never consider each other a commodity if they are to be faithful to who God is and what God does.[35]

Addressing oppression is not, after all, simply about fixing problems. In God's kingdom all are valued, all are loved, there is enough for everyone. In God's kingdom we experience the fullness of life that invites overflowing expression with and toward others. In this fullness of life—this fullness of our true self—we encounter issues and people in new ways. Instead of evoking distrust, we establish trust. Instead of stoking anger and division, we love and hope. Instead of being driven by the autopoietic drives of the systems, or the insufficient attempts to establish our own ego, we experience a substantive peace. In this peace, we experience and express a transforming liberation in our lives and for those around us, whatever their status. Moltmann writes, "Only the person who has found his own self can give himself. What else can he give? It is only the person who knows that he is accepted who can accept others without dominating them. The person who has become free in himself can liberate others and share their suffering."[36] This is life in the kingdom of God, unity and diversity, community and particularity.

The kingdom of God is comprehensive—a meta-system—bringing coherence and integrity to otherwise disparate systems in our life. Because God is Lord of all, there can be neither segmented spheres of our lives nor should we think we are excused from or leave behind the elements of our society. The kingdom is not the church, where religious elements are developed and particular forms of Christian discipline and practices are pursued. The church should be in pursuit of the kingdom within the part of the world it exists. It does not exist as a counter *to* the world; it exists as a witness to the kingdom that is a calling *for* the world. It can never be a contrast to the world without dissolving its own purpose.

The church is in the world, a part of a contextual environment.[37] It is embedded in it as a fractal testimony of the new patterns of God's holistic kingdom.[38] Those in such community are drawn into each other through this love and awaken a new experience of trusting community.[39] This community is the fullness of God's identity and lordship expressed into this world, a perichoretic transformation.[40] The power of death is no longer a substantive threat, and instead we can live in the new way that the cross represents: trust and confrontation in pursuit of a more adequate way of life in this world. In the inbreaking kingdom, "The laws of this world are no longer valid, so one does not have to adapt to them or let oneself be made to conform to them, for one can 'be transformed' through a renewal of life orientation."[41] It is the experience and process of salvation, drawing a person out of anonymized isolation and into a substantive reality that reorients a person within their context in light of eternity. Such an orientation is empowered by the Spirit, oriented in love, and expressed in community.

ORIENTING IN THE KINGDOM

God's community extends into eternity. It begins with silence. "At the heart of prayer and silence," Sarah Coakley writes, "is a simple surrendering of control to God. Instead of a busy setting of one's own agendas, prayer becomes pared down to wanting God alone—'with the sharp darts of longing love,' as the author of *The Cloud of Unknowing* memorably puts it."[42] In surrendering to God, we open ourselves up to a fullness of life. It is a surrender into liberation itself, for both the oppressed and the oppressors. Once again, I come back to Ps. 70:1, that devotional formula that is suitable for all occasions because it orients the person back into the presence of God. Only continual reorientation with God, in God's presence, provides the sustaining orientation that bears fruit. The seed can grow only if it is watered. Without water it will wither and die.[43] And yet, prayer is not generally a key facet of a systematic theology.[44] It is relegated to topics of spirituality and maybe practical theology. It is presumed before meals, bedtimes, sermons, and, if you teach in a Christian school, classes. Yet, prayer has been a core expression of Christian faith for both the most devout and the most influential thinkers in Christian history.

The nature of prayer itself speaks to the reason. Prayer is disempowering, especially in its private form.[45] It is disempowering in both its submission to faith—we speak to a God we cannot experience through our senses—and in admission of insufficiency for our current experiences. This is why prayer is so seemingly natural for those in times of crises, where the insufficiency is radically apparent. There are no atheists in foxholes, as the saying goes.[46] In experiences of privilege, however, God is thought extraneous, and treated as such either explicitly or implicitly, even if the religious system is still operational in providing system-specific perpetuation. This is how oppression becomes prevalent even in places that are broadly confessing the lordship of Christ. It is a representation without consultation, an assumption of authority without reference to the Lord, serving as supposed stewards of a presumably absent king.

In Christian theology, the king is not absent, and assumption of power and privilege in his name is a form of damnable presumption, whether in absolute ways of a totalitarian ruler of nations or in the minuscule ways of a localized despot of a department, organization, church, or home. Earnest prayer orients a person away from this tendency. It is a total perspective vortex, where we are given insight into our real place in light of God's eternal nature and power and love. This perspective is not dehumanizing, not ultimately at least, though it does push against systems-derived perspectives of what it means to be human. It is de-systematizing and then it is re-humanizing as the creator of the universe seeks us out. Thus, in prayer we are, or at least should be, reoriented to our true self and our true calling in our specific context. We become persons in the presence of the triune God. Indeed, we become a people.[47]

Coakley orients her discussion of contemplative prayer within three developmental stages. Prayer is a complex reality because each person is at a different place of selfhood and relationship with God, thus prayer is very personalized. This may point against any possible systematizing, but that is missing the nature of prayer as well. Prayer is personal, but not an isolated experience. It is the practice of participating with God. It is also the practice of joining in with a communion of saints. Over the centuries men and women have been faithful in pursuit of it and drew maps of its nature, with many writing specific treatises on it from the earliest days of the church onward. Just as Clement wrote in three patterns that reflect three stages of Christian conception and focus, Coakley emphasizes how Christian practices go through stages of ascent. These three stages are the "purgative," the "illumative," and the "unitive."[48] Prayer is an expressive practice in each, with each stage revealing a different expression of this communicative communion.

In the purgative stage, a person needs special separation from disordered patterns or defining systems. Forms of legalism help them navigate into a new way of life, just as a child needs rules to help them shape behavior. Coakley notes this stage includes a distinct emphasis on gender binaries in identity and interaction, not in a repressive sense but as part of a rediscovery of self in the context of others, and as a reflection of the dysfunctional patterns in much of society. The status of being "born again" insists on maturing in a way that abandons addictive, defining, or controlling patterns and so requires patterns that push against controlling behaviors. As Vanier writes, "We all have our filters created from our early childhood, protecting our vulnerable hearts and minds. To grow is to let go of these filters and to welcome the reality that is given, no longer through preconceived ideas, theories, prejudgments or prejudices or through our wounded emotions, but just as is."[49] Prayer, and the orientating grace of it, provides a constant reference for this way.[50] Coakley highlights the *Paedagogos* of Clement of Alexandria as a representative writing for this stage, in which a newfound belief in God and participation with God helps people distinguish appropriate behavior from inappropriate.[51]

In the illumative stage, a person is no longer focused on duties that relate to purgation, with its sharply delineated distinctions, but rather engages in a more proactive service, expressions of transformative love pursued in an unsystematic way. Coakley suggests Benedict's Rule as the example, highlighting the "great practical and spiritual subtlety" of this work as a way of leading men and women toward a re-modulation of belief. It helps lead a person "to find 'Christ,' for instance, in new and unexpected places—in the beggar at the door, in one's own spiritual endurance and suffering, in the ministrations of the Abbot."[52] The restrictive practices that enable a separation from systems-derived identity are replaced by a form of developing belief that enables a freedom of practice, where participation with God encourages diverse expressions of liberated interactions.[53]

This leads into the unitive stage, which involves becoming incorporated into the life of the Trinity, drawn by the Spirit into communion with Father and Son. Such transformative participation leads a person even more fully into this present life. Which emphasizes how development with the Spirit does not end with isolation or separation, though may initially include these elements as part of a retuned life. Becoming truly free in Christ awakens a newfound participation in the messianic mission, no longer driven by the narratives of this world and so able to interact with this world in transformative ways. Through prayer, those in this stage are increasingly reflecting the corporeal and intellectual vision of God "that is at a new and deeper level of response than previously known."[54] Prayer is, after all, where theology itself becomes full. "If you are a theologian you will pray truly," Evagrius wrote, "and if you pray truly you are a theologian."[55] As Evagrius's translator notes,

"For Evagrius, the 'theologian' is one who has attained the true knowledge of God in contemplation."[56] More recently, Dumitru Staniloae has emphasized the importance of community in this pursuit of prayer:

> The theologian must take part in this prayer and in the life of the Church, for theology wishes to know God from the experience of his saving activity among men. But the theologian will never know this if he does not enter into a personal relationship of love with God and with the faithful in prayer. Hence one who prays together with the other members of the Church is that much more of a theologian. For in their common love for God, the saving and perfecting work of his love reveals itself all the more.[57]

While Coakley rightly points to Evagrius, John of the Cross, and Theresa of Avila as expressions of this stage, the ultimate model is Jesus himself, whose commitment to prayer is highlighted throughout the Gospels. Unlike we might see in more rigorous monastics, his mode of contemplation is embedded in "the material, the everyday."[58] It leads toward what Moltmann characterizes as "the integration of individual life into the life of the community, and the life of the human community into the warp and weft of all living things on earth."[59] The direct infusion of God's grace in a person's inner and enacted reality orients as a resonating presence of God's life in and for this world. God's being is God's rule, and God's kingdom, his rule, is now a transformative presence among us.

We become alive in a new way, then witness to this enlivening in each part of our lives and places of interactions. Rather than leading us away from the world, contemplation rightly orients us to be truly in this world as God has called us to be. Contemplation leads to discerned action. As Janice McRandal notes, "Coakley's bold assertion is that contemplative practices are truly transformative and empowering, and therefore give rise to the prophetic voice and act."[60] The danger, of course, is that such participatory experiences can themselves become a source of pride, which is why the early monastics noted that pride is among the most dangerous sins of all, as it afflicts those who are otherwise closest to God, and in this affliction may lead to the most precipitous fall.[61] Thus in this life, our contemplative practices should never lead us far from the reorienting statements of Ps. 70:1.

BELONGING IN THE KINGDOM

Belonging is a fundamental experience of human identity, and to experience this sense of belonging we are even willing to abandon our sense of coherent self and adopt patterns framed by the systems. We may become anonymous, but we will be anonymous alongside others, making sense within a system's rationality—not wholly our true self—merely experiencing the seeming validation of communicating the communication to other communicators. It is a comfortable anonymity. Belonging, in this way, can be akin to an addiction, willing to abandon substantive thriving and coherence in order to still "belong" to *something* with others. We may even protest the feelings of anonymity but cannot conceive how to overcome it. It becomes an ever-present source of unspecified discontent, creating friction in the comfort.

The comfort becomes its own goal—to be uncomfortable is a sign we're not fitting in, and that is a source of anxiety. What if people see we don't fit in? Will we lose our place in the production? Thus, we find the counterintuitive tendency in many churches to preach a message of grace while being full of people who put on masks of perfection and hide doubts or disorders as much as they can. This is a symptom of a religious system rather than the kingdom of God. Experiences of weakness, whether by ourselves or by others, disrupt the security of belonging, as weakness in a system often results in being discarded or replaced. Weakness can lead us to anger or emotional distance, or, in another way, weakness leads some toward a possessive love, where we find our identity in the possession of another or by being possessed by another, finding our identity in their accomplishments or charisma.

In light of an identity fulfilled in God, however, we can see weakness as a space for the participation of others, opening our hearts in compassion with others, leading to a greater sense of belonging.[62] In his article on theology and human disabilities, Jürgen Moltmann notes:

> In the Gospels, sickness is part of the understanding of what it is like to be a real person. For wherever the Savior appears, the sick come to light. . . . They come out of the dark corners of cities and villages to which they have been banished, out of the wildernesses to which they have been relegated, and into the spotlight where they reveal themselves to Jesus. Thus Jesus sees the internal and external disabilities of the people. Jesus comprehends us, not from our sunny sides where we are strong and capable, but from our shadow sides, where our weaknesses lie.[63]

This orients belonging in a different way than the systems. Belonging is no longer dependent on performance or inherent attributes; belonging is oriented in an initial invitation of acceptance by God and then becomes a committed condition of trust in God and with others. This is more akin to the kind of belonging experienced in family rather than in a job or school. Such belonging awakens our best self, but also can reveal the worst and most broken parts of our self, as we are comfortable to let down all the pretenses.[64] Belonging can be very messy, especially in its initial experiences.[65]

Vanier notes four signs of healthy belonging.[66] First, we have an openness to those who are weak and needy in our context. Such openness indicates our belonging is not established in system-defining ways but in light of all people being sacred contributors to each other. This prevents the belonging from being manipulated or co-opted if people do not adequately perform. Second, healthy belonging in a group is revealed in how it serves others. Belonging can never involve coercion or paternalistic hierarchy. Each person is free and included as a free person, able to be heard and make decisions, able to share their honest self and respond in honest ways without fear of repression or isolation, empowering rather than diminishing. "It does not impose its vision on others but instead prefers to listen to what they are saying and living, to see in them all that is positive."[67]

Third, we adapt as a community alongside the contributing gifts of others, no longer limited by our own experiences and certitude, but instead learning from each other in words and practices and priorities. The fourth sign of healthy belonging involves an honesty about the past. We make mistakes and every context is filled with the detritus of ill-formed or malformed expressions. If a group refuses to admit error or seek guidance from experienced mentors, it will become locked in its own dysfunction, secure in its self-limiting identity and insisting on conforming and repressing truth, while proclaiming superiority in its idealistic self-understanding. This is, to put it bluntly, idolatry.[68]

In and through all of these signs, healthy belonging is sustained by establishing a mutual respect for each other, an honesty about reality and the contributions and mistakes of the group, and a willingness to always pursue growth in light of a commitment to and with each person. "We are called to grow," Vanier writes, "in order to become fully ourselves and fully alive, to receive from others, and to give to others, not being held back by fears, prejudices, or feelings of superiority or inferiority."[69] Such growth can only occur in a context of committed trust and belonging. The challenges to such goals are persistent and extensive. We who live in the context of the world systems are continually buffeted by the narratives of these systems in demanding our allegiance under threat of identity dissolution. The disempowering experiences of resisting the systems can become overwhelming if we lack support and perspective.

One way of sustaining identity in the midst of this transition is to simply acknowledge the counter-narrative for what it is, a way that cannot make sense to those who do not have an integrative center in Christ. As a hermit once said, "When you flee from the company of other people, or when you despise the world and worldlings, take care to do so as if it were you who was being idiotic."[70] This is essential because if we think our choices to live in a different narrative will ever make sense to those caught in the systems, we will be utterly mistaken and discouraged by the rejection. The path of wholeness is often one that seems foolish and scandalous. As such, the competing narratives engage very deep parts of our unresolved self, jostling our fears of alienation, seeking to drive us back into conformity.[71] We fear dissidents, difference, failure, loss, and change because each of these point to the impermanence of our lives, alternative ways of life in the midst of systems that proclaim themselves as the totality.[72] Indeed this is what makes the so-called deadly sins particularly deadly, not their initial motivation—it is good to eat, it is good to do well at our tasks, there are times to get angry, and so on. Rather, the sin is being driven by distortions about our needs, so we are enslaved and compelled beyond the state of balance and into a competitive, oppressing pursuit of their satiation.[73] Our desires become unmoored from reality, no longer promoting actual good.[74]

Instead of being motivated by these fears back into the corral of anonymous normality, the way of the transformed heart initiates a new pattern of fractal transformation. Little changes accumulate in different areas of our lives. We become enchristened piece by piece, as the Spirit brings renewal and insight. This approach does not require either significance or grandeur of expression, indeed demanding thus may suggest a fear-driven motivation, as we want the significance to give us a sense of meaning in this world. We want to be great and we want to be great *now*. Instead, the fractal transformation of authentic becoming always begins small, a genuine experience of commitment within a sphere where this can take substantive shape. This path of transformative belonging remains open to the world, focusing on the possibilities of genuine human self in relation to other selves.[75] There is no need to negate others, since our identity is not dependent on the favor or disfavor of others. The negation is applied to the systems and the ways we have adopted their sense of meaning. This kind of negation needs others because it is only in the tensions of life together that we become aware of our own lingering dysfunction.

Belonging is a given to be worked out in practice, because the trouble with belonging is the fact that other people make it all so difficult. I've long suggested that a person's true self is openly revealed in how they drive, especially in traffic. We owe little to those in the cars around us and they serve—from an ego-oriented perspective—as barriers to our progress. The more we see them as real people, in a shared experience, the less aggression we feel toward them. But if we are consumed only with our individual progress, we ignite our passion, enable our competitive will, and navigate with aggression—sometimes causing accidents, but almost always causing a frenzy internally. Yet we do so with psychological abandon.

This is why catholicity is such an important confession. It expresses a unity beyond established boundaries of politics, race, time, or geography. Vanier writes, "So, the one-way street, where those on top tell those at the bottom what to do, what to think, and how to be, becomes a two-way street, where we listen to what they the 'outsiders,' the 'strangers,' have to say and we accept what they have to give, that is, a simpler and more profound understanding of what it means to be truly human."[76] A pattern of inclusive trust and vulnerable honesty requires an intimate commitment, and such commitment can extend deeply and broadly as the various networks of such commitments grow within a context. Healthy networks network, drawing in the participants together within a zone of trust, a field of force of God's Spirit that is transforming all, each in light of their particular need and context, toward a shared vision in, with, and for this world. The utopian vision that is impossible when enforced through top-down coercion becomes an authentic possibility from below. "I am suggesting," Vanier continues, "that if each of us, with our gifts and weaknesses, our capacities and our needs, opens our heart to a few people who are different and become their friends, receive life from them, our societies would change. This is the way of the heart."[77] This way is thoroughly transformative and reflects in how we respond in intentional and unintentional moments of community interactions.

This suggests that the real issue in our becoming fully human is not about thinking big enough but rather it is an issue of us not being willing to think small enough. We fear insignificance by limiting our attention to those immediately around us, to take inclusive steps within the reach of our honest possibilities. It is easier to campaign for our favored national candidate than it is to reach out to our immediate neighbor. We want the grand transformation and lapse into an enervating despair when we fall short. We want to control others and fold them within our vision of life. We need freedom from this if we are to find our true self, if we are to be truly open to others, if we are to journey toward thorough liberation and come alongside others on this journey.

Vanier emphasizes this immediate openness is a key part of finding community among disparate populations: "In order to stand by the downtrodden, never to exclude but to include them in our lives, we need to be freed from our compulsive needs to succeed, to have power and approbation. We also need to be free from past hurts that govern our lives and cut us off from some people. We all need to grow to freedom."[78] Our freedom comes from freeing others, inviting them into an empowering community where we seek their best and they seek ours.[79] This involves asking who we have the substantive power to free, in a real sense. How can we free those in our family? In our neighborhood? In our work context? Sometimes these small actions can blossom into great movements, but not often. Thus, the great should not be our goal. Instead, in the little things, in little movements of freedom, we contribute to pockets of new life. If we all participate in these kinds of pockets, we begin to weave together new ways of being across society.

Transformation is more often a resonating and distributional expression—where we contribute to a pattern without being able to see the whole of it. This is not, however, an easy or quick transformation, and so we must commit to this pursuit of freedom in our successes and our failures, established on the trust derived from our belonging. Such change takes substantive faith, both in the direction of this work and trusting that our little contributions are making a difference. We must be patient in applying this amid our immediate setting, in situations that are insignificant in the overall scope, but contribute to substantive change as part of the overall mission of God's extensive work. If every Christian did this throughout history, what a different history we would have!

Patience in the "ferment" of freedom insists on commitment to a rigorous truth: about ourselves, about our context, about God. Commitment involves a breaking of our amalgamated self and a rebuilding as we develop coherence with this truth in our self and our actions.[80] If we see ourselves as masters in the pursuit of our will, we will treat others accordingly. This is not the truth of reality, however. Our will can only reach so far—not even over our own life let alone into eternity. So, true freedom involves a journey, where we construct links that guide us from our current self into new points of discovery of who God has made us to be in the place where we are. As we discover a deeper sense of God and God's work, we enter a mode of transformation. Vanier writes, "As we participate in this, our sense of the true expands. Freedom is to be in awe of this Source, of the beauty and diversity of people, and of the universe."[81] This is the experience and transformation of the Spirit as indicated in 2 Cor. 3:17. Our false self dies, our new self rises, reborn. We experience reinvigoration, often in the same context but with a radically different conception of history, value, and purpose, leading us to engage the systems in a new and integrated way.

Vanier suggests seven steps toward this experience of freedom that is essentially the path of liberation for oppressors.[82] The first step is to see how our fears can be a tool for wisdom and direction and discernment. In fear we are provoked to response. Assessing such fear can give us insight into our values and priorities, where our identity is established in various systems.[83] Second, we must become aware of our "limits and blockages." We want to do and be too much, leading us down a path of dissolution and distraction. An idealistic view can get us started, but this cannot be sustained. Rather than succumb to defeat, however, we can learn our true self and calling rather than abandoning the quest altogether. Third, we should be attentive in unexpected events, looking for wisdom at every turn, even in events that might seem discouraging or alienating. As Basil the Great noted, "Hunting truth is no easy task; we must look everywhere for its tracks."[84] In staying aware, we can learn something new about ourselves and the world at the most curious times.[85]

It is hard to maintain perspective and keep up the discipline of noticing if we are by ourselves, and so Vanier's fourth step is accompaniment. According to Vanier, "An accompanier is someone who can stand beside us on the road to freedom, someone who loves us and understands our life."[86] This is an intentional relationship that can exist in many forms, helping us better understand what God is doing in our lives and in our contexts, highlighting our strengths, helping us in our weaknesses, analyzing our errors. This is necessary throughout our life, as we always need someone to help us better see ourselves and where we are. This can be mutual accompanying as with a friend or spouse, or a mentor, or even paid assistance like with a counselor. The role of spiritual director has long served this function in Christianity.

While having someone alongside is essential, so too is understanding what is ahead, giving us a road map of the transformative journey. This fifth step toward freedom involves having role models, people who are ahead of us in the pursuit of liberation and wholeness, who can serve as both a guide and an inspiration. When the journey seems discouraging or hopeless, or simply confusing, having someone who helps us see beyond our own experiences is essential. "A model," Vanier writes, "is someone who demonstrates new ways of living in spite of all the chaos, someone who remains loving and humble in spite of all the violence, someone who does not judge or condemn."[87] Such people show us the way to liberation in the midst of radical difficulties that often outstrip our own present experiences, thus spurring us to continued growth.

This is not to dismiss our experience of struggles. We must be honest and aware of them, and that is the seventh step. As Vanier puts it, "It is hard work to liberate oneself from inner compulsions, to commit oneself to inner growth, truth, justice, and the service of others."[88] People may have all kinds of struggles, and everyone has a unique set of struggles, so there is not a set template response. We must be attuned and honest with our self and our context, acknowledging the struggles while refusing to be identified by them. Again, the road to liberation is only possible in light of God's life and work, and to be truly liberated we must be in communion with God. "God fortifies our desire to be and to be true," Vanier writes.[89] Moltmann puts it this way:

> I firmly believe that liberation of oneself comes before mutual liberation. One can only accept another when one has first found oneself. One can only accept another person when one has first freed oneself of everything that oppresses and estranges, everything that makes oneself look small, ugly, and worthless in one's own eyes. To "accept one another" presupposes that we have found our independence, our worth, our self-confidence, and that we therefore act out of a sense of mutual acceptance. Only she who has found herself can accept other

people without oppressing them or becoming a burden to them. Only he who is self-aware can allow himself to be helped by others in times of difficulty without feeling demeaned and humiliated.[90]

The need to prove ourselves, to dominate and control, to use systems validation or methods to gain advantage over others is diminished. Nothing is absolute other than God, and in this no one is complete except in God. Our orientation derives from God and in this we learn to view others through the perspective of God, which relativizes our self-perception while not devaluing our contributions.

The final stage of inner liberation is forgiveness, removing the barriers and healing the wounds that prevent honest engagement with others. A lack of honesty results in artificial communication rather than genuine relationship. The festering damage of unforgiveness results in anger, depression, apathy, or other isolating responses formed by moral and psychological guilt.[91] In the experience of forgiveness, we respond to ourselves and others in new ways, ways of freedom and invitation that are vulnerable and transformative. Forgiveness is the gate of liberation, the point at which we either proceed onward into fullness of life with others, or turn back, unable to give up that which has become part of our shadow identity.

Those who feel they have no worth, for whatever reason, will assume they do not have something to contribute and will either let themselves be subsumed by others or seek to dominate in order to assert their being upon others. Forgiveness, in contrast, involves an acceptance derived from love, an awareness of inabilities or deficiencies accompanied by continued presence. Such invitation calls people to take risks in action as well as the often-harder risk of loving and being loved in return.[92] Vanier offers three principles to help orient this process. First, "There can be no forgiveness of ourselves or of others unless we believe that we are all part of a common humanity."[93] Second: "To forgive means to believe that each us can evolve and change, that human redemption is possible." Third: "To forgive means to yearn for unity and peace."

Holding onto guilt, whether our own or the guilt of others, inverts liberation, creating thick walls of isolation, enervating both heart and mind. We become our own oppressors.[94] Ignoring or dismissing guilt helps justify continued personal or systemic injustice. In light of the love of Christ, we can be awakened to a new way of response that affirms and cements community. Vanier writes:

> Forgiveness is unilateral. It begins as the victim, with new-found strength, refuses to seek revenge, or . . . prays that the oppressor may change, refind truth, and admit his evil ways. Forgiveness is then to have hope for the

oppressor, to believe in their humanity hidden under all their brokenness. It becomes reconciliation and a moment of communion of hearts if and when they seek forgiveness.[95]

Such forgiveness is not turning a blind eye to injustice or dismissing the real effects of trauma, caused or received. Rather, such forgiveness is a protest against hatred. Hatred is a counter to love. It likewise is consuming and transforming, but rather than orienting a person toward life it is a trajectory of death. Hatred also promises forms of community, a shared passion against others or another, a community that must defend its narrow interests and so can never be truly open, locking those who are part of it within the restrictive boundaries of their egos and systems-specific priorities. Becoming cognizant of the hurts and fears that result in hatred, expressed in a refusal for forgiveness, is an opportunity to break free from the defining past. This involves embracing truth, not ignoring it, in the context of God's overall mission.[96]

This is not an easy process, and we can withdraw from it at any time as we lapse back into being controlled by our brokenness. "This process," Vanier writes, "can close us up in subtle forms of depression and inertia."[97] To keep from this, we need discipline and commitment, empowered by the Spirit, in order to avoid being controlled by the darkness of hate, anger, and fear. This is a journey of rediscovery, but one that begins, continues with, and ends in love. "This message of love brings with it a secret, gentle ecstasy of love, a new peace of heart, an inner liberation."[98] This love, shared and received, is the hope for the oppressor. In this love is a new kind of human experience, an innervating community where life makes connections with others, spreading wide, gathering and sharing, while at the same time growing and deepening.

CONCLUSION

Life abounds in desire and response. This is the joy of life. Yet this is also the challenge of life. Our desires and our responses can become disordered, malformed, or even co-opted. We get caught in the rules and narratives of competing systems, assuming that our desires reflect our true self. In not really knowing our true self we have no gauge on whether that is really true. Yet, our sensibilities are still our own, so the idea of changing desires or adapting our passions seems to negate our being. In response to this reality, there is a move toward repression—simply saying "Don't!" to our passions. Or there is a move toward libertinism—simply saying "Yes!" to our passions.

Neither way is adequate because both approaches assume that there are no other options, that the passions are what the passions are, and that's what we are left with. The experience of lust, for instance, drives a society to sharply restrict women so as to, purportedly, protect men from themselves. Or, to embrace lust because that's what it means to be human, even though unrestrained sexuality has devastating impacts on families, health systems, and just about everything else. The idea that sex is both everything to human meaning and, at the same time, simply a meaningless act we do, is obviously not coherent, yet because we dance between nonintegrated systems, we have constructed selves that maintain a pseudo-coherence. It makes sense because we've constructed segmented thinking that helps it make sense. This pseudo-coherence is, as the saying goes, built on sand and easily washed away. And lust is just one of the so-called deadly sins. The ways humans engage in this world in disintegration of self and society causes no end of conflicts. But the answer is not to simply turn off our passions and negate all our desires. This robs us of our very nature as creatures—that interplay of emotional and rational physicality.

God's passion for life in creative and engaged participation is not a contrast to the way of the world, it is a confrontation of the patterns of death that feed into who we are told we must be and how the world must function. The patterns of the world—that incoherent, nonintegrated, operationally closed environment of systems—do not offer a sustaining way of hope. They embed oppression and perpetuate oppressing. Life is competition and gain, even if not at the purely individual level, then at the tribal, or the national, or whatever other division happens to give us a sense of meaning over and against the other.

God is whole in God's own self. God's being is eternal unity and eternal diversity. In God's being we find a coherent expression of thought and desire. In God's being we experience God's rule, the reality of the kingdom that provides the orienting truth of how things really should be. We become alive in full while learning how to be wholly who we truly are. This is the path of sanctification, an expression of holiness that embeds us even more into the world that God made, even as it raises confrontations with the way the world thinks it must be. This passion for life celebrates others, seeing possibilities rather than limitations. But if we are not careful, we can easily lapse back into dysfunctional patterns and oppressive behaviors. That is why the kingdom of God is both an experience and a pursuit, with the pursuit enacted in intentional behaviors and a commitment to prayer. People are addicted to the systems, and the function of oppressing is very often outside of rational choice, becoming a compulsive kind of intent that may even be rationally disputed. Social media, of course, takes advantage of this tendency toward compulsion and nonrational accomplishment or comparison. So too does a great deal of our consumerism and vocational ambition. The consumption of products, of others, of our own selves in debilitating patterns abounds, pursuing pursuit because we feel pursued by some nameless, claimless pursuer. The wave is constantly crashing behind us.

Life not only doesn't have to be this way, it wasn't ever intended to be this way. This way that weighs us down and distorts our best selves is actually the wrong way! The kingdom is a way of peace, the call of hope. To turn aside, however, is likewise full of troubles, as we are confronted in every direction by the panic inducing sirens of systems-oriented life. The kingdom is not for us alone, however, it is an expression of who we are to be in the context of others who are likewise in the process of becoming. God's being is by definition communal, and God's rule is by definition communal, and thus the experience of the kingdom is, by definition, a communal pursuit that prioritizes community as the invitation, the method, and the destination.

NOTES

1. See Romans 8.
2. Pannenberg, *Theology and the Kingdom of God*, 55.
3. See Mostert, *God and the Future*, 5. Mostert writes, "In Pannenberg's view, we cannot think of God's being apart from God's rule (kingdom). God's being is God's rule . . . God's rule is an expression of God's power, and the idea of power is implicit in the very idea of deity. If the kingdom of God does not come, God cannot be God." Mostert argues this is a primary interpretive theme throughout Pannenberg's works, even as this phrase is not repeated in the *Systematic Theology*.
4. Cf. Jose Comblin, *The Holy Spirit and Liberation* (Eugene, OR: Wipf & Stock), 44ff. See also Wolfhart Pannenberg, *Ethics* (Philadelphia: Westminster, 1981), 190. Connecting God's Spirit with his kingdom would take on even more interesting analysis in light of Pannenberg's emphasis of Spirit as field.
5. See Pannenberg, *Systematic Theology*, 2:224.
6. Pannenberg, *Theology and the Kingdom of God*, 112–113. Pannenberg continues with this vital point, "Christian ethical failure is closely related to a misunderstanding of the doctrine of God. The idea that God is an entity which has the definite mode of its being in some transcendent realm of its own suggested, inevitably, that love for God moves in another direction than love for fellowmen. Consider the pious literature that speaks of our 'vertical' love for God and our 'horizontal' love for fellowmen. Love for God, it is suggested takes off for heaven, while love for fellowmen remains on earth. Granted that love for God is supposed to generate love for fellowmen, but they are still two distinct acts. We need more clearly to see that love for fellowmen is participation in God's love; that is to say, love for fellowmen is participation in the coming Kingdom of God. The priority of God's coming Kingdom and the possibility of our participating in the coming Kingdom is, properly understood, the meaning of grace."
7. Pannenberg, *Systematic Theology*, 1:245–247.
8. Pannenberg, *Theology and the Kingdom of God*, 112–113.
9. 1 Tim. 3:5.
10. Moltmann, *Sun of Righteousness, Arise!*, 81. Cristoph Blumhardt noted, "The one who is in Christ experiences the tremendous abundance and variety of these

divine powers, and is so filled with the sense of them that it is natural to live by them. Indeed these powers of life can come to us, powers that other people would never think possible. That is what it means to be risen with Christ. That is what we should be, not for our own good but for the world's good, for the good of other people, for those we live with and even suffer from. Therefore, we do not push away the world. We assert our place right among the sons of men—the poorest and lowest of all—trusting that everything can still be different because of the work of the divine powers that we experience. And so our task is to know the power of the resurrection, that power that alone is in Christ." In Christoph Blumhardt, *Action in Waiting* (Farmington, PA: Plough Pub. House, 1998), 144.

11. See, for instance, Dietrich Bonhoeffer, *Ethics* (Minneapolis: Fortress Press, 2005), 90–92.

12. Moltmann, *Sun of Righteousness*, 81.

13. These are found in Moltmann, *Ethics of Hope*, 40–41.

14. Moltmann, *The Spirit of Life*, 201–202.

15. Ibid., 202.

16. Ibid.

17. Evagrius the Solitary, "Texts on Discrimination in Respect of Passions and Thoughts," in *Philokalia*, vol. 1 (London: Faber and Faber, 1979), 38.

18. Kierkegaard, *The Concept of Anxiety*, 123.

19. See Moltmann-Wendel and Moltmann, *God—His & Hers*, chap. 2.

20. This is a particularly insightful list regarding ministers and academics, who may couch their fears and thus their greed in acceptable, religion-laden terms and in doing so embrace the ravages of these demons.

21. György Bulányi and Gyula Simonyi, *Rapture of the Gospel* (Székesfehérvár: BOKOR, BOCS Foundation, 2000), 167.

22. Moltmann, *Ethics of Hope*, 210.

23. Ibid.

24. On the complexity and importance of trust for every element of our life and being, see David DeSteno, *The Truth About Trust: How It Determines Success in Life, Love, Learning, and More* (New York: Hudson Street Press, 2014).

25. See Moltmann, *Ethics of Hope*, 215.

26. Ibid., 210.

27. See Moltmann, *Theology of Hope*, 116–120. The theme of promise is central to Moltmann's entire project.

28. Moltmann, *Ethics of Hope*, 15–17.

29. Ibid., 214.

30. See Romero, *The Scandal of Redemption*, 73–74.

31. On this curious reality, see Anton Blok, *Radical Innovators: The Blessings of Adversity in Science and Art, 1500–2000* (Cambridge: Polity, 2017).

32. See, for instance, Acts 1, where rather than controlling the mission of the church directly, Jesus ascends into heaven, leaving the disciples as the leading figures. A doubtful prospect given what we know of them in the Gospels, but one empowered and led by the Spirit, enabling a mission that is dynamic and powerful but not without its bumps, as the rest of Acts and the epistles illustrate. This is not suggesting God abandons control over the universe, rather that God does not, it seems,

exercise absolute control over human will or actions, making space for freedom and for sin.

33. This certainly is a highly debatable point. It's clear that in the Bible God takes risks on certain people (Saul and David as kings, for instance) but this is not an ontological risk. God is not risking his being as God, so can we talk about real risk at all? Yes, as there is the risk that God made in creating, a risk that distorted but did not destroy. A risk in enabling a freedom that can result in sin, as God certainly does not prefer sin. A risk of separation by humanity that could have been prevented by more rigorous control. After the establishment of Israel as a people intending to reflect God, God also takes a risk in having his revelation distorted by false claims or faithless following. The reality of risk also is a way of understanding the problem of evil. God is in charge, ultimately, but in giving humanity freedom, evil situations develop that cause great pain. God's experience of sorrow at such pain is a result of the risk.

34. Veli-Matti Kärkkäinen, *Christian Theology in a Pluralistic World* (Grand Rapids: Eerdmans, 2019), 308.

35. In this way, forms of human slavery should be considered not merely moral violations, but indeed a form of heresy. The tendency for heresy to primarily address issues of trinitarian concerns (including each Person) ignores how much the biblical testimony emphasizes how we treat others reflects our actual perspective on God. Had the early church (or even later generations) taken the reality of anthropological heresy more seriously, both in how we understand and how we treat others, much of the counter-Gospel expressions of church history likely would not have occurred. See Patrick of Ireland's "Letter to Coroticus" for an early protest against violence and slavery that results in excommunication of a victimizer.

36. Moltmann, *Spirit of Life*, 202.

37. See Oden, *Transformative Church*, 4–6.

38. Moltmann strongly rejects understanding the world and the church as separate. Jürgen Moltmann, interview with the author, Tübingen, Germany, May 17, 2011. I am using the term "fractal" to imply an ordered yet amorphous quality to how the kingdom works in and through this world, especially as it replicates and scales in ways that are both seemingly random and orderly. For a concise definition, see Benoit Mandelbrot, *The Fractal Geometry of Nature*, updated edition (San Francisco: Times Books, 1982), 1–2.

39. Moltmann, *The Living God*, 148.

40. See James E. Loder and W. Jim Neidhardt, *The Knight's Move: The Relational Logic of the Spirit in Theology and Science* (Colorado Springs: Helmers & Howard, 1992), 304–306.

41. Moltmann, *The Living God*, 196.

42. Coakley, "Prayer as Crucible," 37.

43. On this imagery, see John Cassian, "Conference 13:III," in *The Conferences*, trans. Boniface Ramsey (New York: Paulist, 1997), 467–469.

44. Karl Barth is, of course, a notable exception to this. See, for instance, Karl Barth, *Prayer*, 50th Anniversary edition (Louisville: Westminster John Knox Press, 2002). For analysis of his theology of prayer, see the helpful essays by Saliers, Hesselink, Migliore, and McKim in that volume as well as Ashley Cocksworth, *Karl Barth*

on Prayer (New York: T&T Clark, 2018). Cocksworth, 1 writes, "The entire project of Christian theology, for Barth, must be undergirded by the practice of prayer for it to count as Christian theology."

45. The use of prayer as an oppressive act is worth greater study, as its public form can often be an assertion of legalism, power, privilege, dominance, control, or pride. The admonition of Jesus in Mt. 6:5–8 is often ignored by those seeking to be especially seen as devout. In his treatise on prayer, Tertullian writes, "But God is the hearer not of the voice but of the heart, just as he is its inspector." In *On Prayer*, trans. Sydney Thelwall, ANF 3, 17.686.

46. Or, manning anti-aircraft batteries, as Moltmann points to his awakening toward God happening during the bombing of Hamburg in 1944. See Jürgen Moltmann, *A Broad Place* (Minneapolis: Fortress Press, 2009), 17.

47. Oscar Romero, 83 writes, "God wants to save us as a people. He does not want to save each of us in isolation. That is why the church today more than ever before emphasizes what does it mean to be a 'people.' And that is why the church experiences conflicts: the church does not want just crowds; she wants a people . . . she has no intention of being the opium of the people. It is others who drug the people and put them to sleep, and they are happy to keep them that way. The church wants to rouse men and women to the true meaning of being a people. What does it mean to be a people? A people is a community of persons in which everyone works together for the common good."

48. Coakley, *The New Asceticism*, 111.

49. Vanier, *Community and Growth*, 256. Cf. Loder, *The Logic of the Spirit*, chap. 6.

50. Cf. Lk. 18:13 for the specific prayer of the tax collector, with the whole chapter an explication of purgative possibilities for people in various situations. The blind man and the tax collector are more aware of their need for such freedom than the rich man and the Pharisee.

51. Coakley, *New Asceticism*, 112–113. As noted in chapter 6, Clement's writings are themselves directed to different stages of belief. Clement's and Coakley's stages overlap but are not entirely equivalent. Whereas Clement begins with those who are not yet Christian, either as interested parties or as targets of apologetic reasoning, in his *Exhortation to the Heathen*, Coakley begins with those who have already been baptized. Clement moves on to his second stage in the *Paedagogos*, which is Coakley's first stage, of new and relatively immature Christians—those who "drink milk" to use Paul's phrasing. Clement's *Stromatas* are directed to more mature Christians, "true gnostics," those who are able to perceive deeper truths and liberated expressions in their transformative participation with Christ. This coincides more with Coakley's second and possibly third stages, though this latter stage may better relate to an advancement beyond writing and reading, and so would not be as visible in Clement's writings as much as his direct teaching and lifestyle.

52. Coakley, *New Asceticism*, 114.

53. Belief here is not simply intellectual approval. It is an expression of a lived commitment in light of a known reality. See Justo González, *The Apostle's Creed for Today* (Louisville: Westminster John Knox, 2007), 10–12 for a quick summary of the

various levels that the word "belief" can indicate. In saying we believe *in* God, we are asserting something more than rational assent, indeed committing our being within this God. González, 17 writes, "To say that we believe *in* God is to say that it is in God that all our life exists, including our life of faith." This is not a binary of being in or outside of such a belief (though there may be boundaries that these labels clarify). Just as life can be lived more or less fully, so too can our lives express belief in God more or less fully, more or less maturely in different stages of our life.

54. Coakley, *New Asceticism*, 119.

55. Evagrius, "Chapters on Prayer," chap. 60 in *Evagrius of Pontus: The Greek Ascetic Corpus*, trans. Robert E. Sinkewicz (New York: Oxford University, 2003), 199.

56. Sinkewicz, in ibid., 280 n. 44.

57. Staniloae, *Orthodox Dogmatic Theology*, 87. Jean-Marc Ela echoes this, writing, "A theologian must stay within earshot of what is happening within the community so that community life can become the subject of meditation and prayer." In Ela, *My Faith as an African*, 11.

58. Coakley, *New Asceticism*, 120.

59. Jürgen Moltmann, *Experiences in Theology* (Minneapolis: Fortress Press, 2000), 149.

60. Janice McRandal, "Being George Eliot: An Impossible Standpoint?" in *Sarah Coakley and the Future of Systematic Theology*, ed. Janice McRandal (Minneapolis: Fortress Press, 2016), x.

61. See John Cassian, Institutes 12:III:1 in *The Institutes*, trans. Boniface Ramsey (New York: Newman Press, 2000), 255–256.

62. This is often seen and experienced in contexts of tragedy such as occur with natural disasters or the aftermath of disruptive events like September 11, 2001.

63. Moltmann, "Liberate Yourselves by Accepting One Another," 114–115.

64. See Vanier, *Becoming Human*, 58.

65. See M. Scott Peck, *The Different Drum: Community Making and Peace*, 2nd edition (New York: Touchstone, 1998), 90–102.

66. These are found in Vanier, *Becoming Human*, 60–61.

67. Vanier, *Becoming Human*, 60.

68. Ellacuría, *Ignacio Ellacuría*, 153.

69. Vanier, *Becoming Human*, 61.

70. Ward, *The Desert Fathers*, 83.

71. Vanier, *Becoming Human*, 88 writes, "Sometimes we have to forego group approval and even accept rejection, if it should happen, in order to follow what the ancients called '*scientia cordis*,' the science of the heart, which gives the inner strength to put truth, flowing from experience, over the need for approval."

72. Vanier, *Becoming Human*, 71–81.

73. This is why Theophan the Recluse exhorts that "having returned to God, know your sins." In Theophan the Recluse, *The Path to Salvation*, 170–173. On the sins, diagnosing and responding to them in a discerning way John Cassian, *The Institutes*, books 4–12. Cassian lists and discusses eight core sins, following the list compiled by Evagrius.

74. For Vanier's discussion of desire, see Jean Vanier, *Made for Happiness* (Toronto: House of Anansi, 2005), 3–10.

75. Vanier, *Becoming Human*, 82: "One major reason for our mutual distrust, for our propensity to gang together in mutually exclusive groups, is that most of us experience love in only the most imperfect way."

76. Vanier, *Becoming Human*, 84.

77. Ibid., 85.

78. Ibid., 103.

79. Moltmann, "Liberate Yourselves," 122 writes, "Community can heal our divided society, and it can do so on both sides. It is only in fellowship with one another that both the person with disabilities and the one without can experience a new humanity. So may we, with all our strength, build such communities of person with and without disabilities!"

80. See Gerhard Lohfink, *Jesus and Community* (Philadelphia: Fortress Press, 1984), 177–180.

81. Vanier, *Becoming Human*, 117.

82. These are listed in ibid., 125–132.

83. The idea of using a negative to give insight to positive formation was a common one for early monastics, who suggested that if we understand our sins as symptoms of underlying issues, we could actually use our very failings to combat the core issues, thus, as they wrote, putting the demons to flight.

84. Basil the Great, *On the Holy Spirit* (Crestwood, NY: St. Vladimir's Seminary Press, 1980), 16.

85. Vanier, *Becoming Human*, 128 gives the example of parents of disabled children: "Many times parents of people with disabilities have told me about the shock they received at the birth of their child. Then they discovered that their child was leading them from a world of power and competition into a world of tenderness and compassion." This is not generally a quick lesson, and so a person must be willing to press on through the wilderness of struggle, denial, and anger with the hope that God will not leave them in confusion.

86. Vanier, *Becoming Human*, 128. See Roberto S. Goizueta, *Caminemos Con Jesus: Toward a Hispanic/Latino Theology of Accompaniment* (Maryknoll, NY: Orbis Books, 1995), 68. Goizueta writes, "Undertaken actively and in mutual accompaniment, the community's confrontation with suffering can become a source not of despair but of strength. As constituted by his or her relationships with others, the individual person is intrinsically and by definition never alone in his or her struggles." Wealth and power tend to close off and isolate people from genuine community. This can create a context of significant loneliness even when surrounded by others, and leave people feeling alone in their social or emotional struggles, even as others are envious of their financial situation. This is quite apparent, for instance, in how many celebrities become addicted to drugs or even commit suicide. "They had everything," we think, except they clearly didn't. Wealth and fame were not enough, and isolated them from authentic accompaniment in their dysfunctions.

87. Vanier, *Becoming Human*, 121.

88. Ibid.

89. Ibid., 132.
90. Moltmann, "Liberate Yourselves," 106.
91. See Vanier, *Becoming Human*, 136.
92. Ibid., 138.
93. These are described in ibid., 153–155.
94. Vanier, *Becoming Human*, 143.
95. Ibid., 144–145.
96. See Volf, *The End of Memory*, 72–76.
97. Vanier, *Becoming Human*, 151.
98. Ibid., 133.

Chapter 12

Hope among Community

INTRODUCTION

God is holy. That is not to say that God is separate, or distant, or full of isolated wrath. God's holiness is who he is. God is also love. His holiness and his love are unified in his being, his self is holy and his self is love. He is the all-encompassing reality; the infinite whose eternity is a totality of being. In his self he derives his self, needing no one else, nothing else, to give him identity. He has his self in his own self, and as such is the only substantive identity, from which all other selves find their meaning. Sin is the attempt to derive our selfhood from some other source, a source that may promise life and wholeness and identity, but apart from God can only deliver death, and emptiness, and nonidentity. God's wrath is a response to that which contrasts his love, contrasts his self which seeks inclusion in his holiness.[1] God is angered by that which steers people away from their true self, which can only be found in God's self. We are faced continually with our own nonidentity and our own finitude—a perception which begins in the earliest stages of our development. Confronted by this, we form responses which seek to overcome our isolation, asserting ourselves on others, and in doing that finding some meaning in a defensive posture against the world. Our egos clash against God's being. We seek to become what God is, and we are left wallowing as what we are. Wallowing in despair, and also in conflict, as rampaging egos collide in constant attempts at meaning, deflecting and dismissing others, causing more and more ego response in return. Sin abounds.

God does not retreat from this. He continues to reach out. Grace abounds even more. In his holiness, in his selfness, he offers himself to humanity, maintaining an exocentric openness to the world as the hope of salvation. This is seen in the earliest revelations. God reaches out and asks for trustworthy responses so as to embrace his people as reflections of his holiness. They do not understand and continue to soil themselves with self-definition. But in his holiness, God so loves the world he sends his son. Jesus—God and Man—is the very image of God's love and his holiness. In his life, in his teaching, in his sacrifice, in his resurrection we see the wholeness of true identity. In coming to us, God makes possible a holistic restoration for our own identities. We are not left to our egos, to the ravaging, anonymizing nature of sin. "Sin is," Ignacio Ellacuría writes, "the negation of God, and the negation of sin moves, sometimes in unknown ways, toward the affirmation of God, toward the presence of God as the giver of life."[2] God has initiated a new way, a way of substantive life. We are invited to find freedom with God in his eternal being—becoming truly who we are in the power and life of the Spirit.

In the fullness of God's being we encounter the fullness of God's rule, and as we participate with him in our renewed exocentric identity, we become more and more open to others, more and more open to God's being in our life. Jesus promised the kingdom, and the Spirit filled those in the earliest church. Peter was no longer the fearful man who was so insecure of his identity that he would deny his fellowship with Jesus in the face of even the barest opposition. He became a preacher, reaching out to the world in the fullness of the Spirit's gifts, expressing the gospel with power and wisdom and courage. Peter became a new man, in the light of the Spirit's arrival, holy in his identity as finally identifying wholly with Christ, in holy expectation of God's reign, which he was already experiencing in the power of the Spirit.[3] The early Christians, Joel Green writes, "have not been drawn into a new geographical space, but have rather been born anew within the space they had previously inhabited."[4]

Such is God's being realized among us, the gift of the Spirit, life in the kingdom. It is this life that is a life of true holiness. A life with God, for God, lived in fullness and an indescribable wholeness. This emerging holiness is the orientation of a holistic liberation, one that calls the oppressed and the oppressors together into a new pattern of life that reflects the eternal kingdom of God. This emerging holiness is our dance with God, and all those God is dancing with. Thus, this kingdom is oriented in and through community. There is simply no other way to come into Christ's presence other than coming alongside others. This coming alongside involves liberation, a way out of slavery, but for many it also involves alienation, a leaving behind of one's own "country" in pursuit of God's promise. "This divine promise points forward to a 'great people' and the 'blessing for all peoples.' But the way there is a lonely one through the desert," Moltmann emphasizes. "This is not the freedom born out of liberation; it is the freedom that issues from alienation from everything which offers support in the world."[5] This promise goes along the path of the cross. On this path, those who are alienated from the systems of this world find a new basis of meaning and identity in Christ. In Christ, they join with others in a new and freeing way. Life emerges anew, liberated together and free together. In this chapter, I will explore the shape of such a community.

A COMMUNITY OF TRUST

"It is," Moltmann writes, "the task of the Christian community not only to proclaim the gospel of God's love, but also to live it in community."[6] Community is a proactive goal, and not an optional one. It is a required element in order to leave behind the processes of the world and enter into a new narrative. Either we are proactive in community or we fall aside and become co-opted. As Miroslav Volf writes, "Just as a person cannot arise, develop, and live apart from her relationships with others, neither can a Christian exist as a Christian before entering into relation with other Christians; she is first constituted as a Christian *through* these relations."[7] Community is the initiator, the path, and the destination. In the invitation of God's liberation, we trust in Christ and in Christ we are able to trust in the Spirit who works in our context, and in other people. We trust each other in a new way because of the trust Christ has in us, through saving us and pointing us in the new direction of the resurrection.

God who is life leads toward life in ways that coincides with God's being. The way of life is community, because the divine identity is itself communal. God is three in one. The Church lives within God's narrative, God's wide space of being, intentional about God's lordship as the space for living.[8] Moltmann quotes the prayer of Jesus in Jn 17:21, in which he prays for those who believe in him and who will believe in him. Of these Jesus prays "that they may all be one. As you, Father, are in me and I am in you, may they also be in us, so that the world may believe that you have sent me." We who are drawn together in the life of the Spirit are drawn into the divine "us," thus our unity is not a secondary issue or a beneficial side effect. Community is itself the sign of God's presence with us and our presence with God. "In fellowship with Christ, and in the energies of the life-giving Spirit, we experience God as the wide space which surrounds us from every side and leads us to the free unfolding of the new life."[9] We are protected in order that we may proceed, the surrounding allows us freedom to be a new kind of person in a shared orientation toward life.[10]

Moltmann turns to Acts 4:32–37 to show what such a community looks like. This passage highlights community as a primary emphasis of the messianic mission and gives a practical example of it.[11] Moltmann writes that "this was not a social programme; it was the expression of the new Trinitarian experience of sociality."[12] They were not provoked by guilt to prove their righteousness, they were full of a vision of God and the power of the Spirit that freed them to live in transformative patterns. They simply were living, albeit in a brand new way. "They no longer needed these possessions in order to make their lives secure. In the spirit of the resurrection their fear of death disappeared, and with it the greed for life. And so they had enough, more than enough."[13] They were generous because they were joyous.[14] Rather than finding meaning through competition or insecurity, the work of the Spirit in the life of the community orients people within a zone of trust, and in such trust a person can become more fully who they are in fellowship with others also so becoming.[15]

A truly liberated community that is in tune with the work of the Spirit does not have to prioritize community over liberty. The dangers of a person becoming subsumed, losing their self-identity within the community, is no less than the danger of an individualized set of connections that never coalesce into community. Just as with God being one and three, we do not have to abandon unity for the sake of diversity nor sacrifice diversity for the sake of community. We are not conformed into the likeness of a human leader or depersonalized as a cog within a religious system. "The persons can be persons only in community," Moltmann writes, "the community can be free only in its personal members."[16]

The liberated disciples of Christ are truly persons because while individuals are ultimately anonymous, members of autopoietic systems who live to perpetuate and propagate the systems, a person "is a human existence in a field of resonance of his or her social relationships and history. The person has a name, with which he or she can be identified. A person is a being in community."[17] In being free within a context of freedom, we are able to participate with others in their freedom without feeling a need to dominate or control others so as to feed into our own dysfunctions. We who are free in Christ, then, move with Christ in the movements toward the future. The space of community with Christ is a "moved and moving space" which is where our life as community reflects God's eschatological kingdom.[18] We *should* live in the present as we *will* live. In the power of the Spirit this transformative life can take place in the midst of our various contexts, drawing like and unlike together within a zone of trust and fellowship.

This is a worthwhile challenge and a call for all of us, but if it stops as a mere assertion it does not take account of the real contexts and concerns that prevent the persistence of actual community. The issues of oppression leave their own resonating damage, for both the oppressor and the oppressed, and part of finding trust in a community involves finding ways to encounter such experiences in transformative engagement. Moltmann is not blind to such a challenge and is willing to engage the task. In his section on "Christ for the persecutors," Moltmann more directly addresses the issues of a liberation of the oppressor.

He begins with the issue of guilt. "I believe that no one who has become guilty can live with a clear view of his guilt. Once he recognizes it, he begins to hate himself."[19] Such an awareness pursues denial, sometimes through distraction, or "debases us to the depths" if a person sees their acts through the eyes of their victims. For Moltmann, this was most evident in the experience of postwar Germany, where the guilt of Auschwitz became overwhelming. In our current contexts, most would not see their situation as dire as the concentration camps, but oppression does reveal itself in countless ways, whether through national politics or consumeristic obsessions (which is far too often dependent on harsh manufacturing conditions) or any number of other expressions of assumed privilege over against others. In forgiveness in Christ, the guilt is transformed but this does not erase the reality of past injustices. "Mass murder remains mass murder," as Moltmann reminds us.[20] Guilt, however, is not a reason for either avoidance of the past or despair about it in light of the messianic mission. Christ bears the sins of guilt, and such guilt is not a defining weight on the present or future. However, as the church has always taught from the beginning, such a forgiveness is certainly not a rationale for continuing patterns of sin nor an excuse to indulge in new expressions.[21]

We are healed in the light of Christ's work, and in this healing—in this rebirth—Christ calls us to live as new people. "For the perpetrators of injustice and violence this means nothing less than dying to the power of evil, whose servants they have been, and breaking with the systems of injustice, in order to live the new righteousness with the risen Christ."[22] This involves the "sacrament of penance," not as a way to earn salvation but as a way of engaging community in the pursuit of trust and wholeness in light of past concerns. Such penance involves an embrace of truth in order to orient liberation as truly freeing for all involved. Kierkegaard writes, "Viewed intellectually, the content of freedom is truth, and truth makes man free. For this reason, truth is the work of freedom, and in such a way that freedom constantly brings forth truth."[23] Moltmann points to the three steps of this process:[24]

1. Recognition of the sufferings of the victims and confession of his own guilt toward them is the first step into the light of truth.
2. There is a change of mind and a reversal in the direction their lives take. This is bound up with the breaking of the ruling systems producing the injustice, so as no longer to live at the expense of the poor, of the earth, and of children, but to live for them.
3. Perpetrators only arrive at a just community with their victims if they do everything to eliminate the damage they have caused.[25]

Such a process is important because of the nature of human experiences—social and psychological—that are real factors in any attempt at reconciliation and community. We express a new hope in light of our past experiences in the context of people who have been affected and suffered.

Oftentimes in such a discussion, the focus is on systemic evils in society or on unjust overarching structures. In the face of this, it is easy to feel overwhelmed and at a loss. Even so, keeping these in sight is still important as it is the power of the Holy Spirit who works in the communities in transformative ways. We should look for, and fight for, such transformation as the Spirit leads. Yet, the pursuit of social justice itself is not an indicator of actual transformation. Not all paths reflect the work of the Spirit.[26] We can seek change in one realm while indulging dysfunction and oppressing in other ways. Politics especially seems to offer an opportunity for this, demonizing a new other in a supposed defense of an outsider or maximizing one's own wealth through rhetoric about helping the poor. "What good is it for someone to gain the whole world, yet forfeit their soul?" Jesus asks in Mk 8:36.[27] This is where the particularity of the call for community is vital. Jesus repeatedly emphasizes that we are to love *our* neighbors as the beginning of any social engagement. In his musings on 1 Jn 4:20, Kierkegaard argues that the Christian duty is to "find in the world of actuality the people we can love in particular and in loving them to love the people we see."[28]

By emphasizing the particular *first*, the enacting of liberation happens in the context of local oppressing, calling each of us to consider how we oppress those around us. This may not be as dramatic as a societal issue that we see all throughout the news, but is much more directly within our zone of influence. We cannot excuse treating a family member, coworker, or service industry employee poorly even if we are activists for social reform or teachers of theology. That instills an incoherence in our life and strongly suggests our driving concern is something other than genuine love. In effect, it leaves an infection within the wound, and that catches up sooner or later. Our personal liberation is expressed in the contexts of our most intimate interactions or it is not liberation at all, but yet another pose for the sake of another system. This is how even good messages are easily co-opted by the world systems. Jesus refused to be co-opted—and we should not grieve the Holy Spirit in presenting a co-opted pseudo-Jesus to the world. Our particular experience of community should be an active expression of our words, actions, and thoughts. We are to love those around us, even our specific enemies, because they are within our zone of influence, our field of force which can be oriented by ego or by the Spirit. The way of the Spirit orients this power in love and hope.

This love is a love for life, a love for the other and for the whole of cosmos. It is a hospitable love, one that "goes out to meet the stranger and does not depend on reciprocity."[29] Reciprocity depends on similarity, but community involves distinct differences of class and personality and context. In a community, the unlike participate together, an inclusive openness to each other rather than an expectation of like-for-like return in an investment. This love is ordered toward the advantage of the other rather than the self, a giving without expectation of return. Yet in a community that reflects the community of the Divine, we are never depleted or abandoned. We are given that which we did not first give and we are giving that which is not solely ours. Our life together comes to fruition in the giving of the Son and Spirit by the Father.

In such love, we share the loving presence of God, what Michael Welker calls a "domain of resonance."[30] We become the living spaces of love for and with each other. The transforming presence of God draws us together, and together draws us into the divine life of God. Moltmann writes, "Human beings are in harmony with God's love for those God has created when they love life, the life of their neighbor, the life they share, and the life of the earth. They sanctify personal, social, and political life when they give themselves up to the flow of God's love and interpenetrate life with this love."[31] This active and engaged love displays itself in a myriad of ways that constitute lived life. Michael Welker puts it this way:

> The person upon whom the Spirit comes acts directly or indirectly, consciously or unconsciously for the benefit of other persons. The persons immediately affected by the Spirit's action are for their part so "touched," or their services are so powerfully enlisted, that they likewise orient themselves to acting for the benefit of others. The Spirit of God effects a domain of liberation and of freedom (2 Cor. 3:17), a domain not determined by self-relation exercising control, or even merely by intellectual self-relation. People are liberated for action that liberates other people.[32]

Such engagement avoids lofty declarations that exist solely in a theoretical or religious sphere. As Jean-Marc Ela writes, "A magical liberation from one's misery by the incantations of a theory is an escape tactic."[33] The work of the Spirit is not about escape; the goal is transformation. That requires real and engaged love that is interested in each other, that participates together, striving together for the expression of shared hope, a "love for life that makes us happy and at the same time lets us suffer with others."[34] Indeed, this love expresses desires for each other, but not in a corrupted way that uses others for the sake of one's own benefit. When our deepest desire is transformed by the love of God, our participation with others is transformed. It is because of this that Moltmann ends his book *The Living God and the Fullness of Life* with a discussion about prayer. It is in relating to God, interceding and interacting that we find the renewal of our desires and a renewed passion for that which God is passionate about. Such prayer is neither passive nor extraneous to our engaged life. Such prayer is the source of our being with God in the contexts of the world, shaping our awareness and transforming our inner sense of self.[35] It is not a quick process. Cardinal Robert Sarah notes:

> The process of human birth takes a long time and is not a single act. It happens moment by moment. There were stages that gave my life a decisive orientation. But these turning points were the hours, the moments of the day when, one-on-one with the Lord, I became aware of his will for me. The most important moments in life are the hours of prayer and adoration. They give birth to a human being, fashion our true identity; they root our existence in mystery. My daily encounters with the Lord, in supplication and prayer, are the basis for my life.

In this patience persistence, we begin to seek God and desire God's life in the intricacies of every aspect of our experiences. This leads to a discerning, dynamic balance between *via activa* and *via contemplativa* as we journey through life with others.

A COMMUNITY OF EMPOWERING

As part of her developing project, Coakley considers a renewal of Trinitarian theology in light of contemporary challenges. This has taken shape more recently with her choice of sexuality and gender as a topic, because these represent a core element of human experience and because of the significant debate within our churches and society. She points to three interlocking theses that develop her procession from prayer toward a revised experience of desire. First, she suggests "that the revival of a vibrant Trinitarian conceptuality, an 'earthed' sense of the meaningfulness and truth of the Christian doctrine of the Trinity, most naturally arises out of a simultaneous renewal of commitment to prayer, and especially prayer of a relatively wordless kind."[36] This links Christian theology within a context of prayer and orients, ultimately, a substantive liberation within the experience of God's presence with us. In being wordless, she is not suggesting a vaguely spiritualized meditation, but rather a depth of relationship, more akin to two lovers simply enjoying each other's presence.

This analogy is especially apt because of the entangled experiences of sexuality and spirituality, a conflation of desires that is easily disordered and requires attunement in God in order to find enlivening, rather than repressing, resolution. That leads into her second thesis. Coakley suggests "that the close analysis of such prayer, and its implicitly Trinitarian structure, makes the confrontation of a particular range of fundamental issues about sexuality unavoidable."[37] The tendency in Christian history and practice is to dismiss concerns about sexuality and gender as irrelevant or somehow part of our fallen experiences of life. This has led to a repression of both experiences and discussion that leaves potent realities of life left without reflection—or dependent on distinctly non-Christian explications.

Contemplative experience of prayer integrates our being in a way that is in tune with God's created order, and part of this order is understanding our whole being, embodied and sexed as it is, in light of God's holistic reality. As Debra Hirsch notes, "Our sustained quest for God in the world and community, is saturated with sexual metaphor, inarticulate longings, burning desires for connection, the need for healing relationship, the search for true identity and so on. In other words, it cannot be divorced from our sexuality. This is what it means to be truly human."[38] Yet, the response in much of our current society is that being truly human, truly ourselves, involves an unrestrained, unmitigated expression of any and all sexual tendencies, whims, and assumptions. To do otherwise is thought to repress oneself. However, there is no hope in indulgence. Indeed, it tends toward experiences of oppressing and oppression more than boundless freedom. Exploitation of others abounds, trust in relationships diminish, each person maximizing their own expression and then becoming addicted to the behaviors. Libertinism is never nearly as freeing as it supposes, even when it puts on airs of sophistication.

The core issue is to find a way to neither indulge in libertinism in the pursuit of our whimsical—and often systems-constructed—disordered desires, nor indulge in repression by obsessing about negative elements of these desires in ourselves or others.[39] Instead of seeing our own desires or the expressions or temptations of others as distracting us from the divine goal, those who develop a contemplative experience with God are oriented toward a reshaping of desire itself. This is the task of Coakley's third thesis. She writes, "We are seeking a renewed vision of divine desire (a Trinitarian vision, I suggest) which may provide the guiding framework for a renewed theology of human sexuality—of godly sexual relations—rooted in, and *in some sense* analogously related to, Trinitarian divine relations."[40] The challenge here is to be creatures who participate with the divine, to be fully who we are while ordered by the reality and presence of who God is. This is not an easy road. It does not isolate sexuality from the rest of our life nor seek to indulge our every sensual whim, thus initiating complexity in discerning our desires.

Finding balance involves self-knowledge and attentive discipline. Monastic teaching on sin and holiness is quite helpful here, as they highlighted core elements of sinfulness, analyzing their impacts and showing them as interrelated.[41] Rather than a simplistic, legalistic "don't do that," combatting temptation in tactical ways led toward subsequent stages and challenges in succession. Understanding the nuances of sin in one's life is like unknotting a particularly tangled set of threads. It is rarely a quick process, and often very frustrating, as addressing one knot leads to others. Yet, pursuing this unknotting of the self leads to substantive progress in overcoming temptations.

This progression can be seen in the temptation of Jesus, where each of the three temptations represents a triad of intersecting sins.[42] In addressing the initial, Jesus combats the whole. Such combat is initially disempowering, however, because it is a battle of negation. Jesus was, after all, still very hungry after all that process. Immediate satiation was not the goal and so the remaining hunger does not negate the value of the task. In resisting the offer of the immediate, it revealed a way of life that refused to be controlled by impatient passions and reflected how Jesus interacted with people during the rest of his ministry. But, of course, those interactions likewise led to the supremely disempowering experience of crucifixion. That was not the end of the story, but so often we cut our own story short in focusing on the immediate and short-term effects to determine our status.

A reconception of life lived in developing participatory communion with God is indeed uniquely disempowering because it undercuts our assumption of proactive accomplishment. We can only progress by rejecting finding value in the systems of this world while still participating in such systems as embodied people in this world. This task requires a constant reorientation, a retuning where, instead of insisting on establishing our self over against others, we find meaning first in and with God, who then awakens us to a new way to process the challenges of life and live in an enlivening way with and for others. This way of prayer is the path of invitation to the Spirit, who shapes us as we enter into God's presence. "For contemplation," Coakley writes, "is the unique, and wholly *sui generis*, task of seeking to know, and speak of God, unknowingly; as Christian contemplation, it is also the necessarily bodily practice of dispossession, humility, and effacement which, in the Spirit, causes us to learn incarnationally, and only so, the royal way of the Son to the Father."[43]

In being uniquely disempowering, however, it is also uniquely empowering, as the same Spirit leads us to live in a new and more developed way, drawing us into prayer and from prayer into a new conception of this world that reflects God's own perspective. We begin to see as God sees, even if darkly, and love as God loves, though insufficiently, and desire that which God desires, albeit incompletely. Such a development is the definition of a liberated oppressor, to desire differently and, in these new desires, to no longer see a need to oppress. It is not a fight against impulses; it simply does not make any sense to live like that anymore. The way of the cross led into the experience of resurrection. That is the way of true life.

It is the freedom of post-addiction, where the enslaving habit is not indulged, and a person finds themselves feeling better and thinking more clearly. In the pursuit of these reformed desires, there is radical hope that the despaired self can finally and fully experience fulfillment. Hope is not mere optimism. "Authentic Christian hope," Miroslav Volf writes, "is about the promise that the wrongs of the past can be set aright and that the future need not be a mere repetition of the past."[44] That is the resurrection hope that translates into how we live with and for others. Coakley writes, "The contemplative steps wilfully into an act of reflexive divine love that is always going on, always begging Christomorphic shape."[45] This is the experience of continual liberation that orients us within the messianic mission of the Spirit, expressed in relationship with God. Through this divine intersection, relationships with others develop which are no longer constrained or distorted by desires for control. A person is animated by love and experiences substantive belonging, one with another.

A COMMUNITY OF SHARING

In Christomorphic community, there is a balance of the active and contemplative, drawn out from our self, and oriented to being our whole self as God made us. "Communities," Jean Vanier writes, "are a sign that it is possible to live on a human scale, even in the present world. They are a sign that we do not have to be slaves to work, to inhuman economies, or to the stimulations of artificial leisure."[46] There is a better way, a more substantive experience of our humanity, where we become truly ourselves in the contexts of others becoming themselves, both radically particular and bountifully inclusive. Such thorough community is not necessarily an easy or assumed expression for most people. Even as we need community to be whole in our particular self, community engages our ego and defense responses so that we are easily co-opted or seek control, or bask in a persistent shallowness. People must be led to community.

To be led to community, people must experience it and enter into it with a non-idealistic earnestness that is grounded in wisdom.[47] This is the only way a person can be led out of a pattern of oppressing and toward a liberation of the self that is expressed in love.[48] Vanier's approach to community goes well beyond the oft anemic expressions of common experience.[49] Community that enables liberation is neither optional nor arbitrary, and it is not simply about grouping people together in a common place or task. Community is about relationship, real relating with each other in the to-and-fro of love.[50]

"For John," Vanier writes in his collection of musings upon the Gospel, "life is relationship, life is communion—especially the life and communion in

God, with God, and with each other."[51] This is the good news of relationship, he notes, and it is in the growing relationship with Jesus that men and women are able to enter into a transformative relationship with each other. Such interactivity involves purification, letting the other remain other while encouraging the other, and ourselves, to be more truly who we are made to be. This is usually difficult, and often painful, to learn to express this trust. It is in this kind of community that we are able to really enter into a new narrative within our contexts. "Our humanity grows and develops in relationships through which we are transformed and grow in freedom."[52] Indeed, Vanier calls his organizations L'Arche and Faith and Light "schools of relationships."[53]

This again is where liberation takes the shape of the mission of Jesus, who did not focus on meta-political issues but rather always particular personal situations.[54] The mission of Jesus develops from below, creating a new kind of people in the midst of a fractured world, liberating people first from hate, division, desire for power, and all the other symptoms of a systems-derived identity.[55] Only in this new personhood, which he represented in full, could people reconstruct the systems in light of an overarching commitment to God's lordship. As Severino Croatto notes, "The New Person is free from within (through the love that dislodges egoism), from without (from the limitation and the sterility of the law), and toward the future (i.e., from death as ontic limit)."[56] In contrast, the systems depersonalize and anonymize. That is why attempts at liberation through the systems do not result in transformative realities.

Attempts to formulate liberation from above perpetuate the depersonalizing and anonymizing nature of the systems, inverting or reorganizing experiences of power but not bringing real change or substantive peace. They tend to impose a supposed universality, generalizing one particular as being particular for all, which "ends in institutional and canonical rubble, for it is conceived without taking account of the relationship with the Spirit that a church should live in its relationship with a culture."[57] Such can offer a kind of negative peace, as Martin Luther King Jr. spoke of it, which suppresses tension, encouraging people to accept their situation. In contrast to this negative peace, he upended the civil arrangements of his time, disturbing the peace for the sake of a better reality. "For we must come to see that peace is not merely the absence of some negative force, it is the presence of a positive force. True peace is not merely the absence of tension, but it is the presence of justice and brotherhood."[58] True peace—positive peace—is proactive. And this indeed was the mission of Jesus.

But how is this possible in practice?

If we begin with the idea that everyone is sacred—emphasizing the value and personhood of each participant, recognizing those around us for their contributions and gifts, being willing to share with and receive from them—we will find a new pattern of love that begins in small pockets of manageable community. This then spreads through networks of relationships into a new experience of a truly free humanity. The mission of Jesus brings this pattern of relationship into highly localized situations—direct community—as his ministry deals with specific people with specific issues. This invitation is countered by the systems in the experience of the cross. The expressed weakness in his experience is not defeat, but rather triumph, a triumphant entry into a new pattern where it is brokenness that leads to fullness of life rather than application of power or assertions of control.[59]

The cross draws out the ire of the systems while exposing their ultimate inadequacy in the light of God's reality. The resurrection enlivens a community of brokenness into becoming relationships of transformation, where people compete in love for each other.[60] This counterintuitive mission of Jesus raises us up and in raising us up we are newly freed to serve each other, not in slavery or in the model of dominated and dominating, but as friends serving friends, helping and inviting each other in our needs for the benefit of all. In Jesus, then, we can find the meaning that the systems promise but cannot deliver. In calling us, accepting us while leading us to a more complete expression of our true selves, we are no longer consumed with defensive or repressive reactions. We are loved and can thus love, and in this love begin to live lives of peace that construct peace. "This then is the treasure that Jesus wants to reveal, our deepest identity, that of the beloved. Being loved by God liberates us from our need to win, so that we can become artisans of peace in this world."[61] In being artisans of peace, of finding the stillness from the storms, we are better able to take up and participate in the stilling of storms in those around us.

Rather than initiating chaos through extroverting our chaos, we can be bringers of life by exocentric expression of God's work in and through us. This is the continuing work of the Spirit, who continues the mission of Christ in transforming relationships, first in our relationship with the Father, and then transmitting this deeply and broadly. "Through the Spirit we have received," Vanier writes, "we can transmit the Spirit."[62] He continues by orienting this transmission in directly relational terms. "Thus, when we announce the Good News to the poor, it is not to tell them, 'Jesus loves you,' but rather to say, '*I* love you, I commit myself to you in the name of Jesus.'"[63] The kenotic nature of such expression avoids paternalistic service, and instead invites the shared grace of interactive participation. It is in this shared grace together with Christ that we rise with Christ in new experiences of life where there are no longer oppressors or oppressed but simply men and women filled with the Spirit relating to each other as fully formed persons loved by God. This work of the Spirit is the mission of God that awakens us in this present and continues through eternity. The *kenosis* of entering into real relationship with each other draws us into relationship with God. Instead of seeking glory and advancement—trying to be gods within our zone of influence—we embrace humility and participation. Our willingness to let go of that which we think we are owed or deserve makes space for each other to enliven one another with the fruit of the Spirit.

The social nature of the Trinity is not a model for us, but the experience of the Spirit with us, each as particular persons within the diversity of community. As Vanier puts it, "This continuing exchange of divine life with divine life, of divine life with human life, and of human life with human life means that the kingdom community is characterized by a sharing of all we are and all we have. This involves a sharing of love."[64] This sharing of life that is a sharing of love is the deep experience of real relationship and it is this deep experience of real relationship that is the promise to those who experience oppression and those who oppress, the promise to those are caught up in insufficient patterns of identity formation in light of the systems and to those who have been rejected by the systems. The fundamental mission of Jesus invites each person into an experience of transformed relationships and this messianic mission presses onward in the continuing mission of the Spirit. It is not easy, but we are not in it alone. God is truly with us and we are with God.

CONCLUSION

Our hope is in God. God has reached out to us, creating this world and entering into this world. God is not distant nor is God needy, insecure and wanting validation. God is fullness, eternal in nature, and it is out of this richness of being that God seeks us out. God is holy, and this holiness is one of grace and love, seeking a substantive peace and integrative meaning for all of creation. God is Trinity, a revealed nature which defies easy explanation, outside of human conception to fully understand. But we can know in part, and what we know is that God's eternal nature is reflected in divine community: three Persons, one God. We worship one God in Trinity, and Trinity in Unity; neither confounding the Persons, nor dividing the Essence. Yet, as a people we are both confounded and divided. Not only in the broader world, but also in the church itself, that gift of God which invites us into a new pattern of life. We participate in this world as confounded and divided people, and in this we have given way for the world systems to communicate their communication as they always have done. The church has far too often been co-opted by these systems, relegated to a narrow religious sphere or diluted by unreflective participation in other systems, becoming yet another cog in the system or demographic in the mix.

Which drives reflection back to the basics. What is the Gospel? What is the good news to humanity? When John the Baptist was in prison, he sent his disciples to Jesus, and had them ask about what he had heard, wondering if Jesus was the expected one of God. Jesus responded, "Go and tell John what you hear and see: the blind receive their sight, the lame walk, the lepers are cleansed, the deaf hear, the dead are raised, and the poor have good news brought to them. And blessed is anyone who takes no offense at me."[65] What is the good news for the oppressor in this case? That they do not have to give into anxiety or insecurity. That they no longer oppress. As Volf writes, "The good news is that those who hope can acknowledge the dark side of their history because the divine promise frees them from the captivity to the past."[66] This is good news for oppressed and oppressors together. There is a better way, and this is the eternal way of communion with God. Those who distrust can trust. Those who despair find hope. Those who are broken will be made whole. Those who are weary find rest. Those who are lonely will find community.

In this community shaped by the good news of Christ, we live out the new hope in the context of this present world. This is a fractal life, taking a self-similar shape across scales, with the largest scale a reflection of the most intimate. It starts with the beginning of all, the shape and nature of God, as it is the Spirit who enables participation with God and the Spirit who orients people within the context of full life. In the fruit of the Spirit—that orienting description in Galatians 5—we confront the systems of the world and the way they say life must be. The transition is not immediate, as we are people within history there are transitions to endure, and be committed together in seeing them through. Past hurts are lifted off the victims and carried by the perpetrators, who find solace in the grace of Christ and renewal in the power of the Spirit.

In reminding the sufferer that God has offered grace to the oppressor, and in empowering the sufferer to live in a restored identity based on the confrontation of the cross that acknowledges the need for justice, those who suffer are free to forgive. In this forgiveness, the sufferer can be truly reconciled with self and with the perpetrator. Reconciliation, however, is never a one-sided event. For true reconciliation to take place, the perpetrators must themselves "genuinely repent" from their wrongdoing, confessing their own real misdeeds, acknowledging the debt they owe both to the victims and to God. It is only in the cross that this is possible, as the burden of being victimized is otherwise too consuming to forget and the burden of victimizing is too horrible to admit.[67] Reconciliation becomes possible in the freedom that "Christ has reconciled both the wronged and the wrongdoers to God, to themselves and to each other."[68] Peace leads to forgiveness, and forgiveness leads to reconciliation, and reconciliation leads to fruitful celebration of life in all of its many expressions.

This is not a task we can do on our own, as we are caught in the systems that continually divert our rightful orientation. Thus, a liberative community functions in light of prayer, which provides constant reorientation and empowering, leading us back, first, into communion with God—which is God's hope with us—and then into a loving communion with others. We love God, we love neighbors. This trust-filled life is shared with others—not as a burden or a guilt-driven obligation—but as an expression of the fullness of life we are experiencing. Community is the good news, because it is in community that we find fullness in who we have been made to be and are invited to be through eternity. This is the hope of the oppressed and hope for the oppressors.

NOTES

1. See Pannenberg, *Systematic Theology*, 1:439. It is curious to note here how often God's wrath is framed as jealousy. This implies that what is offended is not God's holiness but rather his love. Or, more precisely, it is both his holiness and his love which are offended, but not as judge, rather as one lover by another, who has trusted the other and been betrayed. Sin is betrayal against our identity and against God's trust, more than it is a legal failing. See also Pannenberg, *Systematic Theology*, 2:330.

2. Ellacuría, *Ignacio Ellacuría*, 150.

3. Acts 2:38ff. Cf. 1 Pet. 1:13ff.

4. Joel B. Green, "Identity and Engagement in a Diverse World: Pluralism and Holiness in 1 Peter," *Asbury Theological Journal* 55, no. 2 (Fall 2000): 89.

5. Moltmann, *The Living God and the Fullness of Life*, 106.

6. Ibid., 152.

7. Volf, *After Our Likeness*, 178.

8. Moltmann, *Sun of Righteousness, Arise!*, 162. Oscar Romero makes the bold claim, "The Church is not on earth to gain privileges, to seek support in power and wealth or to integrate herself with the mighty of the world. The church does not exist even to erect great material temples or monuments. The church is not on the earth to teach the wisdom of the earth." Romero, *The Scandal of Redemption*, 93.

9. Moltmann, *Sun of Righteousness*, 163.

10. The idea of surrounding initially may sound restrictive. It need not be seen as such. Any prey animal, for instance, needs protection from predators in order to be what they are. Sheep, for instance, are able to be fully sheep if they are given space and protection within that space. More related to our current contexts is an example I learned from my father who taught literacy in juvenile halls and continuation schools for many years. He noted that teaching in juvenile halls tended to be more productive: because the students were incarcerated they were prevented from the desire or need to express their identity in the patterns that led them to criminal behavior. Removed from gang life, they were more free to be who they were, to show interest and study and learn in ways their usual environment prevented because of the narratives imposed on them. While a dramatic example, this is the case for much of our present society. Being surrounded offers us a space for rest and for contemplative engagement in ways

the frenzied world often prevents. Being surrounded by God's narrative gives us a living space within which we can live most fully within this world.

11. Acts is giving both an example and an admonition to its readers. As we see in the letters of Paul, the earliest Christians struggled with the practice and concept of community as well.

12. Moltmann, *Sun of Righteousness*, 162.

13. Ibid., 162.

14. See Jürgen Moltmann, *Theology & Joy* (London: SCM Press, 1973), 51–54.

15. Moltmann, *Sun of Righteousness*, 162. Moltmann here cautions against the role of the state in imposing such communal realities. He writes, "What comes to an end with this community is also 'the strong hand' of the state, which forcibly keeps people from becoming a 'wolf' for someone else. This community can settle its affairs by itself."

16. Moltmann, *Sun of Righteousness*, 163.

17. Ibid., 164.

18. Ibid., 166.

19. Moltmann, *Ethics of Hope*, 182.

20. Ibid., 182.

21. By no means! See Romans 6.

22. Moltmann, *Ethics of Hope*, 182.

23. Kierkegaard, *The Concept of Anxiety*, 138. See Volf, *The End of Memory*, 56–62.

24. This list is loosely quoted from Moltmann, *Ethics of Hope*, 182–183. Further down, he highlights the process for those who have been oppressed, which while important is not the immediate consideration for this study. See Tutu, *No Future Without Forgiveness*, 30–31.

25. Moltmann notes that some damage can never be repaired nor enough restitution offered. In such cases, the goal is the pursuit of such so as to orient in a trajectory of healing and reconciliation.

26. On discerning the work of the Spirit in a modern global context, see Kirsteen Kim, *The Holy Spirit in the World: A Global Conversation* (Maryknoll, NY: Orbis Books, 2007), chap. 7.

27. Parallel with Mt. 16:26 and Lk. 9:25.

28. Kierkegaard, *Works of Love*, 159.

29. Moltmann, *The Living God*, 138.

30. See Michael Welker, *God the Spirit* (Minneapolis: Fortress Press, 1994), 296–297.

31. Moltmann, *The Living God*, 149.

32. Welker, *God the Spirit*, 296.

33. Ela, *African Cry*, 128.

34. Moltmann, *The Living God*, 151.

35. See Sarah and Diat, *God or Nothing*, 70.

36. Coakley, *New Ascetism*, 85.

37. Ibid., 86.

38. Debra Hirsch, *Redeeming Sex: Naked Conversations about Sexuality and Spirituality* (Downers Grove: IVP, 2015), 208.

39. As Cassian notes, the sin of gluttony includes both excess of eating and over-fastidiousness about it. Thinking about food becomes, one way or the other, a dominating tendency. See *Institutes* 5 in John Cassian, *The Institutes*, trans. Boniface Ramsey (New York: Newman Press, 2000).

40. Coakley, *The New Asceticism*, 87.

41. For a recent, helpful study on this monastic approach, see Dennis Okholm, *Dangerous Passions, Deadly Sins: Learning from the Psychology of Ancient Monks* (Grand Rapids: Brazos, 2014).

42. See Matthew 4. On how the three temptations reflect the intersection of all the sins, see John Cassian, Conference 5.VI.6 in *The Conferences*, trans. Boniface Ramsey (New York: Paulist, 1997), 186–187.

43. Coakley, *GSS*, 46. In the last chapter of *GSS*, 340–343, Coakley notes six theses of privileging contemplation and these are worth noting at least in part as they point to the summation of her first volume and initiate the discussions in subsequent volumes. "Thesis 1: The contemplative is one who is forced to acknowledge the 'messy entanglement' of sexual desire and the desire for God." "Thesis 2: The contemplative acknowledges the leading activity of the Holy Spirit, and so jealously guards the distinctness of the third 'person.'" "Thesis 3: The 'apophatic turn' has the capacity not only to undermine gender stereotypes, but to lead to a form of ever-changing modellings of desire for God." "Thesis 4: Contemplation entails an expansion of the 'self,' a subversion of disengaged reason." "Thesis 5: Contemplation reorders the passions." "Thesis 6: Contemplation presents us with a Trinitarian model of power-in-vulnerability."

44. Miroslav Volf, *Against the Tide: Love in a Time of Petty Dreams and Persisting Enmities* (Grand Rapids: Eerdmans, 2010), 49.

45. Sarah Coakley, *God, Sexuality, and the Self: An Essay "On the Trinity"* (Cambridge, United Kingdom: Cambridge University Press, 2013), 343.

46. Vanier, *Community and Growth*, 310.

47. See Ibid., 5.

48. Ibid., 11. Vanier, *Community and Growth*, chap. 1 develops six elements of community that help construct a person among other persons in the way of true peace and deep love. These are community as openness; community and cooperation; community as a place of healing and growth; community as a place of self-revelation, community as forgiveness; and community as a living body.

49. Not least in Christian circles where the word "community" has devolved into Christianese, a term that is asserted without depth or serious intent.

50. Moltmann writes, "Our self-experiences are embedded in relationship experiences, they are not only made in self-respect. Therefore, hope and patience are not virtues of a lonely subject, but of relationship. I wake up to hope because someone trusts me. I start something new because someone puts his trust in me and expects something from me. I learn the patience of others with me and unfold in the room they give me. I have patience with them because I have hope for them and leave them time and wait. I keep a place in my life open for them and look forward to them This happens from equal to equal in symmetrical living conditions." In Moltmann, *Über Geduld, Barmherzigkeit und Solidarität*, 9. My translation.

51. Vanier, *The Gospel of John, the Gospel of Relationship*, xi.
52. Ibid., xi.
53. Ibid., 4. While L'Arche offers residential care and community for those who are severely disabled, Faith and Light offers non-residential community opportunities for the disabled and their friends and family, organizing monthly meetings and other scheduled activities as a way of support and connection.
54. By this I mean issues that were specifically political, relating to Roman rule. In a broad sense, everything Jesus spoke about was political, but not as part of the communication within the political system.
55. Vanier, *The Gospel of John, the Gospel of Relationship*, 8.
56. Croatto, *Exodus*, 78.
57. Ela, *African Cry*, 111. Cf. Karl Barth, *Church Dogmatics*, 2.1, 602.
58. Martin Luther King, Jr., "Love, Law, and Civil Disobedience," in *A Testament of Hope: The Essential Writings and Speeches of Martin Luther King, Jr.*, ed. James M. Washington (New York: HarperCollins, 1991), 50–51. The rest of the paragraph is worth quoting as he directly relates this task to the mission of Jesus: "But I think what Jesus was saying in substance was this, that I come not to bring an old negative peace, which makes for stagnant passivity and deadening complacency, I come to bring something different, and whenever I come, a conflict is precipitated, between the old and the new, whenever I come a struggle takes place between justice and injustice, between the forces of light and the forces of darkness. I come not to bring a negative peace, but a positive peace, which is brotherhood, which is justice, which is the kingdom of God."
59. See Jean Vanier, *Drawn Into the Mystery of Jesus Through the Gospel of John* (New York: Paulist Press, 2004), chaps. 18–19.
60. Vanier, *The Gospel of John, the Gospel of Relationship*, 93.
61. Ibid., 85.
62. Ibid., 51.
63. Ibid., 51. Emphasis in the original.
64. Vanier, *Community and Growth*, 59.
65. Mt. 11:4–6.
66. Volf, *Against the Tide: Love in a Time of Petty Dreams and Persisting Enmities*, 49.
67. See Miroslav Volf, *Free of Charge: Giving and Forgiving in a Culture Stripped of Grace* (Grand Rapids: Zondervan, 2005), 184–185.
68. Volf, *The End of Memory: Remembering Rightly in a Violent World*, 119.

Chapter 13

Conclusion

IN SEARCH OF THE WAY

"The topic 'Liberation of the oppressors' is a necessary but somehow dangerous project," Moltmann wrote in a letter to me in fall of 2010. "The liberation of oppressed people is self-evident, at least for them, the liberation of oppressors is not; it needs to 'make the blind see.' It is a painful process." Besides being dangerous and painful as a process, the very topic itself invites disagreement. When discussing this project with others, I invariably had to begin by explaining why such a liberation focus is necessary, often without ever getting to the point of explaining what it might look like.

Some do not think there is a real issue while others have told me that this topic evoked negative feelings. Why should we give the oppressors yet more attention when they already dominate cultural and theological conversations? Is this another attempt to co-opt yet more territories in theological discussion? The privileged want liberation too? Others admit it is a real issue—consumerism is a frequently reviled concern—but are suspect about the term "liberation" and the methodology often used to develop the themes. Some assume a liberation of the oppressor must be neocolonial and thus resisted; others assume it must be Marxist and thus resisted. Neither side may be entirely blind but it seems each tends to be nearsighted.

As Moltmann has emphasized, the liberating work of God calls the oppressed out of their oppression and the liberating work of God calls the oppressor out of their oppressing. Oppression has two sides and liberation must begin with each in their own way.

But how can this actually happen?

The challenge of reception is not the only challenge, nor even the most difficult. There are dangers on every side. It is common to assume that the liberation of oppressors must come by force of strength or force of government. Yet, this is to liberate through oppression and is not true liberation, simply a change in the power structure.[1] The ins are out and the outs are in; the systems continue to stand. True liberation of the oppressor can only happen without the application of yet more oppression. If that is the case, why would an oppressor ever give up their power?

A liberation of the oppressor can be in danger of suggesting too little: a gentle push, a mild reprimand, encouraging shifts to a more adequate way of life, applying a little bit of guilt along the way so as to make sure that even if the oppressors do not change at least they feel a little bad about it and make some gestures toward helping others or finding religious restitution. Or it can lead to paternalism, which locks in the systems of oppression while alleviating a sense of guilt about it by providing relief to the symptoms.

A liberation of the oppressor can also be in danger of suggesting, or doing, too much. While prophetic language may sound appealing, it can undermine the goal of enacted liberation. Condemnations, guilt-inducing recriminations about injustices, and participation in dysfunctional societal systems may contain elements of truth, but the communication is either wholly ignored or actively opposed. When such are ignored the historical temptation is to use force, pursuing revolution in overthrowing the establishment and setting up a new society. Oppression rarely goes away, however. The systems do not care who is in power, just that power is applied. History is filled with the oppressed becoming the next oppressors, back and forth the oppressing goes, when it will stop, nobody knows.

The battle lines are drawn, with each side demonizing the other, overlooking the corruption among their own, developing tribal approaches to societal problems, securing perpetual debates while undermining substantive solutions. The goal becomes condemnation not transformation. Many are not necessarily even really concerned about the structures or the patterns or the systems. They are concerned with their place in these structures and patterns and systems. If they have power, they want to keep it. If they do not have power, they want it.

This is the challenge and danger of a liberation of the oppressor because unless real liberation happens for those who are in power, liberation will never be thorough for either the oppressed or the oppressors. These categories are emptied then refilled by a new set of players for another go at the game. Liberation must happen on both sides for it to happen thoroughly for either side, liberating the oppressed from their oppression and liberating the oppressors from their oppressing—at the same time, from both directions—in a substantive way that ends the pattern of oppression for all.

If the attempts at liberation are right on target, then the systems themselves respond, negating any opposition or marshalling their anonymized forces against the voice of substantive change. The systems are not conscious opponents, they are self-perpetuating processes. But, they are reactive nevertheless. The systems defend themselves through the powers and people. This is not new. Jesus, after all, was himself crucified by oppressors and rejected by the oppressed. The liberator became the condemned. But the story of Jesus did not end on the cross. Nor does the story of liberation end with our experiences of history.

Jesus, the firstborn from the dead, was liberated from death, resurrected into life, and in this new life points toward a new way, a way of liberation and a way of renewal for all. This is the way of hope promised to the oppressed and the oppressors together. All those whose guilt is taken up on the cross are invited to be born again in a new way of life with God and with each other, a social salvation as much as it is a personal salvation. We are saved by Christ as particular participants in a new way of life that begins even now and extends into eternity. This is a fractal community of those who are participating in the systems of the world according to a new narrative of the promise of the Triune God. Such a fractal community works from below in renewing a context in light of the Kingdom of God, widening and deepening through the power of the Spirit's work. It is thus liberating, transformative, and expressive across scales.

This is the Way. But what does this way look like in our contexts? How can we navigate the various dangers and difficulties of a liberation of the oppressor? In our era where sides seem intractable, blame replacing dialog and self-righteousness replacing humility, there is no end of recriminations and certainly no small set of examples of the many problems in our society. Texts on such problems abound. But resistance to change continues, so there is a need to first ask why oppression happens. In understanding the impulse, actions become more strategic, addressing the context as it is, providing new perspectives on life and society so that the "blind can see."

To build a distinct approach that begins with the oppressors—arguing that oppressors can in fact, and indeed have, experienced liberation—I gathered together a chorus of contributors to help us all sing a new song, a song of life. "I waited patiently for the Lord," the Psalmist writes, "he inclined to me and heard my cry. He drew me up from the desolate pit, out of the miry bog, and set my feet upon a rock, making my steps secure. He put a new song in my mouth, a song of praise to our God. Many will see and fear, and put their trust in the Lord."[2] This is the song of liberation for both the oppressors and the oppressed.

Throughout this text, I have sought to describe this song in more detail. Yet, it is with an honest humility I acknowledge that I may not have hit every note nor covered all the relevant verses that may be necessary for enacting this chorus in every context. A few key critiques come to mind as tasks for future efforts or other contributors. First, while I have occasionally highlighted issues of concern, I chose to not emphasize critiques about our current political or social realities. Offering such prophetic challenges is indeed vital for practical progress; however, it can also lead to a limiting or even negating discussion, as not everyone shares the same context, the same reach, or the same leading from the Spirit. I also believe that much of what is labeled as prophetic in our era has been co-opted by systems-derived methods. That is not, of course, to dismiss the importance of clear statements about injustice and leading toward reconciliation, more to argue that my goal was to address the underlying issue of method. There is no end of issues to discuss and by reevaluating methodology, through recovering a more wholly *pneumapoietic* pattern, we can be even more effective in addressing these in all of our various contexts.

A second self-critique is that I have a limited number of contributors. I have chosen based on my own experiences of seeking liberation and sought out those who shared a common concern. In doing this, I have knowingly and unknowingly left out many who could have added substantive depth to the discussion at each point. My hope was to treat those contributors I used in a more comprehensive, rather than piecemeal, way, letting their priorities take their intended shape all throughout. As my third self-critique, while I have offered guidance about priorities and perspectives, I have not given any clear action steps that could help construct a liberative process. Although Vanier serves as my practical exemplar, most of us are not called to the same tasks he has been called into, and that leaves it to each of us, as individuals in community, to reach out in prayer for the Spirit's pragmatic leading in our context. This is a theology book and while not impractical, it is not intended as a manual for action but as a guide for emphases and as an encouragement for such to develop.

While this book may lack a clear prophetic challenge in some ways, it is not lacking a challenge altogether. The task at hand, I argue, is one of immediacy and particularity. That is to say that I encourage everyone reading this book to identify elements of oppressing in their life and their context, learn from the discussion of this book, and then live out a new pattern of life in their setting, in your setting. It is easy to address national concerns, indulging a sense of rage and justice while not actually making any changes. "We want to be liberal," Moltmann writes, "and neglect thereby our own liberation. Whoever wishes to help the oppressed to gain their freedom must begin with himself: he must cease being their oppressor."[3] It is much harder to address the particular and immediate, yet it is in the particular and immediate that real change begins.

That is the fundamental challenge of this book. Begin where you are, with your self and with your setting. If everyone initiates liberation, then change will begin in all sorts of places in all sorts of ways. If everyone simply talks about liberation for others, then nothing changes, and the goal stagnates, simply justifying more discussions, grants, seminars, and self-righteousness. The Civil Rights movement had national discussions. However, it was particular acts that galvanized change. What in your zone of oppressing is the equivalent of refusing to go to the back of the bus? What is the equivalent of staying seated at the lunch counter? These were immediate and particular acts that confronted the established narrative of their times.

THE WAY OF THIS BOOK

I began this text by discussing the unique situation of the oppressor, asking why it is they are in need of liberation, and who qualifies as an oppressor. Very few people are purely oppressed or oppressor, and so this conversation is vital for a wide variety of contexts, even those where people are oppressed by others. While each situation offers its own complexity, a basic definition relates to the experience of choice. The oppressed are those who suffer under the dehumanizing choices of others. Oppressors are those who have choice and choose ways that dehumanize others. By pursuing dehumanizing choices, an oppressor engages their context as constant competition. There are winners and losers, a constant flux of ranking that leads to defensive postures and protective pursuits. The apparent freedom of privilege is lost in the consuming dissatisfaction of never having enough or being enough, and so meaning is gained by comparison and acquisition. With this definition, the reality of oppression moves from being a binary—where one is either one or the other—and invites a complexity of interpretation that focuses on the specificity of a given situation.

Understanding the liberation of the oppressor more specifically pursues real liberation for all, rather than merely inverting the power structures in a perpetual cycle of revolution and reformation, because it addresses the destination of liberation: how we are to live if and when we experience freedom. A new kind of discussion is necessary because the entrenched approaches to this topic have tended to divide according to ideological lines and narrow interests, leading to bifurcation rather than transformation as each side claims their portion of perspective as the morally superior. Oppressing becomes entrenched even among those who are seeking resolution.

There must be, then, a better way. I suggest this better way is one of hope. If we are going to ask oppressors to give up power and privilege, we must not first tell them what they must lose. Oppressing seeks a limited kind of freedom, a freedom based on ego and power, showing domination in order to provide a sense of value. To provoke a sense of loss is to enter into the very competition that domination tries to conquer. Instead of loss, the way of hope emphasizes what people will gain. They will gain community, a holistic enlivening that personalizes their contributions and invites a more coherent interaction with God and the whole world. They will gain freedom, real and holistic freedom: a freedom of deliberation, a freedom of responsibility, a freedom of a liberating community.

All these lead into a creative passion for the possible with and for each other. This is a freedom of sociality not systems, a freedom defined in friendship, authenticity, wholeness. As Moltmann writes, "For my part, I shall be free when I open my life for other people and recognize them in their otherness, and like to be with them."[4] When we recognize each other and call each other by name, then "the other person is no longer a restriction of my freedom but complements my own limited life. . . . We call it solidarity or friendship or love."[5] While caught in the systems, we cannot conceive of this freedom in full, and so we continue to eat the fruit, pursuing domination and asserting our choices. The challenge we face in seeking a thorough liberation is to help people understand their fundamental need for real freedom and to seek this freedom in their context. Addressing this challenge is the goal of this book.

In part 1, I describe the context of oppressing. We cannot simply assume oppressing is self-evident, superficial, or somehow a sign of pernicious intent. Why do oppressors oppress? What is it about their contexts that orients toward competition and insatiable consumption? To answer these questions, I offer a different framework of description. First, I highlighted the work of Niklas Luhmann, whose systems theory of society is descriptive rather than prescriptive, an expansive description of how things are, not how things should be or what we should do to get us there. This descriptive framework gives a starting place to examine how and why we rationalize our choices in light of often paradoxical assumptions.

Building on this, I then looked at the work of Søren Kierkegaard and James Loder to help describe the nature of a person. What leads to our fears and insecurities that then are expressed in patterns of oppression and competition? As seems clear, oppressors are not generally seeking to oppress others as their goal, but rather see oppression as an unfortunate result of the necessary realities of living life. Some win, some lose, everyone is on a spectrum of success or failure, so we must do what we must in order to secure the best possible life for ourselves and our family. To simply say "Stop it!" is not enough as there is often no other conception of how to live life. The oppressors are oppressed by the same systems they perpetuate, becoming anonymous in the autopoietic perpetuation, but receiving just enough validation to avoid total despair or identity dissolution. Thus, the oppressors also need liberation and such liberation cannot take place by further application of the systems according to their own narrative values.

Conclusion 281

In part 2, I begin the process of describing a narrative alternative. Scripture points to a pattern of life that is oriented in God and away from oppressing. Indeed, while many have used the Bible to support oppression throughout history, a comprehensive reading makes it clear that God seeks liberation for people. God loves, expressing this love throughout the narrative, not promising an absolute social equality, but certainly insisting on a pattern of life in which all are valued and justice is affirmed at every point. This narrative initiates from the beginning of the world itself, culminating first in the archetype of the Exodus narrative in the Hebrew Scriptures and then in the resurrection narratives of the New Testament. All throughout, we find God giving hope to those who are oppressed and calling those with privilege to use this privilege in wise, community building ways.

I follow my discussion on Scripture by looking at key texts from the early church to explore how they viewed the Christian life and Spirit-led liberation. Clement of Alexandria offers the first and most focused perspective, showing how the issues of wealth and privilege were indeed concerns for the early Christian communities. Yet, they viewed the issue from a different assumption: the oppressed were certainly loved by God, and it was the status of the powerful that was in question. As a teacher himself, Clement was interested in conveying the fundamental Christian teaching while making sure that such teaching was not narrowly understood. Oppression includes topics of wealth and economics, but is not limited to these. Indeed, the motivations that lead to distorted identity can take many forms. We are to find our identity only in God and let go of any desire or possession that impedes. Wealth and power are not themselves evil; it is the application of these in dysfunctional and distorting ways that is the problem.

I follow this with a discussion about Anthony of Egypt, often considered the founder of Christian monasticism. Whereas Clement was a teacher to a broad audience of Christians in Alexandria during the pre-Nicene era, Anthony was seen as a leader to monastics and those seeking separation from society in order to pursue radical Christian devotion. In some ways, he represents the beginning of a bifurcation of Christian devotion, with the regular Christian and the monastic Christian pursuing different experiences with different expectations. Yet, in the writings of Anthony himself this is not the goal. We are to live our calling in full, with different contexts leading us into different expressions of this truly liberated life. Above all we are to know ourselves truly, join in with devotion to God in the power of the Spirit, finding unity with God and our self in prayer and service. This is a calling for all those who are in Christ.

In part 3, I develop these narrative themes in four voices, offering a constructive proposal for theological reflection that leads to liberation of oppressors. Wolfhart Pannenberg provides a perspective on God and holiness that emphasizes exocentricity. God does not depend on anything else for meaning, is secure in identity, and so is the only identity in which we can find security and fullness that will sustain us through eternity. Establishing our identity in God opens us up in relationship with others, free and open to others because of God's identity, presence, and work. In this experience with God, we discover a coherent orthodoxy that leads us into a coherent sense of self and this world.

Sarah Coakley's broad ranging theological acumen is now engaged in the task of constructing a new methodology for theological studies. She calls this method *théologie totale,* and it orients theology as a comprehensive but not totalitarian discussion that has interest in every direction, listening and learning and discovering God's work in multiple ways. In this, she is developing an approach toward freedom in the Triune God that emphasizes a path of liberation without repression or libertinism, a new way of being in which we can be truly ourselves as God has made us. Such a transformation is itself oriented within contemplation, prayer to and with God, an ascetic approach that allows us to be better situated in the world rather than having to flee it.

Jean Vanier initiated a new approach to theology that draws from reflection, action, and transformation through his efforts with L'Arche. Vanier developed a non-idealistic engagement with community in which those with mental disabilities gather together with those willing to come alongside them in their difficulties, sharing life, learning together, contributing to each other as each is able and uniquely suited. He points to a lifelong transformation that he calls the way of the heart. Through this way, those committed to it become vulnerable and open to others in community, overcoming fears and discouragements, and awaken to a new vision of who they truly are. In this fractal community, we need not be doing dramatic or extraordinary tasks in order for there to be a substantive effect. We begin to truly relate to others, and they relate to us, a depth of relationship that then extends across networks in leading toward a broad experience of substantive liberation for both the oppressors and the oppressed.

Jürgen Moltmann provided the initial impetus for this work and has pursued this cause of liberation in almost all of his writings. In examining his newer works, I highlighted four interrelated themes that are essential for a better understanding of God and transformative expression of our life with God in this world. First, we need a renewed vision of God that is oriented relationally based on God's promise. Second, an emphasis on the resurrection deflates the threats of the systems and gives us hope in a narrative identity secure in God. Third, this narrative identity is framed by the kingdom of God, which is already among us and provides the coherent structure that contrasts the incoherent, operationally closed narratives of the world systems. Finally, Moltmann emphasizes the vital nature of community. We are formed in community and our narrative identity emphasizes both our particularity and our unity in forming a cohesive expression of human flourishing in which all are valued and included.

These four themes function as a dialogical framework for my four contemporary theologians. Utilizing this chorus, I explored the theological situation of liberation in five movements: one is a reemphasis on God as loving and exocentric (chapter 8), the second emphasizes how God is alluring and communal (chapter 9). This understanding of God comes to us in power through the enactment and promise of resurrection (chapter 10). A new way forward begins. This calls for our response to live according to God's kingdom (chapter 11). This expression of the Kingdom already among us in the power of the Spirit is through a transforming, fractal community that lives in, with, and for this world (chapter 12).

THE WAY OF LIBERATION

In this text, I am unapologetically pursuing a particularly Christian theology. Such an approach begins with presuppositions about the nature of this world, past and present and future. My fundamental argument is that liberation, true and lasting liberation, happens only in light of the work of Christ, oriented and empowered in the work of the Spirit who leads us to fullness in communion with the Father. Thus, this is also evangelistic. I am, as fits my abilities and the confines of this medium, preaching what has long been called the Good News. What makes this news good? God. Only God is truly good, after all. This nature of God and engagement by God in creating, redeeming, and renewing this world is the heart of a gospel of liberation. Moltmann himself emphasizes this evangelism: "There is no future without hope. There is no life without love. There is no new assurance without faith. It is the task of evangelization and of the witness of the Christian life to proclaim the living Christ and to awaken in us the Spirit of life."[6] This good news is music we play, a rhythm we live, a chorus of like and unlike together joining with each other in celebration with God's freedom. Liberation is indeed a new song.

Such liberation involves a transformation of desires, an empowering and enlivening renewal in which the best of who we are becomes fully realized. This liberation does not negate achievement or pursuit of one's best. If desires are repressed, if a person is restricted, or their ability to achieve their goals is reduced, the tendency is to fall into despair or learned helplessness, where effort is no longer productive. Apathy reigns. In the Spirit's presence, our pursuit of the best endures because we find fulfillment in being in rhythm with God's work in our contexts. We move outside of apathy without a need to dominate others. While seemingly counterintuitive, this is the experience of artists, musicians, and others who are engaged in a task with passion. And maybe not simply in an analogous way. As Rob Johnston notes, "It is in the movement of the Holy Spirit that the artist experiences true freedom."[7] The efforts rarely result in riches but do lead toward a fuller sense of self, in which broader acclaim or validation is not necessary. In the Spirit's work, our desires become integrated with each other and with this world, coherent with God and with others, so that there is no longer a constant clashing of demands and restrictions. We experience a freedom for many that includes many. Liberation is a dance.

Most oppressors are not malicious. They are seeking life as they understand it, conditioned by their context and oriented by their hopes and fears, caught up in patterns and structures that propel them to seek success (defined with certain goals), to seek life (oriented in certain priorities), in ways that offer benefit for a small number while resistant to others. We take on allegiances and associate with those who are similar in order to maximize our own sense of peace. This is understandable. So understandable that when the oppressed do find release from their oppression they themselves take on the same attitudes and goals, seeking freedom through domination, success through resistance, negating and denigrating those who stand in the way of an insatiable drive for a never-ending more. Liberation is achieved in part while the overall cycle continues. Peace for some is paid for by others. This is the way of the world. This is not the way of God.

"Blessed are the peacemakers," Jesus said in his famous sermon, "for they will be called children of God." God's children do not just live in peace, protecting peace for themselves by ignoring others or demanding others bear the burden. Peace is made. The method of this peace-making is exemplified in the mission of the Son of the Father. Jesus set aside what he deserves and entered into life with those who did not know where to turn or who to be. Taking the form of a slave, among those trapped by systems and enslaved by disoriented desires, he was obedient to God's reality, to the way of God's kingdom. He lived the way he did because of who God is, an exocentric holiness that brought renewal as well as confrontation. Jesus was whole in a world filled with amalgamated fragments. He shows us who God truly is, a way of being that invites participation—engaging and creating and restoring. He shows us God is love. This life that was is also the life that is. Jesus is risen and this life presses forward in our lives.

We are to love God. We are to love our neighbor as ourselves. Jesus fulfills all that the law and the prophets were getting at and commends as the way of true life. We are to live in this love. But we can only love when we are freed from our fears, freed from having to rely on the world systems for identity and value and meaning, free to be who we truly are in the company of others. In this freedom, we find ourselves, begin to know ourselves. The oppressing falls away like ragged garments; our old self dissipates and a new self comes alive in the freeing, resurrection power of the Holy Spirit. We become open to others in a new way, seeking to come alongside them and be open to their contributions. We are liberated. The Kingdom of God is already among us. Liberation is peace for all.

Understanding that the oppressors need hope is the first step in a different way of viewing this world. Their experiences of privilege, power, and choice are not sufficient, but they are blind to their needs and others are jealous of their experiences. If we cannot see that oppressors need hope, then we are still viewing the context of the world through the lenses of the world systems. What is this hope? Relationship. Enlivening relationships that provide a context of transformation of self and community. The first step of this is the experience of freedom. We need freedom from systems and desires that proclaim themselves as sustaining our true self, but promise only so much, a small portion of being that cannot be sustained either in time or community. We are constantly buffeted by fears of dissolution and resistance, caught up in storms of our own making and storms of this world as others clash against their despair and distractions. We oppress because we are insecure, afraid, insufficient, trying to find meaning by imposition, competing because we know no other way to establish our relative value. We are anonymous in the systems and we are desperate to be named.

In the experience of God's reaching out to us in Christ—a gift given without any possibility of reciprocity—we are humbled, aware of our deficiency and yet, even still, we discover we are beloved. God loves us, seeks us, invites us. God so loves us the Son is willing to live among us, die for us, confronting the systems on our behalf, conquering our fears because death itself no longer wins. In the confrontation with the systems in which Jesus dies, Jesus wins. The resurrection is the promise that our identity is not dependent on the world systems or satiating our desires for momentary comfort. Our identity derives from God and is sustained in God and God is persistent in applying this promise to us.

We can trust God because the Son shows the obedience that we could not offer. In this obedience, the Son invites us into a new experience of trust, where guilt, blame, despair, and excess no longer define us. In this trust, we begin to trust others, no longer having to compete or dominate, show our greatness or have to establish a show of good works. We trust God and live in this trust by being open to others, free to contribute, free to receive, an experience of reciprocity established in flourishing love. It is a reciprocity of freedom, not one of force or expectation, by those who are beloved. We choose *for* each other, not making our choices a burden on others but making choices that affirm and enrich each other. In this community, each is a fully expressive person, named and unique, weak and strong, able and disabled, all in our own ways so that we can offer to others what they need and receive from others what we need in return.

Such freeing reciprocity invites trust and builds trust, a growing appreciation for each other in a non-idealistic experience of community. Our weaknesses are real, our faults are real, our opinions and assumptions are real. We encounter others in their reality which causes conflict, but this is not determinative conflict. It is inviting. The hope found in God who made us is our hope in finding freedom with and for each other, becoming whole as we learn about our self and learn about others, where we fit together, how we function, willing to engage each other in ways that may bring hurt and frustration, but confident that the Spirit is leading us toward real community. In this experience of real community we begin to know what it truly means to live as God lives. Liberation is life.

The Spirit is the Spirit of Life. Because of this, a liberation of the oppressor requires a substantive theology of the Holy Spirit. In developing a pattern of liberation for our specific context, we must continually ask questions about the Spirit. Where is the Holy Spirit working? How is the Holy Spirit working? Throughout Scripture, we find God's particular presence—the Spirit—with people, filling them and in this filling enlivening them to accomplish specific tasks. In the New Testament, this Spirit is even more expansive, with Pentecost the story of the Spirit in each person, blessing, and using them in a new way.

Those who are free in Christ become named participants, no longer anonymous, sharing and receiving, freeing others and building others up in the particular way the Spirit gives them gifts. This is the body of Christ, which comes together as a community in the name of Christ. The calling of the church is to be a focused fractal community of experienced liberation that reaches out into the world as each person lives in the new way of life of the Spirit. We live the narrative of God together and we live out the narrative of God in the midst of the world systems, no longer anonymous and defined by their autopoietic patterns. We find coherence in the Spirit who integrates our lives according to God's lordship over all creation. The Spirit remakes each context according to the Kingdom's integrating and coherent values.

Because the Spirit is always particular—and the experience of the kingdom is a fractal experience of the small extending within and spreading out among the whole—the emphasis can never be focused on the general goals while negating any person. That is a negating of the Spirit's particularity. It is in the relationship of person to person that the most transformative experience of the Spirit takes place, because it is in each person that the Spirit chooses to dwell. We are gathered together as persons into a unity, and this gathering is what transforms anonymity into identity. Oppression is diminished and eventually dissipates.

Whenever people are oppressed they are repressed, and when they are repressed the systems begin to dominate again. When people are anonymous in churches, it allows patterns of oppression to enter into and be expressed by the Church into the world.[8] By negating each person's participation and contribution—even for seemingly high values—we undermine the very contribution Christianity makes to real and thorough liberation. The Church, the faith, is co-opted by the systems and we worship those systems as our lord—our golden calves. Only in the very humble experience of personal relationships do we push against the systems of oppression and begin to express the real value of each person, each with their gift, each with their role, each with their contribution, everyone engaged in the to-and-fro of liberated love.

Far too often, we have made the service into the goal, the process into the ideal. We have made the method—and as methods they are well-worthwhile—into the purpose. Like the religious leaders of the time of Jesus, who turned the Sabbath into a way of restricting people, making people live for the Sabbath, we have made Christianity into a goal for people, a religious system that tells people what they are to *do*. In this, we have let community become a second or third order task. The community is then constructed so as to worship, with worship taking the priority over relationship—locking people into a religious system among the other systems. We then have descended into patterns of oppressing by neglecting God's calling—choosing sacrifice over obedience—leaving people to the systems which promise a pseudo-identity as each person seeks a semblance of meaning and community on their own in this world. We have sought sacrifice to God in gathering riches, power, complexity of form and description, but have neglected obedience in the radical pursuit of particularized love. Authentic community became an accident of worship—nice if it happens but not essential for our self-definition as followers of Christ—rather than a primary expression of our devotion in Christ together. We have not recognized the body of Christ. And, increasingly, people leave behind the worship, abandoning faith as an empty promise of a never-arriving substance. Falling into death.

The purpose in God's work—whether law or liturgy—is the creation of a people who participate together in the new patterns of the kingdom, patterns of love, peace, joy, patience. As Emerito Nacpil writes, "The intention of the reign of God in His elemental gifts is to make human community possible!"[9] This is the work of the Spirit because this is the experience of the Spirit, the process and the pattern of eternity. God sent the Son for the sake of the people, like a shepherd seeking after lost sheep. Like a father celebrating his lost son who has returned from the far country, God is seeking after community with us. Worship is part of this, but does not offer the liberative hope, because as a purpose it does not give a person that which they are most longing for in their deepest being. For liberation to grow among us, it is vital that the hope of community once again be primary, relegating worship to its secondary function in creating community. This is a potentially scandalous claim, but one that bears out through this study and reflects, I argue, the thrust of Scripture. Worship orients us rightly to God and with others, but the goal of humanity is to love God *and* love others in eternal community.

Community is not a subsidiary or secondary or tertiary effect of a liberated life in light of God's lordship; it is the central goal. Ecclesiology should not result in community as a byproduct but rather the other elements of ecclesiology serve as supporting framework for thorough going, practical, engaged, enlivening community, which is the primary result of the gifts of the Spirit. If we are not liberated into community with God and with others, but instead orient our liberation within another world system, we are not truly liberated at all.

If we pursue Christ in community, there will be challenges and concerns. This should not dissuade us, because it is the life of Christ with us that gives us meaning and it is this life that binds us together, that orients us in thanksgiving, and in this thanksgiving overcomes the entreaties of the systems back toward division and dissolution. In liberation there is the experience of the cross, which is one of pain and forsakenness, but the experience of the cross is not all there is. There is also the experience of resurrection, the hope of life renewed.

We are liberated when each of us participates with each other in becoming fully who we are each made to be. We liberate when we help others become. We are liberated when we let others participate in our becoming. This is true freedom, a freedom that includes and invites, expanding the experience of humanity in particular contexts. Liberation into this kind of freedom happens for the oppressed and the oppressors together, the one taking up as the other lets go, each creating space for the other, resisting the depersonalizing tendencies of social systems as they engage in the truly personalizing movement of the Holy Spirit in their midst. This is the promise to us and for us: liberation is a love story shared between all of creation.

"Now the Lord is the Spirit," Paul writes to the Corinthians, "and where the Spirit of the Lord is, there is freedom. And all of us, with unveiled faces, seeing the glory of the Lord as though reflected in a mirror, are being transformed into the same image from one degree of glory to another; for this comes from the Lord, the Spirit."[10] The Spirit is the Spirit of life. Life is relationship. The Spirit leads us into relationship with God and with others. That is the mission of God. It is this pattern of relationship formation and development that should be the primary mission of the church. We are to live in and invite others into this relationship with God and live in this relationship with God with and for others. This is a mission of freedom, a mission of life, a mission of faith. Let us enter into this life even now, wherever we are at, with and among those who need to experience this life in full.

God loves us. We are to love God and love our neighbor. This is our challenge: if we really want liberation, we need to emphasize the pattern of community that seems to be the method of God. This is our hope. The hope for the oppressors. Let freedom ring.

NOTES

1. Of course, this does not mean that the oppressors should continue oppressing. Addressing specific instances of oppressing is often a necessary first step in liberating the oppressed. It just is not a real liberation from oppressing or a blow to the structures of oppressing.

2. Ps. 40:1–3.

3. Moltmann, "The Liberation of Oppressors," 70.

4. See Moltmann, *God for a Secular Society*, 206–207.

5. Ibid., 207.

6. Ibid., 244.

7. Robert K. Johnston, *God's Wider Presence: Reconsidering General Revelation* (Grand Rapids: Baker Academic, 2014), 198.

8. The sad and pervasive reality of sexual abuse by priests and pastors is a stark example, but not the only one. In these expressions, the victim is used as an object of self-gratification, not treated as a person beloved by God. Moreso, it is the co-opting of God's lordship and using Christ's mission to use another person in this way and is the height of idolatrous heresy. God's name is not just used in vain, it is used for evil. Blaspheming the Holy Spirit.

9. Nacpil, *Jesus' Strategy for Social Transformation*, 242.

10. 2 Cor. 3:17–18.

Bibliography

Alter, Robert. *The Art of Biblical Narrative*. 2nd edition. New York: Basic Books, 2011.

Ashwin-Siejkowski, Piotr. *Clement of Alexandria: A Project of Christian Perfection*. New York: T&T Clark, 2008.

Ayres, Lewis. *Nicaea and Its Legacy: An Approach to Fourth-Century Trinitarian Theology*. Oxford: Oxford University Press, 2006.

Barnett, Christopher B. *From Despair to Faith: The Spirituality of Søren Kierkegaard*. Minneapolis: Fortress Press, 2014.

Barth, Karl. *Prayer*. 50th Anniversary edition. Louisville: Westminster John Knox Press, 2002.

Barton, Stephen C., ed. *Holiness: Past and Present*. New York: T & T Clark, 2003.

Basil the Great. *On the Holy Spirit*. Crestwood, NY: St Vladimir's Seminary Press, 1980.

———. *On Social Justice: St. Basil the Great*. Translated by C. Paul Schroeder. Crestwood, NY: St Vladimir's Seminary Press, 2009.

Bauckham, Richard. "'Only the Suffering God Can Help': Divine Passibility in Modern Theology." *Themelios* 9, no. 3 (April 1984): 6–12.

Bediako, Kwame. *Theology and Identity: The Impact of Culture upon Christian Thought in the Second Century and in Modern Africa*. Oxford: Regnum Books, 1992.

Berkman, Elliot T. "The Neuroscience of Goals and Behavior Change." *Consulting Psychology Journal: Practice and Research* 70, no. 1 (March 2018): 28–44.

Blok, Anton. *Radical Innovators: The Blessings of Adversity in Science and Art, 1500–2000*. Cambridge, UK: Polity, 2017.

Blomberg, Craig L. *Neither Poverty Nor Riches: Illuminating the Riddle*. Grand Rapids, MI: IVP Academic, 2000.

Bonhoeffer, Dietrich. *Ethics*. Minneapolis: Fortress Press, 2005.

Bonino, José Míguez. *Toward a Christian Political Ethics*. Philadelphia: Fortress Press, 1983.

Botterweck, G. Johannes, ed. *Theological Dictionary of the Old Testament, Vol. 12.* Translated by Douglas W. Stott and David E. Green. Grand Rapids, MI: Eerdmans, 2003.

Brakke, David. *Athanasius and the Politics of Asceticism.* Oxford: Clarendon Press, 1995.

Bulányi, György, and Gyula Simonyi. *Rapture of the Gospel.* Székesfehérvár: BOKOR, BOCS Foundation, 2000.

Bundy, David. "Christian Virtue: John Wesley and the Alexandrian Tradition." *Wesleyan Theological Journal* 26, no. 1 (1991): 139–163.

Cassian, John. *The Conferences.* Translated by Boniface Ramsey. New York: Paulist Press, 1997.

———. *The Institutes.* Translated by Boniface Ramsey. New York: Newman Press, 2000.

Castelo, Daniel. *The Apathetic God: Exploring the Contemporary Relevance of Divine Impassibility.* Eugene, OR: Wipf & Stock, 2009.

Cattell, Everett L. *The Spirit of Holiness.* Edited by Evans Wayne. Barclay Press, 2015.

Charleston, Steven, and Elaine A. Robinson, eds. *Coming Full Circle: Constructing Native Christian Theology.* Minneapolis: Fortress Press, 2015.

Chesterton, G. K. *What's Wrong with the World.* New York: Cassell and Company, 1910.

Chinula, Donald M. *Building King's Beloved Community: Foundations for Pastoral Care and Counseling with the Oppressed.* Eugene, OR: Wipf & Stock, 2009.

Chitty, Derwas. *Letters of Saint Anthony the Great.* Oxford: Cistercian Publications, 1978.

Chrysostom, John. *On Wealth and Poverty.* Crestwood, NY: St Vladimir's Seminary Press, 1999.

Clement of Alexandria. *The Exhortation to the Greeks. The Rich Man's Salvation. To the Newly Baptized.* Translated by G. W. Butterworth. Reprint edition. Cambridge, MA: Harvard University Press, 1919.

Coakley, Sarah. *God, Sexuality, and the Self: An Essay "On the Trinity."* Cambridge, UK: Cambridge University Press, 2013.

———. *The New Asceticism.* New York: Bloomsbury, 2015.

———. *Powers and Submissions: Spirituality, Philosophy and Gender.* Malden, MA: Wiley-Blackwell, 2002.

———. "Prayer as Crucible: How My Mind Has Changed." *Christian Century* 128, no. 6 (March 22, 2011): 32–40.

Cocksworth, Ashley. *Karl Barth on Prayer.* New York: T&T Clark, 2018.

Collins, Kenneth J., and Jason E. Vickers, eds. *The Sermons of John Wesley: A Collection for the Christian Journey.* Nashville: Abingdon Press, 2013.

Colonnese, Louis M., ed. *The Church in the Present-Day Transformation of Latin America in the Light of the Council.* 2 vols. Bogota: General Secretariat of CELAM, 1970.

Comblin, José. *The Holy Spirit and Liberation.* Maryknoll, NY: Orbis Books, 1989.

Cooke, Maeve. "Realism and Idealism : Was Habermass Communicative Turn a Move in the Wrong Direction?" *Political Theory* 40, no. 6 (2012): 811–821.
Coppedge, Allan. *The God Who Is Triune: Revisioning the Christian Doctrine of God*. Downers Grove, IL: IVP Academic, 2007.
Coulter, Dale M., and Amos Yong, eds. *The Spirit, the Affections, and the Christian Tradition*. Notre Dame, IN: University of Notre Dame Press, 2016.
Cox, Harvey. *God's Revolution and Man's Responsibility*. Valley Forge, PA: The Judson Press, 1965.
———. *On Not Leaving It to the Snake*. New York: Macmillan, 1969.
Creel, Richard E. *Divine Impassibility: An Essay in Philosophical Theology*. Reprint. Eugene, OR: Wipf & Stock, 2005.
Croatto, J. Severino. *Exodus: A Hermeneutics of Freedom*. Maryknoll, NY: Orbis Books, 1981.
Dallmann, Hans-Ulrich. "Niklas Luhmann's Systems Theory as a Challenge for Ethics." *Ethical Theory and Moral Practice* 1, no. 1 (1998): 85–102.
DeLanda, Manuel. *Assemblage Theory*. Edinburgh: Edinburgh University Press, 2016.
———. *A New Philosophy of Society: Assemblage Theory and Social Complexity*. New York: Continuum, 2006.
DeSteno, David. *The Truth About Trust: How It Determines Success in Life, Love, Learning, and More*. New York: Hudson Street Press, 2014.
Dias, Brian G., and Kerry J. Ressler. "Parental Olfactory Experience Influences Behavior and Neural Structure in Subsequent Generations." *Nature Neuroscience* 17, no. 1 (2014): 89–96.
Disbrey, Claire. "George Fox and Some Theories of Innovation in Religion." *Religious Studies* 25, no. 1 (1989): 61–74.
Downs, David J. *Alms: Charity, Reward, and Atonement in Early Christianity*. Waco: Baylor University Press, 2016.
Du Bois, W. E. B. *John Brown*. Edited by David R. Roediger. New edition. New York: Modern Library, 2001.
———. *The Souls of Black Folk: With "The Talented Tenth" and "The Souls of White Folk."* Reprint edition. New York: Penguin Classics, 1996.
Dutton, Kevin. *The Wisdom of Psychopaths: What Saints, Spies, and Serial Killers Can Teach Us About Success*. Reprint edition. New York: Scientific American/Farrar, Straus and Giroux, 2013.
Eagleson, John, and Philip J. Scharper, eds. *Puebla and Beyond: Documentation and Commentary*. Maryknoll, NY: Orbis Books, 1979.
Efthymiadis, Stephanos, ed. *The Ashgate Research Companion to Byzantine Hagiography: Volume I: Periods and Places*. Burlington, VT: Routledge, 2011.
———, ed. *The Ashgate Research Companion to Byzantine Hagiography Volume II: Genres and Contexts*. Burlington, VT: Routledge, 2014.
Eiesland, Nancy L. *Human Disability and the Service of God*. Nashville: Abingdon Press, 1998.
Ela, Jean-Marc. *African Cry*. Eugene, OR: Wipf & Stock, 2005.

———. *My Faith as an African*. Eugene, OR: Wipf & Stock, 2009.
Ellacuría, Ignacio. *Ignacio Ellacuría: Essays on History, Liberation, and Salvation*. Edited by Michael E. Lee. Maryknoll, NY: Orbis Books, 2013.
Erikson, Erik H. *Childhood and Society*. New York: W.W. Norton, 1993.
Faniran, Adetoye. "Rest: The Biblical Model of Environmental Management and Its Implications for the Kingdom of God." *Ogbomoso Journal of Theology* 12 (2007): 43–58.
Fee, Gordon D. *God's Empowering Presence: The Holy Spirit in the Letters of Paul*. Peabody, MA: Hendrickson, 1994.
Flannery, Austin, ed. *Vatican Council II: The Conciliar and Post Conciliar Documents*. New York: Costello Publishing Company, 1975.
Fowler, James W. "John Wesley's Development in Faith." In *The Future of the Methodist Theological Traditions*, edited by M. Douglas Meeks, 172–208. Nashville: Abingdon Press, 1985.
———. *Stages of Faith: The Psychology of Human Development and the Quest for Meaning*. San Francisco: Harper & Row, 1981.
Fox, George. *The Journal of George Fox*. Richmond, IN: Friends United Press, 1976.
Freedman, David Noel. *Anchor Bible Dictionary*. Vol. 1. 6 vols. New York: Doubleday, 1992.
Freire, Paulo. *Pedagogy of the Oppressed*. 30th Anniversary edition. New York: Continuum, 2000.
Goizueta, Roberto S. *Caminemos Con Jesus: Toward a Hispanic/Latino Theology of Accompaniment*. Maryknoll, NY: Orbis Books, 1995.
Goldingay, John. *Do We Need the New Testament?: Letting the Old Testament Speak for Itself*. Downers Grove, IL: IVP Academic, 2015.
Goldstein, Valerie Saiving. "The Human Situation: A Feminine View." *The Journal of Religion* 40, no. 2 (1960): 100–112.
González, Justo L. *Mañana: Christian Theology from a Hispanic Perspective*. Reprint edition. Nashville: Abingdon Press, 1990.
Graves, Michael. *The Inspiration and Interpretation of Scripture: What the Early Church Can Teach Us*. Grand Rapids, MI: Eerdmans, 2014.
Green, Joel B. *The Gospel of Luke*. Sixth Impression edition. Grand Rapids, MI: Eerdmans, 1997.
———. "Identity and Engagement in a Diverse World: Pluralism and Holiness in 1 Peter." *Asbury Theological Journal* 55, no. 2 (Fall 2000): 85–92.
Green, Joel B., and Max Turner, eds. *Between Two Horizons: Spanning New Testament Studies and Systematic Theology*. Grand Rapids, MI: Eerdmans, 1999.
Gregersen, Niels Henrik. "Guilt, Shame, and Rehabilitation: The Pedagogy of Divine Judgment." *Dialog* 39, no. 2 (2000): 105–118.
Grenz, Stanley J. "Pannenberg on Marxism: Insights and Generalizations." *The Christian Century* 104, no. 27 (September 30, 1987): 824–826.
———. *Reason for Hope: The Systematic Theology of Wolfhart Pannenberg*. 2nd edition. Grand Rapids, MI: Eerdmans, 2005.
———. *The Social God and the Relational Self*. Louisville: Westminster John Knox Press, 2007.

Gutiérrez, Gustavo. *A Theology of Liberation.* 15th Anniversary edition. Maryknoll, NY: Orbis Books, 1988.

———. *We Drink From Our Own Wells: The Spiritual Journey of a People.* Translated by Matthew J. O'Connell. 20th Anniversary edition. Maryknoll, NY: Orbis Books, 2006.

Hall, Timothy. *Separating Church and State: Roger Williams and Religious Liberty.* Urbana: University of Illinois Press, 1998.

Hampson, Daphne. *Kierkegaard: Exposition & Critique.* Oxford: Oxford University Press, 2013.

Harries, Richard. *Is There a Gospel for the Rich?* New York: Andrew Mowbray, 1992.

Haugen, Gary A., and Victor Boutros. *The Locust Effect: Why the End of Poverty Requires the End of Violence.* New York: Oxford University Press, 2014.

Heidegger, Martin. *Being and Time: A Revised Edition of the Stambaugh Translation.* Edited by Dennis J. Schmidt. Translated by Joan Stambaugh. Revised edition. Albany: SUNY Press, 2010.

Heijke, J. P. "Thinking in the Scene of Disaster : Theology of Jean-Marc Ela from Cameroon." *Exchange* 29, no. 1 (2000): 61–88.

Heschel, Abraham Joshua. *Moral Grandeur and Spiritual Audacity: Essays.* Edited by Susannah Heschel. New York: Farrar, Straus and Giroux, 1997.

Hirsch, Debra. *Redeeming Sex: Naked Conversations about Sexuality and Spirituality.* Grand Rapids, MI: IVP Books, 2015.

Holman, Susan R., ed. *Wealth and Poverty in Early Church and Society.* Grand Rapids, MI: Baker Academic, 2008.

Holmes, Michael W., ed. *The Apostolic Fathers in English.* 3rd edition. Grand Rapids, MI: Baker Academic, 2006.

Johnson, Elizabeth A. *Quest for the Living God: Mapping Frontiers in the Theology of God.* New York: Continuum, 2011.

Johnston, Robert K. *God's Wider Presence: Reconsidering General Revelation.* Grand Rapids, MI: Baker Academic, 2014.

Kaplan, Jonas T., Sarah I. Gimbel, and Sam Harris. "Neural Correlates of Maintaining One's Political Beliefs in the Face of Counterevidence." *Scientific Reports* 6 (December 23, 2016): 39589.

Kapolyo, Joe M. *The Human Condition.* Carlisle: Langham Global Library, 2013.

Kärkkäinen, Veli-Matti. *Christian Theology in a Pluralistic World.* Grand Rapids, MI: Eerdmans, 2019.

———. *Hope and Community.* Vol. 5. 5 vols. *A Constructive Christian Theology for the Pluralistic World.* Grand Rapids, MI: Eerdmans, 2017.

———. *Trinity and Revelation.* Vol. 2. 5 vols. *A Constructive Christian Theology for the Pluralistic World.* Grand Rapids, MI: Eerdmans, 2014.

Keener, Craig S. *The Mind of the Spirit: Paul's Approach to Transformed Thinking.* Grand Rapids, MI: Baker Academic, 2016.

Kierkegaard, Søren. *The Concept of Anxiety.* Translated by Reidar Thomte. Princeton: Princeton University Press, 1980.

———. *Practice in Christianity*. Translated by Howard V. Hong and Edna H. Hong. Princeton: Princeton University Press, 1991.

———. *The Sickness unto Death: A Christian Psychological Exposition for Upbuilding and Awakening*. Translated by Howard V. Hong and Edna H. Hong. Princeton: Princeton University Press, 1983.

———. *Works of Love*. Translated by Howard V. Hong and Edna H. Hong. Princeton: Princeton University Press, 1998.

Kim, Kirsteen. *The Holy Spirit in the World: A Global Conversation*. Maryknoll, NY: Orbis Books, 2007.

King, Martin Luther, Jr. *A Testament of Hope: The Essential Writings and Speeches of Martin Luther King, Jr.* Edited by James M. Washington. New York: HarperCollins, 1991.

Kolchin, Peter. *American Slavery: 1619–1877*. Revised edition. New York: Hill and Wang, 2003.

Krawelitzki, Judith. "God the Almighty?: Observations in the Psalms." *Vetus Testamentum* 64, no. 3 (2014): 434–444.

Kreider, Alan. *The Patient Ferment of the Early Church: The Improbable Rise of Christianity in the Roman Empire*. Grand Rapids, MI: Baker Academic, 2016.

Küng, Hans. *The Church*. New York: Sheed and Ward, 1967.

Las Casas, Bartolomé, de. *A Short Account of the Destruction of the Indies*. Translated by Nigel Griffin. New York: Penguin, 2004.

Levinson, Daniel J. *The Seasons of a Man's Life: The Groundbreaking 10-Year Study That Was the Basis for Passages!* New York: Ballantine Books, 1978.

Lewis, C. S. *The Horse and His Boy*. Reprint edition. New York: HarperCollins, 2002.

Loder, James E. *The Logic of the Spirit: Human Development in Theological Perspective*. San Francisco: Jossey-Bass, 1998.

———. *The Transforming Moment*. 2nd edition. Colorado Springs: Helmers & Howard, 1989.

Loder, James E., and W. Jim Neidhardt. *The Knight's Move: The Relational Logic of the Spirit in Theology and Science*. Colorado Springs: Helmers & Howard, 1992.

Lohfink, Gerhard. *The Conversion of St. Paul: Narrative and History in Acts*. Chicago: Franciscan Herald Press, 1976.

———. *Jesus and Community*. Philadelphia: Fortress Press, 1984.

London, Jack. *The Call of the Wild*. New York: Dover Publications, 1990.

———. *The People of the Abyss*. New York: Macmillan, 1903.

Luhmann, Niklas. *Introduction to Systems Theory*. Translated by Peter Gilgen. Malden, MA: Polity, 2013.

———. *A Systems Theory of Religion*. Edited by André Kieserling. Palo Alto: Stanford University Press, 2013.

MacIntyre, Alasdair. *After Virtue: A Study in Moral Theory*. Notre Dame, IN: University of Notre Dame Press, 2007.

Maddox, Randy L. *Responsible Grace: John Wesley's Practical Theology*. Nashville: Kingswood Books, 1994.

Mandelbrot, Benoit. *The Fractal Geometry of Nature*. Updated edition. San Francisco: Times Books, 1982.

Martin, Lee Roy. *A Future for Holiness: Pentecostal Explorations*. Cleveland, TN: CPT Press, 2013.

McEllhenney, John Galen. "Two Critiques of Wealth: John Wesley and Samuel Johnson Assess the Machinations of Mammon." *Methodist History* 32, no. 3 (April 1994): 147–159.

McRandal, Janice. *Christian Doctrine and the Grammar of Difference: A Contribution to Feminist Systematic Theology*. Minneapolis: Fortress Press, 2015.

———, ed. *Sarah Coakley and the Future of Systematic Theology*. Minneapolis: Fortress Press, 2016.

Meeks, M. Douglas. *Origins of the Theology of Hope*. Philadelphia: Fortress Press, 1974.

———, ed. *The Future of the Methodist Theological Traditions*. Nashville: Abingdon Press, 1985.

Moeller, Hans-Georg. *Luhmann Explained: From Souls to Systems*. Chicago: Open Court, 2006.

———. *The Radical Luhmann*. New York: Columbia University Press, 2012.

Moltmann, Jürgen. *A Broad Place: An Autobiography*. Minneapolis: Fortress Press, 2008.

———. *The Coming of God*. Translated by Margaret Kohl. Minneapolis: Fortress Press, 1996.

———. *The Crucified God*. Translated by R. A. Wilson. Minneapolis: Fortress Press, 1993.

———. *Ethics of Hope*. Translated by Margaret Kohl. Minneapolis: Fortress Press, 2012.

———. *Experiences in Theology*. Translated by Margaret Kohl. Minneapolis: Fortress Press, 2000.

———. *God for a Secular Society: The Public Relevance of Theology*. Minneapolis: Fortress Press, 1999.

———. "The Liberation of Oppressors." *The Journal of the Interdenominational Theological Center* 6, no. 2 (1979): 69–82.

———. *The Living God and the Fullness of Life*. Louisville: Westminster John Knox Press, 2015.

———. *The Spirit of Life*. Translated by Margaret Kohl. Minneapolis: Fortress Press, 1992.

———. *Sun of Righteousness, Arise! : God's Future for Humanity and the Earth*. Translated by Margaret Kohl. Minneapolis: Fortress Press, 2010.

———. *Theology and Joy*. London: S.C.M. Press, 1973.

———. *Theology of Hope*. Translated by James W. Leitch. Minneapolis: Fortress Press, 1993.

———. *Über Geduld, Barmherzigkeit und Solidarität*. Gütersloh: Gütersloher Verlagshaus, 2018.

———. *The Way of Jesus Christ*. Translated by Margaret Kohl. Minneapolis: Fortress Press, 1993.

Moltmann-Wendel, Elisabeth, and Jürgen Moltmann. *God–His & Hers*. New York: Crossroad, 1991.

Morgan, Edmund S. *Roger Williams: The Church and the State*. 2nd edition. New York: W.W. Norton & Company, 2006.

Morris, Leon. *The Gospel According to John*. Revised edition. Grand Rapids, MI: Eerdmans, 1995.

Moser, Richard. "Overuse and Abuse of Adjunct Faculty Members Threaten Core Academic Values." *Chronicle of Higher Education* 60, no. 18 (January 17, 2014): A19–20.

Mostert, Christiaan. *God and the Future: Wolfhart Pannenberg's Eschatological Doctrine of God*. New York: T&T Clark, 2002.

Moyo, Dambisa. *Dead Aid: Why Aid Is Not Working and How There Is a Better Way for Africa*. New York: Farrar, Straus and Giroux, 2009.

Murata, Sayaka. *Convenience Store Woman*. Translated by Ginny Tapley Takemori. Kindle edition. Grove Press, 2018.

Murphy, Nancey, and Warren S. Brown. *Did My Neurons Make Me Do It?: Philosophical and Neurobiological Perspectives on Moral Responsibility and Free Will*. New York: Oxford University Press, 2009.

Nacpil, Emerito. *Jesus' Strategy for Social Transformation*. Nashville: Abingdon Press, 1999.

Nason, Shannon. "Opposites, Contradictories, and Mediation in Kierkegaard's Critique of Hegel." *Heythrop Journal* 53, no. 1 (January 2012): 24–36.

Ngong, David Tonghou. "The Theologian as Missionary: The Legacy of Jean-Marc Éla." *Journal of Theology for Southern Africa* 136 (March 2010): 4–19.

Nthamburi, Zablon. "The Relevance of Donatism for the Church in Africa Today." *AFER* 23, no. 4 (August 1981): 215–220.

Nuttall, Geoffrey F. *The Holy Spirit in Puritan Faith and Experience*. Chicago: University of Chicago Press, 1992.

Oden, Patrick. "Liberating Holiness for the Oppressed and the Oppressors." In *A Future for Holiness: Pentecostal Explorations*, edited by Lee Roy Martin, 205–224. Cleveland, TN: CPT Press, 2013.

———. "'Obedience Is Better than Sacrifice': Atonement as the Re-Establishment of Trust." *Wesleyan Theological Journal* 50, no. 1 (2015): 100–115.

———. *The Transformative Church: New Ecclesial Models and the Theology of Jurgen Moltmann*. Minneapolis: Fortress Press, 2015.

Okholm, Dennis. *Dangerous Passions, Deadly Sins: Learning from the Psychology of Ancient Monks*. Grand Rapids, MI: Brazos Press, 2014.

Osborn, Eric. *Clement of Alexandria*. New York: Cambridge University Press, 2008.

Otto, Rudolf. *The Idea of the Holy: An Enquiry into the Non-Rational Factor in the Idea of the Divine and Its Relation to the Rational*. New York: Oxford University Press, 1923.

Palmer, G. E. H., trans. *The Philokalia: The Complete Text*. 4 vols. London: Faber and Faber, 1979.

Pannenberg, Wolfhart. *Anthropology in Theological Perspective*. Translated by Matthew J. O'Connell. Philadelphia: Westminster Press, 1985.

———. *The Apostle's Creed in the Light of Today's Questions*. Eugene, OR: Wipf and Stock, 2000.

———. *Basic Questions in Theology: Collected Essays*. Vol. 1. 2 vols. Philadelphia: Fortress Press, 1970.

———. *Basic Questions in Theology: Collected Essays*. Vol. 2. 2 vols. Philadelphia: Fortress Press, 1971.

———. "Christianity, Marxism, and Liberation Theology." *Christian Scholar's Review* 18, no. 3 (1989): 215–226.

———. "Constructive and Critical Functions of Christian Eschatology." *Harvard Theological Review* 77, no. 2 (1984): 119–139.

———. "Dogmatic Theses on the Doctrine of Revelation." In *Revelation as History*, edited by Wolfhart Pannenberg and translated by David Granskou, 123–158. New York: Macmillan, 1968.

———. *Faith and Reality*. Philadelphia: Westminster Press, 1977.

———. *Jesus–God and Man*. London: SCM Press, 1968.

———. *Systematic Theology*. Translated by Geoffrey W. Bromiley. 3 vols. Grand Rapids, MI: Eerdmans, 1991.

———. *Theology and the Kingdom of God*. Philadelphia: Westminster Press, 1969.

———. *Theology and the Philosophy of Science*. Translated by Francis McDonagh. Philadelphia: Westminster Press, 1976.

———. *What Is Man? Contemporary Anthropology in Theological Perspective*. Translated by Duane A. Priebe. Philadelphia: Fortress Press, 1970.

Pannenberg, Wolfhart, Carl E. Braaten, and Avery Dulles. *Spirit, Faith, and Church*. Philadelphia: Westminster Press, 1970.

Peck, M. Scott. *The Different Drum: Community Making and Peace*. 2nd edition. New York: Touchstone, 1998.

Petts, Richard J. "Trajectories of Religious Participation from Adolescence to Young Adulthood." *Journal for the Scientific Study of Religion* 48, no. 3 (2009): 552–571.

Plantinga, Cornelius. *Not the Way It's Supposed to Be: A Breviary of Sin*. Grand Rapids, MI: Eerdmans, 1995.

Raboteau, Albert J. *Slave Religion: The "Invisible Institution" in the Antebellum South*. Updated edition. New York: Oxford University Press, 2004.

Rack, Henry D. *Reasonable Enthusiast: John Wesley and the Rise of Methodism*. 3rd edition. London: Epworth, 2002.

Reimer, Kevin Scott. *Living L'Arche: Stories of Compassion, Love, and Disability*. Collegeville, MN: Liturgical Press, 2009.

Rhee, Helen. *Loving the Poor, Saving the Rich: Wealth, Poverty, and Early Christian Formation*. Grand Rapids, MI: Baker Academic, 2012.

Rieger, Joerg, ed. *Opting for the Margins : Postmodernity and Liberation in Christian Theology*. New York: Oxford University Press, 2003.

Romero, Oscar. *The Scandal of Redemption: When God Liberates the Poor, Saves Sinners, and Heals Nations*. Walden, NY: Plough Publishing House, 2018.

Rubenson, Samuel. *The Letters of St. Antony: Monasticism and the Making of a Saint*. Minneapolis: Fortress Press, 1995.

Runyon, Theodore. *The New Creation: John Wesley's Theology Today*. Nashville: Abingdon Press, 1998.

Sachs, Jeffrey. *The End of Poverty: Economic Possibilities for Our Time*. New York: Penguin Press, 2005.

Sagan, Carl. *Cosmos*. New York: Ballantine Books, 2013.

Sanders, Fred, and Klaus Issler, eds. *Jesus in Trinitarian Perspective: An Intermediate Christology*. Nashville: B&H Academic, 2007.

Sarah, Cardinal Robert, and Nicolas Diat. *God or Nothing: A Conversation on Faith*. San Francisco: Ignatius Press, 2015.

Schöfthaler, Traugott. "Social Foundations of Morality: Durkheimian Problems and Niklas Luhmann's Systems Theories of Religion, Morality and Personality." *Social Compass* 31, nos. 2–3 (1984): 185–197.

Shults, F. LeRon. *Reforming Theological Anthropology: After the Philosophical Turn to Relationality*. Grand Rapids, MI: W.B. Eerdmans Pub., 2003.

Sinkewicz, Robert E. *Evagrius of Pontus: The Greek Ascetic Corpus*. New York: Oxford University Press, 2006.

Sneed, Joel R., Seth J. Schwartz, and Jr. Cross William E. "A Multicultural Critique of Identity Status Theory and Research: A Call for Integration." *Identity* 6, no. 1 (2006): 61–84.

Sonderegger, Katherine. "God, Sexuality and the Self." *International Journal of Systematic Theology* 18, no. 1 (January 22, 2016): 94–98.

Staniloae, Dumitru. *Orthodox Dogmatic Theology: The Experience of God*. 6 vols. Brookline, MA: Holy Cross Orthodox Press, 1998.

Stewart, Jon. *Kierkegaard's Relations to Hegel Reconsidered*. New York: Cambridge University Press, 2003.

Stolzenberg, Ross M., Mary Blair-Loy, and Linda J. Waite. "Religious Participation in Early Adulthood: Age and Family Life Cycle Effects on Church Membership." *American Sociological Review* 60, no. 1 (1995): 84–103.

Stump, Eleonore. *Aquinas*. New York: Routledge, 2003.

Sugirtharajah, R. S. *Voices from the Margin: Interpreting the Bible in the Third World*. 25th Anniversary edition. Maryknoll, NY: Orbis Books, 2016.

Tanner, Kathryn. *The Politics of God: Christian Theologies and Social Justice*. Minneapolis: Fortress Press, 1992.

Tate, Marvin E. *Psalms 51–100*. Grand Rapids, MI: Zondervan, 2015.

Taylor, Iain. *Pannenberg on the Triune God*. New York: T & T Clark, 2007.

Taylor, John V. *The Go-Between God: The Holy Spirit and the Christian Mission*. Philadelphia: Fortress Press, 1973.

Theophan the Recluse. *The Path to Salvation: A Manual of Spiritual Transformation*. Forestville, CA: St. Herman of Alaska Brotherhood, 1996.

Thompson, Marianne Meye. *John: A Commentary*. Louisville: Westminster John Knox Press, 2015.

Thoreau, Henry David. *Walden, Or, Life in the Woods*. Cambridge, MA: Houghton Mifflin, 1906.

Thulstrup, Niels. *Kierkegaard's Relation to Hegel*. Princeton: Princeton University Press, 1980.

Tolstoy, Sofia. *The Diaries of Sofia Tolstoy*. Translated by Cathy Porter. New York: Harper Perennial, 2010.

Tutu, Desmond. *No Future Without Forgiveness.* New York: Image, 2000.
Vanier, Jean. *Becoming Human.* New York: Paulist Press, 1998.
———. *Community and Growth.* New York: Paulist Press, 1989.
———. *Drawn Into the Mystery of Jesus Through the Gospel of John.* New York: Paulist Press, 2004.
———. *The Gospel of John, the Gospel of Relationship.* Cincinnati: Franciscan Media, 2015.
———. *La bonheur; principe et fin de la morale aristotélicienne.* Paris: Desclée de Brouwer, 1965.
———. *Made for Happiness: Discovering the Meaning of Life with Aristotle.* Translated by Kathryn Spink. Translation edition. Toronto: House of Anansi Press, 2005.
Volf, Miroslav. *After Our Likeness: The Church as the Image of the Trinity.* Grand Rapids, MI: Eerdmans, 1998.
———. *Against the Tide: Love in a Time of Petty Dreams and Persisting Enmities.* Grand Rapids, MI: Eerdmans, 2010.
———. *Free of Charge: Giving and Forgiving in a Culture Stripped of Grace.* Grand Rapids, MI: Zondervan, 2005.
———. *The End of Memory: Remembering Rightly in a Violent World.* Grand Rapids, MI: Eerdmans, 2006.
Ward, Benedicta, trans. *The Desert Fathers: Sayings of the Early Christian Monks.* Revised edition. New York: Penguin Classics, 2003.
———. *The Sayings of the Desert Fathers: The Alphabetical Collection.* Kalamazoo, MI: Cistercian Publications, 1975.
Ware, Frederick L. *African American Theology: An Introduction.* Louisville: Westminster John Knox Press, 2016.
Ware, Timothy. *The Orthodox Church: New Edition.* 2nd edition. New York: Penguin Books, 1993.
Welker, Michael. *God the Spirit.* Minneapolis: Fortress Press, 1994.
White, Carolinne, ed. *Early Christian Lives.* New York: Penguin Books, 1998.
Wilkins, Michael J. "Barabbas." In *The Anchor Bible Dictionary*, edited by David Noel Freedman, 1:607. New York: Doubleday, 1992.
Willard, Dallas. *The Divine Conspiracy: Rediscovering Our Hidden Life In God.* 1st edition. San Francisco: Harper, 1998.
Wong, Kam Ming. *Wolfhart Pannenberg on Human Destiny.* Burlington, VT: Ashgate, 2008.
Wright, N. T. *Paul: A Biography.* San Francisco: HarperOne, 2018.
Yong, Amos. *In the Days of Caesar: Pentecostalism and Political Theology.* Grand Rapids, MI: Eerdmans, 2010.
Žižek, Slavoj, Frank Ruda, and Agon Hamza. *Reading Marx.* Medford, MA: Polity, 2018.

Index

abandonment, 46, 49, 101, 178
Abel, 48
absolute control, 99n30, 250n32
abuse, 3, 10, 18n23, 99n30, 148, 169, 202, 220;
    sexual, 289n8
academia, 7, 10, 19n33, 24, 42n38, 55, 64n33, 65n46, 129, 132, 190, 193, 196, 203n3;
    contingent faculty, 18n23;
    faculty, 10, 19n35;
    labor, 18n23;
    privileged faculty, 41n28;
    students, 10, 20n35, 26, 41n28, 65n46, 132, 136n21, 153n12, 205n31, 270n10;
    superiority, 40n23;
    tenure, 10, 20n35, 65n46, 81n24, 189
academics, 9, 31, 40, 55, 65n46, 130, 133, 203n1, 249n20
acceptance, 32, 103, 211, 214, 239, 245;
    mutual, 244;
    sinner's, 223n5
acclaim, 111, 284
accompaniment, 244, 253n86
accumulation, 75, 92, 130, 216
actions:
    coinherent, 69;
    direct, 121;
    discerned, 238;
    new, 48;
    social, 232
activists, 232, 260
acts:
    creative, 145, 176;
    ecclesial, 200;
    free, 111;
    liberating, 214;
    oppressive, 251n45;
    particular, 248n6, 279;
    physical, 162;
    ultimate rebellious, 108
actuality, 47, 68, 213, 216, 260
actualize, 7, 34
adaptation, 36, 54, 78, 185n86
admirers, 59, 105, 116n14, 127
admonition, 20n44, 110, 125, 127, 144, 202, 251n45, 271n11
advancement, 19n33, 73, 201, 251n51, 268;
    human, 42n36;
    vocational, 24
adversity, 1, 249n31
affections, 134n5
affirmation, 10, 103, 216, 256
afflictions, 143–44, 238
Africa, 3, 18, 41
aggression, 97n15, 232, 241

Alexandria, 124, 126, 154n21, 281
Alexandrian approach, 118n45, 128, 130, 135n12, 135
alienating, 2, 6, 91, 142, 150, 162, 217, 241, 243, 256
aliens, 187n187
allegiances, 2, 116n18, 240, 284
alluring, 10, 50, 180, 190, 193, 283
almighty, 129, 160, 175–77, 186n98
Almsgiving, 153n8
Alter, Robert, 97n7
ambitions, 24, 61n1, 65n47, 110, 247
analogical, 105, 138n53
analysis, 23, 38, 46, 56, 67, 262;
  cooperative, 24;
  rational, 39n10, 115
Ananias, 12, 102, 110–12, 114, 117n34, 125
anger, 115, 147, 169, 208n68, 210, 232, 234, 239, 245–46, 253n85
anonymity, 50–53, 60, 239, 286;
  participation, 29–30, 35, 78, 241, 256, 266
anonymization, 35, 87, 109, 170, 266, 276
Anthony the Great, 12, 124, 126, 134, 139–51, 154n21, 155n31, 198, 281
anticipation, 47, 62n10, 108
anxiety, 46–49, 53, 60, 62n11, 64n39, 73, 79, 232, 239, 269
apatheia, 174, 185n86, 185
apathy, 51, 63n27, 175, 185n87, 216, 245, 283
apologetics, 122–23, 138n58, 251n51
apostles, 12, 111, 163
appeasing, 31, 210
application, 5, 83n48, 88, 112, 121, 130, 160, 163, 175, 198, 223n5, 276, 280–81
appropriation, 133, 160;
  theological, 191
archetype, 214, 281
argument, 15, 23, 36, 38, 58, 107–8, 112, 129;
  common sense, 129;
  fundamental, 283;
  religious, 107
Aristotle, 156n58, 197
Arius, 146
artists, 33–35, 267, 284
asceticism, 142, 152n2, 153n6, 192, 200, 207n55, 282;
  goals, 140, 142, 153n8, 153n13, 193
Ashwin-Siejkowski, Piotr, 96n4, 125, 135n11, 136n32
Aslan, 98n24
aspirations, 4, 134n3, 206n51
Assemblage Theory, 34, 42n40, 42
Athanasius, 126, 140, 142, 153n8, 154n21, 154
atheism, 20n46, 36, 176, 236
atonement, 116n12, 224n15
attributes, 173, 183n43, 212–13, 239;
  classic, 172;
  implied, 167
authenticity, 280, 287
authoritarianism, 93, 98n30, 99, 180
authority, 2, 13, 49, 65n46, 71–72, 106, 110, 121, 236;
  legal, 107;
  religious, 54;
  spiritual, 36, 154n21
automatons, 34, 212
autonomy, 59, 88, 177
autopoiesis, 26–27, 35, 41n32, 42n39, 54–56, 73, 168, 171, 217, 234, 280
awareness, 1, 5–6, 53, 73, 141, 143, 169, 171, 183n51, 194–95, 220, 225n29, 245, 259, 262;
  conscious, 69, 76, 149, 207n60;
  passive, 179;
  theological, 164, 171, 202
Ayres, Lewis, 96n3

balance, 99, 133, 161, 201, 241, 262, 265
Barabbas, 108–9
Barnabas, 110, 117n28

barriers, 78, 81n28, 103, 132, 163, 194, 203, 232, 241, 245
Barth, Karl, 250n44, 273n56
Basil the Great, 136n26, 243
Bauckham, Richard, 185n86, 185
Bediako, Kwame, 18n23, 124
behavior, 6, 20n44, 26–27, 33, 41n29, 47, 77, 183n51, 187n119, 192, 217, 225n29, 237, 263;
  changed, 6, 160;
  criminal, 270n10;
  defensive, 39n5;
  human, 23, 80n21, 115n5, 222, 247;
  oppressive, 219, 247
belief, 13, 70, 129, 192, 237, 251n51
believers, 114, 118, 124–25, 169, 171, 211
Belkin, Lisa, 63n25
belonging, 221–22, 230, 238–41, 243
benefits, 3–4, 20n47, 25, 32, 107, 113, 117n30, 127, 130, 137n40, 138n58, 142, 203, 261, 267;
  claimed, 95, 116n18
benevolence, 144–46, 149
Bible, 20n40, 70, 88, 93–94, 163, 171–72, 175, 217, 234, 281;
  injunctions, 128, 136n31.
  See also Scripture
bifurcation, 126, 279, 281
biology, 26–27
birth, 116n10, 253n85, 262;
  new, 92, 101–2, 105, 112, 117n30, 237;
  physical, 104, 262
blasphemy, 58, 107, 289n8
blessings, 92–94, 105, 129–30, 133, 148, 229, 256, 284, 286
blind, 17n19, 102, 209, 246, 251n50, 258, 269, 275, 277, 285
Blok, Anton, 249n31
Blomberg, Craig, 96n6
Blumhardt, Christoph, 231, 248n10
bodies, 1, 24, 28–29, 47, 53, 111, 114, 142–43, 148, 207n65
Boethius, 183n47

bondage, 8, 150, 211, 229
Bonhoeffer, Dietrich, 231
boundaries, 26, 28, 33, 56, 60, 88–89, 93, 167, 171, 205n31, 215, 217, 252n53;
  cultural, 162, 167, 195;
  limited, 82n31, 89, 131, 151, 191, 193, 246;
  operational, 56, 166;
  relational, 89;
  spiritual, 107, 162
bounty, 3, 94, 129
bourgeois attitude, 64n33
Boutros, Victor, 18n23
brain, 26, 28, 69
brokenness, 91, 246, 267
brother, 140, 142, 154n23, 171, 186n96
brotherhood, vii, 131, 266, 273n57
Brown, John, 7
Browning, Don, 77
bureaucracy, 2, 185
business, 31, 65n46, 77
Butterworth, G. W., 128

Caesar, 40n24, 50
Cain, 48
California, 199
Calvin, John, 155n33
capability, 175–76
capacity, 3–4, 70, 231, 242, 272n43;
  human, 96n3, 96
capitalism, vii, 41n28
care, 25, 33, 45, 49, 94, 107, 126, 143, 145, 177, 197–99, 240, 276;
  health, 24;
  medical, 4;
  residential, 273n52
careers, 19n33, 64n33, 139, 193;
  academic, 197
caretakers, 94, 199, 207n58
Cassian, John, 38, 152n3, 153n14, 154n23, 250n43, 252n73, 272n42
Castelo, Daniel, 185n86
Cattell, Everett, 110
celebration, 110, 207n58, 269, 283

celebrity, 29–30, 35, 253n86
cells, 26–27
change:
    possibility of, 173, 209, 215, 279;
    real, 31, 243, 266, 277–78;
    social, 37, 82n33, 231
chaos, 51, 114, 244, 267
childhood, 63n27, 71–72, 80n6, 115n8, 154, 198, 237, 253;
    early, 237.
    See also children
children, 3, 76–77, 81n28, 83n47, 103–4, 147, 186n96, 202, 253n85, 259, 284
Chinula, Donald M., 79n31
choices, 3–6, 9, 30, 47–48, 58–59, 64n30, 72–73, 105, 123, 207n65, 221, 240, 262, 279–80, 285;
    forced, 2, 218;
    making, 3–4, 6, 15, 27, 30, 48, 70, 130, 247, 285
chorus, 13, 160–61, 230, 277, 283
Christ, 10–13, 56–61, 101–14, 121–22, 124–33, 144–46, 148–49, 169–71, 177–79, 199–200, 209–14, 237–40, 256–60, 266–69, 284–88;
    body of, 286–87;
    crucified, 185n88;
    liberating, 151;
    life of, 13, 38, 113, 118n46, 149–50, 202, 209, 211, 224n15, 283, 288;
    lordship of, 133, 185n88, 236;
    mind of, 113, 118n47;
    mission of, 95, 113, 176, 192, 203, 267;
    risen, 202, 259;
    trust in, 24, 102, 105, 148, 257, 259
Christendom, 24, 55, 57, 116n14, 127, 151, 205n30
Christian communities, 13, 79, 121, 123, 133, 134n6, 138, 257, 281.
    See also church
Christian devotion, 40n24, 126, 139, 141, 235, 281
Christian doctrine, 262

Christian experience, 171, 176
Christian faith, 123, 181n23, 191, 193, 226n34, 236
Christianity:
    almost, 37, 43n43, 156n59, 184n65;
    altogether, 38, 116n14, 125, 151;
    history of, 18n23, 150;
    popular, 95, 141
Christian life, 15, 122, 124, 129–30, 133–34, 135n15, 141, 151, 153n8, 183n40, 281, 283
Christian Perfection, 96n4, 133, 134n2
Christian practices, 121, 161, 236
Christian priorities, 25, 132
Christians, 9–10, 13, 23, 59, 104, 109–10, 112–14, 121–24, 126, 128, 138, 148, 151, 217–18, 257;
    baptized, 136n21, 281;
    early, 40, 95, 110, 122, 124, 167, 174, 190, 256, 271n11;
    immature, 124, 251n51
Christian teaching, 124, 128–29, 135n15, 192–93, 209, 281
Christian testimony, 180, 195
Christian theology, 2, 19, 36, 38, 46, 60, 124, 159–60, 165, 171, 174, 190–91, 194, 217–18, 236
Christian Tradition, 15, 18n23, 119n57, 173, 192
Christology, 20n44, 59–60, 105, 113n2, 113, 118n46, 140, 174, 185, 191–92, 213–16, 259, 289n8
Chrysostom, John, 136n26
church, 4, 7, 14–15, 109, 111, 114, 123–25, 160–61, 170, 218, 235–36, 238–39, 257, 268, 286–88;
    apathetic, 175;
    earliest, 110, 136n31, 256;
    gathered, 31, 76, 127, 130, 191.
    See also Christian communities
city, 3, 98n22, 124, 150–51, 239
Civil Rights, 279
Clark, Elizabeth A., 128, 136n31
classes:
    higher, 3, 65n44;

Index

impoverished, 16, 65n44, 74, 117n41
Clement of Alexandria, 12, 17n20, 96, 96n4, 98, 124–33, 135n12, 135n15, 136n21, 136n31, 138n53, 150–51, 155n58, 236–37, 281
clergy, 19n33, 170, 218
Coakley, Sarah, 14, 180, 190–91, 193–97, 217–19, 230, 235–38, 262–65, 282
Cocksworth, Ashley, 251n44
coercion, 233, 240, 242
cognition, 47, 57
cogs, 10, 170, 220, 258, 268
coherence, 6, 33, 49, 54, 72, 77, 92, 96, 114, 151, 173, 221–23, 235, 239, 243;
   internal, 45, 161;
   rational, 28, 39n9
cohesion, 34, 49, 58, 69;
   personal, 31
collegiality, 64n33, 189
Comblin, Jose, 248n4
comfort, 9, 52, 57, 81n26, 149, 151, 239, 285
command, 18, 105, 130–31, 162–63
commandments, 10, 18n20, 103, 143
commission, 152n3, 197
commitment, 10, 35, 46, 88, 95, 106, 110, 125, 133, 169, 238, 240–43, 246–47, 262, 266;
   intimate, 242;
   lived, 111, 251n53, 252;
   moral, 201
commodification, 234
communal, 87, 197, 203, 229, 257, 271n15, 283
communication, 26, 28–31, 35, 50–53, 55–56, 60, 72, 77, 160, 165, 197, 199, 239, 268, 276
communicative expressions, 28, 91
communion, 8, 44, 79, 101, 105, 199–200, 219, 225n31, 236–37, 244, 246, 265, 269–70, 283
community:
   beloved, vii;

   cohesive, 6, 82n31, 111, 122, 258;
   eternal, 288;
   finding, vii, 82n31, 111, 123, 226n54, 238, 242, 281, 287;
   fractal, 277, 282–83, 286;
   gathered, 114, 202;
   innervating, 78, 246;
   liberating, 258, 280;
   nature of, 14, 79n1, 179, 248, 258, 282;
   particular, 7, 114, 123, 149, 267;
   real, 8, 59, 102, 115, 121, 124, 201, 219, 235, 242, 253n86, 257, 286
companionship, 144, 166, 170
compassion, 89, 119n61, 175, 200–201, 206n45, 239, 253n85;
   love, 137n32, 199–202, 207n51
competition, 8–9, 15, 24, 75, 140, 178, 189, 200, 221, 232, 247, 258, 279–80
complexity, 25, 33, 38, 75, 122, 193, 196, 236, 263, 279, 287
compulsion, 117n30, 247
compulsions, inner, 244
confession, 35, 92, 98n23, 104, 167, 171, 223n5, 241, 259n1
conflict, 4, 23, 40n24, 46, 69–70, 90, 116n19, 159, 182n28, 213, 247, 251n47, 255, 273n57, 286;
   direct, 110;
   internal, 32, 61, 71;
   social, 61, 168, 195
conformity, 78, 81n28, 241
confrontation, 38, 57, 60, 89, 105–9, 121, 209, 213, 217, 235, 247, 262, 269, 284–85;
   fundamental, 25, 83n48;
   radical, 91, 203
confusion, 24, 40n24, 116n14, 253n85;
   relational, 90
consciousness, 28, 183
consensus, 32–33, 54
constancy, 177, 202
Constantine, 133, 139, 141

constraints, 4, 25, 98n30, 102, 149, 205n34
consumerism, 10, 15, 30, 92, 184n63, 189, 216, 247, 259, 275, 280
contemplation, 96n3, 189, 194, 203, 207n60, 217, 238, 262, 264, 272n43, 282;
　privileging, 194, 272n43
contempt, 128, 147
contexts, 6–7, 9–14, 37–38, 71–74, 77–79, 101–2, 104–6, 112–13, 191–92, 233–37, 240, 242–44, 257–62, 277–81, 283–86;
　definitive, 9, 170;
　ecological, 74, 93;
　particular, 13–14, 79n1, 101, 106, 114, 221, 223, 258, 288;
　religious, 82n45
contextualization, 27–28, 30, 35, 38, 124, 128, 195
contradictions, 65n41, 88, 132, 174, 183n51, 213–14, 225n29
control, 4, 7–8, 165–67, 170, 173, 175, 177, 212–13, 232–35, 242, 245, 258, 261, 265, 267
conversation, 1, 7, 11, 16n1, 103–4, 128, 191, 204n14, 279;
　theological, 104, 162, 275
conversion, 112, 141
cooperation, 161, 179, 272n48;
　human, 59
co-opting, 59, 178, 275
co-opting Jesus, 110, 260
Coppedge, Allan, 181n17
core members, 199–201, 206–7
Corinthians, 39n8, 215, 226n34, 288
corporations, 3, 7, 18n23, 41n29, 99n30
correspondence, 178, 226n54
corruption, 54, 57, 151, 163, 166–67, 173, 183n40, 210–12, 276
cosmos, 10, 57, 88, 90, 96n3, 169, 187n113, 223, 225n23, 231, 260
cost, 6–7, 177, 216
counsel, 15, 94, 170
counselling, 18n20, 79n1

counselor, 94, 179, 198, 244
counterintuitive activities, 114, 127, 133, 148, 283
covenant, 89, 94, 98n23, 169
Cox, Harvey, 20n47, 119n59
creation, 88–89, 105, 111, 133, 144, 163, 165, 167–68, 172–73, 176–77, 212, 231, 268, 286–88;
　new, 65n41, 129, 172, 214, 219
creator, 38, 39n6, 131, 133, 138n58, 144–46, 148, 166, 236
creatures, 138n58, 144–45, 165, 176, 183, 211–13, 225n29, 247, 263
Creel, Richard E., 185n86
crises, 25, 37, 45–47, 76, 78, 81n28, 102, 113, 180, 207n68, 236
critiques, 25, 27, 32, 37, 46, 54–55, 57, 127–28, 130, 132, 172, 176, 193, 215, 217
Croatto, Severino, 97n17, 266
cross-cultural applicability, 79n1
Crowder, Collin, 181n25
crucifixion, 41n33, 54, 106–7, 109, 211, 264
cultures, 9, 15, 30, 43n54, 95, 112, 121, 124, 128, 160, 181n19, 217, 266
cultus, 164–65
cycles, 3, 5, 10, 30, 57, 60, 70, 160, 211, 232, 279, 284
Cyprian, 118n46

Dallmann, Hans-Ulrich, 41
dance, 51, 162, 174, 247, 256, 284
dangers, 51, 81n26, 117n30, 231, 238, 258, 275–77
darkness, 38, 106, 110, 145, 148, 178, 192, 202, 246, 269, 273n57
deaf, 209, 269
death, 29, 50–51, 88, 90, 102, 104, 108–9, 114–15, 145, 147, 212, 215–17, 221–23, 231, 246–47;
　body of, 5, 53;
　power of, 145, 235;
　social, 216
debt, 41n28, 64n37, 112, 138n58, 269

deception, 31, 89, 147
deeds, 122, 147
defense, 53, 61, 73, 76, 132, 177, 211, 260
defensive postures, 8, 68, 76, 222, 232, 255, 265, 279
defiance, 51–53, 216
deficiencies, 53, 173, 203, 245, 285
dehumanizing, 87, 231, 236, 279
deity, 36, 166, 182n34, 248n3
DeLanda, Manuel, 34, 42n40
demons, 146–48, 218, 232, 249n20, 253n83
denial, 33, 166, 253n85, 259
dependence, 55, 64n37, 93, 125, 154n21, 218
depersonalizing, 15, 39n5, 60, 93, 206n49, 219, 266, 288
depression, 81n28, 97n15, 245–46
desert fathers, 141, 143, 153n12, 154n20
despair, 49–56, 60–61, 69, 71–72, 74, 89, 92, 167–68, 199, 201, 216, 220, 222, 283, 285;
total, 53–54, 280
desperate, 10, 51, 94, 132, 285
despot, localized, 94, 236
DeSteno, David, 249n24
destiny, 20n47, 182n28, 211
destruction, 16n9, 43n54, 167, 183n40;
social patterns, 24
development, 2, 50, 58, 75, 77, 81n29, 192, 197, 204n14, 215, 221–22, 233–34, 237, 255, 264;
individual, 40n23, 70, 77, 81n29, 221;
societal, 75, 77, 118n46
devotion, 1, 134, 150, 153n12, 165, 191, 235–36, 251n45, 281, 287
dialog, 18n22, 79, 221, 277
Didache, 117n28
differentiation, 28, 40n20
disabilities, 197, 199–201, 206n45, 207n58, 207n65, 239, 253n79, 253n85, 282

disappointment, 202, 208n68
disassociation, 28, 79
disasters, 161;
natural, 3, 252n62
Disbrey, Claire, 43
discernment, 47, 122, 131, 142, 144, 146, 153n14, 195, 202, 243
disciples, 77, 102, 106, 111, 121, 125, 138n53, 146, 149, 207n60, 249n32, 258, 269
discipline, 87, 140, 170, 189, 203, 244, 246, 263
discord, 49, 225n31
discouragements, 81n25, 160, 202, 203n3, 282
discourse, 27, 42n39;
theological, 2, 14, 192, 194, 197
disease, 15, 47, 54, 211
disempowering, 236, 240, 264
dis-integration, 28, 57, 71, 213, 247
dissatisfaction, 221, 232, 279
dissolution, 46, 51, 57, 68, 72, 89–90, 95, 109, 167, 243, 285, 288;
potential, 69, 216;
social, 73, 87
dissonance, 32, 70, 159, 213–14
distortions, 20n46, 36, 99n30, 174, 196, 213, 241, 281
distractions, 48, 52, 126, 139, 145, 216, 243, 259, 285
distrust, 42n36, 90, 234, 253n75, 269
diversity, 14, 79, 111, 123, 196, 234, 243, 258, 268;
eternal, 247
divine attributes, 96n3, 129, 159, 167, 172, 174–75, 178, 182n30, 185n86, 211–12, 214, 257, 261, 265, 268
divinity, 36, 59–60, 62n10, 65n49, 80n16, 118n45, 165, 171, 173, 175, 177–78, 183n43
Docetism, 174
doctrines, 12–13, 15, 18n20, 127, 174, 184n73, 192, 195, 202, 204n10, 248n6

dominance, 64n27, 113n2, 175, 194, 234, 251n45
domination, 8, 14, 79, 89, 151–52, 159, 165, 168, 213–14, 218, 220, 279–80, 284
Donatism, 35, 41n27, 41
Downs, David J., 136n21
dream, 71–73, 81n25, 222
Du Bois, W. E. B., 7, 16n7
duties, 16, 18n20, 102, 237
Dutton, Kevin, 19n33
dysfunctions, 11, 15, 25, 45, 53, 69, 74, 78, 160, 171, 232, 240–41, 258, 260;
  ecclesial, 46;
  psychological, 31, 73;
  social, 6, 41n28, 55

early monasticism, 12, 14, 93, 151, 238, 253n83
earth, viii, 87, 145, 176, 217, 222, 229–31, 238, 248n6, 259, 261, 270n8
ecclesiologies, 35, 37, 43n47, 288
economics, 9, 24, 29, 31–32, 41n312, 69, 92, 130, 133, 218, 281
education, 18n20, 42n38, 76, 132, 153n12, 154n21
  higher, 18n23, 19n35, 20n36, 41n28, 64n37
Efthymiadias, Stephanos, 152n5
ego, 7, 60–61, 68–70, 76, 165, 169, 211–14, 222, 229–30, 232, 234, 246, 256, 260, 265;
  colliding, 69, 89, 211–12, 229, 232;
  fragile, 34, 211;
  human, 110, 168, 212, 232
egocentrism, 63n27, 73, 82n29, 182n28, 220
egoism, 97, 97n15, 232, 255, 266
Éla, Jean-Marc, 105, 111, 252n57, 261
election, 167–68
Elizondo, Virgilio P., 17n19, 17
Ellacuría, Ignacio, 2, 10, 37, 44n55, 256
emotions, 1, 12, 147, 153n6, 174, 216, 237

empowerment, 98n29, 171
encouragement, 15, 142, 144, 148, 202, 278
Encyclopedia Galactica, 178
endurance, 59, 132, 186n96, 237
enemies, 6, 53, 73, 102, 111, 144, 221, 260
energies, 76, 111, 216, 257
engagement, 95, 162, 164, 175, 202, 207n65, 261, 283;
  committed, 38, 201;
  constructive, 32, 173, 258, 260;
  non-idealistic, 32, 53, 245, 282;
  positive, 34, 62n3, 71;
  spiritual, 201, 270n10
enlivening, 88, 149, 163, 183n40, 219, 238, 262, 268, 285–86, 288
entertainment, 29–30, 65n47
Ephesians, 202, 208n69
equality, 7, 31, 227n57, 281
Erikson, Erik H., 68–69, 73, 75, 81n29
escape, 11, 153n11, 261
eschatology, 72, 96n3, 187n115, 209, 214, 221, 230
essence, 43n51, 45, 73, 144, 149, 156n58, 163, 181n17, 211, 268
establishment, 4, 58, 124, 209, 250n33, 276
eternal life, 68, 103, 127, 146, 172, 180, 214, 236, 268
eternity, 7, 52, 56, 78, 167–68, 172, 213–14, 229, 235, 243, 267, 270, 277, 282, 287;
  of God, 168, 225n23
ethics, 73, 97n20, 132, 137n45, 162, 192, 195, 232, 271
Eucharist, 170
Evagrius, 232, 237–38, 252n73
Evangelicals, 153n12, 226n49
evangelization, 43n54, 283
evil, 4, 8, 15, 89, 92, 102–3, 129–30, 144–45, 148, 221–22, 259, 281
excess, 219, 272n39, 285
exclusiveness, 16n5, 104, 109
exhortation, 121, 138, 144, 170

existentialism, 46, 61, 160, 203, 209
exocentric, 14, 76, 113, 174, 182n28, 210–13, 219–21, 229–30, 256, 267, 282–83
Exodus, 82n35, 89–92, 97, 98n20, 104, 114, 162, 164–65, 206n43, 214, 281
experience:
    contemplative, 192, 263;
    fundamental, 221, 229, 238;
    new, 132, 216, 235, 267, 285;
    substantive, 230, 265;
    transformative, 201, 286
exploitation, 4, 18n23, 263

factions, 6, 223n5
failure, 9, 115, 241, 243, 280
faith, viii, 57, 59–60, 67, 70, 112–14, 121–24, 126, 131–32, 161, 166, 214–15, 231, 233, 287–88;
    stages of, 70–71, 80n16
faithfulness, 91–93, 133, 173, 177
faithlessness, 147, 233, 250n33
fame, 29, 50, 63n24, 129, 139–40, 164, 253n86
father, 94, 139, 143, 145–46, 149, 197, 199, 210–12, 218–19, 257, 261, 264, 267, 270, 283–84
fears, 53, 104–5, 143–44, 174, 222, 233, 240–41, 243, 246, 258, 277, 280, 282, 284–85
Fee, Gordon D., 97n13
fellowship, 166, 169, 171, 211–12, 224n18, 230–31, 253n79, 256–58;
    exocentric, 168, 211, 230
Fiddler on the Roof, 129, 137n38
fight, 15, 74, 138n58, 199, 220, 260, 264
figurehead, 57, 160
filioque clause, 218, 226n51
financial decisions, 72, 111
finitude, 167, 255
flesh, 20n40, 62n5, 87, 143, 145, 167, 224n10;
    desires of the, 87, 90

flourishing, 101, 283, 285
followers, 77, 140–41, 176, 287
food, 4, 34, 78, 137n45, 138n58, 143, 147, 170, 192, 272n39
forgiveness, 7, 54, 94, 98n29, 115, 119n61, 138n53, 178, 203, 221, 245–46, 259, 269, 272n48
formation, 31, 160, 164, 195, 207n60, 253n83
Fowler, James W., 70, 74, 80n16, 82n29, 82
Fox, George, 36, 43n51, 43
fractal, 12, 250n38, 269
freedom, 1–11, 47–48, 88–91, 99, 144, 146, 148–49, 202–3, 213–14, 231–34, 242–45, 256–59, 278–80, 282–85, 288–89;
    academic, 18, 234;
    boundless, 99n30, 263;
    context of, 10, 258;
    entangled, 47, 62n11;
    experience of, 3–5, 231, 243, 285;
    holistic, 92, 280;
    individualized, 89, 93;
    liberating, 13, 47, 57, 59, 110, 117n41, 123, 145, 148, 212–13, 234, 242, 259, 263, 285–86;
    true, 14, 146, 213–14, 243, 284, 288
Freire, Paulo, 26
fruit:
    forbidden, 89;
    spiritual, 154n53
fulfillment, 10, 28, 45, 49, 51, 59, 68, 89, 128, 170, 210, 221–22, 283
fullness, 149, 168, 171–72, 174–75, 177–79, 183–84, 203, 210–12, 214, 216, 229, 234–35, 256, 267–68, 270
fundamentalists, 6, 233

Galatians, 87–88, 97n9, 112, 114, 207n63, 269
Gaudium et Spes, 64n40, 134n3
gender, 51, 63n27, 135n11, 195, 226n49, 237, 262–63, 272n43

generosity, 110, 131–32
Genesis, 89–90, 156n58, 162, 186n98
Germany, vii, 31, 259
Gervais Principle, 64n34
gifts, 131–32, 138n58, 151, 199, 201, 210, 213, 220, 229, 240, 242, 256, 266, 268, 285–88
glory, 94, 102, 112, 149, 182n30, 288;
   glorification, 220, 225n31;
   seeking, 268
gluttony, 137n37, 232–33, 272n39
gnostic, 24, 124, 128, 135n11, 137n32, 214, 251n51
God:
   calls, 1–2, 111, 147, 162, 275;
   eternal, 127, 212;
   punishing, 7, 183, 225;
   trust in, 89, 101–2, 105–6, 212, 215, 233, 239;
   worshiping, 114, 145
Goizueta, Roberto S., 202, 208, 253
Goldingay, John, 95–96, 99, 185
Goldstein, Valerie Saiving, 63n27
González, Justo, 17, 251
good news, 6–7, 129, 196, 266, 269–70, 283.
   See also gospel
goods, 114, 142, 233, 267
gospel, 6, 106, 116, 121, 127–30, 134–35, 206, 214–15, 238–39, 249, 256–57, 265, 269, 273, 283
governance, 18, 99, 107
government, 32, 34, 42n38, 64n30, 99n30, 276;
   oppressive, 33
grace, 93, 129, 141, 143–44, 149, 154, 154n23, 171, 194, 238–39, 248n6, 255, 267–69, 273;
   orientating, 237;
   responsible, 93, 98n29, 137n45
gratitude, 138, 207n60
Green, Joel B., 97n7, 116n19, 256
Grenz, Stanley J., 19n26, 39n9, 183n43
growth, 199, 221, 240, 244, 272n48
guidance, 26, 38, 69, 79, 94, 180, 203, 216, 240, 278

guilt, 5–6, 9, 30, 48–49, 53, 142–43, 203, 245, 258–59, 259n1, 276–77, 285
guilty, 90, 125, 149, 259
gullibility, 132
Gutiérrez, Gustavo, 16n5, 17n9, 43n54, 82n35

Habermas, Jürgen, 41–42
habits, 15, 62n5, 104–5, 138n58, 143;
   religious, 15, 20n45
Hägg, Tomas, 143
hagiography, 126, 140, 142, 153n5
Hampson, Daphne, 61n2
happiness, 9
harmony, 213, 225n31, 261
Harries, Richard, 215
hate, 115, 246, 259, 266
Haugen, Gary A., 18n23
healing, 18, 61, 145, 199, 207n58, 211, 221, 245, 259, 271n25, 272n48
healing ministry, 82n46
hearts, 57, 126, 128, 145–47, 199–200, 216, 218, 221, 233, 235, 239, 242, 245–46, 282–83
heaven, 15, 103, 140, 217, 229–30, 248n6, 249n32
Hebrew Bible. *See* Old Testament
Hegel, Georg Wilhelm Friedrich, 29, 39n9, 42n39, 46, 61n3, 108, 196
Heidegger, Martin, 60
heresy, 32, 42n34, 167, 219, 250n35, 289n8;
   anthropological, 250n35
heroism, 112, 123–24, 126, 128
Heschel, Abraham, 174
hierarchy, 176, 180, 218;
   religious, 166
Hinterberger, Martin, 153n5
Hirsch, Debra, 263
history, 31, 33, 88, 90, 122, 124, 149, 151, 163, 179–80, 209, 214, 243, 269, 276–77
Hitchhiker's Guide to the Galaxy, 178
holiness, 14, 54–55, 110–11, 149–51, 162–63, 166–69, 174, 179,

Index 313

210–14, 219, 222–23, 229–30, 255–56, 263, 268;
  exocentric, 169, 210–11, 284;
  of God, viii, 168–69, 174, 222
holocaust, 161, 205n27
Holy Spirit, 110–11, 143, 146, 163, 172, 194, 198, 201–2, 212, 220, 223, 230, 260, 284–86, 288–89
homo religious, 81
homo sympatheticus, 174
honesty, 58, 111, 202, 207n51, 220, 240, 242
honor, 7, 129, 140, 200, 226n51
Horrell, Scott, 227n57
hospitality, 153n8
human beings, 4, 26, 40n14, 57, 105, 179, 224n7, 233, 261.
  See also humanity
human development, 67, 76
human ingenuity, 179
humanity, vii–viii, 8, 14–15, 67, 89–90, 92–93, 101, 144–45, 159–60, 166–67, 173–74, 210, 233–34, 265–66, 288;
  existence, 10, 224n18, 258;
  experience, 10, 12, 23, 153n6, 221, 246, 262;
  identity, 14, 56, 63n27, 79, 211, 217, 238
human life, viii, 38, 98, 98n12, 125, 169, 173, 190, 201, 222, 224n7, 234, 268
human meaning, 247
human nature, 1, 5, 11, 20n40, 96n3, 221
humiliation, 171
humility, 65n47, 131, 140–41, 148, 153n11, 206n45, 220, 264, 268, 277
hunger, 50, 160, 171, 264

idealism, 20n40, 29, 31, 33, 41n25, 67, 75, 121, 150, 201, 216, 222, 230, 240, 243
ideals, 23, 59, 203, 206n51;
  monastic, 140

identity, 34–35, 55–56, 93, 101–4, 126, 131–33, 146–47, 167–68, 198–200, 210–16, 229–30, 239, 255–57, 281–82, 284–86;
  eschatological, 214, 267;
  narrative, 201, 282–83;
  new, 92, 110, 114, 150, 231;
  real, 88, 221, 229, 269;
  systems-derived, 33, 57, 59, 72, 74, 92, 111, 147, 201, 237, 240, 245, 266;
  true, 151, 256, 262–63
identity dissolution, 215, 240, 280
identity formation, 29, 32–33, 51, 79, 93, 109, 174, 206n49, 213, 268
ideologies, 208n70, 222, 232
idols, 50, 159, 170, 184n66
ignorance, 52–53, 64n39, 132, 134n2, 145, 204n10
image, 7, 27, 61, 71, 149, 162, 165, 173–74, 176–77, 179, 256, 288
imagery, 119n58, 177
immanence, 170–71, 202
immutability, 173
impatience, 145, 230, 232–33
implications, 24;
  expressive, 171;
  radical, 126;
  social, 113n2, 218;
  vocational, 215
impossibility, 5, 49, 74, 83n49, 104, 198;
  moral, 126
impulses, 189, 264, 277
impurity, 163, 223n5, 224n10
inadequacy, 60, 81n28, 173, 223, 245
incarnation, 96n3, 106, 124, 174, 195, 220
inclusion, 168–69, 215, 255;
  absolute, 71;
  perichoretic, 118n47
incoherence, 41n28, 260
incompleteness, 76, 103, 168, 213
India, 65n65, 138n58
individualization, viii, 26, 29, 45–46, 77, 81n28, 82n31, 83n49, 95, 142

individuals, 7–8, 30, 43n54, 45–46, 60, 83n49, 123–24, 207n58, 214, 222, 258, 278
indulging, 47, 111, 189, 259, 263, 278
inequality, 30, 91, 240
infinity, 6, 52, 112, 116n14, 166–69, 183n43
infirmities, 20n40, 134n2
inheritance, 48, 149, 186n96
injustice, 5, 41n27, 65n41, 91, 133, 159, 209, 211, 221–22, 246, 259, 273n57, 276, 278
insecurities, 8, 48, 220, 258, 269, 280
instinct, 78, 82n82, 154n21
institutions, 10, 18n23, 20n35, 24, 42n38, 76, 79n1
instruction, 123–24, 206n47;
    catechetical, 17n17, 135n15, 140
insufficiency, 48–49, 53, 180, 236
integration, 17n12, 30, 35, 58–59, 69, 71–72, 79, 97n7, 194, 238
integrative meaning, 36, 38, 268
intellectual, 18n20, 42n39, 62n10, 159, 193, 195, 198, 251n53
intelligence, 62n10, 130, 136n21
intensification, 51, 53–54, 219
intention, 178–79, 251n47, 287;
    moral, 27, 110
intentional, 27, 121, 242, 257
intercession, 89, 261
interconnectedness, 92, 97n7
intimacy, 68–74, 81n28, 131, 174, 260
investments, 72, 75–76, 261
invitation, 11, 13, 38, 54, 57, 59, 123, 133, 138, 147, 245, 248, 257, 264, 267;
    eschatological, 90, 115;
    new, 215, 239
Isaac the Solitary, 1
Isaiah, 117n25
isolation, 3, 29, 31, 69, 72–74, 109, 121, 162, 168–69, 215, 222, 237, 240, 245, 255;
    anonymized, 235;
    prophetic, 132;
    well-defended, 73
Israel, 82n35, 88, 90–93, 98n24, 105, 109, 114, 167, 169, 174, 176, 250n33

Jabez, 95
Jenson, Robert, 163
Jesus. *See* Christ
Jillette, Penn, 226n43
Johnson, Elizabeth A., 160
Johnston, Robert K., 289n7
Jong-un, Kim, 99
Jose Miguez Bonino, 177
Joseph, 90
Joshua, 92, 98n22
journey, 12, 59, 72, 96n3, 194, 198, 201, 221–22, 242–44, 246, 262;
    transformative, 244
joy, 115, 145, 171, 174, 186n96, 201, 204n10, 216, 246, 287
Jubilee, 92–93, 98n12, 103
Judaism, 9, 41n33, 101, 106–9, 125, 165
Judas, 106
judgment, 11, 13, 25, 29, 55, 58, 98n24, 126, 132, 145, 168, 177, 183n51, 213, 225n31;
    final, 177
justice, 109, 115, 123, 130, 177, 186n96, 193, 198, 244, 266, 269, 273n57, 278, 281;
    pursuits of, 2, 105, 108
justification, 27, 41n27, 65n46, 108, 124, 129, 159, 162, 219

Kalu, Ogbu, 18n23
Kant, Immanuel, 42, 231
Kapolyo, Joe M., 3
Kärkkäinen, Veli-Matti, 186n102, 234
Keener, Craig S., 155n58, 213
kenosis, 8, 14, 91, 102, 113, 118n45, 199, 220, 267
Kernnell, Chebon, 182n29
kids, 3, 80n21, 112, 177.
    See also childhood

Kierkegaard, Søren, viii, 24, 39n9, 45–53, 56–60, 62n3, 67–68, 82n29, 83n47, 105, 115n8, 116n14, 119, 259–60
Kim, Kirsteen, 271n26
King, Martin Luther, Jr., vii, 2, 4, 79n1, 81n25, 266
kingdom of God, 7, 38, 56, 75, 103, 108, 114, 126, 217, 222–23, 230–31, 233–35, 247, 277, 282
knowledge, 45, 62n10, 89, 96n3, 131, 137n32, 144–46, 156n58, 160, 164, 178–79, 194–95, 197, 199; true, 18n20, 147, 167, 238
Krawelitzki, Judith, 175
Kreider, Alan, viii, 12, 20n45, 42n43, 123, 134n6

language, 31, 87, 110, 134n3, 179–80
l'Arche, viii, 14, 197, 199–201, 206n46, 207n58, 220, 266, 273n52, 282
las Casas, Bartolomé de, 16n9
Latin America, vii, 17n9, 43n54, 129
law, 34, 36, 92–93, 95, 101, 103, 145, 169, 171, 210–11, 213, 220, 222, 284, 287
leadership, 4, 9, 19n33, 99, 107, 109, 151, 180, 182, 197, 258, 281, 287
legalism, 54, 102, 122, 136n31, 166, 192, 204n10, 229, 237, 251n45
lepers, 210–11, 269
Letter of Barnabas, 110, 117n28
Letter to Coroticus, 250n35
Levinson, David, 80
Leviticus, 92
liberated life, 105, 141, 150, 281, 288
liberation:
 continual, 93–94, 265;
 holistic, 4, 10, 25, 38, 60–61, 140, 234, 256, 262, 276, 279, 282, 289n1;
 pattern of, 11, 79, 88, 102, 282, 286;
 pursuit of, 6, 146, 181n21, 189, 220, 244;
 theme of, 124, 161, 176

liberation theologians, 17n19, 129
liberation theology, vii–viii, 7, 37, 43n54
liberator, 93, 176–77, 277
libertinism, 192, 217, 219, 246, 263, 282
liberty, 7, 258
likeness, 214, 224n9, 258
limitations, 4, 6, 47, 56, 89–90, 138n53, 179, 193, 201–2, 220, 247, 266
Lindström, Harald, 135n12
living, 5–6, 13–15, 112, 114–15, 122–23, 132–33, 147–48, 150–51, 199–201, 211, 213, 231, 233–34, 238, 257–58
living life, 4, 74, 110, 112, 280
living space, 172, 186n96, 233, 261, 271n10
location, 24, 118n46, 141, 151
Loder, James E., 11, 61, 67–68, 70–73, 75–76, 118n52, 280
logic, 40n20, 41n33
Lohfink, Gerhard, 117n34, 119n56
London, Jack, 16n8, 186n94, 220
loneliness, 221, 253n86
longing, 31, 61n1, 62n10, 219, 222, 235, 263, 287
lordship, 58, 89, 91, 93, 102, 106, 111, 217, 223, 233, 235, 257, 266, 286, 288;
 active, 127;
 overarching, 89, 93;
 universal, 129
Lord's prayer, 94
losers, 51, 177, 279
Losie, Lynn, 117n34
loss, 35, 48, 51–52, 75–76, 105, 111, 113, 138, 172, 174, 177, 219, 231, 241, 279–80;
 weight, 226n43
love, 50–51, 68, 124–26, 131–32, 147–52, 167–69, 174–77, 198–202, 210–11, 229–30, 233–36, 245–46, 255–57, 260–61, 264–68;
 of Christ, 199–200, 245;

liberative, 200;
non-naïve, 68;
prevenient, 234;
transformative, 200, 237;
unconditional, 231
lovers, 15, 171, 216, 262, 270n1
loving, 123, 148, 150, 178, 221, 244–45, 260–61, 283
Luhmann, Niklas, vii, 23, 25–29, 35–37, 40n23, 41n31, 42n39, 50
Luke, 106, 111–12, 115n6, 116n22, 122, 136n26, 186n96, 223n5
lukewarm, 39n8, 110

machinations, 137n45, 148
MacIntyre, Alasdair, 43n46
Maddox, Randy L., 98, 137n45, 137
Magnesians, letter to the, 121
maintenance, 27, 29, 52
Mandelbrot, Benoit, 250n38
manifestation, 50, 52, 146, 165, 183n51, 212, 225n29
maps, 67, 125, 236
Marvel Comics, 187n116
Marxism, vii, 39n3, 41n31, 65n51, 275
masculinity, 51, 63n27
masks, 7, 52, 193, 239
master, 149, 164, 243
Maturana, Humberto, 26
maturity, 110–11, 122, 221;
    moral, 201, 206n47;
    spiritual, 122, 141–42
Maximos the Confessor, 62n10
McRandal, Janice, 65n52, 238, 252
meaningfulness, 124, 262
media, 61n1, 192, 196;
    social, 117n30, 131, 247
meditation, 252n57, 262
memory, 116n10, 187n111
mentors, 240, 244
messy entanglements, 195, 272n43
meta-system, 93, 127, 235
methodology, 13, 64n33, 107, 109, 161, 169, 196, 209, 217, 275;
    systems-derived, 278

mind, 15–16, 20, 26, 28, 33, 64–65, 128, 131, 143, 147, 150, 187, 189, 192, 203–4;
    irrational, 146
ministers, 19, 64, 130, 249
ministry, 104, 106–7, 111–12, 126, 135, 137, 154, 170, 207, 264, 267
miracles, 104, 142
misdeeds, 57, 130, 160
misery, 216, 261
mission, 7–8, 13, 112–13, 127–28, 149–50, 174–75, 177, 180–81, 223–24, 232, 234, 243, 249, 266–68, 288;
    messianic, 223, 237, 257, 259, 265, 268
mission of God, 128, 144, 182, 267, 288
Moeller, Hans-Georg, 26, 40–41
Moltmann, Jürgen, 5, 8, 169–78, 185n86, 186n96, 214, 216, 230–34, 250n38, 251n46, 256–59, 275, 278, 280, 282–83
monasticism, 124, 132, 139–43, 150, 152n2, 153n12, 154n21, 191–92, 200, 238, 263, 281
money, 28, 103, 111, 117n30, 128, 137n44, 142
morality, 6, 31, 95, 163, 215, 229, 250n35
Morris, Leon, 104
mortality, 76, 103, 215
Moser, Richard, 18n23
Moses, 12, 90–91, 117n34, 145, 162, 165, 171, 210
Mostert, Christiaan, 224n18, 225n23, 248n3
mothers, 72, 198, 226n51
motivations, 7, 46, 54, 65n46, 69, 71, 117n30, 131, 135n11, 140, 206n49, 210, 241, 281
Moyo, Dambisa, 18n23
multiplicity, 72, 101, 114, 147
multitude, 9, 146, 229
Murata, Sayaka, 32
Murphy, Nancey, 42n37
music, 196, 283

mutuality, 75, 197, 199–201
mystery, 81n26, 185n88, 197, 262
mysticism, 190, 192

Nacpil, Emerito, 103, 287
narratives, 88–89, 92, 94, 96n3, 101, 106, 116n19, 136n21, 151, 179, 237, 240–41, 246, 270n10;
  early Jewish, 88, 101;
  understanding, 88, 114, 122, 127, 150
Nason, Shannon, 61
nations, 3, 17n19, 90, 94, 98n24, 161, 236
naughty scenes, 177
necessity, 30, 47–48, 62n11, 137n45, 138n58, 221
negation, 23, 90–91, 202, 220, 231, 241, 256, 264
neighbor, 3, 5, 8, 10, 105, 114, 123, 131, 138n53, 142, 148, 187n119, 260–61, 284, 289
neighborhoods, 184n63, 223, 242
networks, 26, 197, 242, 267, 282
New Testament, viii, 88, 95, 106, 112, 113n2, 118n46, 121, 163, 212, 281, 286
Ngong, David, 195
Nicodemus, 104
Nietzsche, Friedrich, 42n39, 60
nitty-gritty realities, 223
nonidentity, 102, 167, 255
Nuttall, Geoffrey F., 43n51

obedience, 18n20, 105–6, 109, 113–14, 142–43, 217–18, 220, 224n15, 233, 285, 287
obligation, 92–93, 111, 122–23, 270
obsessing, 34, 64n33, 137n37, 263
the Office, 64n35
Okholm, Dennis, 272
Old Testament, 88, 95, 97n7, 116n20, 117n34, 163, 214, 224n7, 281
omnipotence, 167, 175, 179
omnipresence, 167, 177–78

omniscience, 178–79
ontology, 47, 113n1, 128, 149, 174, 182n30;
  task-oriented, 103
openness, 12, 68, 72, 110, 166, 168, 175, 182, 194, 201, 212–13, 221, 240, 242, 272n48
open theism, 178, 187n112
operational closure, 26, 29, 33, 71, 165
operations, 26–28, 31, 91, 136n31, 168, 213;
  autopoietic, 31, 33
opposition, 33, 87, 116n22, 132, 165, 232, 276
oppress, 4–5, 15, 24, 31, 59, 92–93, 152, 244, 260, 264, 268, 280, 285
oppressed people, vii, 97n20, 275
oppressing, 2, 4–5, 7–12, 24–25, 36–37, 58, 67, 73, 91, 93–94, 159–60, 189–90, 217–19, 275–76, 278–81
oppressing behaviors, 10, 23, 45–46, 52, 59, 102, 166, 200, 232
oppression, 1–2, 4–5, 7–8, 13, 36–37, 73–74, 88, 91–93, 95, 101–2, 161–63, 217–20, 258–59, 275–77, 279–81;
  indulging, 7, 47, 75, 78, 151, 207n65, 218, 247, 281;
  systems of, viii, 9, 11, 13, 26, 37, 46, 78, 115n3, 170, 180, 227n57, 276, 280, 287
oppressors, 4–12, 14–15, 35–36, 48, 53–54, 73–74, 77–79, 91–94, 122–25, 151, 178–79, 245–46, 269–70, 275–80, 284–86;
  liberated, vii, 5, 12, 85, 264, 275–76, 281
order, 27, 32, 34, 58, 74, 89, 107, 195, 257, 263;
  social, 107–8
orientation, 6, 13–15, 38, 75, 90, 105, 141–42, 160, 203, 233, 235, 245, 256–57, 262, 270;
  transcendent, 70

orienting philosophies, 25, 36, 47, 56, 69–70, 80n16, 141, 247
Origen, 135n12
Original Sin, 20n40, 20
Orthodox Church, 184n73
orthodoxy, 5, 12–13, 143, 171, 190, 192, 195–96, 204n10, 282;
  radical, 40n23, 191
orthopathy, 6, 12–14, 17n20, 171, 190, 192, 204n10, 204
orthopraxy, 5, 12–14, 171, 190, 192, 204n10
Osborn, Eric, 125, 129, 135n15
Otto, Rudolf, 164
outcasts, 36, 170, 207n52
outsiders, 121, 123, 242, 260

pain, 159, 185n88, 186n96, 250n33, 288
panentheism, 172, 178
panic, 216, 248
Pannenberg, Wolfhart, 14, 25, 39n9, 63n27, 161, 163–69, 172, 182n40, 211–13, 221, 224n7, 230, 248, 248n4
paraclete. *See* Holy Spirit
paradox, 29, 34–36, 49, 60–61, 69, 76, 160, 202, 205n24, 217, 220, 280;
  possible, 59–61
parasitoid wasps, 54
parents, 72, 76, 139, 176, 186n96, 253n85
participation, 26, 28–29, 35–36, 38, 49, 51, 59, 68–69, 165, 201–3, 212–13, 219, 229–30, 237, 268–69;
  anonymized, 34;
  communal, 196, 199;
  engaged, 195, 247;
  human, 194, 287;
  transformative, 237, 251n51
particularity, 6, 10, 14, 23, 29, 35, 46, 77, 147, 173, 234, 260, 278, 283
passions, 12, 14, 18, 128, 130, 173–74, 190, 192, 196, 210, 213, 217, 219, 241, 246–47;
  creative, 8, 280;

negative, 129, 264;
renewed, 261;
right, 6, 14, 190
passivity, 26, 273n57
Passover feast, 91
paternalism, 2, 4, 26, 82n33, 240, 276
patience, viii, 11, 20n45, 134n6, 151, 175–76, 186n96, 199, 201, 216, 220, 243, 262, 272n50, 287
Patrick of Ireland, 154, 250
patripassianism, 186n96
Paulo Freire, 74, 117n41
pax Christi, 83n48, 108
pax Romana, 83n48, 107–8
peace, 14, 57, 71, 77, 89, 107–9, 221, 232, 234, 245, 248, 266–67, 269, 284–85, 287;
  negative, 78, 266, 273n57, 273;
  positive, 266, 273n57;
  substantive, 59, 107, 210, 234, 266, 268, 272n48
Pelagianism, 141
penance, 259
Pentateuch, 162n3
Pentecost, 110, 286
perfection, 102–3, 125, 127–28, 133, 134n2, 136n21, 139, 142–43, 150, 224n18, 239
perpetrators, 23, 171, 259, 269
perpetuation, 26, 28, 31–32, 54, 74, 76, 108, 132, 236
persecution, 112, 122, 133–34, 139, 147, 217, 259
perseverance, 142, 216
persistence, 76, 91, 105, 125, 132, 149, 179, 201, 258;
  eternal, 74
personalities, 163, 201, 231, 233, 261
personhood, 7–8, 12, 25, 30, 39n5, 68, 73–74, 82n33, 90, 92, 124, 170, 217, 219, 266;
  new, 8, 127, 266
perversion, 166, 183n40
Pharaoh, 90–91
Pharisee, 104, 223n5

Philippians, 20n44, 113n2, 118n46, 206n43, 213
philistine-bourgeois mentality, 52
philosophers, 129, 140, 154n21, 173
philosophies, 25, 39n9, 39n11, 44n5, 125, 129, 161, 173, 184n66, 193–94, 197
Picasso, 193, 204, 204n12
piety, 164, 215
Pilate, 108
Plotinus, 167, 172, 183n47
pneumapoietic, 88, 110
pneumatology, 172, 185.
    See also Holy Spirit
poiesis, 27, 30, 37
political action, 32, 55
political climate, 4, 16n5
politicians, 31, 34, 54, 83n50
politics, 11, 24, 31–33, 54, 92, 94, 131, 133, 231, 241, 260–61
possessions, 103, 114, 125–26, 130, 142, 175, 239, 258, 281
poverty, 12, 18n23, 55, 65n47, 96n6, 123, 129, 137n46, 145, 149, 216;
    voluntary, 129
power, 3–10, 32–34, 55, 93–94, 107, 113–14, 127, 164–67, 175–78, 209–10, 217–18, 232–34, 256, 258–60, 276–77;
    application of, 175, 198, 267;
    assumption of, 91, 236;
    position of, 91, 194, 198;
    transforming, 109, 113, 164, 214;
    worldly, 108, 193
power encounters, 140
power structures, 16n5, 127, 217, 276, 279
practice:
    abusive, 170;
    contemplative, 14, 41n27, 153n10, 166, 238;
    expressive, 236
praxis, 27, 30–31, 37, 202;
    liberative, 35, 44n55

prayer, 93, 95, 139–40, 192, 197, 199, 203, 235–38, 247, 250n44, 251n45, 257, 261–64, 278, 281–82;
    contemplative, 1, 192, 236;
    dangerous, 94;
    isolated, 139;
    nature of, 236;
    unceasing, 1, 191
preaching, 6, 9, 13, 43n46, 129, 187n107, 239, 283
preexistence, 118n46
prejudices, 73, 174, 206n51, 232, 237, 240
pride, 65n44, 92, 102, 126, 142, 147–48, 203, 238, 251n45
priests, 106–7, 162, 210–11, 224n10, 289n8
privilege, 5, 7, 12, 24, 72, 78, 91–92, 113, 133, 139, 141, 236, 279, 281, 285;
    relative, 102, 198
Process Theology, 176
Procksch, Otto, 163
proclamation, 196, 241, 257, 283, 285
prodigal son, 186n96, 287
production, 14, 27–28, 30, 32, 51, 54, 56, 68, 76, 78, 234, 239
progress, 29, 31, 49, 54, 73, 75, 77, 108, 113, 142–44, 147, 221, 234, 241, 264;
    personal, 136n23, 241;
    spiritual, 141
prohibitions, 6, 36, 47–48
promise, 73–74, 77–78, 88–89, 109, 114, 144–46, 148–49, 168–71, 175, 178–79, 214–17, 231, 233–34, 285, 287–88;
    false, 219, 287;
    fulfilled, 49, 201, 216
property, 87, 125, 138n58
prophetic, viii, 12, 77–78, 276, 278
prophets, 5, 95, 106, 117n117, 144–45, 169, 284
prosperity, 1, 94, 103

protest, 10, 30, 34, 54, 108, 130, 137n37, 222, 239, 246, 250n35
Protestants, 3, 43n46, 141
Psalms, 12, 57, 89, 93–94, 99n32, 127, 177, 184n58, 206n43, 277
pseudo-self, 28, 30, 50, 68–69, 73, 89, 247, 287
psychological development, 11, 24, 47, 61, 67–68, 75, 77–78
psychology, 67, 79
psychopathology, 19n33, 73, 83n49
public theology, 204n8
punishment, 107, 143, 198
purgation, 194, 237, 251n50
purification, 134, 266
purity, 152n3, 223n5

race, 9, 241
racism, 9
Rahab, 92, 98n23
rationality, 32–34, 49, 54, 56, 65n46, 106, 112, 121, 247;
    system-derived, 26, 33, 38, 55, 200, 239
rationalization, 11, 19, 25, 28, 53, 77–78, 129, 280
reactionary, 72, 168, 180n3
realism, 25, 75
rebirth, 8, 20n45, 54, 68, 92, 105, 110, 122, 133, 134n6, 212, 214, 243, 259
recapitulation, 224n7
reciprocity, 132, 175–76, 199, 220, 260, 285;
    exocentric, 174, 179;
    theological, 172
recognition, 7, 19n33, 199, 259
reconciliation, 6, 8, 79, 88, 115, 164, 203, 213, 246, 260, 269, 278
recreation, 54, 68
redemption, 6, 92, 96n3, 101, 110, 214, 217, 220–21, 230, 245
reformation, 6, 48, 212, 279;
    partial, 48
Reimer, Kevin Scott, 200–202, 206n51, 207n58, 222

rejection, 54, 56, 72, 109, 181n25, 184n66, 241, 252n71;
    professional, 75
relationality, 177
relationship, 59–60, 68, 72–73, 79, 88, 94, 149–50, 166–67, 175–77, 199–200, 211, 263, 265–68, 282, 285–88;
    personal, 79n1, 166, 238, 287;
    real, 175, 198, 267–68;
    social, 215, 258;
    transformative, 263, 266–68
relationship of trust, 2, 98n23, 142, 166, 175, 224n15, 245
relativism, 58, 72, 119, 130, 194, 245
religion, 31, 35–36, 50, 55, 58, 70, 80n16, 91, 99, 105, 133, 138, 164–66, 209;
    basic function, 35, 47, 50, 58, 69, 101–2, 161, 164–66, 175, 183n40, 193–94;
    system of, 27–28, 30, 33, 35–37, 46, 54–55, 57, 63, 65, 107, 110–12, 132, 165–66, 191, 287
renewal, 7–8, 13–14, 56, 105, 148, 200, 202, 216, 234–35, 241, 261–62, 269, 277, 284
renewed life, 105, 144, 214
renunciation, 130, 136n31
reorientation, 93, 105, 126, 144, 203, 235
repentance, 11, 48, 143, 173, 269
repression, 7, 102, 189, 192, 196, 217–21, 237, 240, 246, 262–63, 267, 282
reputation, 19n33, 111, 125, 140
resentments, 61, 76
resignation, 39n5, 142, 200
resistance, 45, 54, 61, 61n3, 146, 149, 152, 189, 192, 196, 231–32, 240, 277, 284–85, 288
resolution, 32, 53–54, 56, 70–71, 73, 75, 91, 115n4, 221, 262
resonance, 24, 47, 89, 102, 118, 146, 180, 203, 233, 238, 243, 258, 261

responsibility, 3, 15, 75–76, 81n26, 89, 92–94, 99n30, 117n30, 134n3, 170, 208n68, 280;
   moral, 24;
   personal, 31, 201
restitution, 125, 271n25, 276
restoration, 6, 93, 139, 190, 211
restrictions, 10, 56, 165, 280, 284
resurrection, 13, 101, 105, 109, 114–15, 212, 214–17, 219, 223, 231, 233, 256–58, 265, 285, 288;
   experience of, 214, 264;
   protests, 216
retuning, 189, 203n2, 264
reunification, 64n30
revelation, 88, 95–97, 107, 110, 163, 165, 167, 169–70, 173, 179, 191, 194–95, 210–11, 222, 230;
   of God, 39n6, 150, 165, 171, 174, 179–80;
   indirect, 169
revenge, 160, 245
revolution, 33–34, 58, 119, 160, 177, 186, 209, 221, 276, 279
Rhee, Helen, 123, 134n9
rhetoric, 6–7, 18n23, 82n33, 119n58, 121, 161, 260;
   guilt-emphasizing, 127
righteousness, 75, 130–31, 143, 151, 224n10, 258–59
risk, 10, 35, 72, 77, 81n26, 91–92, 106, 111, 116n16, 129, 161, 174, 234, 245;
   ontological, 250n33
road map, 12, 141, 244
Rogers, Eugene F., 193
roles, 8, 25, 30, 32–33, 35, 38, 94, 99, 107, 124, 132, 145, 171, 189, 199;
   archetypical, 30, 34;
   confusion, 82n29
Roman Empire, 123, 151
Roman gods, 172
Roman government, 40n24, 41n33, 109

Romans, 11, 20n41, 30, 107, 109, 165, 213
Rome, 107–11, 123, 222
Romero, Oscar, 7, 251n47, 270n8
Royal Canadian Navy, 197
rule, 32, 92, 94, 103, 108–9, 114, 130, 175–77, 213, 229–30, 233, 237–38, 246–48, 248n3, 256;
   golden, 94
rulers, 99, 107, 176–77, 185n86, 211;
   totalitarian, 177, 236
Runyon, Theodore, 17n20

Sabbath, 92, 287
Sachs, Jeffrey, 18n23
sacrifice, 45, 48, 76–77, 194, 212, 256, 258, 287
safeguards, 163, 166
saints, 114, 124, 126, 143, 236
salvation, 6, 8, 79, 105–6, 125, 129, 131, 145, 148–49, 151, 160, 166, 170, 255, 259;
   eternal, 60, 125, 168;
   securing, 30, 123;
   social, 48, 277.
   See also soteriology
sanctification, 87, 179, 247
Sapphira, 110–12, 114, 117n30
Sarah, Robert , 262
Satan, 106
satiation, 31, 51, 54, 241, 264;
   anemic, 45, 216
Saul, 102, 111–12, 117n34
savior, 38, 124, 140, 239
Schleiermacher, Friedrich, 164, 181n23, 191
Schöfthäler, Traugott, 23
scholars, 97n7, 184n73, 190–91
scholarship, 10, 20n35, 88, 97n7
science, 47, 178, 194, 208n70, 252n71
Scripture, 96n3, 101, 103, 105–6, 115n4, 122–23, 144–45, 149, 159–61, 170, 176, 179–80, 281, 286, 288
secularization, 35, 58, 164–65, 205n24

security, 76, 81n24, 89, 93, 109, 121, 166, 178, 207n51, 233, 239, 282
self, 34, 45–56, 58–61, 68–72, 74–79, 89–90, 105, 144–49, 163–64, 166–69, 171–75, 196–97, 219–22, 255, 264–65;
    amalgamated, 60, 74, 78, 147, 191, 243;
    coherent, 35, 56, 58–60, 168, 220, 238–39, 282;
    despaired, 46, 50, 56, 69, 173, 265;
    inner, 12, 74, 212;
    loving, 148;
    true, viii, 49–50, 56, 72, 128, 147–50, 168, 234, 236, 239, 241–43, 246, 255, 285
self-awareness, 29, 34, 51, 53–54, 60, 67–69, 71–73, 75, 90, 105, 168, 171, 194, 200, 284
self-centeredness, 182, 222
self-contradictions, 183n51, 225n29
self-deception, 62n5, 73, 147
self-definition, 26, 77, 88, 210, 256, 287
selfhood, 28, 45, 168, 236, 255
self-identity, 34, 51, 258
self-knowledge, 147, 263
self-perception, 90, 245
self-perpetuation, 29, 31, 49, 110
self-production, 27, 29, 31, 33
self-protection, 110, 163
self-righteousness, 277, 279
separation, 109, 133–34, 142, 151, 162–63, 178, 200, 211, 222, 224n10, 225n29, 237, 250n33, 281
separatist, 109, 192, 216
sermons, 24, 47, 50, 236, 284
serpent, 45, 89–90, 170
servants, 9, 51, 92–93, 106, 149, 259
service, 10, 27, 50, 52, 71, 199, 202, 217, 244, 261, 281, 287
setbacks, 146, 150
sexuality, 68, 80n21, 192–95, 247, 262–63;
    and spirituality, 262
shalom, 47, 119n59

shame, 5–6, 53, 89, 129
sheep, 270n10, 287
Shekinah, 174
shepherd, 91, 165, 287
Shittim, 98n23
silence, vii, 108, 141, 235
Simon bar Kokhba, 108
Simonyi, Gyula, 233
sin, 7–8, 11, 36, 38, 46–49, 51–58, 60, 63, 148–49, 165, 171, 211–13, 233, 255–56, 263–64;
    deadly, 152n3, 241, 247;
    expression of, 52, 54, 56, 65n49, 90, 198, 259
sinfulness, 60, 101, 263
singing, 3, 29, 50, 277
sinner, 7, 183n51, 213, 223n5, 225n29
slave owners, vii, 4, 129
slavery, vii, 4, 51, 54, 88, 90, 97n20, 105–6, 114, 129, 149, 250n35, 256, 265, 267
sleep, 143, 251n47
smoke, 68, 162
social environment, vii, 3, 7, 23, 26, 28, 30–31, 37–38, 45, 47, 56, 69, 92, 195, 200
social identity, 9, 29, 76
social issues, 11, 77, 80n11, 91, 107, 109, 136, 195, 197, 221, 260
sociality, 12, 50, 78, 219, 221, 258, 268, 280
social systems, 15, 26, 28–31, 41n31, 51, 106, 191, 276, 288
social trinitarianism, 219, 227n57
societal problems, 77–78, 128, 276
society, 2, 7, 9, 11–12, 24–27, 29–30, 32–33, 35–36, 38, 45–46, 50–51, 58, 67–68, 92–95, 197–99;
    modern, 9, 12, 23, 69, 79, 87, 90, 270, 276
sociology, 11, 24–25, 31, 45, 106, 115, 184n66
solidarity, 8–9, 16n5, 32, 177, 210, 215, 224n10, 280
Solomon, 93–94, 99n32, 99

solutions, viii, 12, 25, 35, 37, 46, 49, 55, 57–58, 60, 61n1;
destructive, 232;
effective, 23, 276;
supposed, 15, 23, 36, 39n8
Son, vii, 68, 94, 129, 143, 167, 175, 211–12, 218–20, 224, 256, 261, 264, 284–85, 287.
See also Christ
Sonderegger, Katherine, 197, 206
songs, 277, 283
soteriology, 39n8, 113
souls, 18n20, 38n1, 57, 62n5, 126–27, 130, 143, 147, 174, 260
Spirit, work of, 7, 144, 149, 179–80, 194, 197–99, 224n19, 225n23, 256, 260–61, 277, 284, 286.
See also pneumatology
Spirit Christology, 10, 70, 110
Spirit of life, 171–72, 213, 219, 229, 231, 283, 286, 288.
See also Holy Spirit
spirituality, 195, 235, 262
spiritual pursuits, 139, 192, 244
stagnation, 31, 75–76
Staniloae, Dumitru, 219, 238
starving, 50, 220
status, 2, 10, 24, 35, 48, 50–51, 57–58, 77–78, 141, 168, 174, 211, 218, 234, 237
status quo, 10, 52, 108, 129, 221
steps, 70, 102–3, 114–15, 143, 162n3, 165, 169, 201, 203, 243–44, 259, 277;
clear action, 103, 115n3, 242, 278;
first, 243, 259n1, 285, 289n1
Stewart, Jon, 62n3
stillness, 114, 189, 191, 267
story, 13, 95, 98n24, 104, 110, 112, 126, 139, 141, 144–45, 223, 264, 277, 286;
new, 105, 109–10, 113n1;
world's, 90, 139
strength, 48, 149, 164, 244, 253n86, 276;

human, 181n19, 245, 252n71
spiritual, 75
stresses, 31, 72, 81n28
structures, 32, 36–37, 48, 68, 102, 129, 132, 199, 219, 260, 276, 284;
ecclesial, 118n46, 134;
narrative, 77, 96n3;
sinful, 54, 218;
social, 37–38, 44n44, 132, 218
Stump, Eleonore, 183n47
subjugation, 81n25, 176, 217–18, 220
submission, 54, 194, 217–19, 236
subordination, 58, 218, 226n51
subservient, 27, 36, 130
substantiation, 35, 70, 173, 217, 219, 287
suburban life, 81n28
success, 1, 9, 19n33, 33, 52, 75, 94–95, 103, 112, 115, 121, 198, 243, 280, 284;
societal, 1, 33, 56, 90, 198
succumbing, 47–48, 114, 212, 216, 243
suffering, 113n1, 128, 147, 171, 173–75, 177–78, 185n88, 186n96, 220, 234, 237, 253n86, 259, 269
suffering servant, 177
Sugirtharajah, R. S., 98n20
suicide, 31, 63n24, 64n30, 253n86
superiority, 220–21, 240
surrendering, 235
symptoms, 15, 23, 180, 239, 253n83, 266, 276
synthesis, 49, 76, 109, 196
systems, 25–38, 48–60, 67–79, 90–93, 105–14, 130–33, 165–66, 168, 191–95, 197–200, 233–34, 238–41, 266–70, 276–77, 287–88;
academic, 27, 42n38, 65n46, 161, 189, 191, 234. *See also* academia;
anonymizing, 36, 60, 232;
autopoietic, 26, 32, 50, 65n46, 258;
caste, 65n44;
closed, 27–28, 30, 33, 101, 191;
communication, 26, 34, 53–54;
distinct, 28–29, 71, 101, 235;

entertainment, 27, 29, 65n47;
environment of, 46, 79, 105, 132–33, 165;
legal, 15, 24, 26–27, 29–30;
political, viii, 4, 15, 31, 55, 65n47, 132, 165, 273n53

Tabernacle, 162–63
Tanner, Kathryn, 43n50, 170
Taylor, John V., 155n56
teacher, 26, 123–24, 126, 139, 154n21, 201, 260, 281
teaching, 10, 12, 15, 106, 110, 122–23, 127, 130–31, 135n15, 137n41, 145, 150–51, 152n1, 209, 211–12;
moral, 105;
spiritual, 143
televangelists, 61
temptations, 15, 59, 89, 101, 116n18, 140, 149–50, 153n11, 177, 215, 218, 263–64, 272n42, 276
tension, 4, 8, 30, 34–35, 45, 101, 114, 121, 166, 179, 189, 232–33, 241, 266
terminology, 40n23, 92, 106, 163, 178, 187n112
Tertullian, 115, 119n58, 122, 138n58, 172, 251n45
testimony, 112, 114–15, 127, 138, 141, 171, 177, 180, 186n94, 210;
biblical, 164, 178, 250n35
Tevye, 129
thanksgiving, 3, 288
theologians, vii, 14, 19n33, 160–61, 175, 190, 196, 203, 204n14, 237–38, 252n57;
contemporary, 181n25, 283
theological discussion, 25, 37, 146, 161, 164, 169–70, 174, 190, 196, 207n51, 218, 229, 275, 282–83
théologie totale, 191, 194–96, 203
theology, 2, 13–15, 38, 152, 160–62, 169–72, 174, 176, 180, 189–97, 205, 215, 217–18, 235, 237–39;
academic, 160, 180n3, 193;
contemporary, 11, 115, 191, 204n14;
dysfunctional, 20n46;
task of, 191, 217, 219
Theophan the Recluse, 62, 252n73
Theresa of Avila, 238
Thompson, Marianne Meye, 105
Thoreau, Henry David, 15
threat, 18, 73, 108, 116n18, 167–68, 215, 235, 240, 282
thriving, 7–8, 77, 89, 102, 138, 239
time, 2–3, 5, 112, 114, 141–42, 144, 155, 155n39, 168, 172, 179–80, 213–14, 222–23, 241, 245–47
Tolstoy, Sofia, 186n94
tongue, 146, 179
totality, 32, 58, 167–68, 174, 197, 241, 255
total perspective vortex, 236
traditions, 11–12, 70, 72, 81n26, 97n20, 119n57, 154n21, 179, 192, 218
tragedy, 216, 252n62
trajectory, 15, 46, 74, 79, 190, 231, 246
transcendence, 35, 38, 47, 49, 71–72, 131, 167, 170–71, 193, 248n6
transcendent disintegration, 58
transcendent immanence, 38
transformation, 8, 10, 12–14, 37–38, 56–57, 59, 74–75, 102, 160–61, 191–92, 215, 230–32, 243, 260–61, 282–83;
concomitant, 215;
fractal, 110, 241;
orthopathic, 216;
pneumapoietic, 233;
resonating, 13
Transformative Church, 118n46, 170
transformative ways, 170, 214, 237, 260, 266
transforming, 14, 24, 63, 194, 203, 215, 223, 229–30, 242, 246, 261–62, 283
trauma, 41n29, 202, 246
treasure, 131, 145, 267
trials, 41n33, 106–7, 112, 116
Trinity, 14, 171–72, 185, 194, 196, 214, 217–19, 226, 226n54, 227n57, 236–37, 262–63, 268, 277, 282

triumphalism, 180
trust, 6–8, 77, 89, 92–93, 101–2, 105–6, 166, 173, 177, 211–12, 214–16, 232–35, 243, 257–59, 285–86;
  basic, 212;
  committing, 70, 77, 89, 240, 242, 258, 270
truth, 11, 18, 57–59, 72, 124–28, 131, 133, 195, 199, 217, 222, 243–44, 251, 259, 262
tuition, 42n38, 130

ultimacy, 80n21, 106, 129
ultimate inadequacy, 34, 76, 108, 267
uncertainties, 47, 104–5, 131
uncleanness, 210–11
United States, 41n29, 99n30
unity, 1, 34, 40n20, 166, 169, 221, 225n23, 225n31, 234, 241, 245, 257–58, 268, 283, 286
universality, 16n5, 34, 195, 266
universe, 70, 156n58, 236, 243, 249n32
U.S. Constitution, 81, 99n31

vainglory, 129, 140, 152n3
validation, 50–51, 168, 176, 193, 211, 233, 239, 280, 284;
  societal, 34, 245, 268
valuation, vii, 27, 29, 132, 201, 206, 233, 284
values, 7–9, 27, 51–52, 54–55, 93, 95, 169, 171, 199–201, 206–7, 215, 217, 220–22, 243, 264;
  transcendent, 70;
  world's, 133
Vanier, Jean, viii, 14, 190, 197–99, 202, 206–8, 220–22, 227, 230, 240–46, 251–54, 265, 267–68, 272–73, 282
Varela, Francisco, 26
Vatican Council II, 64
veneer, 29, 39, 69
victims, vii, 65n41, 171, 245, 259, 269, 289n8
Victorian England, 65n44, 186n94

victory, 54, 92, 113n1, 113, 174, 216
vigilant, 145, 148
violence, 83n49, 90, 107–8, 159, 244, 250n35, 259
vision:
  idealistic, 73, 210, 242;
  integrated, 61, 237;
  transformative, 1, 14, 128–29, 133, 203, 242, 263, 282
vocation, 68, 76, 190, 200, 203n1
voices, prophetic, 197, 238
Volf, Miroslav, 68, 257, 265, 269
volition, 30–31, 48
vulnerability, 68–69, 72, 90, 93, 106, 174, 201, 218, 220

walls, 163, 245
Ware, Frederick L., 10, 20
Ware, Timothy, 184n73
Watchers, 179, 187n116
water, 171–72, 221, 233, 235
waves, 52, 57, 247
weakness, 48, 51–52, 140, 145, 149, 173, 176–77, 220, 231, 239, 242, 244, 286;
  expressed, 161, 267
wealth, 12, 16n5, 54–55, 74, 123, 126–30, 132–33, 136, 137n45, 139, 149–50, 260, 281;
  issues of, 17n19, 96n6, 104, 126, 129–30, 136n31;
  and poverty, 135n11, 137n46, 149
wealthy, 16, 65n47, 99, 109, 126, 129, 136n21, 160, 207n52
weary, 57, 147, 269
web, 79n1, 87
welcoming, 128, 130, 141, 237
Welker, Michael, 261
Wesley, John, 20n40, 37, 63n25, 82n29, 98n29, 130, 134n2, 135n12, 137n44, 184n65
Wesleyan tradition, 124, 135n12, 137n46, 153n9
Western contexts, 35–36, 79, 141, 227n57
whims, 202, 263

wholeness, 34, 47, 49, 71, 74, 87, 89–90, 144, 150–51, 197, 221, 241, 244, 255–56, 259
Wilkins, Michael J., 108
Willard, Dallas, 25, 39n5
wills, 7, 24, 29, 57, 232
winners, 32, 51–52, 92, 140, 279
wisdom, 15, 45, 104, 124, 141, 144, 148–50, 154n21, 206n45, 220, 243, 256, 265, 270n8;
dead, 129;
gracious, 143, 146
witness, 102, 235, 238, 283
women, vii, 1, 19, 58, 83, 137n41, 218, 226n51, 247, 266;
subordinating, 218
Wong, Kam Ming, 182n28, 224n7
work, 1–2, 6–7, 10–14, 27, 59–61, 88, 148, 150–51, 154n23, 159, 161–62, 198–99, 203, 211–12, 231–32;
counter-rational, 146;
liberating, 1, 194, 234, 275;
transformative, 67, 88, 105, 131, 155n27, 209, 238
world, 11–13, 24–26, 36–39, 47–48, 67–71, 105–7, 109–11, 148–52, 162–67, 169–77, 209–23, 230–33, 235, 255–57, 280–87;
broken, 38, 145, 169, 174, 196, 266, 271n10;
present, 11, 159, 265, 269
world systems, 58–59, 122, 126–27, 146, 148, 150, 170, 177, 199, 218, 260, 268, 282, 284–86, 288
World War II, 81n28, 161, 180n4
worry, 48, 185n86
worship, 50, 65n49, 107, 145, 162, 184n66, 219, 268, 287–88
wounds, 12, 145, 148, 245, 260
wrath, 48–49, 147, 225n31, 255, 270n1
Wright, N. T., 94

yearnings, 69, 134n3, 198
YHWH, 98n23, 167, 171, 173. *See also* God
yoke, 57, 94, 114
Yong, Amos, 110
young adulthood, 51, 67–72, 75–77, 80–81, 83, 161

Zacchaeus, 125, 130
zealots, 107–9, 141
zealous, 103, 141, 145–46
Žižek, Slavoj, 34

About the Author

Patrick Oden is a visiting assistant professor of theology at Fuller Theological Seminary and a minister in the Wesleyan Church. He is the author of *The Transformative Church: New Ecclesial Models and the Theology of Jürgen Moltmann* (2015) and other works.